Health and Safety –
The New Legal Framework

Health and Safety –
The New Legal Framework

Ian Smith, MA, LLB (Cantab)
Barrister, Devereux Chambers; Reader in Law, University of East Anglia

Christopher Goddard, LLB (Hons)
Barrister, Devereux Chambers

Nicholas Randall, LLB (Hons)
Barrister, Devereux Chambers; part-time Lecturer in Law at the
London School of Economics

Butterworths
London, Dublin, Edinburgh
1993

United Kingdom	Butterworth & Co (Publishers) Ltd, 88 Kingsway, LONDON WC2B 6AB and 4 Hill Street, EDINBURGH EH2 3JZ
Australia	Butterworths, SYDNEY, MELBOURNE, BRISBANE, ADELAIDE, PERTH, CANBERRA and HOBART
Belgium	Butterworth & Co (Publishers) Ltd, Brussels
Canada	Butterworths Canada Ltd, TORONTO and VANCOUVER
Ireland	Butterworth (Ireland) Ltd, DUBLIN
Malaysia	Malayan Law Journal Sdn Bhd, KUALA LUMPUR
New Zealand	Butterworths of New Zealand Ltd, WELLINGTON and AUCKLAND
Puerto Rico	Equity de Puerto Rico, Inc, HATO REY
Singapore	Butterworths Asia, SINGAPORE
USA	Butterworth Legal Publishers, AUSTIN, Texas; BOSTON, Massachusetts; CLEARWATER, Florida (D & S Publishers); ORFORD, New Hampshire (Equity Publishing); ST PAUL, Minnesota; and SEATTLE, Washington

A CIP Catalogue record for this book is available from the British Library.

ISBN 0 406 02299 2

Typeset by Doublestruck Ltd, London
Printed in Great Britain by Redwood Books, Trowbridge, Wiltshire

Foreword

Those of us who have practised over the years in the field of personal injury law know how important it has always been to have available in our briefcases a reliable guide dealing with the many, sometimes improbable, not always wholly intelligible regulations covering the wide range of activities in which people are employed.

The new health and safety regulations, with which this book deals, mark a wholesale reconstruction of the statutory edifice, and all those concerned with the regulation of working conditions or with the litigation of injuries and diseases which may be attributable to a failure to meet its objectives will need a guide to the resulting architecture – both its broad sweep and its nooks and crannies including those reflecting the different style of the European dimension. Such a guide this book admirably provides. It is the product, I must admit, of three hardworking members of my own Chambers. What midnight oil must have been burned in its timely production I can only guess. I am proud to be given the opportunity to commend it, not only to our fellow practitioners at the Bar and to solicitors, whether advising, instructing or advocating, but to all those who have an interest in the health and safety of our working populations.

Peter Weitzman QC

Preface

This book is intended for lawyers, workers, Trade Unionists and employers who are concerned with the law of health and safety. The introduction of the new health and safety Regulations which are the subject matter of this book is nothing short of a revolution in this very important area of the law. This is so not only because of the replacement of the pre-existing law but also because of the European origin of the new protections.

One of our main objectives has been to stress the important interrelationship between the domestic Regulations and the European Community Directives from which they have been taken. We cannot overemphasise the importance for all concerned to keep abreast of developments in European law. Indeed, at the very time that this Preface is being written the European Court of Justice is reconsidering the effect of Directives in domestic law and this is likely to be a continuing process. There is also little doubt that the European Court will be called upon at some time in the future to interpret individual Articles from the relevant Directives and these decisions will need to be observed by the domestic courts.

The aim of this book is to provide an introductory guide to the new legal framework. These radical changes have given rise to many interesting questions and it will be a long time before many of them are resolved. As a result we have largely attempted to give guidance and provoke awareness rather than to offer solutions.

The introductory chapters set out the new Regulations in their context – both from an historical and a European perspective – and the remaining chapters are meant to provide a handy guide to each set of new Regulations. At the end of the text we have also provided some guidance to practitioners on the overall impact of the new Regulations on the conduct of personal injury litigation.

At the end of the book we have provided the full text of the relevant Directives and the Regulations and the substantial body of the Approved Codes of Practice and Guidance Notes which have been produced to accompany the Regulations. The Regulations are set out separately, for ease of reference; each set of Regulations is then followed by the relevant guidance, for cross-reference.

We would like to express our thanks to all the staff at Butterworths without whom this book would never have been possible. Thanks also go to our colleagues in Chambers, the University of East Anglia and the London School of Economics for their encouragement and support. The Approved Codes of Practice and Guidance Notes are Crown copyright. We remain responsible for any errors, omissions or false prophecies.

The law is stated as at 1 February 1993.

Ian Smith
Christopher Goddard
Nicholas Randall

Devereux Chambers, London

Contents

Table of statutes

Table of statutory instruments

Table of EC legislation

List of cases

Chapter 1
Introduction

The new health and safety Regulations which form the subject matter of this book represent a wholesale reform in this important area of the law. A substantial body of the pre-existing law has been repealed or revoked and that which remains has often been amended and qualified. These changes are likely to have a substantial impact on the way in which personal injury litigation is conducted and will require a different approach from practitioners, employers, workers and unions.

CONCENTRATION ON THE RISK

The new Regulations represent a major shift away from the pre-existing system of looking to the type of workplace or premises in which an accident has occurred in order to establish which, if any, statutory provisions apply. This is because, as their titles suggest, the new Regulations concentrate on combating a specific type of risk rather than looking to the premises in which the risk has occurred. This universality of coverage represents a substantial extension of health and safety provisions and large numbers of workers who did not previously enjoy specific protections will now be covered under the new Regulations.

THE EUROPEAN DIMENSION

The new Regulations are also of significance because of their European origin. In many instances they will represent the first major exposure for practitioners, employers and employees to the influence of the European Community and this is likely to have far-reaching consequences. It is now clear, for example, that when considering the coverage and impact of the Regulations, account must be taken of the wording and overall scheme of the Directives. There are also wider implications for practitioners and it is no longer possible to advise or practise in this area without a working knowledge of European Community law. This cultural change will also be accentuated by the fact that the jurisprudence of the Community is still at a relatively early stage of development and in many relevant areas there will be no specific authorities and only general principles to guide the practitioner.

IMPACT ON CIVIL LIABILITY

The influence of the Regulations is also likely to filter through into the law of negligence and civil liability. The Directives can be seen as setting not only specific legal standards but also as setting acceptable standards for health and safety practice throughout the Community. It is certainly now arguable, for example, that a failure to meet the standards required by the Directives will represent a breach of duty in negligence even if the risk in question is not directly covered by the provision. In addition, the requirement on employers and others to carry out risk assessments is likely to be of considerable significance when considering questions of foreseeability at common law.

It is hoped that this book will provide a useful introduction to the new legal framework for all those who work in the area of health and safety. Wherever possible the authors have attempted to highlight the areas in which difficulties are likely to arise as well as providing a general commentary on the substance of the new Regulations. A destination table is also included which it is hoped will provide an at-a-glance view to illustrate where the new equivalents of some old friends can be found.

Chapter 2

Interrelationship with existing provisions

It is important to realise that the new Regulations do not exist in isolation; in spite of the fact that they constitute the single most important development in health and safety law in nearly two decades (and to a large extent stand together under the umbrella of the Management of Health and Safety Regulations 1992, enacting the 'Framework' Directive[1]), they are primarily meant to fit into much of the existing legislation.

Large parts of the old statute law are, of course, repealed and replaced (subject to transitional provisions), in particular the old factory legislation; on the other hand, the Health and Safety Commission were concerned that the enactment of the new Regulations should not compromise the more modern legislation (for example, the Control of Substances Hazardous to Health Regulations 1988) which had been produced as a result of domestic initiatives.[2] Thus, although efforts are made in some contexts to rationalise the coverage of old and new,[3] as a general rule it is

---

1 Council Directive 89/391/EEC; see p 33, below.
2 Ironically, one of the Commission's fears about qualified majority voting under Article 118A was that it could result in a setting of *lower* health and safety standards than those already applying in the UK, usually recognised as having the most highly developed system in the EC: '... our large body of recently achieved law is at risk to the rapid counterplay of argument and compromise, with the risk that less carefully constructed and industrially acceptable solutions will emerge' (HSC, 'Plan of work for 1990–91 and beyond', para 95). Of course, the desire for higher Community-wide standards is only partly altruistic or social in its nature; it is also based on economic ideas of the 'level playing field', ie that firms in one EC country should not be able to undercut firms in other EC countries through having lower health and safety obligations and hence lower unit labour costs. On this latter basis, the Regulations can be seen as part of the 'single market' philosophy, without the need to stray into the 'social dimension' minefield.
3 See, eg, the Personal Protective Equipment at Work Regulations, reg 3(3) (p 55, below) which provides that the new Regulations do not apply to six specified areas where existing Regulations already require the provision of specified items of protective equipment.

accepted that there may well be overlaps and that this in turn may well be no bad thing, given that the overall aim is to produce a matrix of modern laws applying to all industrial undertakings. This is made clear in the first paragraph of the first Approved Code of Practice, 'Management of Health and Safety at Work':

'The duties of the Management of Health and Safety at Work Regulations, because of their wide-ranging general nature, overlap with many existing regulations. Where duties overlap, compliance with the duty in the more specific regulation will normally be sufficient to comply with the corresponding duty in the Management of Health and Safety at Work Regulations. However, where the duties in the Management of Health and Safety at Work Regulations go beyond those in the more specific regulations, additional measures will be needed to comply full with [the new Regulations].'

Similarly, there may be areas of overlap within the six new sets of Regulations themselves, particularly in relation to the very general requirements of the 'framework' Regulations.[4]

The most important area of overlap, however, is with the Health and Safety at Work Act 1974 itself. This Act, the product of the deliberations of the Robens Committee,[5] began the process of revolutionising our industrial safety laws, and continues to act as the basis and framework for all subsequent Regulations, even those as fundamental as the new sets. The relationship between the Act and the new Regulations may conveniently be explained in three stages: (1) what the Act has already achieved; (2) how the Regulations take these achievements further; and (3) how the Regulations advance the law beyond the Act.

WHAT THE ACT HAS ALREADY ACHIEVED

The Act was based on a philosophy of active accident prevention, rather than the traditional role of the law of tort in largely reacting to accidents that have occurred, by concentrating on the awarding of compensation. The following are the main practical applications of the philosophy.

---

4   See, eg, the Guidance on the Provision and Use of Work Equipment Regulations, paras 13ff, p 300, below.
5   Report of the Committee on Safety and Health at Work, Cmnd 5034, 1972. For fuller consideration of the report and the resultant Act, see Smith & Wood *Industrial Law* (5th edn, 1993), Ch 13.

(i) Comprehensive coverage of workplaces and processes

One of the first criticisms by the Robens report was of the vast complexity of the existing system,[6] which had grown up piecemeal, with the result that certain types of workplace or process were well covered but certain other areas were left uncovered, possibly because no major disaster had yet occurred in that area prompting Parliament to cover it in yet another piece of specific, reactive legislation.[7] The Health and Safety at Work Act, by contrast, applies generally to all workplaces, employers and employees, and extends to many self-employed persons, and also to others such as manufacturers, designers and importers of articles to be used at work. Moreover, the domestic regulations already enacted reflect this approach by covering certain hazards or processes *as such*, wherever they arise or are carried out. Good examples are the regulations covering the protection of eyes,[8] noise,[9] the use of lead,[10] the use of asbestos,[11] the control of industrial major hazards[12] and the control of substances hazardous to health.[13] Likewise, provisions relating to first aid[14] and the reporting of accidents, diseases and dangerous occurrences[15] are in common, *not* reliant on the detailed nature of the workplace in question.

(ii) Comprehensive duties on employers and self-employed

Sections 2–6 of the Act place general duties on employers, the self-employed, persons otherwise in control of premises and designers, manufacturers, importers or suppliers of articles for use at work. These duties are owed not just to employees, but also to others who

---

6 It was contained in 11 major statutes and nearly 500 statutory instruments.
7 For example, the Factories Act 1961 contained exhaustive provisions, but their application depended on the premises in question qualifying as a 'factory' within s 175(1); that definition, with voluminous case law on the meaning of phrases such as 'manual labour', 'for trade or gain' and 'close, curtilage or precinct', took seven pages of previous editions of Smith & Wood's *Industrial Law* to explain in outline only. On the other hand, before the 1974 Act, universities were covered by no protective legislation, in spite of the fact that science faculties frequently had the potential ability to devastate the surrounding countryside for miles around.
8 Protection of Eyes Regulations 1974, SI 1974/1681.
9 Noise at Work Regulations 1989, SI 1989/1990.
10 Control of Lead at Work Regulations 1980, SI 1980/1248.
11 Control of Asbestos at Work Regulations 1987, SI 1987/2115.
12 Control of Industrial Major Accident Hazards Regulations 1984, SI 1984/1902.
13 Control of Substances Hazardous to Health Regulations 1988, SI 1988/1657.
14 Health and Safety (First Aid) Regulations 1981, SI 1981/917.
15 Reporting of Injuries, Diseases and Dangerous Occurrences Regulations 1985, SI 1985/2023.

may be affected by work activities. They are cast in terms of reasonable practicability for the most part, and the principal provision, the duty in section 2(1) on 'every employer to ensure, as far as is reasonably practicable, the health, safety and welfare of all of his employees', is then filled out in section 2(2) to cover the main areas traditionally covered by the common law duty of employer to employee, namely safe plant, systems of work, storage and transport of substances, training and supervision, place of work, access and working environment. What has always marked this off, however, from its common law background is that it is specifically provided[16] that these duties do *not* support civil liability. Instead, they are the basis for criminal prosecution and administrative enforcement by the Health and Safety Executive (HSE).

(iii) Self-regulation

Section 16 of the Act provides for the HSC to approve codes of practice giving guidance on the practical application of the general duties in the Act. This element of self-regulation and practical guidance was an important element in seeking to maximise safety, rather than relying on an 'attitude of minimum compliance' engendered by the older, more technical approach to the drafting of industrial safety legislation. Any such codes of practice are specifically made admissible in criminal proceedings, and may, of course, be relevant also in civil proceedings, subject to the usual caveat that they are not in themselves law, and so a failure to follow a suggested practice does not in itself render the employer liable.[17]

(iv) Joint regulation

The involvement of employees through recognised trade unions (where appropriate) was another key idea behind the Act. This is advanced by means of safety representatives and safety committees, with statutory rights to be consulted and to have time off work for the necessary training and exercise of their functions.[18] The government took the view that these existing provisions largely

---

16 Health and Safety at Work Act 1974, s 47(1).
17 Ibid, s 17. In criminal proceedings where a provision of an ACOP is not complied with there is a reversal of the burden of proof on to the employer to show that he has complied with the statutory obligation in question in some other way: s 17(2).
18 Safety Representative and Safety Committees Regulations 1977, SI 1977/500.

complied with the new EC initiatives and so made only minor amendments; it is, however, argued later in the book that these have not fully implemented the Directive in question, particularly where there is no recognised trade union.[19]

(v) Duties on employees

Sections 7 and 8 of the Act place statutory duties on employees: (1) to take reasonable care for their own and other people's safety; (2) to co-operate with the employers to the extent necessary to allow those employers to comply with their statutory obligations; and (3) not intentionally or recklessly to interfere with or misuse 'anything provided in the interests of health, safety or welfare in pursuance of any of the relevant statutory provisions'. As with the general duties on the employer, breach of these provisions does not give rise to civil liability, but could lead to criminal liability.

(vi) Enforcement agencies and powers

A priority under the Act was the unification of the inspectorates, and the modernisation of their administrative powers. The Health and Safety Commission (HSC) was established as the governing body, with the Health and Safety Executive (HSE) as the executive arm. Wide powers are given to inspectors;[20] although in most cases they will proceed by way of education and suggestion, legal teeth are given in the form of the inspector's powers to issue an improvement notice[21] or (where there is a risk of serious personal injury) a prohibition notice[22] or physically to seize and render harmless any article or substance which is a cause of imminent danger of serious personal injury.[23]

---

19 Management of Health and Safety at Work Regulations 1992, reg 17, Schedule; see Chapter 12, below.
20 Health and Safety at Work Act 1974, s 20. Subsection (2) specifies remarkably wide powers of entry, investigation, sampling, etc in heads (a) to (l), followed by (m): 'any other power which is necessary for the purpose mentioned in subsection (l) above'.
21 Ibid, s 21; such a notice specifies the contravention in question and requires the person to remedy it within a set period.
22 Ibid, s 22; such a notice actually requires the cessation of the activity in question unless and until the situation is remedied. Appeal against both kinds of notice lies to an industrial tribunal but in the case of a prohibition notice it remains in force pending the appeal: s 24(3). Such appeals are extremely rare. In 1991/92 inspectors issued 8,377 improvement notices and 4,005 prohibition notices.
23 Ibid, s 25.

(vii) Criminal penalties

Part of the Robens philosophy was that, given the aim of encouraging the maximisation of safety, criminal enforcement should be relegated to a longstop *but* at the same time the available penalties should be made realistic and effective in case of need.[24] A long series of offences is set out in section 33 of the Act, including breach of the general provisions in sections 2–8, contravention of any health and safety Regulations,[25] obstruction of an inspector and breach of an improvement or prohibition notice. The desire to increase the 'ultimate deterrent' effect was achieved in two ways: (1) although some offences are summary only, the principal offences can now be tried on indictment, in which case the penalty is an unlimited fine (particularly important in the prosecution of a large company in a high-profile case) and/or a maximum of two years' imprisonment;[26] (2) the *level* of the responsibility within an organisation is kept deliberately vague and, although the policy is invariably to prosecute the organisation not an individual, there is nothing in law to *prevent* an individual being prosecuted and, ultimately, imprisoned.

(viii) Health and safety Regulations

Finally, the Act laid the basis for the progressive replacement of *all* the existing (largely outmoded[27]) legislation by modern health and safety Regulations. The procedure is laid down[28] and, once they are

---

24 For many years the maximum penalty under the factories legislation was £40.
25 Thus the six new sets of Regulations do *not* contain enforcement provision, but instead are enforceable under these established provisions. Section 40 contains another reversal of the burden of proof; where the allegation is of failure to do something as far as practicable or reasonably practicable, it is for the accused to prove that it was *not* practicable or reasonably practicable to do more, or that there was no better practicable means than was in fact used.
26 The normal penalty maximum in summary proceedings is a fine up to level 5 on the standard scale, but as from March 1992 certain stiffer penalties were introduced; thus, breach of sections 2–6 of the Health and Safety at Work Act 1974 (the general duties on employers) carries a maximum of £20,000 or six months' imprisonment or both. In 1991/92 there were 2,407 prosecutions, leading to 2,122 convictions; the average fine was £1,134.
27 The principal safety provisions in the Factories Act 1961, ss 12–14 still reflected a nineteenth-century cotton mill, ie s 12 'prime movers' (steam boilers), s 13 'transmission machinery' (overhead belts) and s 14 'dangerous parts of machinery other than prime movers or transmission machinery' (the actual machines powered by the belts).
28 Health and Safety Act 1974, ss 15, 82.

enacted, not only are they criminally enforceable in the normal way (above) but also it is specifically provided that they *do* support civil liability unless they provide otherwise.[29]

HOW THE NEW REGULATIONS TAKE THESE ACHIEVEMENTS FURTHER

(i) Replacement of existing legislation

The original aim at the time of the 1974 Act was for the repeal and replacement of all of the old legislation within two decades. Although a great deal of work was done in producing health and safety Regulations, these tended to be concerned with new areas, or only repealed and replaced specific parts of the old legislation, so that by the mid-1980s we still had with us most of the original factory legislation, etc, and it seemed that the original aim would not be realised. However, this most recent involvement of the EC through Article 118A revitalised that aim and produced, with effect from 1 January 1993, the new overall framework that has been so long awaited.

(ii) Use of codes of practice

As already seen the device of the code of practice was an essential element of the Robens philosophy. One original idea was that such codes could be used *instead* of Regulations, but that did not come to fruition. Instead, codes have been used in the more traditional way to flesh out certain sets of Regulations. However, it is arguable that the dependence on ACOPs or guidance notes in the new structure is quantitatively different and comes at least several steps closer to that original idea – the six sets of Regulations are themselves of course fundamental *but* it may be that in practice it is the extensive guidance that assumes the dominant role, certainly in the minds of those charged with the day-to-day application of the

---

29 Ibid, s 47(2). The Management of Health and Safety at Work Regulations do exclude civil liability for their breach (reg 15, see p 212, below), but the other five sets of new Regulations do not, and so will support civil liability in an action for breach of statutory duty. Moreover, it is the contention in this book that, despite reg 15, breach of the framework Regulations *will* be relevant in establishing common law negligence.

new rules. This is arguably shown simply by the form of presentation of the six ACOPs or guidance notes which include within them the (short) text of each regulation which is then expanded upon to a very considerable extent.[30]

(iii) Comprehensive coverage

The comprehensive, cross-industries nature of the new obligations is obvious on first reading. The Management of Health and Safety Regulations could hardly have been cast in wider terms, and the same approach can be seen in, for example, the definitions of 'workplace',[31] 'work equipment'[32] and VDU 'user'.[33]

(iv) Maximisation of safety

The emphasis on accident *prevention* can be seen not just in the modernised forms of requirements in relation to particular machinery or processes, but more generally in the importance given to positive steps to *assess risk*, act upon such assessments and act so as to eliminate, avoid or (at the least) lessen perceived risks.[34] This can be seen particularly in the Management of Health and Safety Regulations, which also reflect the modern concerns not just with accidents but also with industrial *health* risks.

(v) Information and written policies

The 1974 Act introduced a requirement of more openness in health and safety measures, and placed a statutory obligation on

---

30 Prime examples of this are the Workplace Health, Safety and Welfare ACOP with its extensive explanations of standards etc actually required in the light of the Regulations, and the Manual Handling guidance and Display Screen guidance with their use of diagrams.

31 '[A]ny premises or part of premises which are not domestic premises and are made available to any person as a place of work': Workplace (Health, Safety and Welfare) Regulations, reg 2(1).

32 '[A]ny machinery, appliance, apparatus or tool and any assembly of components which, in order to achieve a common end, are arranged and controlled so that they function as a whole': Provision and Use of Work Equipment Regulations, reg 2(1).

33 '[A]n employee who habitually uses display screen equipment as part of his normal work': Health and Safety (Display Screen Equipment) Regulations, reg 1(1). 'Use' means 'use for or in connection with work': ibid.

34 This appears especially in the Manual Handling Operations Regulations, reg 4(1), see p 395, below. Of major importance legally is the emphasis placed throughout the new Regulations on providing, to use the old common law terminology, safe *systems* of work.

employers to produce written health and safety policies.[35] A similar approach can be seen in the requirement of written risk assessments and health and safety arrangements in the framework Regulations.[36]

(vi) Statutory duties on employees

In addition to the general duties on employees in the 1974 Act, there are new obligations:

(a) to use equipment in accordance with training or instructions and to inform the employer of serious and imminent dangers or shortcomings in protective arrangements;[37]

(b) to use personal protective equipment in accordance with training or instructions and to report any loss of or obvious defect in that equipment;[38] and

(c) to make full and proper use of any system provided by the employer for manual handling of loads.[39]

HOW THE REGULATIONS GO BEYOND THE ACT

Although a great deal needs to be worked out in practice before forming definite views on the overall impact of the Regulations, it is suggested that the following may be significant ways in which they constitute an advance on the Act.

(i) Their origin in EC harmonisation

The initial reaction of the HSC to the proposed EC Directives was that the UK already complied substantially in one way or another, in other words that it was all there somewhere if you looked hard

---

35 Health and Safety at Work Act 1974, s 2(3). Employers of less than five employees are exempt: Employers' Health and Safety Policy Statements (Exemptions) Regulations 1975, SI 1975/1584.
36 Management of Health and Safety at Work Regulations, regs 3(4) and 4(2); again, employers of less than five employees are exempt. See also reg 8 on the 'comprehensible and relevant information' that must be given to employees.
37 Management of Health and Safety at Work Regulations, reg 12.
38 Personal Protective Equipment at Work Regulations, regs 10, 11.
39 Manual Handling Operations Regulations, reg 5.

enough; in particular, much of it was already at least implicit in the wide general duties in the 1974 Act. In the event, of course, the Directives led to a major reformulation and modernisation, in which the EC origins of the new Regulations can be seen in at least two ways. First, although some of the new Regulations retain traditional formulations such as 'reasonably practicable' and most are compatible with the long-standing UK approach of adopting the 'best practicable means', many of the new Regulations adopt novel formulations taken from the Directives such as 'effective and suitable' and 'suitable and sufficient', the meaning of which will have to be litigated. Second, harmonisation in this context includes making these Regulations harmonious with EC requirements and Directives in other areas, particularly those of product liability and industrial standards. Thus, one of the obligations of an employer under the Provision and Use of Work Equipment Regulations[40] is to ensure that work equipment complies with any applicable product Directives,[41] and personal protective equipment is to comply with relevant EC design or manufacture standards.[42]

(ii) Greater emphasis on the concept of risk

Although the 1974 Act was more positive and proactive than the previous legislation, much of it was still concerned with what might be termed the 'static condition' approach to industrial safety. More advanced ideas of hazard analysis and risk assessment have already appeared in domestic legislation since the Act,[43] but they now occupy a much more central place in the scheme of the new Regulations.

---

40 Reg 10(1). 'Existing national legislation on the manufacture and supply of new work equipment is increasingly being supplemented by new and more detailed Regulations implementing EC Directives made under Article 100A [the 'Single Market' powers]: Work Equipment Guidance, para 97. On the importance of Article 100A Directives, see ibid, paras 102–106.

41 The aim eventually is to have harmonised standards for the production of work equipment (bearing the 'CE Mark'); reg 10(2) provides that where equipment complies with harmonised standards the detailed requirements of regs 11 to 24 only apply 'to the extent that the relevant Community Directive . . . is not applicable to that item of work equipment'. Thus, the health and safety provisions and the standards provisions are meant to be integrated.

42 Personal Protective Equipment at Work Regulations, reg 4(3)(e), Sch 1. Harmonised European standards (ENs) are increasingly to replace existing British standards: Guidance on PPE, paras 33–35 and Appendix 3.

43 See, eg, the Control of Substances Hazardous to Health Regulations 1988.

(iii) Inclusion of temporary workers

In addition to the six specific Directives, the new Regulations are also intended to comply with Council Directive 91/383/EEC which requires the extension of the usual level of health and safety protection to (a) employees on fixed-term contracts, and (b) temporary employees provided by an 'employment business'. There is a specific provision in the Management of Health and Safety at Work Regulations[44] requiring the giving of health and safety information to such employees; other requirements of the Directive are presumably to be read into other parts of the Regulations by implication, at least where this is legally possible (see Chapter 11).

(iv) Nature of the obligations

In line with the EC approach generally, the new requirements are in some ways more prescriptive than the older domestic legislation that they replace. As mentioned above, the guidance given is certainly more voluminous and detailed. With regard to the level of duty in the Regulations themselves, some vestiges remain of existing 'as far as reasonably practicable' duties, and strict liability continues to apply in certain areas where it applied before.[45] However, there is one shift of emphasis which may impart more elements of strict (though not absolute) liability. Where a new regulation is cast in terms of the provision of something to a 'suitable and sufficient level' (rather than providing it 'as far as reasonably practicable') the drafting tends to state that it *shall* be provided to that level.[46] Where this is the case, the obligation to *provide* it is strict, with any argument being as to whether that which was in fact provided was 'suitable and sufficient' (whereas before there could have been arguments as to whether it was

---

44 Reg 13.
45 Thus, reg 11 of the Provision and Use of Work Equipment Regulations ('Dangerous parts of machinery') is a modernised form of the strict liability regime of the old Factories Act 1961, s 14, though of course now applicable to any workplace (unless specifically excluded); even here, however, it is arguable that the nature of the duty may have changed, see p 50.
46 For example reg 21 of the Provision and Use of Work Equipment Regulations states that 'Every employer shall ensure that suitable and sufficient lighting . . . is provided at any place where a person uses work equipment'. Another form of wording used in conjunction with a strict requirement is 'where appropriate': 'Every employer shall ensure that where appropriate work equipment is provided with suitable means to isolate it from its sources of energy' (ibid, reg 19(1)).

'reasonably practicable' to provide it *at all*); it is unlikely that the 'suitable' level of provision would be held to be nil. Moreover, in at least one place the Regulations themselves seem to accept that the new 'suitable and sufficient' type of duty is higher than the old reasonably practical duty – regulation 17(2) of the Workplace Regulations states that there must be suitable and sufficient traffic routes, but then regulation 17(5) qualifies this by saying that that requirement only applies to certain premises 'as far as reasonably practicable'. Thus, one of the key areas in the legal application of these Regulations is likely to be the interpretation to be placed by the courts on the new terminology of suitability, sufficiency, effectiveness, adequacy and appropriateness. Dictionary definitions might be a starting point, but at the end of the day these terms will have to be interpreted in the light of the Regulations overall, being heavily questions of fact, on which the guidelines given in the appropriate ACOP or Guidance Notes could well be determinative in practice.

Chapter 3
The European dimension

INTRODUCTION

The new Regulations represent the attempts of the UK government to implement the first group of Directives made under Article 118A of the Treaty of Rome and adopted by the Council of Ministers of the EC for implementation by the Member States by 31 December 1992. Article 118A was introduced by the Single European Act 1986 (SEA). The aim of the SEA was to transform the existing relationships between the Member States of the EC into a European Union in accordance with the principles of the Stuttgart Solemn Declaration of June 1983. In support of this aim the SEA contains new policy objectives in the fields of social policy and economic and social cohesion.

Article 118A of the Treaty obliges the Member States to 'pay particular attention to encouraging improvements, especially in the working environment, as regards the health and safety of workers' and provides for the adoption of Directives to achieve this purpose on the basis of majority voting in the EC Council of Ministers.

The Directives which form the subject matter of this work can therefore be seen as the first fruits of Article 118A. A number of other measures are currently under discussion and it is likely that Article 118A will be the source of further legislative measures in the future.

IMPLEMENTATION IN THE UK

The UK has sought to implement the first series of Directives by means of statutory Regulations made under section 15 of the Health and Safety at Work etc Act 1974. The Regulations were laid before Parliament by the Secretary of State for Employment on the basis of proposals submitted to her by the Health and Safety Commission which had carried out consultations in accordance with its powers and duties under the 1974 Act.

The stated aim of the Health and Safety Commission in implementing the Directives in the UK was to propose Regulations which did not go beyond the strict requirements of the Directives in order to minimise the impact of any changes in the law. This approach has left the Commission open to criticism and it is certainly arguable that, in a number of areas, the Regulations as proposed by the Commission fail to meet the standards required by the Directives. This is an area which will be dealt with in greater detail later on in this text.

In view of the increasing influence of the EC in the area of health and safety it is important to consider the relevant Community standards and how these interact with domestic law and some consideration of the law of the EC is therefore necessary. Indeed, it is now clear that any practitioner working in this field will require a working knowledge of EC law and procedure. Although a detailed consideration of the law of the EC is beyond the scope of this work, a brief outline of the law of the Community and, in particular, the role and legal effect of Directives is of vital importance when considering the new legal framework of health and safety in the UK.

THE EUROPEAN COMMUNITIES ACT 1972

EC legislation has force in the UK by virtue of the provisions of the European Communities Act 1972. The Act is of major constitutional importance and has had a number of important repercussions. It is now clearly established that the supreme judicial authority in respect of any legal issues which involve EC law and its interaction with the law of the UK is the Court of Justice of the European Community (ECJ). It is also now generally accepted that in the event of any conflict between EC law and domestic law then EC law will normally prevail and should be enforced as such by the domestic courts.

DIRECTIVES

Article 118A provides that its objectives should be achieved by the use of Directives. A Directive is primarily intended to create legal relationships between the EC and the Member State to which it is addressed. Article 189 of the Treaty of Rome states that a Directive 'is binding as to the result to be achieved upon each Member State to which it is addressed but shall leave to the national authorities choice of form and methods'.

It was originally thought that Directives did not provide any directly enforceable rights for individuals but this view has now been revised as a result of a series of landmark decisions from the ECJ which have established that private individuals can obtain directly enforceable rights from Directives in certain circumstances. It is now possible for a private individual to invoke the provisions of a Directive directly against the state or an employer in the public sector and, to an extent which is not yet clearly defined, an individual may further rely upon the provisions of a Directive in an action against the state in circumstances where they can show that they have suffered loss or have had their rights infringed by reason of the failure of the Member State to implement the Directive effectively. It needs to be remembered that this is an expanding area of jurisprudence, the limits of which are currently undefined.

When considering the practical application of the new Regulations the practitioner will be primarily concerned with the following issues:

(a) to what extent should the court look to the relevant provisions of the Directive when interpreting the Regulations?

(b) what is the position if the standards required by the Regulations appear to fall below those set in the Directive?

(c) what is the position if the standards required by the Regulations go beyond those set in the Directive?

(d) what if the Regulations fail to implement the relevant Article of the Directive at all?

INTERPRETATION

It is only in a very few instances that the wording of a particular regulation has been taken directly from the wording of the Directive and, as a result, in a large number of cases there is likely to be some difference between the wording of the regulation and the equivalent article of the Directive. In the vast majority of such cases the differences can effectively be eliminated in the process of interpretation. It is now clearly established that domestic law which has been introduced to meet the UK's Community obligations is to be construed in accordance with the applicable Community law. This principle will obviously apply to the new health and safety Regulations. The position has been clearly stated by the House of Lords in *Litster v Forth Dry Dock and Engineering Co Ltd* [1989] IRLR 161:

> 'The approach to the construction of primary and subordinate legislation enacted to give effect to the United Kingdom's obligations under the EEC Treaty has been the subject matter of recent authority in this House (see *Pickstone v Freemans plc* [1988] IRLR 357) and is not in doubt. If the legislation can reasonably be construed so as to conform with those obligations – obligations which are to be ascertained not only from the wording of the Directive but from the interpretation placed upon it by the European Court of Justice at Luxembourg – such a purposive construction will be applied even though, perhaps, it may involve some departure from the strict and literal application of the words which the legislature has elected to use.' [Lord Oliver at 165]

The 'purposive' approach may well create some initial difficulties for those domestic lawyers who are used to a more 'literal' approach to construction. The 'purposive' approach to construction requires the court to look at the object and purpose of the particular provision as well as the instument as a whole. This necessarily involves some consideration of the preamble to the Directive and a willingness to depart from the literal application of the words used by the legislature even to the extent of inserting new words into the domestic provision in order to achieve the desired effect. These points are all well illustrated by *Litster* in which the House of Lords upheld an appeal on a point of construction of a regulation giving effect to a Community Directive on the ground that the lower courts had erroneously interpreted the instrument in a literal fashion instead of adopting the proper 'purposive' approach. This approach is likely to resolve issues of intepretation of the Regulations in favour of plaintiffs in view of the overall scheme and aim of the Directives and Article 118A to promote and ensure the health and safety of workers at work.

However, there are still limits to the ambit of the 'purposive' approach to construction. In *Litster* Lord Oliver suggests that the relevant legislation must be capable of being reasonably construed in such a manner so as to conform with the necessary Community obligations, and this has been further emphasised by Lord Keith in *Webb v Emo Air Cargo (UK) Ltd* [1993] 1 WLR 49 and by Lord

Templeman in *Duke v GEC Reliance Systems Ltd* [1988] AC 168. However, it is also clear from these authorities that the courts will not be willing to adopt interpretations which distort the domestic provision. It would appear to follow from this that the courts will not be willing to strike out words from the domestic provisions even if they do not comply with Community obligations as a result. This may well lead to some difficulties in a number of areas in the Regulations.

WHAT IS THE POSITION IF THE REGULATIONS FAIL TO MEET THE STANDARDS OF THE DIRECTIVE AND ANY DIFFERENCES CANNOT BE SOLVED BY INTERPRETATION?

If the Regulations fall below the standard required by the Directive and the differences in wording cannot reasonably be resolved through the approach of interpretation, then it is necessary to consider to what extent the individual can rely directly on the Community provision. This requires some consideration of the principle of 'direct effect'. As previously noted, it is now established that Directives are capable of giving rise to enforceable individual rights in certain circumstances.

The guiding principle as to whether a provision is capable of direct effect is the extent to which the Member State has been left with any discretion as regards implementation. In principle, if no real discretion has been left to the Member State, then the provision is capable of direct effect. This is well illustrated by the case of *Van Duyn v Home Office*: 41/74 [1975] Ch 358, ECJ in which it was held that a Directive could be enforced directly by a private individual against a Member State in certain circumstances. For such a position to arise the Article of the Directive must be 'clear, precise, and permit of no exceptions' so as not to require the intervention of the national authorities in order to be enforceable. Regard must also be had to the 'nature, general scheme, and wording of the provision'.

It is, therefore, important to consider each Article of the Directive in isolation. Some Articles in the same Directive may be enforceable and others not. This point is well illustrated by the cases of *Marshall v Southampton And South West Hampshire Area Health Authority (Teaching)*: 152/84 [1986] IRLR 140 and *Marshall v Southampton And South West Hampshire Area Health Authority (No 2)* [1990] IRLR 481, both of which involved consideration of the direct effect of different Articles of the Equal Treatment Directive (76/207). The first *Marshall* decision decided that Article 5 of the Directive was capable of direct effect whereas the *Marshall (No 2)* decision held that Article 6 of the same Directive was not.

The first *Marshall* decision also established that a Directive can have direct effect as against a Member State but cannot have direct effect as between private individuals. This approach has been confirmed by the more recent decision of the ECJ in *Officer Van Justitie v Kolpinghuis Nijmegen BV* [1989] 2 CMLR 18 in which it was observed that Article 189 of the Treaty provided that the obligations contained in a Directive exist only in relation to the Member State to which it is addressed. It is therefore clear that a Member State cannot defend itself in any proceedings on the grounds of its own failure to implement a Directive. In other words, a Directive is capable of having what is termed 'vertical effect', ie as against the state, but is not capable of 'horizontal effect', ie as between individuals.

What constitutes the state?

The *Marshall* case, therefore, raised the issue of what organisations are capable of being the state or its emanations. The leading case in this area is the decision of the ECJ in *Foster and Others v British Gas plc* [1990] IRLR 353 in which it was held that a Directive may be directly relied upon against an entity which provides a public service under the control of the state and which has powers in excess of those which result from the normal rules applicable in relations between individuals. The legal form of the entity is irrelevant for these purposes. Whether any particular organisation falls within the definition or not is a matter for the domestic courts. As a result of the decision of the ECJ the House of Lords had little difficulty in deciding that British Gas, prior to privatisation, was an emanation of the state for these purposes.

However, it is important to remember that the control of the state is not the sole determining factor, and this is well illustrated by the case of *Doughty v Rolls-Royce* [1992] IRLR 126 in which it was held that Rolls-Royce was not an emanation of the state even though the state had a controlling shareholding because it failed to meet two of the three criteria laid down by the ECJ. However, it is strongly arguable that an organisation may still fall within the definition if some but not all of the criteria are established.

The position is now relatively clear if an employee of the state or an emanation of the state brings a claim under the new health and safety Regulations. If there is a difference between the wording of the Directive and the Regulations and the relevant Article of the Directive is sufficiently clear and precise then the employee is entitled to rely upon the Directive directly.

Employees in the private sector

As a result of these authorities the position emerged in which employees in the public sector appeared to be in a more advantageous position than their counterparts in the private sector because they could enforce rights contained in Directives against their employer in certain circumstances. Indeed, this apparently arbitrary and unfair distinction between private and state employees was noted in the *Marshall* decision. However, as a result of important new developments, it is now arguable that this distinction has been removed by the decision of the ECJ in *Francovich v Italian Republic* [1992] IRLR 84.

The *Francovich* case establishes the principle that there is a Community law right to compensation against a Member State where it has failed to implement a Directive and an individual has suffered loss or damage as a result of the state's failure to act. A claim on this basis should be brought in the domestic courts. The right to recover from the state depends upon the nature of the breach of Community law. Liability for damages will result if three conditions are satisfied:

'The first of these conditions is that the result required by the Directive includes the conferring of rights for the benefit of individuals. The second condition is that the content of these rights may be determined by reference to the provisions of the Directive. Finally, the third condition is the existence of a causal link between the breach of the obligation of the state and the damage suffered by the persons affected.'

Although *Francovich* involved a complete failure by the Italian government to implement the Directive, the principle would also appear to extend to cases in which ineffective attempts to implement have been made even if such attempts have been made in good faith. This view coincides with that put by the Advocate General in the case. Such a finding would also be consistent with the principle that the basis of enforcement is implicit in the Treaty of Rome and also expressly in Member States' obligations under Article 5 of the Treaty. It also needs to be noted that it was established in *Francovich* that the relevant provisions of the Directive were *not* capable of direct effect.

Although the position needs to be clarified, it would appear that:

(a) health and safety Directives confer rights on individuals;

(b) the nature of these rights are capable of identification from the Directives; and

(c) circumstances can easily be envisaged in which a causal link could be established between the breach of the Member State and the damage suffered by the individual.

It would, therefore, appear that a *Francovich*-type action would be available to a plaintiff in an action under the Regulations if they could show that they have suffered some detriment by reason of the failure of the Member State to implement the Directive adequately.

It would also appear that the arbitrary distinction between employees in the state sector and the private sector may have been eradicated by *Francovich*, although it will still be incumbent upon the private employee to commence fresh proceedings against the Member State in the domestic courts. It also needs to be borne in mind that state employees should also be able to rely upon *Francovich* in cases in which the relevant provision of Community law is not capable of direct effect.

In summary then, it would appear that, if the provisions of the Regulation fall below the standards required by the Directive and the difference cannot be overcome by adopting a 'purposive' approach to construction, then a party which has a cause of action against the state or an emanation of the state can rely directly on that provision so long as it is capable of direct effect. If the provisions of the Directive are not capable of direct effect but the conditions set out in *Francovich* are satisfied, then a remedy can be obtained from the Member State in a separate action in the domestic court. In all other cases a remedy can be obtained from the state if the conditions of *Francovich* have been met. There would also appear to be no reason why the principle in *Francovich* should not apply to provisions capable of direct effect.

WHAT IS THE POSITION IF THE STANDARDS REQUIRED BY THE REGULATIONS GO BEYOND THOSE REQUIRED BY THE DIRECTIVES?

If the regulation goes beyond the standards required by the Directive then the regulation should be construed in the normal way. In other words the purposive approach to interpretation should be used so that the regulation does not fall below the standard required by the Directive.

WHAT IS THE POSITION IF THE REGULATIONS FAIL TO IMPLEMENT THE DIRECTIVE AT ALL?

In general terms if there has been no attempt to implement the terms of the Directive at all in the Regulations, then the position is the same as if the Regulations fall below the requirements of the Directive. In other words if the provisions of the Directive are capable of direct effect then they can be relied upon by any party which has commenced proceedings against the state or an emanation of the state. In all other circumstances an action against the Member State will lie if the requirements of *Francovich* are met.

It is important that the practitioner keeps abreast with the current developments in EC law. There is some suggestion that in all cases in which there is a conflict between domestic law and Community law the domestic law provisions must be interpreted in a manner consistent with Community law (see *Marleasing SA v La Commercial Internacional de Alumentacion SA* [1992] 1 CMLR 305 although this is not the interpretation that has been put on the case by the House of Lords in *Webb v Emo Air Cargo (UK) Ltd* [1993] 1 WLR 49) even if this means striking out the relevant provisions of domestic law. If this view is confirmed by the ECJ then it would effectively mean that Directives would be capable of 'horizontal' effect by indirect means, ie through the machinery of interpretation. If this approach was confirmed by the ECJ then in all cases it would be open to individuals to rely directly on the Directives. However, this approach would appear to conflict with the reasoning of the previous authorities and, in particular, would impose liabilities on private individuals who have never been put under any obligation to comply with Community provisions by their Member State. Such a step would therefore appear to conflict with the reasoning so far adopted by the ECJ.

THE ROLE OF THE ECJ

It is also important to bear in mind that any question of the interpretation of Community law is a matter for the ECJ and not the domestic court. It is therefore only in the most simple of cases that the domestic court can interpret the meaning of a provision of Community law. If such a question is in doubt then the question should be referred to the ECJ.

Chapter 4
Civil liability

Although the primary legislative aim of industrial safety legislation has always been to prevent accidents, it has to be conceded that its main significance to the personal injury lawyer has always been as a basis for civil liability once an accident has happened. The new Regulations are obviously aimed at improving industrial safety and are, as is made clear elsewhere in this book, deliberately made more pro-active and positive in their approach than much of the legislation that they replace. At the same time, however, it is exactly that widened scope that may (1) extend the scope of the action for breach of statutory duty, (2) increase the importance of certain facets of common law negligence, and (3) have an effect on the defence of contributory negligence. These matters are now considered in turn.

BREACH OF STATUTORY DUTY

The action for breach of statutory duty is usually a more precise and focused action in an industrial accident than common law negligence, and has often also had the advantage of imposing a stricter duty on the employer.[1] The first question, therefore, is whether the new Regulations themselves support civil liability. The Health and Safety at Work Act 1974, section 47(2) provides:

'Breach of duty imposed by health and safety Regulations shall, so far as it causes damage, be actionable except in so far as the Regulations provide otherwise.'

---

1 For the elements of breach of statutory duty, see Munkman *Employer's Liability* (11th edn, 1990); for the author of that work's strong views on the failings of the action for negligence and its current dominance, see the Foreword at pp vi and vii.

The five subsidiary sets of Regulations do not have any such exclusion of civil liability and so can be relied on as the basis for actions for breach of statutory duty. However, the head Regulations, the Management of Health and Safety Regulations, do provide in regulation 15 as follows:

> 'Breach of a duty imposed by these Regulations shall not confer a right of action in any civil proceedings.'

Thus, a breach of one of the very general duties in these Regulations (in particular, the obligation under regulation 3 to undertake risk assessments which arguable is central to the whole scheme of the new regulatory system, with its emphasis on *risk*) will not give rise directly to an action for breach of duty. This restriction was not contained in the original draft of the Regulations, but appeared in the final version. From the point of view of a plaintiff's lawyers this is unfortunate, but on the other hand it may be that this late amendment will not have the desired effect of rendering the head Regulations of criminal and administrative effect only,[2] for two reasons:

(i) it may be arguable that the insertion of this restriction is in breach of EC law, as being a failure to implement fully the Framework Directive; remedies are usually left largely to the Member State *but* there is a general requirement that whatever remedies are enacted must be realistic[3] and so, although the Management Regulations are amenable to criminal and administrative enforcement, it could be argued that without the possibility of a civil liability in favour of those injured by a breach of the Regulations, they do not in fact provide full and adequate remedies;

(ii) in any event, it is argued below that breach of the Management Regulations may be actionable indirectly through the medium of a common law negligence action.

Where one of the new Regulations does support civil liability directly, it will be necessary for a plaintiff seeking to rely on it to prove the usual requirements of the tort of breach of statutory duty.

---

2 Presumably the desire was to impose the same limitation on liability as has always applied to the general duties in sections 1–8 of the Health and Safety at Work Act 1974, by virtue of section 47(1); see Chapter 2, above.

3 *Von Colson v Land Nordrhein-Westfalen* Case 14/83 [1984] ECR 1891, [1982] 2 CMLR 430, ECJ.

(i) *The duty was owed to that plaintiff, either individually or as a member of a class meant by Parliament to be protected.*
This should not normally be difficult because of the breadth of coverage of the new Regulations.

(ii) *The duty was owed by that defendant.*
Again, this should not normally be difficult in the light of the extended coverage of the new Regulations which are *not* now tied to specific industries, processes or types of workplace.

(iii) *The defendant was in breach of the statutory duty.*
The ACOPs and Guidance Notes may well give very useful material on this point, given their extensive nature and, in some cases, very detailed suggestions. They are admissible generally in civil actions as evidence. One potentially significant point relates to the burden of proof. By virtue of the Health and Safety at Work Act 1974, section 17(2), where in any *criminal* proceedings it is proved that there was a failure to observe a provision of an ACOP[4] covering the allegation of breach in question, then that allegation is to be taken as proved 'unless the court is satisfied that the requirement or prohibition was in respect of that matter complied with otherwise than by way of observance of that provision of the code', ie there is a statutory reversal of the burden of proof. This does not apply in civil proceedings. However, it has long been held under the old factory legislation[5] that, where a duty is imposed to do or provide something 'as far as reasonably practicable' the onus is generally on the defendant employer to satisfy the court as to any question of reasonably practicability. From the plaintiff's point of view, it is to be hoped that this approach will now also be applied to the many new Regulations that adopt standards, not of reasonable practicability, but of the new terminology of suitability, sufficiency, adequacy, etc.

(iv) *Causation.*
There is no presumption of causation in a breach of statutory duty action.[6]

---

4 Note that section 17(2) does not specifically include Guidance Notes.
5 *Nimmo v Alexander Cowan & Sons Ltd* [1968] AC 107, [1967] 3 All ER 187, HL; *Jenkins v Allied Ironfounders Ltd* [1969] 3 All ER 1609, [1970] 2 WLR 304, HL; *Bowes v Sedgefield District Council* [1981] ICR 234, CA. This was recently reaffirmed in *Larner v British Steel plc* (1993) Times, 19 February, CA.
6 *Caswell v Powell Duffryn Associated Collieries Ltd* [1940] AC 152, [1939] 3 All ER 722, HL; see Munkman *Employer's Liability* (11th edn, 1990) at pp 207–212.

(v) *The damage caused was the type to be prevented by the statute
or Regulations.*

This requirement (usually known as the rule in *Gorris v
Scott*[7]) had certain unfortunate results under the old factory
legislation, especially the fencing requirements, since it could
lead to a narrow and arguably over-technical interpretation of
the scope of the legislative protection. In particular, it was
held that the central provisions of the Factories Act 1961,
section 14 on the fencing of dangerous machinery, only
applied to keep the worker out, not to keep the machine in.[8]
The over-subtleties of this approach were strongly criticised in
later cases,[9] but by that time there was little that the courts
could do about it. It is hoped that there should be less scope
for such an approach under the new Regulations, with their
wider coverage and frequent overlap. Thus, for example,
regulation 11 of the Workplace Equipment Regulations is still
concerned with keeping the worker out of machinery, *but*
regulation 12 now goes on to cover the ejection of material
from the machinery. On the other hand, it must be assumed
that the rule in *Gorris v Scott* will still apply and so it may in
some cases still be important to sue under the right
Regulation (or combination of Regulations).

NEGLIGENCE

Common law negligence has always been important in personal
injury litigation, though in the context of industrial accidents it has,
arguably, been secondary to the action for breach of statutory duty.
Ordinary principles apply (duty–breach–damage; the standard of
reasonable care, not a guarantee of safety), but in this particular
area the applications of these principles have evolved in certain
specific directions. Since the seminal case of *Wilsons and Clyde Coal
Co Ltd v English*[10] the usual approach is that the employer is under
a personal, non-delegable duty to take a reasonable care to provide:

(a) a safe workplace;

---

7 (1874) LR 9 Exch 125, ExCh.
8 *Nicholls v Austin (Leyton) Ltd* [1946] AC 493, [1946] 2 All ER 92, HL.
9 See particularly the speech of Lord Hailsham LC in *Callow (Engineers) Ltd v
Johnson* [1971] AC 335 at 341, [1970] 3 All ER 639 at 641.
10 [1938] AC 57, [1937] 3 All ER 628, HL; see Munkman *Employer's Liability* (11th
edn, 1990) Chapters 3 and 4.

(b) safe equipment;[11]

(c) competent and safe fellow employees;

(d) a safe system of work in all the circumstances.

The first two heads concern what may be considered to be the 'static condition' of the premises and the equipment. These matters are now covered in detail by the new Regulations, particularly the Workplace Regulations and the Work Equipment Regulations, with their extensive ACOP and Guidance Notes; these should provide much evidential material not just for an action for breach of statutory duty but also for a common law negligence claim. Thus, as can be seen from several of the precedents in Chapter 17, it may well be possible to re-plead the particulars of breach of statutory duty also as particulars of negligence under these first two heads.

The third head, the provision of competent and safe fellow employees, is different. It is not per se covered by the new Regulations and so the existing (sometimes quite bizarre) case law may well still be of considerable importance in any case where the plaintiff is injured by the negligence of a fellow employee/practical joker/homicidal maniac.[12] That fellow employee's propensity must, of course, have been known to the employer or, at the least, the employer must reasonably have been expected to have known of it, for the employer to be liable.[13]

---

11 Latent defects in machinery or tools provided by the employer caused problems where that defect could not have been discovered by reasonable inspection and the machinery or tool had been bought from a reputable supplier and was of reputable make: *Davie v New Merton Board Mills Ltd* [1959] AC 604, [1959] 1 All ER 346, HL. However, there is now a stricter duty on the employer to provide safe work equipment by virtue of the Employer's Liability (Defective Equipment) Act 1969 under which the employee injured through a defect in equipment provided by the employer may sue that employer (if he can show that the defect is attributable to the fault of a third party), leaving it to the employer then to seek to sue the manufacturer. This Act has, in the few reported cases, been applied widely: *Coltman v Bibby Tankers Ltd, The Derbyshire* [1988] AC 276, [1987] 3 All ER 1068, HL (includes a whole ship as 'equipment'); *Knowles v Liverpool City Council* [1993] IRLR 6, CA (includes *material* provided by the employer for the purpose of the work, in that case a flagstone that the employee was laying).

12 It is possible that the employer may also be vicariously liable for the acts of the fellow employee, but the problem is, of course, that the more idiotic the practical joke the more likely it is that the employee will be held to have been 'on a frolic of his own', rather than being in the course of his employment.

13 In the wider context of employment law this raises the interesting question not just whether it would be fair to dismiss the practical joker in these circumstance, but whether there would be a positive *obligation* at common law to dismiss him if that was the only effective way of protecting the workforce.

It is, however, when one turns to the fourth head, the provision of a safe *system* of work, that the possible effects of the new regulations can be seen most clearly. In the past, this head has been something of a 'makeweight', a final, residual allegation in a statement of claim. Now, however, it could be about to receive renewed emphasis for the following reasons.

(i)   It is in line with the new Regulations in looking not at the static condition of the workplace but instead at the way work is *organised*; it is thus capable of reflecting the more dynamic, pro-active approach to industrial safety that is to be found in the Regulations, particularly in the key concepts of *risk* and risk assessment.

(ii) Moreover, it is argued in this book that, although the Management Regulations do not themselves support civil liability, there is no reason why they should not be relied upon as *evidence* of required practice, failure to follow which can constitute negligence. For one thing, the actual wording of the exclusion of civil liability in regulation 15 does not preclude this indirect use of the Management Regulations in a negligence action;[14] for another, certain other parts of the Regulations as a whole assume that key concepts in the Management Regulations (especially on risk assessment) are an integral part of the overall scheme of protection.[15]

(iii) Thus, although the absence of a necessary risk assessment is not itself actionable as a breach of statutory duty, it is so central to the whole scheme that it should be considered important evidence of a failure to provide a safe system of work in all the circumstances, and therefore common law negligence. This argument is also applicable to other parts of the Management Regulations, such as health and safety arrangements, health surveillance and the need for procedures to deal with serious and imminent dangers.

---

14 Regulation 15 only states that breach of a duty imposed by the Regulations is not to *confer* a right of action in any civil proceedings. It is submitted that this only means that the Regulations cannot be relied upon *directly*, in order to maintain an action for breach of statutory duty. In the case of an action for negligence, that cause of action already exists by virtue of the employer's want of care, and the Regulations are only being used to *substantiate* that want of care, not to 'confer' the right of action.

15 See, eg, the notes to the Work Equipment Regulations, regulations 11 and 12, paras 110 and 122, pp 318–320, below.

(iv) Further, it may even be possible to argue that if in a particular respect one of the sets of Regulations does not fully implement the appropriate EC Directive, failure by an employer to comply with the *Directive* may also be evidence of negligence; it is argued later[16] that this may be the case with consultation with employees on health and safety matters.[17]

CONTRIBUTORY NEGLIGENCE

The partial defence of contributory negligence is, of course, of great importance in industrial accident cases, particularly as it has long been established that it applies to breach of statutory duty actions as well as negligence actions.[18] What constitutes contributory negligence and what deduction should be made from damages in respect of it are heavily questions of fact for the trial judge.

Of particular relevance here is the rule that breach by the *employee* of a statutory duty placed upon him may well constitute contributory negligence.[19] Such duties have long been found in industrial safety legislation, including the Health and Safety at Work Act 1974, sections 7 and 8. Now, however, there are more extensive duties on employees under the new Regulations, both in regulation 12 of the general Management Regulations and also in the other, more specific regulations.

These duties are considered in Chapter 13, below. For present purposes they are mentioned to show the increased scope for reliance on them in order for a defendant to establish contributory negligence. With regard to the duties on employees in regulation 12 of the Management Regulations, that is covered by the general

---

16 See Chapter 12 below.
17 The statutory obligation to consult is restricted in domestic law to cases where there is a recognised trade union. However, Directive 89/391/EEC (the Framework Directive), art 11(1) states that 'employers shall consult *workers* and/or their representative and allow them to take part in discussions on all questions relating to safety and health at work'. If an employer has no machinery whatsoever for (non-unionised) workers to air their thoughts or grievances about safety, and if that could be shown to have at least contributed to an accident, could that be alleged to be common law negligence (evidenced by the directive) even though in domestic law there is still no direct obligation to have such machinery where no union is recognised?
18 See Munkman *Employer's Liability* (11th edn, 1990) Ch 23.
19 *Norris v Syndic Manufacturing Co* [1952] 2 QB 135, [1952] 1 All ER 935.

exclusion of civil liability by regulation 15 of those Regulations. However, repeating the argument made above in relation to negligence, that only means that the employee cannot be sued *directly* for any breach; it is again submitted that it does *not* mean that breach of regulation 12 cannot be used by a defendant as evidence to establish a defence of contributory negligence.

Chapter 5

The Management of Health and Safety at Work Regulations 1992

SOURCE

The Management of Health and Safety at Work Regulations 1992 implement EC Directive 89/391/EEC in the UK and are made under the provisions of the Health and Safety at Work etc Act 1974.

DATE OF IMPLEMENTATION

The Regulations came into effect on 1 January 1993 and are of immediate application (see regulation 1(1)).

CIVIL LIABILITY

Regulation 15 provides that a breach of duty imposed by the Regulations shall not confer a right of action in any civil proceedings.

APPROVED CODE OF PRACTICE

The Regulations are accompanied by an extensive Approved Code of Practice which has been supplied by the Health and Safety Executive.

OVERVIEW

The Regulations, in common with the Framework Directive from which they are directly related, have to be seen in the context of the other Directives and Regulations which have been passed in accordance with the stated aims of Article 118A of the Treaty of Rome. They essentially create a framework of provisions within which the remaining Directives and Regulations are set by creating broad and general duties on employers, employees and the self-employed which provide the backdrop against which the more specific Directives and Regulations operate.

The approach to implementation in the UK has been on a largely piecemeal basis. This is because it was felt by the Health and Safety Commission that a number of the requirements of the Framework Directive were already in force in the UK through the Health and Safety at Work etc Act 1974 and it was felt that the best method of implementation was to work within the existing framework of the 1974 Act. This has meant that the obligations contained in the Framework Directive are to be found in a number of separate domestic provisions including the 1974 Act, the Safety Representatives and Safety Committees Regulations 1977 as well as the 1992 Regulations. In view of the fact that the Regulations work within the existing structure of health and safety law in the UK there are no repeals or revocations of any existing domestic provisions brought about by the Regulations.

COMMENTARY

The Regulations are of very broad scope covering all employers and all forms of work apart from sea transport (see regulation 2). The centrepiece of the Regulations is the obligation on all employers and the self-employed to carry out a risk assessment under regulation 3. The risk assessment must be suitable and sufficient and must consider the risk to the health and safety of all employees and other persons arising out of the conduct of the business or undertaking by the employer or self-employed person. The purpose of the assessment is to identify the measures which need to be taken in order to comply with the relevant statutory provisions. The 'statutory provisions' are defined in the ACOP as including the general duties under the 1974 Act as well as any more specific provisions (paragraph 7).

The risk assessment has to be reviewed if there is any reason to believe that it is no longer valid or if there has been any significant change in the matters to which it relates (see regulation 3(3)). The significant findings of the assessment have to be recorded if the employer employs five or more employees.

Regulation 4 obliges employers to give effect to arrangements for the effective planning, organisation, control, monitoring and review of the measures which they need to take as a result of the findings of the risk assessment. These arrangements need to be recorded by any employer who employs five or more employees.

The employer is also under a duty to ensure that his employees are provided with appropriate health surveillance in accordance with regulation 5. This is particularly important in cases in which the risk assessment has identified any identifiable disease or adverse health condition related to the work. The ACOP states that the minimum requirement for health surveillance is the keeping of an individual health record (see paragraph 32).

Regulation 6 requires the employer to appoint one or more 'competent persons' to assist him in taking the relevant measures that he needs to take in order to comply with the relevant statutory obligations. The persons appointed by him must be sufficient in number and be given sufficient time and the necessary means to fulfil their obligations. If the competent person appointed is not an employee in the undertaking then they must be given information on any special factors which may affect the risks to health and safety in the undertaking as well as information on any temporary workers who may be working in the undertaking.

A 'competent person' is defined in regulation 6(5) as being someone who has sufficient training and experience to enable him to assist properly in the undertaking. The ACOP gives some guidance in this area and states that simple situations will only demand a person who has a basic understanding of current best practice, who is aware of their own limitations and who has the willingness and ability to supplement existing experience and knowledge. This definition will obviously vary depending on the nature of the undertaking and in more complex situations experts may well be required.

Regulations 6(6) and 6(7) provide for employers to carry out the function of the competent person in very limited circumstances.

Regulation 7 lays down a specific requirement for employers to establish appropriate procedures which are to be followed in the 'event of serious and imminent danger to persons at work in his undertaking'. The ACOP refers to the need to set out clear guidance on when employees and others at work should stop work and how they should move to a place of safety (paragraph 41). The type of risks that need to be covered should have been revealed by the risk assessment but would obviously include fire and bomb risks. The employer is required to nominate a sufficient number of competent persons to implement the necessary procedures and to ensure that his employees are unable to enter any dangerous areas in his undertaking without first having been given adequate health and safety training. The ACOP defines a danger area as a working environment 'where the level of risk is unacceptable without special precautions being taken' (paragraph 51). This is a potentially broad definition and would clearly cover areas where there are dangerous substances present as well as areas with dangerous structures or other hazards.

Regulation 7(2) lays down some guidance on what the appropriate procedures should involve. This includes the provision of information and the opportunity for employees to immediately leave their workstation in cases of danger.

The competent person or persons appointed under regulation 7(1)(b) must have sufficient training and experience and possess the necessary qualities to be able to carry out their functions properly (regulation 7(3)).

Regulation 8 is of importance and requires every employer to provide his employees with comprehensible and relevant information on the risks to which they are exposed and the measures which the employer has taken in accordance with the risk assessment which he has carried out. Information must also be provided on the procedures to be taken in cases of serious and imminent danger as well as any risks to which the employee may be exposed as a result of the conduct of any other employer who may be sharing the workplace.

Specific requirements are laid down in regulation 9 for employers to co-operate on health and safety matters with other employers who may be sharing the same workplace. The duty also extends to the self-employed and applies whether the sharing is on a temporary or part-time basis. The respective parties must provide each other with sufficient information and should co-ordinate the steps taken when appropriate. Detailed guidance is included in the ACOP.

Regulation 10 is also of significance and it extends the employer's duty to provide information to include the provision of adequate health and safety information to employers of any employees from another undertaking who are working in his undertaking. This will obviously include groups such as contractors and employees of employment businesses who are hired to work under the user's control.

Regulation 10(3) requires every employer and every self-employed person to provide any person working in his undertaking who is not his employee with adequate health and safety information and instruction on any risks which that person faces as a result of the conduct of the undertaking. This will clearly include information on the steps and procedures which are to be taken in cases of serious and imminent danger and the persons who are to operate any evacuation procedures.

Regulation 11(1) requires employers to consider the capabilities of their employees as regards health and safety before entrusting any tasks to them. This is clearly a duty which has to be met on an individual-by-individual basis. The employer must ensure that the demands of any job do not put the employee at risk. This will require consideration of the individual's capabilities, level of training, knowledge and experience (see ACOP paragraph 70). The employer is also now under a duty to provide his employees with adequate health and safety training in a number of specific instances. These are set out in regulation 11(2) and include the time of recruitment, on exposure to new risks, on introduction of new technology and on changes to any system of work. This training must be carried out in working hours.

New obligations are placed on employees by regulation 12. Every employee is under a duty to use any equipment provided to him by his employer in accordance with the instruction and training that has been given to him. The employee is also under a duty to report, to his employer or to any fellow employee with specific responsibilities for health and safety, any shortcomings or defects which the employee considers exist in the health and safety measures taken by his employer.

Regulation 13 creates new specific obligations on employers and the self-employed towards temporary workers. Three tiers of obligation are created which all relate to the provision of comprehensible information on any special occupational qualifications or skills which are required for the work to be carried out safely and any health surveillance which may also be necessary. The relevant information must be supplied by any employer to any of his employees who are employed on fixed-term contracts (regulation 13(1)). The same obligation also applies to any employer and any self-employed person who is to use the services of any employee of an employment business. In such a case the employer or self-employed person must provide the necessary information to not only the relevant employee but also to the employment business itself (regulations 13(2) and 13(3)).

The person carrying on the employment business is also under a duty to make sure that the relevant information is supplied to their employee.

Regulation 14 permits the Secretary of State for Defence to produce exemption certificates in certain circumstances.

Regulation 15 excludes civil liability for any breach of the Regulations.

IMPLEMENTATION OF THE DIRECTIVE

As has previously been mentioned it is important to note that the Management of Health and Safety at Work Regulations 1992 only implement certain sections of the Framework Directive. The view was taken by the Health and Safety Commission that some of the general duties which are set by the Directive, and in particular the general duties which are placed upon employers in Article 6, are already in place in the UK under section 2 of the Health and Safety at Work etc Act 1974. Similarly, the requirement set out in Article 6.5 of the Directive that measures taken in relation to health and safety at work may in no circumstances involve workers in financial cost has a domestic equivalent already in place in section 9 of the 1974 Act. Other areas of the Directive are also met by the Fire Precautions Act 1971 and The Health and Safety (First Aid) Regulations 1981.

One of the other major differences between the Management of Health and Safety at Work Regulations 1992 and the other Regulations which have been introduced is the fact that a breach of the Management Regulations will not result in civil liability (although this will not prevent the Regulations from having an impact in the area of civil liability (see further page 25)). The Regulations are admissible in any criminal proceedings but it is certainly arguable that by failing to provide for civil liability the Regulations have failed to meet the requirements of the Directive. This is because it has been established that Member States must provide realistic remedies in domestic law in order to make Community rights a reality. There has been some consideration of this in relation to Article 6 of the Equal Treatment Directive in the case of *Von Colson and Kamann v Land Nordrhein-Westfalen*: 14/83 [1984] ECR 1891 ECJ. However, it would appear that this is a matter for the European Commission to take up through infraction proceedings against the UK government if appropriate under Article 169 of the Treaty of Rome rather than for individuals through actions in the domestic courts. The remedies provided by the UK government are criminal and administrative in nature but it is certainly arguable that the aim and purpose of the Directive is to provide rights for workers and others which they should be entitled to enforce directly against their employers. In principle, however, it would appear that there is no reason why an employee of the state or an emanation of the state should not be able to rely upon a breach of the Directive directly in the relevant circumstances (further reference should be made to Chapter 3). Again, this is an area in which the practitioner must keep abreast with developments as they occur.

The Framework Directive also includes a number of provisions on consultation and employment protection. These are areas which are dealt with in detail in Chapters 12 and 15. Reference is also made to Chapter 11 in relation to temporary workers. In all of these areas it is arguable that the Regulations fail to meet the requirements of the Directive.

It is also arguable that the Regulations fail to implement adequately the standards required by the Directive on health and safety assistance. This is because the Regulations only require the employer to appoint 'competent persons' under regulation 6. There is no requirement that this person is an employee of the employer in question. It is arguable that this falls below the requirements of the Directive which requires the employer to appoint designated 'workers' to carry out the relevant health and safety duties. 'Worker' is clearly defined in Article 3 of the Directive as being an employee. The Directive only permits outside assistance if the protective and preventative measures cannot be organised for lack of competent personnel in the undertaking (Article 7.3). This requirement is not included in the Regulations and again appears to permit an employer to perform their functions under the domestic Regulations without directly involving their own workforce. This is, arguably, contrary to the wording and spirit of the Directive.

Regulations 3(4) and 4(2) only require employers with five or more employees to record the findings of the risk assessment and the arrangements made as a result. This is, arguably, contrary to the Directive which contains no such exception. It is also important to note that Article 9.2 of the Directive refers to the requirement for documents to be provided. This also appears to be correct in principle because the seriousness of the hazards faced by people at work is not necessarily linked, if at all, with the size of the undertaking.

It is also important for the practitioner to note the areas in which the Directive creates more specific duties than domestic law. This is particularly relevant to the specific duties set out in Article 6 of the Directive which have been left to the very general duties in the 1974

Act. Even though the broad general duty would appear to cover the requirements of the Directive the more specific duties may well have an impact on the law of negligence and civil liability. Article 6.2 is of particular interest in this regard because it lays down a hierarchy of measures and general principles of prevention which should be observed. The question of civil liability is considered in more detail in Chapter 4.

Chapter 6

The Workplace (Health, Safety and Welfare) Regulations 1992

SOURCE

The Workplace (Health, Safety and Welfare) Regulations 1992 implement Directive 89/654/EEC. The Regulations are made under the Health and Safety at Work etc Act 1974.

DATE OF IMPLEMENTATION

This is defined in regulation 1. The Regulations came into effect on 1 January 1993. All the Regulations apply to any new workplace or new part of a workplace, and in respect of a workplace or part of a workplace which is a modification, extension or a conversion where work started after 31 December 1992. There is a transition period for existing workplaces. Regulations 5 to 27 will apply from 1 January 1996 to workplaces in existence before 1 January 1993 which have not been modified, extended or converted.

There is a trap for the unwary, despite the clear and explicit terms of regulation 1. By regulation 17(5) it is provided that regulation 17(2), dealing with the suitability of traffic routes, shall apply so far as is reasonably practicable to a workplace which is not a new workplace, a modification, an extension or a conversion.

CIVIL LIABILITY

Breach of the Regulations creates civil liability.

APPROVED CODE OF PRACTICE

The Regulations are accompanied by an Approved Code of Practice (ACOP). The Approved Code of Practice has been approved by the Health and Safety Commission, with the consent of the Secretary of State under section 16 of the Health and Safety at Work etc Act 1974.

OVERVIEW

By regulation 4 the Regulations apply to employers, occupiers of factories, and persons in control of workplaces in connection with the carrying on of a trade, business or other undertaking, whether for profit or not. Thus, the Regulations apply to workplaces not previously the subject of specific statutory provisions, such as hospitals, schools, universities, hotels, and courthouses. The Regulations contain some extensions of familiar provisions in the Factories Act and the Offices, Shops and Railway Premises Act.

The Regulations do not apply to ships, building operations, works of engineering construction, mines, quarries, or other mineral extraction. Temporary worksites, which are not defined by the Regulations, need only comply with the welfare provisions in regulations 20 to 25 so far as is reasonably practicable. Aircraft, locomotive, rolling stock and road vehicles used as a means of transport are not covered by the Regulations, unless stationary in a workplace, for example when being loaded or unloaded. Agricultural and forestry workplaces which are not inside a building and are situated away from the undertaking's main building are excluded from the ambit of the Regulations, save for the provision of sanitary conveniences, washing facilities and drinking water so far as is reasonably practicable.

COMMENTARY

Regulation 5 requires that the workplace, equipment, devices and systems shall be maintained in an efficient state, in efficient working order and in good repair. Where appropriate there shall be a suitable system of maintenance. The Code of Practice makes it clear that this is intended to apply to matters of health and safety, and not to the efficiency of production or working.

Regulation 6 requires effective and suitable provision for the ventilation of every enclosed workplace by a sufficient quantity of fresh or purified air. Plant used for ventilation must have an effective device to give visible or audible warning of any failure of the plant where necessary for reasons of health or safety. The regulation does not apply to enclosed or confined spaces as variously defined in section 30 of the Factories Act 1961, regulations 49 to 52 of the Shipbuilding and Ship-Repairing Regulations 1960, regulation 21 of the Construction (General Provisions) Regulations 1961, and regulation 18 of the Docks Regulations 1988. For protection from hazardous substances it is necessary to consider the Control of Substances Hazardous to Health Regulations and other specific regulations dealing with asbestos, lead and ionising radiation.

Regulation 7 provides for a reasonable temperature in all workplaces, and for the provision of thermometers. What is reasonable must depend upon the nature of the process and the general circumstances. Areas near blast-furnaces cannot be compared directly to an office nor to a cold-store. The ACOP provides some useful guidance. The aim is to provide reasonable comfort without the need for special clothing. Where workrooms have extremes of temperature the area should be limited, insulation should be provided, and local ventilation or heating made available. Protective clothing and rest areas are a last resort.

Regulation 8 requires suitable and sufficient lighting, so far as is reasonably practicable by natural light. The provision relating to natural light is an advance on previous legislation.

Regulation 9 relates to the cleanliness of the workplace and equipment, and the removal of waste materials.

Regulation 10 provides that every room where persons work shall have sufficient floor area, height and unoccupied space for the purposes of health, safety and welfare. The regulation does not specify any area or volume, but there is some guidance in the ACOP.

Regulation 11 provides that the workstation shall be suitable both for the person at work and for the work that is likely to be done there. The term 'workstation' is not defined in the Regulations. It clearly covers a static work position, and layouts such as a machine and adjacent workbench. It is debatable whether it could apply to the whole of a production line, although it would apply to individual control points. Every workstation outdoors shall be so arranged that it ensures that any person at the workstation is not likely to slip or fall. Thus, its application might be more restrictive than the meaning attached to 'place of work'. There is no requirement of reasonable practicability. The test is one of suitability. The regulation also provides for a suitable seat, and where necessary a footrest, where the work must or can be done while sitting.

Regulation 12 relates to the condition of the floors and traffic routes. Regrettably, it is necessary to turn back to regulation 2 to discover that traffic route means a route for pedestrian traffic, vehicles or both and includes any stairs, staircase, fixed ladder, doorway, gateway, loading bay or ramp. Moveable ladders are likely to be regarded as work equipment, and will be covered by other regulations. The floor and surface of every traffic route must be of a construction that is suitable for the purpose for which it is used, and this includes a requirement that there shall be no hole or slope, unevenness or slipperiness so as to expose any person to a risk to his health or safety. There is no test of reasonable practicability. The determining factor is whether there is a risk. It can be expected that there will be arguments that the risk must be more than minimal. No account shall be taken of a hole where adequate measures have been taken to prevent a person falling. Account is to be taken of any handrail provided in connection with a slope. The regulation protects persons other than employees, such as visitors or outside contractors. Regulation 12(3) requires, so far as is reasonably practicable, floors and surfaces of traffic routes to be kept free from obstruction and from any article or substance which may cause a person to slip, trip or fall. This is an extension of previous provisions in some respects.

Regulation 13 relates to falls by a person of a distance likely to cause personal injury. The real change effected is that no distance is specified. The test is of likelihood to cause personal injury, and factors such as the nature of the surface or equipment upon which the person may fall are going to be of great importance. The protection requires the provision of fences or covers so far as is reasonably practicable, before resort to personal protective equipment, information, instruction, training or supervision. The regulation also requires measures to prevent the fall of objects likely to cause personal injury. Both the fall of persons and of objects are subject to reasonable practicability, except that tanks, pits or structures where there is a risk of falling into a dangerous substance must be securely covered or fenced so far as is practicable, and traffic routes over them must be securely fenced. The ACOP provides a great deal of guidance material.

Regulation 14 relates to windows and other transparent or translucent surfaces in walls or doors, and provides for safety material or protection against breakage, and for the marking or indicating of their presence.

Regulations 15 and 16 relate to the safe opening of windows and skylights and ventilators, and the safe cleaning of windows and skylights.

Regulation 17 contains new and important material. Regulation 17(1) provides that every workplace shall be organised in such a way that pedestrians and vehicles can circulate in a safe manner. Regulation 17(2) requires that traffic routes in a workplace shall be suitable for the persons or vehicles using them, sufficient in number, in suitable positions and of sufficient size. By regulation 17(5) it is provided that regulation 17(2) shall apply so far as is reasonably practicable to a workplace which is not a new workplace, a modification, an extension or a conversion. The regulation envisages the separation of pedestrians and vehicles at doors or gates, and the separation of pedestrians and vehicles using the same traffic route. The ACOP contains a wealth of relevant material.

Regulation 18 provides that doors and gates shall be suitably constructed, which includes being fitted with any necessary safety device. In particular, a sliding door or gate must have a device to prevent it coming off its track during use, and any upward opening door must have a device to prevent it falling back. Powered doors must have suitable and effective features to prevent them causing injury by trapping, and must be capable of being operated manually. Doors or gates which open both ways must provide a view when closed of the space on the other side.

Regulation 19 provides that escalators and moving walkways shall function safely, and be equipped with safety devices and one or more emergency stop controls.

Regulations 20 to 25 contain provisions relating to sanitary conveniences, washing facilities, drinking water, accommodation for clothing, facilities for changing clothing, and facilities for rest and to eat meals. Of particular note is that rest rooms and rest areas shall include suitable arrangements to protect non-smokers from discomfort caused by tobacco smoke.

Regulation 26 makes provision for the Secretary of State for Defence to make any necessary exemptions in the interests of national security.

IMPLEMENTATION OF THE DIRECTIVE

The Directive

Article 1.2 does not exempt transport used in the undertaking, but regulation 3(3) appears to exempt transport used in the under-taking except when stationary and in relation to falls covered by regulation 13.

In respect of the provision of information to workers, Article 7 and the consultation envisaged by Article 8, reference should be made to the detailed chapter covering these points.

Annex one

Point 6.2 requires air-conditioning or mechanical installation systems to operate in such a way that workers are not exposed to draughts which cause discomfort. This provision is not contained in the Regulations although it is mentioned in the ACOP.

Point 12.5 requires that, where workplaces contain danger areas in which, owing to the nature of the work, there is the risk of the worker or objects falling, the places must be equipped, as far as possible, with devices preventing unauthorised workers from entering those areas. Regulation 13 only provides for clear indication of such an area. The Guidance Notes state that additional safeguards may be necessary in places where unauthorised entry is foreseeable.

Point 14.2 requires a loading bay to have at least one exit point. This is only referred to in the ACOP.

Point 17 requires that pregnant women and nursing mothers must be able to lie down to rest in appropriate conditions. Regulation 25(5) only requires suitable facilities to rest. The ACOP says that where necessary this should include the facility to lie down. It is to be wondered whether the necessity is to be measured by the needs of the woman or someone else.

Point 20 states that workplaces must be organised to take account of handicapped workers, particularly in relation to doors, passageways, staircases, showers, washbasins, lavatories and workstations. This is not specifically mentioned in the Regulations, and it is left to interpretation of words such as 'sufficient' and 'suitable', and reference in the ACOP.

Annex two

This sets minimum standards for workplaces already in use. The following matters do not appear to be covered:

(a) Point 6 requiring that a breakdown of a forced ventilation system must be indicated by a control system where it is necessary for the worker's health;

(b) Point 10 which requires that, where workplaces contain danger areas in which, owing to the nature of the work, there is the risk of the worker or objects falling, the places must be equipped, as far as possible, with devices preventing unauthorised workers from entering those areas;

(c) Point 11 in relation to rest areas;

(d) Point 12 which requires that pregnant women and nursing mothers must be able to lie down to rest in appropriate conditions;

(e) Point 13 relating to the provision of changing-rooms and lockers.

Chapter 7

The Provision and Use of Work Equipment Regulations 1992

SOURCE

The Provision and Use of Work Equipment Regulations 1992 implement EC Directive 89/655/EEC. The Regulations are made under the Health and Safety at Work etc Act 1974.

DATE OF IMPLEMENTATION

This is defined in regulation 1. The Regulations came into force on 1 January 1993. Regulations 5 to 10 are of immediate effect. There is a transition period for work equipment first provided for use in the premises or undertaking before 1 January 1993 in that regulations 11 to 24 and 27 and Schedule 2 will not come into force until 1 January 1997.

CIVIL LIABILITY

Breach of the Regulations creates civil liability.

GUIDANCE NOTES

There is no Approved Code of Practice, but the Health and Safety Executive have provided Guidance Notes.

OVERVIEW

The Regulations impose many new obligations, and warrant careful study. They replace such well-known provisions as sections 12 to 16 of the Factories Act 1961, and section 17 of the Offices Shops and Railway Premises Act 1963, as well as replacing or affecting a host of regulations. The Regulations apply to premises and under-takings. The Regulations do not apply to sea-going ships, but do apply to offshore oil and gas installations and associated vessels. The requirements of the Regulations are also imposed on self-employed persons, those in control of non-domestic premises, and the occupiers of factories.

COMMENTARY

The definition of 'premises' in the Health and Safety at Work etc Act 1974 is very wide, and regulation 2 puts very wide definitions on the words 'use' and 'work equipment'. 'Work equipment' can include items as diverse as a pair of scissors, a steel rolling mill, and a lathe. Work equipment is defined as any machinery, appliance, apparatus or tool and any assembly of components, which in order to achieve a common end are arranged and controlled so that they function as a whole.

Regulations 5 to 10 are of immediate effect. Regulation 5(1) provides that an employer shall ensure that work equipment is so constructed or adapted as to be suitable for the purpose for which it is used or provided. By regulation 10 the employer is required to ensure that any item of work equipment provided for use complies with enacted safety requirements.

Regulation 5(3) imposes an obligation upon an employer to ensure that work equipment is used only for the operations for which, and under conditions for which, it is suitable, meaning suitable in any respect which it is reasonably foreseeable will affect the health or safety of any person, not just the user. Regulations 8 and 9 require an employer to provide adequate health and safety information and training to those who use the work equipment, and to those who supervise or manage the use of work equipment. The regulation goes further than Directive 89/655/EEC in its requirements relating to supervisors and managers. It is not enough to have a foreman transferred or promoted from another department; he must have been given information and training relevant to the tasks being performed by those that he supervises.

Where work equipment is likely to involve a specific risk to health or safety, regulation 7 requires the employer to restrict its use and maintenance to specific persons. This is likely to have wide implications.

Regulation 6 imposes a duty to ensure that work equipment is maintained in an efficient state, in efficient working order and in good repair. The Guidance Notes indicate that 'efficient' relates to conditions affecting health and safety, and is not concerned with matters of productivity. It is a pity that this was not made clear in the regulation itself.

Regulation 11 provides for protection from dangerous parts of machinery and rotating stock bars. The duty is not absolute, but provides for a hierarchy of measures governed by the standard of practicability. Thus, there has been a weakening of the protection offered by provisions such as section 14 of the Factories Act 1961 where there was an absolute duty to fence. The hierarchy of protection given by the Regulations starts with fixed guards enclosing the danger. If that is not practicable then other guards or protection devices, for example micro-switch cut-outs, may be used. If that is not practicable jigs, holders, push-sticks or similar appliances may be used. If that is not practicable then the final level of protection is the provision of information, instruction, training and supervision. Regulation 11(3) provides the standards to be met by the guards and protection devices. It appears open to argument that push-sticks, for example, are not devices which prevent access to danger zones such as those created by circular saws, because if they slip then access can be gained to the saw blade. The saw blade must be exposed to cut the wood, but is it not practicable to provide a tunnel guard through which the wood can be fed to the saw blade?

The difficulty in applying the hierarchy of protection measures arises from having provisions which cover such a wide range of work equipment outside factory premises. An oft-quoted example is the mowing machine. It cannot cut the grass if completely guarded, and there remains the risk of pulling the mower over a foot. It seems open to argument that a long handle at arms length is what is required by the provisions of regulation 11(2)(c). It is perhaps only items such as the mechanical hand-held tools that will attract the last rank of protection provided in the Regulations, namely the provision of information, instruction, training and supervision.

Regulation 12 is a considerable advance and provides measures to prevent or control hazards created by articles or substances falling or being ejected from work equipment, or by discharge from the work equipment, fire or explosion. However, the regulation does not apply where particular substances are governed by other specified regulations, namely asbestos, ionising radiation, lead, and substances hazardous to health, and in relation to noise and head protection in the construction industry.

Regulation 13 provides protection to prevent injury from burns, scalds, and searing from high or low temperature work equipment, parts of work equipment, and articles and substances produced, used or stored. Its universal application is a substantial increase in the protection afforded.

Regulations 14 to 18 relate to controls and control systems for work equipment. Previously, regulation of these matters was limited to particular areas such as woodworking machines. Regulation 14 requires the provision of controls for starting or making a significant alteration to the operating conditions of work equipment, and save in the case of the normal operation of automatic devices, deliberate action on the control is required. Regulation 15 relates to stop controls, and regulation 16 relates to emergency stop controls. These provisions need to be considered in relation to each type of work equipment. Regulation 17 provides that controls shall be clearly visible and identifiable, and that its positioning shall not expose the operator to a risk to his health or safety. Regulation 18 requires that control systems shall be safe as far as is reasonably practicable, and that where reasonably practicable any failure should lead to a fail safe condition. The Guidance Notes are of particular interest when considering regulations 14 to 18.

Regulation 19 governs isolation from sources of energy. The means of isolation must be clearly identifiable and readily accessible. Appropriate measures must be taken to ensure that reconnection does not expose any person using the work equipment to any risk to his health or safety. 'Use' is defined by regulation 2 as any activity involving work equipment and includes starting, stopping, programming, setting, transporting, repairing, modifying, maintaining, servicing and cleaning.

Regulation 20 requires that work equipment or any part of it shall be stabilised by clamping or otherwise to prevent fall or collapse.

Regulation 21 provides that every employer shall ensure that suitable and sufficient lighting, which takes account of the operations to be carried out, is provided at any place where a person uses work equipment. This is more specific than the requirement for suitable and sufficient lighting for every workplace in regulation 8 of the Workplace (Health, Safety and Welfare) Regulations 1992.

Regulation 22 requires appropriate measures to ensure that work equipment is so constructed or adapted that, so far as is reasonably practicable, maintenance operations can be carried out while the work equipment is shut down, or without exposing the person to risk, or taking appropriate measures for protection of the person.

Regulation 23 requires work equipment to be marked in a clearly visible manner with any marking appropriate for reasons of health and safety. Regulation 24 requires work equipment to incorporate any warnings or warning devices which are appropriate for reasons of health and safety.

Regulation 25 makes provision for the Secretary of State for Defence to make any necessary exemptions in the interests of national security.

IMPLEMENTATION OF THE DIRECTIVE

The terms of the Directive are implemented only in part by these Regulations. Some of the terms of the Directive were already covered by existing legislation, in particular the Health and Safety at Work etc Act 1974, the Control of Substances Hazardous to Health Regulations 1988, the Electricity at Work Regulations 1989, and the Fire Precautions Act 1971 and associated regulations.

Article 4.2 requires that the employer take measures necessary to ensure that, throughout its working life, work equipment is kept, by means of adequate maintenance, at a level such that it complies with the provisions of this and other Directives. It is not clear to what extent the terms of regulation 6 comply with the requirements of the Directive. The regulation imposes a duty to ensure that work equipment is maintained in an efficient state, in efficient working order and in good repair.

There is one part of the Directive that is not easy to interpret. Point 2.8 of the Annex to the Directive provides that, where there is a risk of mechanical contact with moving parts of work equipment which could lead to accidents, those parts must be provided with guards or devices to prevent access to danger zones or to halt movements of dangerous parts before the danger zones are reached. The difficulty is in the meaning to be given to the word 'mechanical'.[1] It does not seem to have a specialised meaning.

If 'mechanical' is meant to include bodily contact as well as contact with clothing, as where a loose sleeve is drawn into a machine, then it has an effect similar to that given by section 14 of the Factories Act 1961. However, it could have a more restrictive meaning. Depending upon the view taken as to the meaning of the

---

1   The same word is used in the French version of the Directive.

Directive, it can be argued that regulation 11 either exceeds the requirements of the Directive, or falls short of full implementation.

In respect of the consultation envisaged by Article 8, reference should be made to the chapter on consultation.

Chapter 8

The Personal Protective Equipment at Work Regulations 1992

SOURCE

The Personal Protective Equipment at Work Regulations 1992 implement EC Directive 89/656/EEC and are made under the Health and Safety at Work etc Act 1974.

DATE OF IMPLEMENTATION

The Regulations came into force on 1 January 1993 and are of immediate effect. There are no transitional provisions.

CIVIL LIABILITY

A breach of the Regulations will create civil liability.

GUIDANCE NOTES

There is no Approved Code of Practice but the Health and Safety Executive have provided full Guidance Notes.

OVERVIEW

The provision of personal protective equipment ('PPE') is an area in which there were already pre-existing statutory protections. The approach to implementation has therefore been varied. Some existing provisions, such as the Control of Lead at Work Regulations 1980 and the Control of Substances Hazardous to Health at Work Regulations 1988, have been amended, whereas others, such as the famed Foundries (Protective Footwear and Gaiters) Regulations 1971, have been revoked (see Schedule 3 to the Regulations). The Regulations also dovetail with other Community provisions such as EC Directive 89/686/EEC on the approximation of the laws of the Member States relating to PPE. These Directives and the Regulations made to implement them will therefore provide a unified code on the standards of design and manufacture required for PPE.

COMMENTARY

Regulation 2(1) defines personal protective equipment in very broad terms as including:

'all equipment (including clothing affording protection against the weather) which is intended to be worn or held by a person at work and which protects him against one or more risks to his health or safety, and any addition or accessory designed to meet that objective.'

This very broad definition is limited to a certain extent by regulation 3(2) which excludes certain items such as uniforms which do not specifically protect the health and safety of the wearer and equipment used during the playing of competitive sports from the ambit of the Regulations.

Regulation 3(3) also provides that regulations 4 and 6 to 12 will not apply if the relevant situation is covered by some specified pre-existing provisions, notably the Control of Lead at Work Regulations 1980, the Control of Asbestos at Work Regulations 1987 and the Noise at Work Regulations 1989.

The central obligation of the Regulations is contained in regulation 4, which requires every employer to ensure that suitable PPE is provided to his employees who may be exposed to a risk to their health or safety while at work except where and to the extent that such risk has been adequately controlled by other means which are equally or more effective. This obligation can, therefore, be seen to fit in with the overall scheme of the various Directives that the primary aim should be to attack the risk at source rather than to provide palliative measures. The use of PPE should therefore be seen as being a last resort within a hierarchy of measures. This approach is also well illustrated by the Manual Handling Operations Regulations (see Chapter 9).

Regulation 4(2) places an obligation on the self-employed to ensure that they are also provided with suitable PPE. It is important to note at this stage that the obligation on the employer under regulation 4(1) is only owed to his employees. Employees of employment businesses would not, therefore, appear to be covered. This is arguably in breach of the Temporary Workers Directive and readers are asked to turn to Chapter 11 for a further consideration of this issue.

Regulation 4(3) provides a list of requirements which have to be met if the equipment is to be suitable. It must be appropriate for the risk, take into account the ergonomic requirements of the person who is to wear it, it must fit the wearer correctly, be effective and must comply with any Community standards which have been implemented in the UK. A note on existing British and European standards is included at Appendix 3 of the Guidance Notes.

Regulation 5 requires both employers and the self-employed to ensure that if more than one item of PPE has to be worn at any one time that such equipment is compatible and continues to be effective against the various risks.

Regulation 6 requires any employer or self-employed person to carry out an assessment of any PPE before it is provided. The assessment must ensure that any PPE provided is suitable. The requirements for the assessment are listed in regulation 6(2). It should take account of health and safety risks which have not been avoided by other means and should consider the characteristics which will be required of the equipment. The assessment should be reviewed if appropriate. The Guidance Notes to the Regulations include a specimen risk survey table.

Any PPE provided must be maintained in an efficient state, in efficient working order and in good repair in accordance with regulation 7. Appropriate accommodation should also be provided for the PPE when it is not in use (see regulation 8). The Guidance Notes include a detailed section on the selection, use and maintenance of PPE and has specific sections on head protection, eye protection, foot protection, hand and arm protection and protective clothing for the body.

Regulation 9 contains requirements on information, instruction and training. In any case in which PPE must be provided by an employer he must also provide the employee with appropriate and comprehensible instruction, training and information on the risks which the PPE will limit, the purpose and manner of the use of the PPE and any steps which the employee must take to keep the PPE in an efficient state.

Further obligations are placed on the employer by regulation 10(1) which requires him to take all reasonable steps to ensure that any PPE provided is properly used and a corresponding obligation is placed on employees in regulation 10(2) to use any PPE provided to them in accordance with the training and instruction which has been given to them. These obligations are also placed upon the self-employed.

Employees who have been provided with PPE are also under a duty to report to their employer any loss of or obvious defect in any PPE which has been provided to them under regulation 11.

The Secretary of State for Defence may produce exemption certificates in the interests of national security under regulation 12. Regulation 14 provides for the various amendments and revocations which are contained in Schedules 2 and 3 to the Regulations.

IMPLEMENTATION OF THE DIRECTIVE

As has been mentioned, the Regulations appear to fall below the standards required by the Temporary Workers Directive and this issue is discussed in detail at Chapter 11. In general terms, the Regulations appear effectively to implement the provisions of the Directive. However, this does not mean that the practitioner can disregard the terms of the Directive. This is because in a number of areas the Directive provides more detailed provisions than the Regulations and this needs to be borne in mind when interpreting the more general principles of the Regulations (see for example Article 4.6 of the Directive). In general terms, however, the Regulations provide a welcome clarification of the law on PPE although the practitioner must keep in mind the fact that several of the pre-existing provisions will remain in force.

A number of pleading precedents for the Regulations are included at page 96.

Chapter 9

The Manual Handling Operations Regulations 1992

SOURCE

The Manual Handling Operations Regulations 1992 implement Directive 90/269/EEC of the Council of the European Communities. The Regulations are made under the Health and Safety at Work etc Act 1974.

DATE OF IMPLEMENTATION

This is defined in regulation 1. The Regulations came into force on 1 January 1993 and are of immediate effect. There is no transition period.

CIVIL LIABILITY

Breach of the Regulations creates civil liability.

GUIDANCE NOTES

There is no Approved Code of Practice, but the Health and Safety Executive have provided very full Guidance Notes.

OVERVIEW

The Regulations apply to every employment except those on sea-going ships. Previously, legislation was limited to work in defined locations such factories, shops, and offices, or to particular occupations such as agricultural, construction or shipyard workers. The new Regulations cover occupations as diverse as nurses, delivery drivers, and university technicians. Duties are imposed upon the self-employed. Manual handling operations are defined as any transporting or supporting of a load, including the lifting, putting down, pushing, pulling, carrying or moving of the load by hand or bodily force. Loads include animals and people.

The Regulations do not apply to a master or crew of sea-going ships. However, they will apply to other persons loading ships or working on ships in territorial waters. The Regulations apply to offshore oil and gas installations and associated vessels.

COMMENTARY

Manual handling operations are defined by regulation 2 as any transporting or supporting of a load, including the lifting, putting down, pushing, pulling, carrying or moving of the load by hand or bodily force. Thus, using a foot or pushing with the back are activities covered by the Regulations.

It is made clear by regulation 2 that these Regulations do not cover injury caused by a toxic or corrosive substance that has leaked or spilled from a load, or is present on a load, or is a constituent part of a load. The intention is to cover strain injuries, common examples of which are strains to the back, shoulder, and groin.

The assessment required by the Management of Health and Safety at Work Regulations 1992 should have indicated work activities which entail a risk of injury from manual handling. Where there is a risk of injury from manual handling operations regulation 4(1)(a) requires the employer to avoid that manual handling operation so far as reasonably practicable. Where it is not reasonably practicable to avoid such manual handling operations, the employer must make an assessment having regard to the factors set out in the Schedule to the Regulations. There are four main factors: the task, the load, the working environment, and individual capability. Other factors may include hindrance by clothing or protective equipment. In many ways the approach needs to be inverted. Consideration of the factors and questions set out in the Schedule will help in assessing whether there is a risk of injury, as well as identifying individual matters which can be altered or avoided so as to reduce the risk of injury. The Guidance Notes offer an assessment checklist which can be copied and completed during the assessment.

The Regulations do not specify maximum weights. Nor is there any emphasis on the relative strengths of men and women, or the young and the old. The Schedule to the Regulations requires consideration of whether the job requires unusual strength, height, etc, or whether it might create a hazard for persons who are pregnant or who have a health problem. Being of small stature is not a health problem. Regulation 11 of the Management of Health and Safety at Work Regulations does require an employer to take into account their employees' capabilities when entrusting them with tasks, but there is no civil liability for breach of this regulation. Emphasis on unusual strength, height, etc, gives the impression that the consideration is only as to whether the task needs to be performed by a giant or by an average employee. An ordinary employee may be small or relatively weak by reason of any number of factors which do not amount to a health problem, but which may affect his lifting capability.

The employer's duty under regulation 4(1)(b)(ii) is to take steps to reduce the risk of injury to the lowest level reasonably practicable, and where it is reasonably practicable to give precise information on the weight of the load and the position of the centre of gravity if it is not located centrally in the load. It is debatable whether this can be interpreted to include an obligation to train employees on the proper handling of loads.

Regulation 4(2) requires a review of the assessment if there is any reason to suspect that it is no longer valid or there has been a significant change in the manual handling operations. Thus, any injury sustained while carrying out that manual handling operation would necessitate a review. So would a relevant complaint. Any change in a manual handling operation might be significant, and thus the obligation to review the assessment is needed to assess its significance.

Regulation 5 imposes a duty on employees to make a full and proper use of any system of work provided for his use by the employer following an assessment.

Regulation 6 makes provision for the Secretary of State for Defence to make any necessary exemptions in the interests of national security.

IMPLEMENTATION OF THE DIRECTIVE

There are a number of respects in which it is arguable that the Regulations fail to implement the terms of the Directive.

Article 3 provides for a hierarchy of measures. The emphasis is on avoiding manual handling, in particular by the use of mechanical equipment. It is only where the need for the manual handling of loads by workers cannot be avoided that the employer must consider organisational measures.[1] The Regulations impose the requirement of reasonable practicability.

Article 6 requires that workers and/or their representatives shall be informed of all measures to be implemented, pursuant to this Directive, with regard to the protection of safety and of health. An explanatory note to the Regulations concedes that this requirement has not been included in the Regulations. It is arguable that the requirements of this Article are covered by the terms of regulation 8 of the Management of Health and Safety at Work Regulations, but there is no civil liability for breach of this regulation.

Article 6.2 requires employers to ensure that workers receive proper training and information on how to handle loads correctly and the risks that arise with incorrect handling. This is not included in the Regulations as a positive requirement. The only direct reference to training comes in the Assessment Checklist in the Guidance Notes, which raises the question whether special information/training is required. There is a duty on employers under regulation 4(1)(b)(ii) to take steps to reduce the risk of injury to the lowest level reasonably practicable. It is debatable whether this can be interpreted to include an obligation to train employees on the proper handling of loads. It is arguable that the requirements of this Article are covered by the terms of regulation 8 of the Management of Health and Safety at Work Regulations, but there is no civil liability for breach of this regulation. It is regrettable that the opportunity has been missed to emphasise the obligation to train by having it spelt out in the Regulations dealing with manual handling.

In respect of the consultation envisaged by Article 7, reference should be made to the chapter on consultation.

Annex two identifies workers who may be at risk if they are physically unsuited to carry out the task in question. This risk is not identified in a positive way in the Regulations, the Schedule or the Assessment Checklist contained in the Guidance Notes. The Schedule to the Regulations requires consideration of whether the job requires unusual strength, height, etc. Thus, the emphasis is on whether someone larger or stronger than the ordinary is required, rather than on the physical capabilities of the existing employee, who may be smaller or weaker than the average.

---

1 See Chapter 3 for consideration of the interpretation of the terms of the Directives.

The Regulations appear to fall below the standards required by the Temporary Workers Directive, and reference should be made to Chapter 15 where this issue is discussed in detail.

Chapter 10

The Health and Safety (Display Screen Equipment) Regulations 1992

SOURCE

The Health and Safety (Display Screen Equipment) Regulations 1992 implement EC Directive 90/270/EEC in the UK and are made under the provisions of the Health and Safety at Work etc Act 1974.

DATE OF IMPLEMENTATION

The Regulations came into effect on 1 January 1993 and are of immediate effect (regulation 1(1)). However, there is a lead-in period for meeting the minimum requirements for workstations as set out in regulation 3. If the workstation was already in use prior to 1 January 1993, then it has to comply with the necessary requirements by not later than 31 December 1996. The requirements apply in full to all new workstations introduced on or after 1 January 1993.

CIVIL LIABILITY

Breach of the Regulations creates civil liability.

GUIDANCE NOTES

There is no Approved Code of Practice but the Health and Safety Executive have produced full Guidance Notes.

OVERVIEW

The Regulations create new duties on employers in an area of health and safety which has not been covered by any previous statutory provisions. There are, therefore, no repeals or revocations of any existing provisions and the Regulations represent a new start in this area. The Regulations are likely to have a significant impact in the areas of repetitive strain injuries and risks to eyesight as a result of working for long periods with computers and other display screen equipment. This is an area in which some form of legal regulation has been long overdue.

COMMENTARY

The Regulations cover all persons who habitually use display screen equipment as a significant part of their normal work. 'Display screen equipment' is defined in regulation 1(2)(a) as any alpha-numeric or graphic display screen, regardless of the display process involved. This definition therefore covers computers and microfiche but would not cover television or film pictures. Whether an individual is an 'habitual' user or not is a question of fact and degree in each individual case. The main onus should be on the relative intensity of the work that the individual is required to perform. An obvious example of an habitual user would be a word processing pool worker but a wide variety of individuals may be covered from a data input operator to a financial dealer. Useful indicators are included in the accompanying Guidance Notes. If there is any doubt as to the precise status of the individual an assessment should be carried out. The Guidance Notes give a general guide figure of three hours' use a day as being a sufficient period to qualify. However, there would appear to be no reason in principle why a shorter but more intense period may not also be sufficient.

The Regulations create different standards of protection for 'users' and 'operators'. These categories are defined in regulations 1(1)(b) and 1(1)(d). In essence, the 'operator' is self-employed and the 'user' is an employee. It is important to note that the duties owed by an employer to 'users' are not only duties owed to his employees but also cover employees of other employers if those employees are working in his undertaking. This, therefore, covers employees of employment businesses in accordance with the requirements of the Temporary Workers Directive (see further paragraph 9 of the Guidance Notes and the discussion at Chapter 11).

Regulation 2 requires the employer to carry out an analysis of the workstations in his undertaking which are used by operators or users. A workstation is defined in regulation 1(2)(e) as an assembly which comprises display screen equipment, any optional accessories, any disk drive, telephone, workchair or other peripheral items and the immediate work environment around the equipment. The assessment must be suitable and sufficient and for the purpose of assessing the relevant risks to health and safety from the operation. The Guidance Notes recommend that the individual users and operators should take part in the assessment after they have received appropriate training. The employer is under a duty to reduce the risks revealed by the assessment to the 'lowest extent reasonably practicable' (regulation 2(3)). A list of possible risks is included in Appendix B to the Guidance Notes.

Regulation 3 sets out minimum requirements which every workstation must meet. The requirements are set out in the Schedule to the Regulations and include provisions on the supply of equipment (including the display screen, the keyboard, the work desk and work chair), on the environment (including requirements as to space, lighting, reflections and glare, noise and heat), and the interface between computer and operator/user. These standards must be met by any workstation which is put into service on or after 1 January 1993 but workstations which are already in use prior to that date have to comply by not later than 31 December 1996. The requirements in the Schedule are to be met to the extent that the 'inherent requirements or characteristics of the task make compliance appropriate'. The Guidance Notes indicate that this proviso will not affect compliance in normal office conditions.

Regulation 4 is of great importance. It requires employers to plan the activities of their 'users' at work in their undertaking so that there are periodic interruptions in their work on the display screen equipment. These interruptions can be breaks or changes of activity. This duty is not owed to the self-employed. The Guidance Notes state that shorter, more frequent breaks are to be favoured.

Regulation 5 requires employers to provide appropriate eye and eyesight tests to their employees. It is important to note that the obligation does not extend to the employees of other employers who may be working in the undertaking. The onus would appear to be on the employee to request the test. New employees should be tested before they commence work. The Guidance Notes set out the necessary requirements for the test and the competent person who is qualified to carry out the test. These should be a registered ophthalmic optician or a registered medical practitioner with suitable qualifications (see paragraph 50 of the Guidance Notes).

Regulation 5(5) requires the employer to provide every user employed by him with appropriate special corrective appliances when any test shows that such provision is necessary. The employer should not make any charge for any such appliance unless the employee requests appliances which are more luxurious than those that are necessary on purely health and safety grounds (see further section 9 of the Health and Safety at Work etc Act 1974 and Article 6.5 of the Framework Directive).

Regulation 6 requires the employer to provide adequate training on the health and safety aspects of the workstation and to ensure that adequate training is also given whenever the organisation of any workstation is substantially modified. The general obligation to train under regulation 6(1) only applies as between an employer and his employee whereas the obligation to train in the event of any substantial modification in circumstances under regulation 6(2) applies as between the employer and any 'user' at work in his undertaking. The substantial modification of circumstances would include any alterations to software, hardware, location, furniture or tasks (see further paragraph 64 of the Guidance Notes).

Regulation 7 imposes a requirement on employers to provide adequate information on health and safety matters and on the assessment and steps that they have taken under the Regulations to all operators and users in their undertaking.

Regulation 8 makes provision for the Secretary of State for Defence to make any necessary exemptions in the interests of national security.

IMPLEMENTATION OF THE DIRECTIVE

It is arguable that in a number of respects the Regulations fail to meet the strict requirements of the Directive. When considering these aspects, the practitioner needs to be aware of the comments made on Community law and its interrelationship with domestic law in Chapter 3.

Regulation 2(3) requires the employer to reduce the risks which are apparent from the assessment to the lowest extent reasonably practicable. Article 3.2 of the Directive, however, appears to set the higher standard of 'practicable' because it requires employers to take appropriate measures to 'remedy the risks found'. This is, clearly, a debatable point and much will depend upon the interpretation that is given to the word 'appropriate'. It is also important to remember that the preamble to the Framework

Directive states that health and safety at work 'is an objective which should not be subordinated to purely economic considerations'.

It is also arguable that regulation 3 fails to meet the standards of the Directive because it only requires the minimum standards for workstations to be met for those workstations which may be used by 'operators' or 'users'. In other words, the requirements only have to be met for workstations which may be used by individuals who work with display screen equipment on an habitual basis. It is arguable that Article 4 of the Directive requires the standards to be met by all workstations regardless of who is using them. This is of obvious importance for workstations which may be used by individuals who do not cross the 'habitual' threshold.

It is also important to note that the extent to which workstations must comply with the minimum requirements set out in the Schedule to the Regulations arguably falls short of the requirements of the Directive. This is because paragraph 1(c) of the Schedule refers to the extent that the 'inherent characteristics of a given task make compliance with those requirements appropriate as respects the workstation concerned' and this appears to permit some consideration of the workstation as well as the task. This is not permitted by the Directive which only refers to the task itself. It is interesting to note that paragraph 38(c) of the Guidance Notes applies the apparently more limited test as laid down in the Directive and this will, therefore, probably be an area in which the differences between the Regulations and the Directive can be ironed out through the process of interpretation (see further Chapter 3).

Readers are referred to the relevant chapter on the question of consultation.

In general, the Regulations follow the general scheme of the Directive and would appear to have considerably increased the levels of protection in this area.

Example pleadings are included at page 107 onwards.

Chapter 11
Temporary workers

INTRODUCTION

It is important when considering the impact of the new health and safety Regulations to keep in mind the provisions of Directive 91/383/EEC ('The Temporary Workers Directive'). The Directive applies to workers on fixed-term contracts as well as those who are subject to temporary employment relationships 'between a temporary employment business which is the employer and the worker, where the latter is assigned to work for and under the control of an undertaking and/or establishment making use of his services' (Article 1). The Directive provides that workers which fall into these categories shall be accorded the same level of protection as other workers in the same undertaking as regards health and safety and, accordingly, the Framework and all the other Directives made under Article 118A of the Treaty of Rome 'shall apply in full' to such temporary workers (Article 2.3). This is obviously of great importance when considering questions of interpretation (see further Chapter 3).

The Directive also contains a number of additional provisions which apply exclusively to temporary workers as defined by the Directive. Article 3 creates an obligation on any undertaking in which such a temporary worker is to work to provide that worker with information on any special risks that the worker may face in the undertaking and any special qualifications which may be required. Article 4 further provides that training should be given to the temporary worker in order that such standards can be met. Article 5 provides for such workers to be given medical surveillance where appropriate.

Article 7 of the Directive also places additional obligations on the undertaking which is making use of the services of a temporary worker to provide to the employment business the necessary information on the occupational qualifications and specific features of the job to be filled and to further ensure that the employment business brings this information to the attention of the workers concerned.

Article 8 is of vital importance because it provides that the user undertaking is 'responsible, for the duration of the assignment, for the conditions governing performance of the work' and this is defined in Article 8.2 as meaning those conditions connected with safety, hygiene and health at work.

IMPLEMENTATION IN THE UK

A piecemeal approach to implementation has been taken in the UK. The major provisions are contained in the Management of Health and Safety at Work Regulations but other matters have been left to each individual set of Regulations. This approach has created some difficulties because, although some of the Regulations deal with temporary workers specifically, others do not. It is, therefore, necessary to consider each set of Regulations in turn.

The Management of Health and Safety at Work Regulations 1992

The Management of Health and Safety at Work Regulations 1992 include definitions for 'employment business' and 'fixed-term contract of employment' in regulation 1(2). Both categories of temporary worker would appear to be covered by the requirements in relation to risk assessments because regulation 3(a) covers employees of the relevant employer and regulation 3(b) covers the 'risks to the health and safety of persons not in his employment arising out of or in connection with the conduct by him of his undertaking'. However, it is also worth noting at this point that it would appear that an employment business is under an obligation to conduct a risk assessment for all its employees and that such an assessment will have to include all of the separate undertakings in which they work. This is because regulation 3(1)(a) is not limited to the specific undertaking but includes all risks to which employees are exposed 'whilst they are at work'.

The requirement to provide appropriate health surveillance under regulation 5 rests on the employer and only extends to his employees. The obligation for agency workers would, therefore, seem to rest only on the employment business and not on the user.

This may well conflict with Article 8 of the Temporary Workers Directive which requires that the responsibility for any health and safety conditions rests on the user for the duration of the assignment. Although a corresponding provision is not contained in Article 5, it is arguable that it is implicit.

Regulation 6(4)(b) implements Article 6 of the Directive by requiring that designated workers and competent persons with responsibility for carrying out health and safety functions are informed of any temporary workers who are working in the undertaking for the purposes of carrying out their functions. Regulation 13, which deals specifically with temporary workers, implements Article 7 of the Directive by requiring that information on any special occupational qualifications and any health surveillance required should be provided to both the relevant worker and the employment business.

Temporary workers will also be covered by regulation 10 as regards the provision of information on the risks to which they are exposed in the undertaking and the measures taken by the user of the undertaking as regards health and safety. Information must also be provided on the necessary steps which are to be taken in circumstances of imminent danger and in relation to danger areas.

It is important to note that the obligations as regards capabilities and training contained in regulation 11 do not rest upon the user but only upon the employment business. As regards the taking into account of an individual's capabilities before entrusting any tasks to that individual, regulation 11 would appear to fall below the standards required by the Directive because this would appear to be a health and safety responsibility which should fall on the user during the period of the assignment in accordance with Article 8 of the Directive. It is also arguable that regulation 11(2) fails to meet the requirements of Article 4 of the Directive which requires that temporary workers must be provided with appropriate training in relation to the activities which they are to perform in the user's undertaking. Regulation 11(2) places the obligation on an employer towards his employees only and not towards any employees of an employment business who may be working in his undertaking. Furthermore, the regulation only requires the training to be given in relation to the risks which are present in the employer's own undertaking. It would, therefore, appear that the requirements of Article 4 of the Directive, which requires temporary workers to be given training which is appropriate to the risks which they will encounter in the user's undertaking, have not been met.

The Provision and Use of Work Equipment Regulations 1992

The provisions of the Work Equipment Regulations would appear to apply in full to temporary workers. This is because regulation 4 imposes the requirements of the Regulations not only upon employers but also upon 'any person who has control, to any extent, of non-domestic premises made available to persons as a place of work, in respect of work equipment used in such premises by such persons and to the extent of his control' (regulation 4(1)(b). It is also clear that none of the obligations contained in the Regulations is limited by being only applicable to the employees of a particular employer.

The Personal Protective Equipment at Work Regulations 1992

It would appear that, as drafted, the Personal Protective Equipment Regulations fail to meet the requirements of the Temporary Workers Directive. This is very much to be regretted, particularly in view of the fact that Article 2.2 of the Directive specifically states that temporary workers must not be treated differently as regards health and safety matters 'especially as regards access to personal protective equipment'. The Regulations appear to fall short because the central requirement to provide suitable personal protective equipment only rests upon an employer to his employees. It is therefore clear that in the case of employees of an employment business, the obligation to provide suitable personal protective equipment rests upon the employment business and not the user. This is clearly in breach of the Directive which requires that the responsibility for health and safety conditions rests upon the user during the assignment. This apparent error is repeated in regulations 5 (compatibility of personal protective equipment), 7 (maintenance and replacement), 8 (accommodation), 9 (information, instruction and training), 10 (use of equipment), and 11 (reporting of loss or defect).

However, it is clear that these obligations do extend to employment businesses themselves because they are not limited to protective equipment which is used in their own undertaking. The employment business is, therefore, under a duty to provide suitable equipment to all its workers regardless of where they are to work, to ensure that such equipment is properly maintained and to ensure that proper information and training is provided. This is a very onerous obligation and would appear not to be necessary within the terms of the Directive because the obligation should rest on the user for the period of the assignment. However, this does not mean that the employment business can raise the Directive in its defence because a Member State is perfectly entitled to introduce measures which go beyond the terms of the Directive.

The Manual Handling Operations Regulations 1992

The comments which have been made in relation to the Personal Protective Equipment Regulations apply equally to the Manual Handling Regulations. This is because regulation 4 specifically only applies to employers and employees. This error is again repeated in regulation 5.

The Health and Safety (Display Screen Equipment) Regulations 1992

The Display Screen Regulations appear to cover temporary workers because of the definition of 'user' contained in the Regulations. A 'user' is defined in Regulation 1(2)(d) as an employee who habitually uses display screen equipment as a significant part of his normal work. This would, therefore, appear to cover both types of temporary worker as defined in the Directive. This view is also expressed in the published guidance to the Regulations (see paragraph 9). However, it is important to note that the obligations contained in regulations 2, 3, 4, 6(2) and 7 will rest upon the user employer and regulations 5 and 6(1) (obligations regarding training and the provision of appropriate eye tests) will rest upon the employment business.

The Workplace (Health, Safety and Welfare) Regulations 1992

The provisions of the Workplace Regulations would appear to apply in full to both categories of temporary worker included in the Temporary Workers Directive. This is because the obligation to comply with the requirements of the Regulations rests upon not only the relevant employer who is in control but also on 'every person who has, to any extent, control of a workplace' and that the breach in question relates to matters within that person's control (see regulation 4(2)).

CONCLUSION

It is, therefore, clear that the practitioner will have to tread a careful path when considering the legal position of temporary workers under the new Regulations. This area illustrates clearly the need for the practitioner to be fully aware not only of the terms of the Regulations but also of the central position occupied by the Temporary Workers Directive. All of the comments in Chapter 3 on the interaction of domestic and Community law need to be borne in mind.

Chapter 12
Consultation

INTRODUCTION

The Directives contain a number of new provisions on consultation. The primary obligations are included in the Framework Directive and these are then referred to in each of the individual Directives. The general aim of the provisions can be gleaned from the preamble to the Framework Directive which includes reference to the need for workers and/or their representatives to take part in balanced participation on matters concerned with health and safety at work.

The UK government has sought to implement the provisions of the Directives through amendments to the Safety Representatives and Safety Committees Regulations 1977 which are contained in a Schedule to the Management of Health and Safety at Work Regulations. The overall approach has, therefore, been to act through the existing structures for health and safety representatives. This is an approach which has left the government open to criticism because the various rights and protections accorded to safety representatives depend upon the willingness of the employer to recognise an independent trade union for the purposes of consultation on health and safety matters. There is no legal mechanism currently available in the UK to force an employer to recognise a trade union even if all of his workforce want this. The unsatisfactory position therefore remains that, if an employer does not want to consult with his workforce on health and safety matters, he does not have to do so, and it is arguable that this position is not permitted by the Directive.

THE PRE-EXISTING POSITION

The pre-existing law on consultation on health and safety matters at work was contained in the Safety Representatives and Safety

Committee Regulations 1977 (SI 1977/500) which were made under section 2(6) of the Health and Safety At Work etc Act 1974. The 1977 Regulations placed a duty on an employer to consult with appointed safety representatives from recognised unions as regards arrangements for the promotion, maintenance and monitoring of improvements in health and safety at work.

The 1977 Regulations grant to safety representatives the right to represent their fellow workers, to carry out inspections and investigations and to receive information on health and safety matters. The role of safety representatives is supposed to be on a continuing day-to-day basis and is not intended to apply only after a major accident or incident has actually taken place.

The right of appointment of safety representatives is restricted to independent unions who are already recognised by their employers for the purposes of collective bargaining. It is for the union to decide on the method of selection and appointment of safety representatives although the employer must be informed in writing of the names of the representatives appointed and the groups they represent.

The Regulations are industrial relations orientated and there are few existing methods of legal enforcement. It would only be in the most unusual of circumstances that the Health and Safety Executive would consider prosecuting an employer for failing to consult. This has to be seen against the background of the absence of any legal method of forcing an employer to recognise the union in the first instance. This approach of keeping the law at arm's length is further illustrated by the blanket legal immunity given to safety representatives by the 1977 Regulations (regulation 4(1)).

Safety representatives are also entitled to reasonable time off with pay in order to undergo training and in order to carry out their functions. If these facilities are not provided then a complaint can be made to an industrial tribunal (regulation 11). The employer is also under a general duty to provide 'such facilities and such assistance as the safety representative shall require' (regulation 5(3)) and to disclose information to safety representatives which is necessary for them to carry out their functions (regulation 7(2)). The employer is also under a duty to establish a Safety Committee if requested to do so, in writing, by at least two of his safety representatives (regulation 9(1)).

The pre-existing law therefore provided reasonably extensive obligations on an employer to consult with his workers' representatives on health and safety matters, providing that the initial hurdle of recognition had been passed.

THE DIRECTIVES

The primary obligations are contained in Article 11 of the Framework Directive and have to be read in context with the definitions of 'worker' and 'workers' representative with specific responsibility for the safety and health of workers' as set out in Article 3 of the Directive. The Directive appears to provide for one level of rights for 'workers' and one level of rights for 'workers' representatives'. Article 11.1 contains the general principle that employers shall consult workers and/or their representatives and allow them to take part in discussions on all questions relating to health and safety at work. It presupposes the consultation of workers and balanced participation 'in accordance with national laws and/or practices'.

Article 11.2 provides for more specific duties on consultation and states that the employer must consult on a broad range of issues including any measure which may substantially affect health and safety, the appointment of designated workers and those with specific responsibilities in cases of serious and imminent danger as provided for in the Framework Directive, information on the risk assessment (see further Article 10.3) and the planning and organisation of health and safety training. Article 11.3 provides additional rights for workers' representatives to ask the employer to take appropriate measures to mitigate hazards and remove sources of danger. Article 11.5 provides for workers' representatives to have time off without loss of pay in order to carry out their duties and Article 11.6 provides for the right of appeal to the 'authority responsible for safety and health protection at work' in circumstances where workers or their representatives feel that their employer has taken inadequate steps for the purposes of ensuring health and safety at work.

IMPLEMENTATION

The UK government has purported to implement the Directive by means of amendments to the 1977 Regulations. The pre-existing structure, therefore, largely remains, save that a new regulation 4A has been inserted into the 1977 Regulations. The new regulation 4A is contained in a Schedule to the Management of Health and Safety at Work Regulations 1992 (see regulation 17).

THE NEW REGULATION 4A

The new regulation 4A provides for additional specific matters on which an employer shall consult with safety representatives 'in good time'. These specific matters essentially mirror the provisions contained in Article 11.2 of the Framework Directive, namely: the introduction of any measure which may substantially affect the health and safety of workers; arrangements for the appointment of the competent person(s) required under the Management of Health and Safety at Work Regulations 1992; any health and safety information which has to be provided under any statutory enactment; the planning and organisation of training; and the implications of the introduction of any new technologies in the workplace.

MEETING THE STANDARDS REQUIRED BY THE DIRECTIVES

As has previously been stated the approach to implementation in the UK is clearly open to criticism. This is because, although substantial rights on consultation are provided to safety representatives, these rights are dependent on the employer having taken the significant step of recognising the union. Where the employer has not taken this step, the rights do not apply. This is arguably contrary to the terms of the Framework Directive which draws distinctions between 'workers' and 'representatives'. This is clearly illustrated in Article 11.2 which arguably does not permit the situation to arise in which there is no consultation at all – a situation which is clearly permitted after purported implementation in the UK. This is an area which is likely to be hotly contested in view of the current debate on subsidiarity within the Community and the present ideological reluctance of the UK government to extend current practices on union recognition in the workplace.

Chapter 13

The duties of employees

The Regulations have created civil liability for breaches of duty by employees in respect of personal protective equipment and manual handling. The other duties on employees are unchanged.

The Health and Safety at Work etc Act 1974 imposed duties on employees in sections 7 and 8.

'7. It shall be the duty of every employee while at work,
(a) to take reasonable care for the health and safety of himself and of other persons who may be affected by his acts or omissions at work; and
(b) as regards any duty or requirement imposed on his employer or any other person by or under any of the relevant statutory provisions, to co-operate with him so far as is necessary to enable that duty or requirement to be performed or complied with.

8. No person shall intentionally or recklessly interfere with or misuse anything provided in the interests of health, safety or welfare in pursuance of any of the relevant statutory provisions.'

By section 47 of the Act these sections do not confer a right of action in civil proceedings. They provide the means of bringing prosecutions against employees.

Regulation 12 of the Management of Health and Safety at Work Regulations 1992 provides:

'12.(1) Every employee shall use any machinery, equipment, dangerous substance, transport equipment, means of production or safety device provided to him by his employer in accordance both with any training in the use of the equipment concerned which has been received by him and the instructions respecting that use which have been provided to him by the said employer by or under the relevant statutory provisions.

12.(2) Every employee shall inform his employer or any other employee of that employer with specific responsibility for the health and safety of his fellow employees –

(a) of any work situation which a person with the first-mentioned employee's training and instruction would reasonably consider represented a serious and immediate danger to health and safety; and

(b) of any matter which a person with the first-mentioned employee's training and instruction would reasonably consider represented a shortcoming in the employer's protection arrangements for health and safety,

insofar as that situation or matter either affects the health and safety of that first-mentioned employee or arises out of or in connection with his own activities at work, and has not previously been reported to his employer or to any other employee of that employer in accordance with this paragraph.'

Regulation 15 of the Management of Health and Safety at Work Regulations states that breach of a duty imposed by those Regulations does not confer a right of action in any civil proceedings. Criminal prosecutions can be brought, however.

Regulation 19(2) of the Personal Protective Equipment at Work Regulations requires that every employee shall use any personal protective equipment provided to him by virtue of the Regulations in accordance with any training or instruction given to him. Regulation 19(4) imposes an obligation upon the employee to take all reasonable steps to ensure that the personal protective equipment is returned to the accommodation provided for it after use. Regulation 11 requires an employee to report any loss or obvious defect in personal protective equipment provided to him. These obligations add civil liability to the pre-existing liability to criminal sanctions.

The Manual Handling Operations Regulations by regulation 5 require an employee to make full and proper use of any system of work provided for his use by his employer in taking steps to reduce the risk of injury after making an assessment. These obligations add civil liability to the pre-existing liability to criminal sanctions.

Chapter 14

Duties of the self-employed

The Regulations have added to the duties imposed upon self-employed persons. There are important additions to their civil liability for breaches of Regulations.

The Health and Safety at Work etc Act 1974 imposed duties on self-employed persons in section 3(2) and (3).

> '3.(2) It shall be the duty of every self-employed person to conduct his undertaking in such a way to ensure, so far as is reasonably practicable, that he and other persons (not being his employees) who may be affected thereby are not thereby exposed to risks to their health or safety.
>
> 3.(3) In such cases as may be prescribed, it shall be the duty of every employer and every self-employed person, in the prescribed circumstances and in the prescribed manner, to give to persons (not being his employees) who may be affected by the way in which he conducts his undertaking the prescribed information about such aspects of the way in which he conducts his undertaking as might affect their health or safety.'

By section 47 of the Act these subsections of section 3 do not confer a right of action in civil proceedings. They provide the means of bringing prosecutions against self-employed persons.

No regulations were made relating to section 3(3) until these 1992 Regulations.

Regulation 9(1) of the Management of Health and Safety at Work Regulations 1992, as construed by regulation 9(2) of the same Regulations, provides:

> '9.(1) Where 2 or more [self-employed persons][or one or more employers and one or more self-employed persons] share a workplace (whether on a temporary or a permanent basis) each such [self-employed person or] employer shall –

(a) co-operate with the other [self-employed persons or] employers concerned so far as is necessary to comply with the requirements and prohibitions imposed upon them by or under the relevant statutory provisions;

(b) (taking into account the nature of his activities) take all reasonable steps to co-ordinate the measures he takes to comply with the requirements and prohibitions imposed upon them by or under the relevant statutory provisions with the measures the other [self-employed persons or] employers concerned are taking to comply with the requirements and prohibitions imposed upon them by or under the relevant statutory provisions;

(c) take all reasonable steps to inform the other [self-employed persons or] employers concerned of the risks to their employees' health and safety arising out of or in connection with the conduct by him of his undertaking.'

Regulation 10(1) of the Management of Health and Safety at Work Regulations 1992, as construed by regulation 10(2) of the same Regulations, provides:

'10.(1) Every . . . self-employed person shall ensure that the employer of any employees from an outside undertaking [or any self-employed persons] who are working in his undertaking is [are] provided with comprehensible information on –

(a) the risks to those employees' [or self-employed persons'] health and safety arising out of or in connection with the conduct by . . . that first mentioned self-employed person of his undertaking; and

(b) the measures taken by . . . that self-employed person in compliance with the requirements and prohibitions imposed upon him by or under the relevant statutory provisions insofar as the said requirements and prohibitions relate to those employees [or self-employed persons].

. . .

10.(3) Every . . . self-employed person (not being an employer) shall ensure that any person working in his undertaking is provided with appropriate instructions and comprehensible information regarding any risks to that person's health and safety which arise out of the conduct by that . . . self-employed person in his undertaking.'

Regulation 13 of the Management of Health and Safety at Work Regulations 1992 provides:

'13.(2) Every employer and every self-employed person shall provide any person employed in an employment business who is to carry out work in his undertaking with comprehensible information on –

    (a) any special occupational qualifications or skills required to be held by that employee if he is to carry out his work safely; and

    (b) any health surveillance required to be provided to that employee by or under any of the relevant statutory provisions.

13.(3) Every employer and every self-employed person shall ensure that every person carrying on an employment business whose employees are to carry out work in his undertaking is provided with comprehensible information on –

    (a) any special occupational qualifications or skills required to be held by those employees if they are to carry out their work safely; and

    (b) the specific features of the jobs to be filled by those employees (insofar as those features are likely to affect their health and safety);

and the person carrying on the employment business concerned shall ensure that the information so provided is given to the said employees.'

Regulation 15 of the Management of Health and Safety at Work Regulations states that breach of a duty imposed by those Regulations does not confer a right of action in any civil proceedings. Criminal prosecutions can be brought, however.

Regulation 4(2) of the Workplace (Health, Safety and Welfare) Regulations does not impose any requirement upon a self-employed person in respect of his own work or the work of any of his partners, but where a self-employed person has control, to any extent, of a workplace, he must ensure compliance with the Regulations in respect of the workplace in matters within his control.

The Provision and Use of Work Equipment Regulations 1992 apply to work equipment used by self-employed persons, by regulation 4(2)(a). Thus he must provide suitable equipment, maintain it, obtain information, instructions and training, and ensure that his equipment complies with the requirements as to guarding, provision of controls, and stability.

The Manual Handling Operations Regulations 1992 impose duties under the Regulations on a self-employed person in respect of himself, by regulation 2(2).

By regulation 4(2) of the Personal Protective Equipment at Work Regulations, every self-employed person shall ensure that he is provided with suitable personal protective equipment where he may be exposed to a risk to his health or safety while at work, except where the risk is controlled by other means which are equally or more effective. By regulation 5(2) the self-employed person shall ensure that his personal protective equipment is compatible with other items of protective equipment that he wears. Regulations 6 and 7 on assessment, maintenance and replacement, and regulation 8 on accommodation for protective clothing, all apply to the self-employed person. Regulation 10 requires the self-employed person to make full and proper use of any personal protective equipment provided to him, and to return it to the accommodation provided. Curiously, there is no duty upon a self-employed person to obtain training, nor for an employer who provides personal protective equipment to train a self-employed person.

A self-employed person is an operator within the meaning of the Health and Safety (Display Screen Equipment) Regulations 1992. The self-employed person must look to those who carry out the business or undertaking in which they are engaged for the assessment of workstations and the provision of workstations meeting the requirements of the Regulations. There is no requirement for breaks for the self-employed, nor for eye-tests, or training, although they must be provided with health and safety information, by regulation 7.

A failure by a self-employed person to meet the requirements of applicable regulations which results in injury to others will provide evidence of negligence. It has been doubted that such a breach gives rise to an action for breach of statutory duty, the argument being that the Regulations are to provide protection for the self-employed person. This restrictive approach does not seem to accord with the general approach of the Commission, nor with the distinction made between the Health and Safety at Work etc Act and the Management Regulations on the one hand, and the deliberate addition of statutory duties on the other.

Chapter 15
Employment protection

INTRODUCTION

The Framework Directive contains new protections for employees who carry out health and safety duties and who leave their workstations in the event of serious and imminent danger. These provisions are contained in Articles 7.2, 8.4, 8.5, and 11.4 of the Directive. These measures have not been implemented in the various health and safety Regulations but proposals for reform have been included in the Trade Union Reform and Employment Rights Bill 1992. It is important to note at this stage that, in failing to implement the necessary protections by 1 January 1993, the UK government is in breach of its Community obligations and in the interim period it would appear that any worker who suffers a detriment within the scope of the Directive would be able to commence proceedings against the state in accordance with the principle in *Francovich* (see Chapter 3).

Although there is insufficient space in this work for a detailed analysis of employment law, the new proposed protections are worthy of comment. At present, the vast majority of employees do not have any specific employment protection rights with respect to any steps which they might take in relation to health and safety matters. They will, therefore, have to rely upon the general law of unfair dismissal. This creates many difficulties and can often leave an employee unprotected because of the two years' service qualification for unfair dismissal rights. There is also no protection for action short of dismissal taken against employees on health and safety grounds. These difficulties are well illustrated by the case of *Chant v Aquaboats* [1978] ICR 643. Mr Chant was a skilled shipwright who complained to his employers that the woodworking machinery did not comply with the required safety standards. He subsequently organised a petition which was signed by a number of his fellow workmen and he was later dismissed by his employer for slow work. Although the industrial tribunal had little difficulty in finding that the real reason for Mr Chant's dismissal was his health and safety activities his claim for unfair dismissal did not succeed. This was because he did not have the necessary length of service to qualify for unfair dismissal protection and his actions did not fall within the ambit of protection for taking part in the activities of an independent trade union because he was seen to be acting in an individual capacity.

However, it should not be forgotten that an employee with the necessary length of service to bring a claim for unfair dismissal will have good prospects of succeeding with his or her claim under section 57(3) of the Employment Protection (Consolidation) Act 1978 if they can show that the reason for their dismissal was related to health and safety matters. It is also well established that an employee who leaves his employment because the system of work is unsafe in some serious respect may claim constructive dismissal and is therefore entitled to pursue an unfair dismissal claim. However, the breach will have to be serious enough to amount to a fundamental breach of contract before the employee leaves his employment (see *British Aircraft Corporation v Austin* [1978] IRLR 332 and *Graham Oxley Tool Steels Ltd v Firth* [1980] IRLR 135).

The one area in which there has been some effort to create statutory employment protection beyond existing unfair dismissal rights for workers who have engaged in health and safety activities has been in relation to employees working on offshore installations. The Offshore Safety (Protection Against Victimisation) Act 1992 provides additional protections for safety representatives and members of safety committees who have been dismissed or had action short of dismissal taken against them as a result of their having performed functions in accordance with their duties under the relevant health and safety legislation. The approach of the Act is to mirror the existing provisions contained in sections 146(1) and 152(1) of the Trade Union and Labour Relations (Consolidation) Act 1992 which grant additional levels of protection for employees who have taken part in or propose to take part in the activities of an independent trade union. This removes the service qualification and provides for substantially increased levels of compensation as well as providing protection for workers who have had action short of dismissal taken against them. However, it needs to be remembered that these provisions do not create a general level of protection for all workers as they only apply to safety representatives and members of safety committees. Indeed, it can be argued that such employees are already protected because their functions would appear to fall within the definition of taking part in the activities of an independent trade union. This is because (unlike Mr Chant) they would be officially linked with the union and would not therefore be seen as acting in an individual capacity. Activities relating to health and safety matters are capable of coming within the section (see the comments of Slynn J in *Drew v St Edmundsbury Borough Council* [1980] ICR 513 at 517).

THE DIRECTIVE

The protections contained in the Directives are potentially far-reaching. However, the various provisions need to be seen in context and, in particular, against the background of other provisions in the Directives on consultation and participation of workers and/or their representatives on health and safety matters. The perspective of the European initiatives on these matters can be gleaned from the preamble to the Framework Directive which refers to the need for workers and/or their representatives to be able to contribute, through participation, to ensure that any necessary protective measures are taken and to take part in a balanced dialogue with their employers. These aims also dovetail with the provisions in the Framework Directive on the appointment of designated workers to assist in health and safety matters, the provision of information to workers and the requirement for employers to consult with workers and/or their representatives on all questions relating to health and safety at work. The method of implementation of these proposals chosen by the UK government is certainly open to question (see further Chapter 12) and this certainly has to be borne in mind when considering the proposed employment rights protections. This is because it is certainly arguable that the level of protection offered is severely reduced because, in most cases, in order to be protected, the worker concerned has to be a safety representative from a recognised trade union and there is no existing legal obligation on an employer to recognise a trade union.

The provisions of the Directive state that workers and workers' representatives who take part in health and safety consultations with their employers 'may not be placed at a disadvantage' because of their activities (Article 11.4). A similar protection is also provided for 'designated' workers (Article 7.2). Further protections are also provided for workers who leave their workstation or a dangerous area in the event of serious, imminent and unavoidable danger or take steps to avoid that danger (Articles 8.4 and 8.5). The wording of the Directive is somewhat inelegant and permits a lower level of protection where a worker takes steps to avoid the consequences of such danger when the immediate supervisor cannot be contacted. This is because the worker is protected from any disadvantage unless 'they acted carelessly or there was negligence on their part' (see Article 8.5). The test to be used when deciding what is negligent or careless would appear to be subjective because account should be taken of the knowledge and technical means at the disposal of the worker.

THE PROPOSED PROVISIONS CONTAINED IN THE 1992 BILL

The proposed changes are included in section 24 and Schedule 5 of the 1992 Bill. The new provisions essentially mirror the approach taken in the Offshore Safety (Protection Against Victimisation) Act 1992, namely to provide a form and level of protection similar to that currently in place for workers who take part in the activities of an independent trade union. The proposed provisions are also universal in scope, covering employees in all sectors, and the Offshore Safety (Protection Against Victimisation) Act 1992 will be repealed as a result.

Action short of dismissal

The Bill includes the right for designated workers, (presumably this means the 'competent persons' appointed by the employer to assist in health and safety matters under the Management of Health and Safety at Work Regulations 1992) safety representatives and members of safety committees to 'not be subjected to any detriment by any act, or any deliberate failure to act, by his employer' done on the ground that the employee carried out any of his relevant health and safety duties. The protection is further extended to employees who leave their place of work in circumstances of 'danger which was serious and imminent and which he could not reasonably have been expected to avert' and to those employees who take appropriate steps to protect themselves from any such danger. However, an employee who has taken such steps will not be regarded as having been subjected to any detriment if the employer 'shows that it was, or would have been, so negligent for the employee to take the steps which he took, or proposed to take, that a reasonable employer might have treated him as the employer did'.

Dismissal

If an employee is dismissed by his employer and the reason or, if more than one, the principal reason for the dismissal falls into one of the categories already discussed above, then the dismissal is automatically unfair. This will also apply if it is the reason for a redundancy selection.

Remedies

Proceedings will be brought by way of an application to the industrial tribunal and the normal three-month time limit will apply. In cases involving a detriment short of dismissal the tribunal will have the power to grant a declaration and make an award of compensation. The level of compensation should be 'just and equitable in all the circumstances having regard to the infringement complained of and to any loss which is attributable to the act or the failure to act'. The normal duty to mitigate will apply and the level of compensation may further be reduced if the detriment 'was to any extent caused or contributed to by action of the complainant'. A wide discretion is therefore envisaged for the tribunal. The ability to reduce the level of compensation for contributory fault is arguably contrary to the Directive which specifically states that an employee shall suffer 'no detriment' and any questions relating to the negligence of the employee should be considered at the liability stage.

The remedies proposed for the dismissed employee mirror those currently available in trade union dismissal cases. In addition to the standard basic and compensatory awards, the tribunal also has the power to make a special award and an additional award in certain circumstances. The remedies of reinstatement and re-engagement are also available. It is proposed that the two-year service qualification will not apply. The procedure for interim relief will also available.

MEETING THE STANDARDS OF THE DIRECTIVE

The proposed reforms are certainly open to criticism. This is because the Directive states that employees should not suffer any detriment. Industrial tribunals, however, do not have the power to compel an employer to reinstate or re-engage a dismissed employee. This, therefore, means that an employee who has lost his or her employment by reason of carrying out health and safety duties will often only be able to obtain compensation. It is certainly arguable that the loss of a job still represents a detriment even though some compensation may be available. This is particularly so in times of high unemployment when the dismissed employee may have difficulty in finding alternative work. These measures also arguably fall below the requirements of the Directive because they fail to offer any real protection for employees who work for an employer who refuses to recognise a trade union and who refuses to appoint one of his employees as the 'competent person' to assist him with his health and safety obligations (see further Chapters 3 and 12). It is certainly arguable that the Directives do not permit the situation to exist in which the workforce has no role in health and safety matters and it is these workers who are given protection under the terms of the Directive. This is not the position as currently proposed by the government. It is also arguable that the Directive only permits consideration of the negligence of the employee when they have taken steps to protect themselves 'when the immediate superior cannot be contacted'. When advising in this area it is obviously important for the practitioner to keep the Directive clearly in mind.

Chapter 16
Practical impact upon personal injury litigation

It is believed that the effect of these Regulations will alter the approach of the practitioner to litigation. Sometimes it will require a change of emphasis; in other respects it requires a new approach.

TRANSITIONAL PROVISIONS

There are transitional provisions for the following Regulations:

Work Equipment, regulations 11 to 24;

Display Screen Equipment, regulation 3;

Workplace (Health, Safety and Welfare), regulations 5 to 27.

Where there is a claim based on an accident or events occurring between 1 January 1993 and 31 December 1995 it is important to ascertain whether these new Regulations apply. The Workplace Regulations apply to any new workplace, or to a modification, an extension or a conversion of a workplace which was already in existence on 1 January 1993. A new workplace is defined as a workplace used for the first time as a workplace after 31 December 1993. Thus, where a business takes occupation of different premises after 1 January 1993, the Regulations will not apply if the premises had been previously used as a workplace. The Regulations will only apply to premises in which the modification, extension or conversion started after 31 December 1992 and will only apply when the works of modification, extension or conversion are complete. The words 'modification, extension or conversion' are not defined. The interpretation of the words 'extension' and 'conversion' is likely to be straightforward. Whether or not premises have been modified is a matter of fact and degree, and is likely to give rise to litigation in a number of cases.

For the plaintiff's lawyers some evidence as to these matters may be available from the plaintiff, his witnesses, and his trade union. It may be difficult in some cases to make a judgment as to whether the Regulations apply. While pre-action Discovery is available in theory, the better practice is probably to plead the Regulations and to plead the old statutory provisions in the alternative. Some examples are given in the section on pleadings.

Once the proceedings have been commenced then the plaintiff's lawyers can pursue the issue through Discovery, and if necessary through Interrogatories.

The possible application of the new Regulations will also be an important matter for the defendant's lawyers. They will need to obtain evidence of the relevant matters from the defendants. It will be important to obtain evidence, both from witnesses and from available documentation. This will need to be done at an early stage if the defence is to deal with the issues adequately. The practical difficulties in obtaining adequate information at an early stage may necessitate the service of an amended defence at a later date.

PARTIES

When the plaintiff's lawyers are satisfied that it is appropriate to rely upon the Regulations, they need to consider whether the Regulations do implement the terms of the Directives. Attention is drawn to such failures elsewhere in this book. The plaintiff will only be able to sue his employer, or the person in control of, or the occupier of, premises by reliance upon the Regulations, as interpreted by reference to the Directives. Where the regulation fails to implement the terms of the Directive an action may well lie against the Member State for this failure. An employee of the state or an emanation of the state may be able to rely upon the provisions of a Directive directly.[1] Employees who are in the private sector will have to show that the failure to implement the terms of the Directive has resulted in loss or damage. In many cases it may be possible for the plaintiff to succeed against the employer, controller or occupier without reliance upon the faulty regulation. It may be

---

1   There is an example pleading at precedent no 9 in Chapter 17.

necessary to take such proceedings and obtain a judgment before any right against the Member State crystallises. The above matters are dealt with in greater detail in Chapter 3 on the European dimension.

PLEADINGS

The pleadings are governed by the terms of RSC Order 18. Every pleading must contain a statement in a summary form of the material facts on which the party pleading relies for his claim or defence. A party may by his pleading raise any point of law. It would be good practice to plead any competing interpretation of the Regulations, particularly where they are new and untested.

The Management Regulations require a suitable and sufficient assessment of the risks to health and safety. The Display Equipment Regulations require a suitable and sufficient analysis of work-stations for the purpose of assessing the health and safety risks. The Personal Protective Equipment Regulations require an assessment to determine whether the personal protective equipment that it is proposed to provide is suitable. The Work Equipment Regulations require an employer to have regard to the risks to the health and safety of persons which exist in the premises and any additional risk posed by the use of the work equipment. The Manual Handling Regulations require assessment of the risks of injury and a suitable and sufficient assessment of manual handling operations which involve a risk of injury.

An employer, or other person owing a duty under the Regulations, may purport to have carried out an assessment, but it must be sufficient and suitable or assess equipment as suitable. If the assessment does not measure up to the standard set in the Regulations it is evidence of negligence, and, save in respect of the Management Regulations, is a breach of statutory duty which is actionable if it caused or contributed to the plaintiff's injury.

Unless there has been pre-action Discovery or voluntary disclosure of the documents relating to the assessment, a plaintiff cannot be sure that there has been such an assessment. Defendants who employ more than five people must keep a record of the assessment required by the Management Regulations. If the plaintiff's lawyers requested a copy of the assessment from the defendants before commencing proceedings, then any failure by the defendants to provide a copy would be evidence of a failure to have carried out such an assessment. The Particulars of Claim will have to make a general allegation if there is some evidence that there was no assessment.

Without a copy of the assessment, it will not be possible for a plaintiff to plead to the respects in which it is to be said that the assessment was insufficient or unsuitable. It is recommended that the Particulars of Claim contain an allegation of failure to carry out a suitable and sufficient risk assessment where the facts justify such an allegation.

Once the proceedings have been commenced then the issues can be pursued through Discovery and, if necessary, through Interrogatories.[2] An Amended Particulars of Claim may well be required later. In some circumstances it may prove possible to provide adequate Further Particulars, either voluntarily, or in response to a Request.

Similar considerations will apply where there has been a review of an assessment of risks, or where it is alleged that there should have been a review because the assessment was no longer valid or where there have been significant changes in relevant factors.

It is suggested that breaches of the Management Regulations and any ACOP are pleaded as allegations of negligence.[3]

The defence must plead to any issue of practicability, reasonable practicability. The burden of proof is on the defendants, and they must plead the material facts upon which they wish to rely in support of a contention that something was not practicable, or that it was not reasonably practicable. It appears likely that the courts will take the same view in relation to terms such as 'suitable and sufficient'.[4]

DISCOVERY

Discovery is governed by RSC Order 24 and CCR Order 14. Discovery will be an important procedure in any case to which the Regulations apply. The defendants will need to disclose documents relating to risk assessment, and any reassessment, health and safety arrangements, health surveillance, health and safety assistance, any procedures set up for serious and imminent danger and danger areas, information for employees, and health and safety training, as

---

2 There is an example pleading at precedent no 6 in Chapter 17.
3 See Chapter 17, and the example pleading at precedent no 1.
4 There are example pleadings at precedents no 5 and 10 in Chapter 17.

envisaged by the Management Regulations. Discovery will also focus on any particular assessments under specific regulations.

Discovery will also assist in the determination of the issues likely to arise under the transitional provisions. There are likely to be many documents shedding light upon whether the premises were new, or whether they were modified, extended or converted. Similarly, there should be documents shedding light on whether work equipment is new to the undertaking.

The appointment of competent persons to assist in applying the provisions of health and safety law under regulation 6 of the Management Regulations is likely to have given rise to documentation relevant to the issues in a personal injury action.

The requirements for suitable work equipment and suitable personal protective equipment may have involved an employer in a comparative study of different types of equipment. There may have been consideration of brochures, catalogues and data sheets.

It is suggested that the occurrence of an accident of the type intended to be covered by these Regulations will give rise to the need for a reassessment. Such a reassessment should have considered the circumstances of the accident and made recommendations. Documentation relating to such a reassessment is discoverable. Where a previous accident has led to a disputed court hearing, it is suggested that a finding on liability against the defendants is a matter which requires a reassessment of the risks to health and safety in the defendant's undertaking.

Maintenance records may be of value in showing whether work equipment or personal protective equipment was kept in an efficient state. There may have been correspondence or notices from the Health and Safety Executive. All these categories of documents are discoverable.

INTERROGATORIES

Interrogatories are governed by RSC Order 26, subject to CCR Order 14 rule 11. Interrogatories are likely to be an important tool for the plaintiff. Interrogatories are available without order, although the opposite party may take objection to the Interrogatories sought. Interrogatories are allowed where they relate to any matter in question between the parties and they are necessary for disposing fairly of the cause or matter or for the saving of costs.

If a document is no longer in the possession, custody or control of the other party, then Interrogatories can be administered as to the content of the document. Where no records were kept of an assessment, Interrogatories can be directed to discover what matters were considered, what facts were assumed, and what factors were weighed in the balance.

Where there are pleaded issues as to whether it was practicable, or reasonably practicable to take certain measures, a full picture might not be gained by Further and Better Particulars, and it will be necessary to consider whether Interrogatories can yield relevant information.

EXPERTS

The expert can only provide a full report if he is able to consider the assessments made by the defendants, and to make comparison with the Regulations, any Approved Code of Practice, and the Guidance Notes. Comparison with risk assessments by others operating a similar business or undertaking may be helpful in determining whether the risk analysis or assessment was suitable and sufficient.

REFERENCE TO THE EUROPEAN COURT

Reference is governed by RSC Order 114, and CCR Order 19 rule 11. The Rules confer a discretion upon the Judges of the county court and the High Court concerning referral. A Reference to the European Court should only be made where it is necessary to enable the national court to determine the litigation. The Reference will need to have a determination of the essential facts, and, where necessary, of the national law. However, an application for a Reference to the European Court cannot be made after the court has given judgment.[5]

---

5   See Chapter 3 on the European dimension.

Chapter 17
Precedents

PRECEDENT NO 1

IN THE EVERYWHERE COUNTY COURT   Case No 930002

BETWEEN

REX HALLUX   Plaintiff

and

NEWTON MECHANICS LIMITED   Defendants

PARTICULARS OF CLAIM

1. At all material times the Plaintiff was employed as a finisher by the Defendants at their premises at Appletree Industrial Park, Everywhere.

2. The provisions of the Workplace (Health, Safety and Welfare) Regulations 1992 and the Personal Protective Equipment at Work Regulations 1992 applied.

3. On or about 1 April 1993 whilst in the course of that employment the Plaintiff had placed a casting on his workbench. The casting weighed 5 kilograms. The casting was cylindrical. The casting rolled along the workbench and fell off the edge onto the Plaintiff's foot, causing injury to the Plaintiff.

4. The injury to the Plaintiff was caused by the breach of statutory duty and/or negligence of the Defendants, their servants or agents.

PARTICULARS OF BREACH OF STATUTORY DUTY

a) contrary to regulation 11(1) of the Workplace (Health, Safety and Welfare) Regulations 1992 the Plaintiff's workstation was not so arranged that it was suitable for the work that was done there; the workbench was not provided with a rail or raised edge to prevent components rolling off.

b) contrary to regulation 4(1) of the Personal Protective Equipment at Work Regulations 1992 failed to provide suitable personal protective equipment, namely boots with steel toe-caps, to the Plaintiff.

c) contrary to regulation 6(1) of the Personal Protective Equipment at Work Regulations 1992 failed to make an assessment to determine whether the personal protective equipment he intended to provide was suitable. The boots provided did not have a strengthened toe-cap.

d) contrary to regulation 6(2) of the Personal Protective Equipment at Work Regulations 1992 failed to make a reassessment of the suitability of the boots provided when cylindrical castings were first worked upon in about early March 1993.

PARTICULARS OF NEGLIGENCE

a) the Plaintiff repeats as allegations of negligence the allegations of breach of statutory duty.

b) failed to provide the Plaintiff with information upon the weight of the casting and the risk to his health of dropping the casting or letting the casting fall on his foot; the Defendants had a duty to provide information under regulation 11(2) of the Management of Health and Safety at Work Regulations 1992.

c) failed to devise and operate a safe system of work.

5. By reason of the Defendant's breach of statutory duty and/or negligence the Plaintiff, who was born on 29 February 1952, has suffered a fracture of the right great toe. A medical report is served with this pleading. The Plaintiff has experienced pain, suffering and disability.

6. By reason of the Defendant's breach of statutory duty and/or negligence the Plaintiff has suffered loss and damage, a schedule of which is served with this pleading.

7. The Plaintiff claims interest on damages pursuant to section 69 of the County Courts Act 1984. The Plaintiff claims interest on general damages at the rate of 2% or such higher figure as may be necessary to compensate the Plaintiff for the loss of use of the money since the date of the service of these proceedings. The Plaintiff claims interest on Special Damages from the date of each claimed loss at the full Special Account rate as varied from time to time, on the grounds that the Plaintiff has lost the use of the money and its value has been diminished by inflation.

And the Plaintiff claims DAMAGES exceeding £5,000 and INTEREST.

PI HACKE

Dated this day of 1993 by KLAIM, KLAIM & PARTNERS, Station Road, Everywhere, EV1 5CH, Solicitors for the Plaintiff.

PRECEDENT NO 2

IN THE EVERYWHERE COUNTY COURT   Case No 930003
BETWEEN

ROBERT CLUMSEY   Plaintiff

and

THE WIDGET MANUFACTURING   Defendants
CO LTD

PARTICULARS OF CLAIM

1. At all material times the Plaintiff was employed as a machine operator by the Defendants at their premises at the Riverside Industrial Estate, Everywhere.

2. The Provision and Use of Work Equipment Regulations 1992 applied.

3. Alternatively, the provisions of the Factories Act 1961 applied to the Defendant's premises.

4. On or about 1 April 1993 whilst in the course of that employment the Plaintiff was working a drilling machine, drilling holes in widgets. As the Plaintiff was placing a widget in the machine the splonger descended and crushed the Plaintiff's hand. The guard descended and trapped the Plaintiff's arm. The drill bit descended and drilled a 1mm hole in the Plaintiff's thumb.

5. The injury to the Plaintiff was caused by the breach of statutory duty and/or negligence of the Defendants, their servants or agents.

PARTICULARS OF BREACH OF STATUTORY DUTY

a) contrary to regulation 11(1) of the Provision and Use of Work Equipment Regulations 1992 effective measures were not taken to prevent access to any dangerous part of machinery, namely the splonger.

b) contrary to regulation 11(1) of the Provision and Use of Work Equipment Regulations 1992 effective measures were not taken to prevent access to any dangerous part of machinery, namely the drill.

c) contrary to regulation 11(3)(c) of the Provision and Use of Work Equipment Regulations 1992 the guard provided for the drilling machine was not maintained in an efficient state in that it tended to stick and did not descend before the operational cycle of the machine commenced.

d) contrary to regulation 11(3)(d) of the Provision and Use of Work Equipment Regulations 1992 the guard provided gave rise to an increased risk to health or safety in that it trapped and held the Plaintiff's arm.

e) contrary to regulation 15(1) of the Provision and Use of Work Equipment Regulations 1992 the machine was not provided with a readily accessible control the operation of which would have brought the drilling machine to a safe condition. The control to stop the operating cycle of the drilling machine was situated at the side of the machine, and could not be reached by the Plaintiff when his arm was trapped by the guard.

f) contrary to regulation 16(1) of the Provision and Use of Work Equipment Regulations 1992 the machine was not provided with a readily accessible emergency stop control.

g) contrary to regulation 8(1) of the Provision and Use of Work Equipment Regulations 1992 failed to ensure that the Plaintiff had available to him adequate health and safety information or written instructions pertaining to the use of the work equipment.

Alternatively:

h) contrary to section 14 of the Factories Act 1961, the splonger was a dangerous part of the machine which was not securely fenced.

i) contrary to section 14 of the Factories Act 1961 the drill was a dangerous part of the machine which was not securely fenced.

j) contrary to section 16 of the Factories Act 1961 the fencing was not constantly maintained, in that it tended to stick and did not descend before the operational cycle of the machine commenced.

PARTICULARS OF NEGLIGENCE

a) the Plaintiff repeats as allegations of negligence the allegations of breach of statutory duty.

b) failed to carry out a suitable and sufficient assessment of the risks to the health and safety of their employees to which they were exposed whilst they were at work; the Defendants had a duty to carry out an assessment under regulation 2 of the Management of Health and Safety at Work Regulations 1992.

c) failed to devise and operate a safe system of work.

d) caused or permitted the Plaintiff to work at the drilling machine when they knew or ought to have known that the Plaintiff was unfamiliar with the operation of the machine and the sequence of its operating cycle.

e) failed to provide and maintain safe plant and equipment.

[to be completed as in Precedent No 1]

PRECEDENT NO 3

IN THE EVERYWHERE COUNTY COURT   Case No 930003
BETWEEN

ROBERT CLUMSEY   Plaintiff

and

THE WIDGET MANUFACTURING   Defendants
CO LTD

DEFENCE

1. Paragraph 1 of the Particulars of Claim is admitted.

2. The application of the Provision and Use of Work Equipment Regulations 1992 is denied. The drilling machine had been in use at the Defendant's factory premises in Grantham since December 1991, and had been transferred to the premises at the Riverside Industrial Estate in February 1993.

3. The application of the provisions of the Factories Act 1961 is admitted.

4. No admissions are made as to the facts and matters alleged in Paragraph 4 of the Particulars of Claim.

5. It is denied that the Defendants their servants or agents were in breach of statutory duty or negligent whether as alleged in the Particulars of Claim or at all. Causation is denied.

6. Without prejudice to the denial of the application of the Provision and Use of Work Equipment Regulations 1992, the Defendants will contend as follows:

a)   a guard was provided to prevent access to the splonger and drill.

b)   the guard was maintained in an efficient state; any sticking of the guard was caused by the application of a wedge by the Plaintiff.

c)   the guard only held the Plaintiff's arm because the Plaintiff had interfered with the mechanism. The splonger and drill should not have descended unless the guard was fully closed and activating a micro-switch. The Plaintiff had inserted a match in the micro-switch.

d)   a readily accessible stop control was not appropriate given the provision of the guard and the micro-switch.

e)   a readily accessible emergency-stop control was not appropriate given the provision of the guard and the micro-switch.

f)   the Plaintiff was an experienced machine operator who had used machines with an almost identical function and operation for many years.

7. The Defendants deny breaches of sections 14 and 16 of the Factories Act 1961. The Defendants will contend that the dangerous parts of the drilling machine were securely fenced by fencing that was constantly maintained. The Plaintiff had attempted to wedge the guard open, and had inserted a match into the micro-switch.

8. Any injury suffered by the Plaintiff was caused wholly or in part by his own negligence.

PARTICULARS OF NEGLIGENCE

a)   attempted to wedge open the machine guard.

b)   inserted a matchstick in the micro-switch.

c)   failed to heed the training given by the Defendants upon the function and operation of this type of drilling machine.

d) failed to inform the Defendants if the guard was sticking. The Plaintiff was required to report any shortcoming in the Defendant's protection arrangements for health and safety by regulation 12(2) of the Management of Health and Safety at Work Regulations 1992.

9. No admissions are made as to the alleged injury.

10. No admissions are made as to the alleged loss and damage.

11. No admissions are made as to the claimed entitlement to interest.

ROD IRONGATE

Served this day of 1993 by DOUGHTER & DENAI, Thomasville, SN1 1PE, Solicitors for the Defendants.

PRECEDENT NO 4

IN THE EVERYWHERE COUNTY COURT　　　　　　Case No 930004
BETWEEN

ADIE TRIPPER　　　　　　Plaintiff

and

THE EVERYWHERE　　　　　　Defendants
HOSPITAL TRUST

PARTICULARS OF CLAIM

1. At all material times the Plaintiff was employed as a nurse by the Defendants at their premises at the Everywhere Hospital, Caring Road, Everywhere.

2. The Workplace (Health, Safety and Welfare) Regulations 1992 applied to the Defendant's premises.

3. On or about 1 February 1993 whilst in the course of that employment the Plaintiff was walking from the car-park along the path towards the Maternity Wing. There was a pothole in the path. The Plaintiff tripped in the pothole and fell, and as a consequence she sustained injury.

4. The injury to the Plaintiff was caused by the breach of statutory duty and/or negligence of the Defendants, their servants or agents.

PARTICULARS OF BREACH OF STATUTORY DUTY

a)   contrary to regulation 12(2)(a) of the Workplace (Health, Safety and Welfare) Regulations 1992 the path was a traffic route which contained a hole so as to expose a person to a risk to his health or safety.

PARTICULARS OF NEGLIGENCE

a)   the Plaintiff repeats as allegations of negligence the allegations of breach of statutory duty made above.

b)   failed to warn the Plaintiff by means of a sign, notice or otherwise of the presence of the pothole in the path.

c)   failed to prevent the Plaintiff walking along the path by the use of barriers, fencing, or cones, or by marking off the area.

d)   failed to inspect, repair or maintain the path.

e)   failed to provide and maintain safe means of access to the Plaintiff's place of work.

[to be completed as in Precedent No 1]

PRECEDENT NO 5

IN THE EVERYWHERE COUNTY COURT   Case No 930004
BETWEEN

ADIE TRIPPER   Plaintiff

and

THE EVERYWHERE   Defendants
HOSPITAL TRUST

DEFENCE

1. Paragraph 1 of the Particulars of Claim is admitted.

2. The application of the Workplace (Health, Safety and Welfare) Regulations 1992 is denied. The premises had been in use prior to 1 January 1993 and had not been modified, extended or converted within the meaning of regulation 1(3) of the Regulations.

3. No admissions are made as to the facts and matters alleged in Paragraph 3 of the Particulars of Claim.

4. It is denied that the Defendants their servants or agents were in breach of statutory duty or negligent whether as alleged in the Particulars of Claim or at all. Causation is denied.

5. Without prejudice to the denial of the application of the Workplace (Health, Safety and Welfare) Regulations 1992, the Defendants will contend as follows:

a)   any hole on the path was not of a size or depth to expose any person to a risk to his health or safety.

b)   the hole had been marked with yellow paint and that was an adequate measure to prevent persons falling within the meaning of regulation 12(4)(a) of the Workplace (Health, Safety and Welfare) Regulations 1992.

6. Without prejudice to the general denial of negligence, the Defendants will contend that it was not reasonably practicable to fill every hole within a period of a week and that any hole had only become apparent some three days before the Plaintiff's alleged accident.

7. Any injury suffered by the Plaintiff was caused wholly or in part by her own negligence.

PARTICULARS OF NEGLIGENCE

a)   failed to keep any or any proper lookout.

b)   failed to observe the hole or its markings.

c)   failed to watch where or how she placed her feet.

d) failed to keep her balance.

[to be completed as in Precedent No 3]

PRECEDENT NO 6

IN THE EVERYWHERE COUNTY COURT   Case No 930004
BETWEEN

ADIE TRIPPER   Plaintiff

and

THE EVERYWHERE   Defendants
HOSPITAL TRUST

INTERROGATORIES

The Plaintiff requires the answers to these Interrogatories to be
provided by Affidavit or Affirmation by a responsible officer of
the Defendants within 28 days of service of these Interrogatories.

Look at the Defence and the contention that the premises had
been in use prior to 1 January 1993 and had not been modified,
extended or converted within the meaning of regulation 1(3) of the
Workplace (Health, Safety and Welfare) Regulations 1992.

1. Was the area which is now used as a car park formerly used as an
area to store old beds?

2. Was not the area which is now used as a car park cleared of old
beds and rubbish?

3. If the answer to the second Interrogatory is yes, were not the old
beds removed and the rubbish cleared in about the second week of
January 1993?

4. Was the area which is now used as a car park resurfaced on or
about 19 and 20 January 1993?

5. Was the path from the car park to the Maternity Wing used by about 23 people daily after about 21 January 1993?

Dated etc

PRECEDENT NO 7

IN THE EVERYWHERE COUNTY COURT   Case No 930005
BETWEEN

BASIL DONNE   Plaintiff

and

SCROOGE LIMITED   Defendants

PARTICULARS OF CLAIM

1. At all material times the Plaintiff was employed by the Defendants as a typist using a word-processor at their premises at Canary Wharf.

2. The provisions of the Offices, Shops and Railway Premises Act 1963 applied.

3. The provisions of the Health and Safety (Display Screen Equipment) Regulations 1992 applied.

4. The Plaintiff worked in an office at 1 of 2 glass-topped tables which faced a window. The Plaintiff sat on a 4-legged wooden chair. The window was without curtains or blinds.

5. The Plaintiff worked from 9am to 5pm with a break of 1 hour for lunch. His work was brought to his table, and completed work was collected from his table.

6. The Plaintiff commenced work on 4 January 1993. The Plaintiff experienced eye strain and tiredness after the first week. In about April 1993 the Plaintiff began to experience aching in his upper back, neck and shoulders, and suffered headaches and irritability.

7. The Plaintiff's symptoms were caused by the breach of statutory duty and/or negligence of the Defendants, their servants or agents.

PARTICULARS OF BREACH OF STATUTORY DUTY

a) contrary to regulation 2(1) of the Health and Safety (Display Screen Equipment) Regulations 1992 failed to perform any or any suitable and sufficient analysis of the Plaintiff's workstation for the purpose of assessing the health and safety risks to which the Plaintiff was exposed in consequence of his use of the workstation. The risks which should have been identified were that his seat was not adjustable in height, that the table caused distracting glare and reflections, and that the windows were not fitted with a system to attenuate the daylight that fell on the workstation.

b) contrary to regulation 2(3) of the Health and Safety (Display Screen Equipment) Regulations 1992 failed to reduce the risks identified in consequence of any assessment made under regulation 2(1).

c) contrary to regulation 3(1) of the Health and Safety (Display Screen Equipment) Regulations 1992 failed to ensure that the Plaintiff's workstation met the requirements laid down in the Schedule to the Regulations. The requirements that were not met were the provision of a seat which was adjustable in height, the provision of a table which did not cause distracting glare and reflections, and the windows were not fitted with a system to attenuate the daylight that fell on the workstation.

d) contrary to regulation 4 of the Health and Safety (Display Screen Equipment) Regulations 1992 failed to plan the activities of the Plaintiff at his work so that his daily work on display screen equipment was periodically interrupted by such breaks or changes of activity as to reduce his workload at that equipment.

e) contrary to regulation 5(1) of the Health and Safety (Display Screen Equipment) Regulations 1992 failed to provide the

Plaintiff with an appropriate eyesight test by a competent person following the request made by the Plaintiff on 13 January 1992.

f) contrary to regulation 6 of the Health and Safety (Display Screen Equipment) Regulations 1992 failed to provide the Plaintiff with adequate health and safety training in the use of the workstation upon which he was required to work. The Plaintiff should have been trained to adopt and maintain a comfortable position.

g) contrary to regulation 7 of the Health and Safety (Display Screen Equipment) Regulations 1992 failed to provide the Plaintiff with adequate information about all aspects of health and safety relating to the workstation upon which he was required to work. The Plaintiff should have been informed that the work could cause eye symptoms and musculo-skeletal symptoms and that he should report the first onset of any such symptoms to the Defendants.

h) contrary to section 14 of the Offices, Shops and Railway Premises Act 1963 failed to provide a seat of a design, construction and dimensions suitable for the Plaintiff. The Plaintiff will rely upon the fact that it was not adjustable for height.

PARTICULARS OF NEGLIGENCE

a) the Plaintiff repeats as allegations of negligence the allegations of breach of statutory duty.

b) failed to provide safe plant and equipment; the Plaintiff will rely upon the matters pleaded above.

c) in the above respects failed to make and keep safe the Plaintiff's workstation.

d) failed to devise and operate a safe system of work.

[to be completed as in Precedent No 1]

PRECEDENT NO 8

IN THE EVERYWHERE COUNTY COURT   Case No 930006
BETWEEN

SHARON SHOEBURY   Plaintiff

and

TEMPS UNLIMITED   First Defendants

and

SCROOGE LIMITED   Second Defendants

PARTICULARS OF CLAIM

1. At all material times the Plaintiff was employed by the First
Defendants as a 'Temp' typist using word-processors and was
contracted to work at the premises of the Second Defendants in
Canary Wharf.

2. The provisions of the Health and Safety (Display Screen
Equipment) Regulations 1992 applied.

3. The provisions of the Offices, Shops and Railway Premises Act
1963 applied to the Second Defendant's premises.

4. The Plaintiff worked in a small office at 1 of 2 glass-topped tables
which faced a window. The Plaintiff sat on a 4-legged wooden
chair. The window was without curtains or blinds. The screen
display was of poor contrast.

5. The Plaintiff worked from 9am to 5pm with a break of 1 hour for
lunch. Her work was brought to her table, and completed work was
collected from her table.

6. The Plaintiff commenced work at the premises of the Second
Defendants on 4 January 1993. The Plaintiff experienced eye strain
and tiredness after the first week. In about April 1993 the Plaintiff
began to experience aching in her upper back, neck and shoulders,
headaches and irritability.

7. The Plaintiff's symptoms were caused wholly or in part by the breach of statutory duty and/or negligence of the First Defendants, their servants or agents.

PARTICULARS OF BREACH OF STATUTORY DUTY

a)   contrary to regulation 5(1) of the Health and Safety (Display Screen Equipment) Regulations 1992 failed to provide the Plaintiff with an appropriate eyesight test by a competent person following the request made by the Plaintiff on 13 January 1992.

b)   contrary to regulation 6(1) of the Health and Safety (Display Screen Equipment) Regulations 1992 failed to provide the Plaintiff with adequate health and safety training in the use of the workstation upon which she was required to work. The Plaintiff should have been trained how to adjust the screen display.

PARTICULARS OF NEGLIGENCE

a)   the Plaintiff repeats as allegations of negligence the allegations of breach of statutory duty made above.

b)   failed to ensure that the Second Defendants had performed a suitable and sufficient analysis of the Plaintiff's workstation for the purpose of assessing the health and safety risks to which the Plaintiff was exposed in consequence of her use of the workstation. The risks which should have been identified were that her seat was not adjustable in height, that the table caused distracting glare and reflections, and that the windows were not fitted with a system to attenuate the daylight that fell on the workstation.

c)   failed to ensure that the Second Defendants had reduced the risks identified in consequence of the analysis made under regulation 2(1).

d)   failed to provide the Plaintiff with adequate health and safety training in the use of the workstation upon which she was required to work. The Plaintiff should have been trained how to adjust the screen display.

e)   failed to provide the Plaintiff with adequate information about all aspects of health and safety relating to her workstation upon which she was required to work. The Plaintiff should have been informed that the work could cause eye symptoms and musculo-skeletal symptoms and that she should report the first onset of any such symptoms to the First and/or Second Defendants.

f)   failed to warn or instruct the Plaintiff to plan her activities at her work so that her daily work on display screen equipment was periodically interrupted by such breaks or changes of activity as to reduce her workload at that equipment.

g)   failed to devise and operate a safe system of work.

8. The Plaintiff's symptoms were caused wholly or in part by the breach of statutory duty and/or negligence of the Second Defendants, their servants or agents.

PARTICULARS OF BREACH OF STATUTORY DUTY

a)   contrary to regulation 2(1) of the Health and Safety (Display Screen Equipment) Regulations 1992 failed to perform any or any suitable and sufficient analysis of the Plaintiff's workstation for the purpose of assessing the health and safety risks to which the Plaintiff was exposed in consequence of her use of the workstation. The risks which should have been identified were that her seat was not adjustable in height, that the table caused distracting glare and reflections, and that the windows were not fitted with a system to attenuate the daylight that fell on the workstation.

b)   contrary to regulation 2(3) of the Health and Safety (Display Screen Equipment) Regulations 1992 failed to reduce the risks identified in consequence of any analysis made under regulation 2(1).

c)   contrary to regulation 3(1) of the Health and Safety (Display Screen Equipment) Regulations 1992 failed to ensure that the

Plaintiff's workstation met the requirements laid down in the Schedule to the Regulations. The requirements that were not met were the provision of a seat which was adjustable in height, the provision of a table which did not cause distracting glare and reflections, and the windows were not fitted with a system to attenuate the daylight that fell on the workstation.

d) contrary to regulation 6(2) of the Health and Safety (Display Screen Equipment) Regulations 1992 failed to provide the Plaintiff with adequate health and safety training in the use of the workstation upon which she was required to work. The Plaintiff should have been trained how to adjust the screen display.

e) contrary to regulation 7 of the Health and Safety (Display Screen Equipment) Regulations 1992 failed to provide the Plaintiff with adequate information about all aspects of health and safety relating to her workstation upon which she was required to work. The Plaintiff should have been informed that the work could cause eye symptoms and musculo-skeletal symptoms and that she should report the first onset of any such symptoms to the First and/or Second Defendants.

f) contrary to section 14 of the Offices, Shops and Railway Premises Act 1963 failed to provide a seat of a design, construction and dimensions suitable for the Plaintiff. The Plaintiff will rely upon the fact that it was not adjustable for height.

PARTICULARS OF NEGLIGENCE

a) the Plaintiff repeats as allegations of negligence the allegations of breach of statutory duty made against the Second Defendants.

b) failed to ensure that the Plaintiff's workstation met the requirements laid down in the Schedule to the Health and Safety (Display Screen Equipment) Regulations 1992. The Plaintiff contends that it would have been reasonable for the Defendants to meet the requirements of the Schedule because the Defendants only operated 3 workstations with display screen equipment and the costs and time expended to meet the requirements would have been modest.

c) failed to plan the activities of the Plaintiff at her work so that her daily work on display screen equipment was periodically interrupted by such breaks or changes of activity as to reduce her workload at that equipment.

d) failed to provide safe plant and equipment; the Plaintiff will rely upon the matters pleaded above.

e) in the above respects failed to make and keep safe the Plaintiff's workstation.

f) failed to devise and operate a safe system of work.

[to be completed as in Precedent No 1]

PRECEDENT NO 9

IN THE EVERYWHERE COUNTY COURT   Case No 930007
BETWEEN

ABLE LYFTER   Plaintiff

and

STATE RAILWAY COMPANY   Defendants

PARTICULARS OF CLAIM

1. At all material times the Plaintiff was employed as a production worker by the Defendants at their workshop premises at Railway Cuttings, Everywhere.

2. The provisions of the Manual Handling Operations Regulations 1992 and the Workplace (Health, Safety and Welfare) Regulations 1992 applied.

3. On or about 1 April 1993 whilst in the course of that employment the Plaintiff was attempting to move a K9 casting from a pallet beside his workbench onto his workbench. The casting weighed 50

kilograms. The pallet had been placed on the floor by a forklift truck. The surface of the workbench was 80 centimetres above the level of the floor.

4. As the Plaintiff was lifting the casting from the pallet by holding it at each end he suffered a strain to his back.

5. The injury to the Plaintiff was caused by the breach of statutory duty and/or negligence of the Defendants, their servants or agents.

PARTICULARS OF BREACH OF STATUTORY DUTY

a) contrary to regulation 4(1)(a) of the Manual Handling Operations Regulations 1992 failed to avoid the need for the Plaintiff to undertake a manual handling operation which involved a risk of the Plaintiff being injured.

b) contrary to regulation 4(1)(b)(i) of the Manual Handling Operations Regulations 1992 failed to make a suitable and sufficient assessment of the manual handling operations to be undertaken by their employees.

c) contrary to regulation 4(1)(b)(ii) of the Manual Handling Operations Regulations 1992 failed to take appropriate steps to reduce to the lowest level reasonably practicable the risk of injury to employees arising out of manual handling operations; without prejudice to regulation 4(1)(a), the pallet should have been placed at a height level with the surface of the Plaintiff's workbench.

d) contrary to regulation 4(2) of the Manual Handling Operations Regulations 1992 failed to make a reassessment of the manual handling operations in relation to castings when the Plaintiff's workbench was moved away from the conveyor; it had been possible to slide castings from the conveyor onto the workbench.

e) contrary to regulation 4(2) of the Manual Handling Operations Regulations 1992, if there was a reassessment of the manual handling operations in relation to castings when the Plaintiff's workbench was moved away from the conveyor, failed to make any changes to the manual handling operations.

f)   contrary to regulation 11(1) of the Workplace (Health, Safety and Welfare) Regulations 1992 the Plaintiff's workstation was not so arranged that it was suitable for the work that was done there; it should have been arranged so as to avoid the need for the Plaintiff to undertake a lift from close to the floor; the pallet should have been placed at a height level with the surface of the Plaintiff's workbench.

g)   contrary to Article 6.2 of the Council Directive 90/269/EEC failed to ensure that the Plaintiff received proper training and information on how to handle loads correctly and the risks that he might be open to if these tasks are not performed correctly.

PARTICULARS OF NEGLIGENCE

a)   the Plaintiff repeats as allegations of negligence the allegations of breach of statutory duty.

b)   failed to provide the Plaintiff with information upon the weight of the casting and the risk to his health in attempting a manual lift of the casting; the Defendants had a duty to provide information under regulation 8 of the Management of Health and Safety at Work Regulations 1992.

c)   failed to provide adequate health and safety training for the Plaintiff in the aspects of safe lifting and handling of heavy loads; the Defendants had a duty to provide information under regulation 11(2) of the Management of Health and Safety at Work Regulations 1992.

d)   if, contrary to the Plaintiff's contention that Article 6.2 of the Council Directive 90/269/EEC has direct effect upon these Defendants, the Plaintiff will contend that failure to comply with the terms of the Directive constitutes evidence of negligence.

e)   failed to devise and operate a safe system of work.

[to be completed as in Precedent No 1]

PRECEDENT NO 10

IN THE EVERYWHERE COUNTY COURT   Case No 930007
BETWEEN

ABLE LYFTER   Plaintiff

and

STATE RAILWAY COMPANY   Defendants

DEFENCE

1. Paragraph 1 of the Particulars of Claim is admitted.

2. The application of the Manual Handling Operations Regulations 1992 is admitted.

3. It is denied that the K9 casting weighed 50 kilograms. It will be contended that the casting weighed 20 kilograms. No admissions are made as to the remaining allegations in Paragraph 3 of the Particulars of Claim.

4. It is denied that the Plaintiff suffered any injury whilst lifting a casting.

5. It is denied that the Defendants their servants or agents were in breach of statutory duty or negligent whether as alleged in the Particulars of Claim or at all. Causation is denied.

6. It is denied that the Plaintiff can rely directly upon the provisions of Article 6.2 of the Council Directive 90/269/EEC.

7. The lifting of the 20 kilogram weight of the K9 casting from the pallet to the surface of the workbench did not create a risk of injury to the Plaintiff.

8. Alternatively, if the lifting of the K9 casting did create a risk of injury it was not reasonably practicable to avoid manual lifting of the casting for the following reasons:

a) the Defendants worked upon a K9 casting only once every 6 months.

b) the overhead hoist did not travel to the Plaintiff's workbench.

c) the Plaintiff's workbench needed to be sited near the exhaust appliances for the purpose of his other work.

d) there were other employees in the area who could and would assist the Plaintiff in lifting the casting onto the workbench.

9. The Defendants took steps to reduce to the lowest level reasonably practicable the risk of injury to the Plaintiff from handling a K9 casting by:

a) delivering the casting on a pallet to a position beside the Plaintiff's workbench.

b) instructing the Plaintiff only to lift the casting with the assistance of one or more fellow employees.

10. Any injury suffered by the Plaintiff in lifting the K9 casting was caused wholly or in part by his own breach of statutory duty and/or negligence.

PARTICULARS OF BREACH OF STATUTORY DUTY

(i) contrary to regulation 5 of the Manual Handling Operations Regulations 1992 failed to make full and proper use of the system of work provided by the Defendants, namely the assistance of one or more fellow employees in lifting a K9 casting.

PARTICULARS OF NEGLIGENCE

a) the Defendants repeat as an allegation of negligence the allegation of breach of statutory duty.

b) failed to heed the training given by the Defendants upon the aspects of safe lifting and handling of heavy loads.

c) failed to inform the Defendants if the lifting of the casting represented a risk to the Plaintiff. The Plaintiff was required to report any shortcoming in the Defendant's protection arrangements for health and safety by regulation 12(2) of the Management of Health and Safety at Work Regulations 1992.

[to be completed as in Precedent No 3]

Chapter 18

Destination table

This does *not* purport to be a complete destination table. Its purpose is a quick reference guide to take the user to those regulations which, in whole or in part, now cover the most well known statutory provisions. Care will need to be exercised when looking at the less commonly used regulations and statutes, for there are repeals, revocations and amendments to many of them. It will be necessary to check the Schedules to the new Regulations to see whether or to what extent they are affected.

The following abbreviations are used below.

Management of Health and Safety at Work Regulations	=	MHSWR
Personal Protective Equipment at Work Regulations	=	PPE
Provision and Use of Work Equipment Regulations	=	PUWER
Workplace (Health, Safety and Welfare) Regulations	=	Workplace
Manual Handling Operations Regulations	=	M Handling

Factories Act 1961

section 1	reg 9 Workplace
section 2	reg 10 Workplace
section 3	reg 7 Workplace
section 4	reg 6 Workplace
section 5	reg 8 Workplace
section 6	reg 12(2)(b) Workplace
section 7	reg 20 Workplace
section 12 to 17	PUWER

Factories Act 1961 (cont)

section 18	reg 13(5) Workplace
section 19	PUWER
section 28(1) & (2)	reg 12 Workplace
section 28(3) & (4)	reg 13 Workplace
section 28(5)	reg 5 Workplace
section 29(1)	regs 5, 12, 17 Workplace
section 29(2)	reg 13 Workplace
section 57	reg 22 Workplace
section 58	reg 21 Workplace
section 59	reg 23 Workplace
section 60	reg 11(3) Workplace
section 65	PPE
section 69	regs 8, 10 Workplace
section 72	M Handling

Offices, Shops and Railway Premises Act 1963

section 4	reg 9 Workplace
section 5	reg 10 Workplace
section 6	reg 7 Workplace
section 7	reg 6 Workplace
section 8	reg 8 Workplace
section 9	reg 20 Workplace
section 10	reg 21 Workplace
section 11	reg 22 Workplace
section 12	reg 23 Workplace
section 13	reg 11(1) Workplace
section 14	reg 11(3) Workplace
section 15	reg 25 Workplace
section 16	reg 12 Workplace
section 17	PUWER

The Mines and Quarries Act 1954

sections 81(1) and 82	PUWER

The Abrasive Wheels Regulations 1970

regulation 3(2), 3(3), 3(4), 4, 6–8, 10–16	PUWER

The Abrasive Wheels Regulations 1970 (cont)

regulation 17   reg 12 Workplace
regulations 18 & 19   PUWER

The Construction (General Provisions) Regulations 1961

regulations 42, 43,
  and 57   PUWER

The Shipbuilding and Ship-Repairing Regulations 1960

regulation 67   regs 5, 11, and 12 PUWER

The Woodworking Machines Regulations 1974

regulations 1(2), 1(3),
  3(2), 5–9   PUWER
regulation 10   reg 10 Workplace
regulation 11   reg 12 Workplace
regulation 12   reg 7 Workplace
regulations 14–19,
  21–38, 40–43   PUWER

Chapter 19

The Directives

COUNCIL DIRECTIVE OF 12 JUNE 1989
on the introduction of measures to encourage improvements in the safety and health of workers at work (89/391/EEC)

The Council of the European Communities,

Having regard to the Treaty establishing the European Economic Community, and in particular Article 118a thereof,

Having regard to the proposal from the Commission drawn up after consultation with the Advisory Committee on Safety, Hygiene and Health Protection at Work,

In cooperation with the European Parliament,

Having regard to the opinion of the Economic and Social Committee,

Whereas Article 118a of the Treaty provides that the Council shall adopt, by means of Directives, minimum requirements for encouraging improvements, especially in the working environment, to guarantee a better level of protection of the safety and health of workers;

Whereas this Directive does not justify any reduction in levels of protection already achieved in individual Member States, the Member State being committed, under the Treaty, to encouraging improvements in conditions in this area and to harmonizing conditions while maintaining the improvements made;

Whereas it is known that workers can be exposed to the effects of dangerous environmental factors at the work place during the course of their working life;

Whereas, pursuant to Article 118a of the Treaty, such Directives must avoid imposing administrative, financial and legal constraints which would hold back the creation and development of small and medium-sized undertakings;

Whereas the communication from the Commission on its programme concerning safety, hygiene and health at work provides for the adoption of Directives designed to guarantee the safety and health of workers;

Whereas the Council, in its resolution of 21 December 1987 on safety, hygiene and health at work, took note of the Commission's intention to submit to the Council in the near future a Directive on the organization of the safety and health of workers at the work place;

Whereas in February 1988 the European Parliament adopted four resolutions following the debate on the internal market and worker protection; whereas these resolutions specifically invited the Commission to draw up a framework Directive to serve as a basis for more specific Directives covering all the risks connected with safety and health at the work place;

Whereas Member States have a responsibility to encourage improvements in the safety and health of workers on their territory; whereas taking measures to protect the health and safety of workers at work also helps, in certain cases, to preserve the health and possibly the safety of persons residing with them;

Whereas Member States' legislative systems covering safety and health at the work place differ widely and need to be improved; whereas national provisions on the subject, which often include technical specifications and/ or self-regulatory standards, may result in different levels of safety and health protection and allow competition at the expense of safety and health;

Whereas the incidence of accidents at work and occupational diseases is still too high; whereas preventive measures must be introduced or improved without delay in order to safeguard the safety and health of workers and ensure a higher degree of protection;

Whereas, in order to ensure an improved degree of protection, workers and/or their representatives must be informed of the risks to their safety and health and of the measures required to reduce or eliminate these risks; whereas they must also be in a position to contribute, by means of balanced participation in accordance with national laws and/or practices, to seeing that the necessary protective measures are taken;

Whereas information, dialogue and balanced participation on safety and health at work must be developed between employers and workers and/or their representatives by means of appropriate procedures and instruments, in accordance with national laws and/or practices;

Whereas the improvement of workers' safety, hygiene and health at work is an objective which should not be subordinated to purely economic considerations;

Whereas employers shall be obliged to keep themselves informed of the latest advances in technology and scientific findings concerning workplace design, account being taken of the inherent dangers in their undertaking, and to inform accordingly the workers' representatives exercising participation rights under this Directive, so as to be able to guarantee a better level of protection of workers' health and safety;

Whereas the provisions of this Directive apply, without prejudice to more stringent present or future Community provisions, to all risks, and in particular to those arising from the use at work of chemical, physical and biological agents covered by Directive 80/1107/EEC, as last amended by Directive 88/642/EEC;

Whereas, pursuant to Decision 74/325/EEC, the Advisory Committee on Safety, Hygiene and Health Protection at Work is consulted by the Commission on the drafting of proposals in this field;

Whereas a Committee composed of members nominated by the Member States needs to be set up to assist the Commission in making the technical adaptations to the individual Directives provided for in this Directive.

HAS ADOPTED THIS DIRECTIVE:

SECTION I

General provisions

Article 1

OBJECT

1.   The object of this Directive is to introduce measures to encourage improvements in the safety and health of workers at work.

2.   To that end it contains general principles concerning the prevention of occupational risks, the protection of safety and health, the elimination of risk and accident factors, the informing, consultation, balanced participation in accordance with national laws and/or practices and training of workers and their representatives, as well as general guidelines for the implementation of the said principles.

3.   This Directive shall be without prejudice to existing or future national and Community provisions which are more favourable to protection of the safety and health of workers at work.

Article 2

SCOPE

1.   This Directive shall apply to all sectors of activity, both public and private (industrial, agricultural, commercial, administrative, service, educational, cultural, leisure, etc).

2.   This Directive shall not be applicable where characteristics peculiar to certain specific public service activities, such as the armed forces or the police, or to certain specific activities in the civil protection services inevitably conflict with it.

In that event, the safety and health of workers must be ensured as far as possible in the light of the objectives of this Directive.

Article 3

DEFINITIONS

For the purposes of this Directive, the following terms shall have the following meanings:

(a)   worker: any person employed by an employer, including trainees and apprentices but excluding domestic servants;

(b)   employer: any natural or legal person who has an employment relationship with the worker and has responsibility for the undertaking and/or establishment;

(c)   workers' representative with specific responsibility for the safety and health of workers: any person elected, chosen or designated in accordance with national laws and/or practices to represent workers where problems arise relating to the safety and health protection of workers at work;

(d)   prevention: all the steps or measures taken or planned at all stages of work in the undertaking to prevent or reduce occupational risks.

Article 4

1.   Member States shall take the necessary steps to ensure that employers, workers and workers' representatives are subject to the legal provisions necessary for the implementation of this Directive.

2.   In particular, Member States shall ensure adequate controls and supervision.

SECTION II

Employers' obligations

Article 5

GENERAL PROVISION

1.   The employer shall have a duty to ensure the safety and health of workers in every aspect related to the work.

2.   Where, pursuant to Article 7 (3), an employer enlists competent external services or persons, this shall not discharge him from his responsibilities in this area.

3.   The workers' obligations in the field of safety and health at work shall not affect the principle of the responsibility of the employer.

4.   This Directive shall not restrict the option of Member States to provide for the exclusion or the limitation of employers' responsibility where occurrences are due to unusual and unforeseeable circumstances, beyond the employers' control, or to exceptional events, the consequences of which could not have been avoided despite the exercise of all due care.

Member States need not exercise the option referred to in the first subparagraph.

Article 6

GENERAL OBLIGATIONS ON EMPLOYERS

1.   Within the context of his responsibilities, the employer shall take the measures necessary for the safety and health protection of workers, including prevention of occupational risks and provision of information and training, as well as provision of the necessary organization and means.

The employer shall be alert to the need to adjust these measures to take account of changing circumstances and aim to improve existing situations.

2.   The employer shall implement the measures referred to in the first subparagraph of paragraph 1 on the basis of the following general principles of prevention:

(a)   avoiding risks;

(b)   evaluating the risks which cannot be avoided;

(c)   combating the risks at source;

(d) adapting the work to the individual, especially as regards the design of work places, the choice of work equipment and the choice of working and production methods, with a view, in particular, to alleviating monotonous work and work at a predetermined work-rate and to reducing their effect on health;

(e) adapting to technical progress;

(f) replacing the dangerous by the non-dangerous or the less dangerous;

(g) developing a coherent overall prevention policy which covers technology, organization of work, working conditions, social relationships and the influence of factors related to the working environment;

(h) giving collective protective measures priority over individual protective measures;

(i) giving appropriate instructions to the workers.

3. Without prejudice to the other provisions of this Directive, the employer shall, taking into account the nature of the activities of the enterprise and/or establishment:

(a) evaluate the risks to the safety and health of workers, inter alia in the choice of work equipment, the chemical substances or preparations used, and the fitting-out of work places.

Subsequent to this evaluation and as necessary, the preventive measures and the working and production methods implemented by the employer must:

–   assure an improvement in the level of protection afforded to workers with regard to safety and health,

–   be integrated into all the activities of the undertaking and/or establishment and at all hierarchical levels;

(b) where he entrusts tasks to a worker, take into consideration the worker's capabilities as regards health and safety;

(c) ensure that the planning and introduction of new technologies are the subject of consultation with the workers and/or their representatives, as regards the consequences of the choice of equipment, the working conditions and the working environment for the safety and health of workers;

(d) take appropriate steps to ensure that only workers who have received adequate instructions may have access to areas where there is serious and specific danger.

4. Without prejudice to the other provisions of this Directive, where several undertakings share a work place, the employers shall cooperate in implementing the safety, health and occupational hygiene provisions and,

taking into account the nature of the activities, shall coordinate their actions in matters of the protection and prevention of occupational risks, and shall inform one another and their respective workers and/or workers' representatives of these risks.

5.   Measures related to safety, hygiene and health at work may in no circumstances involve the workers in financial cost.

Article 7

PROTECTIVE AND PREVENTIVE SERVICES

1.   Without prejudice to the obligations referred to in Articles 5 and 6, the employer shall designate one or more workers to carry out activities related to the protection and prevention of occupational risks for the undertaking and/or establishment.

2.   Designated workers may not be placed at any disadvantage because of their activities related to the protection and prevention of occupational risks.

Designated workers shall be allowed adequate time to enable them to fulfil their obligations arising from this Directive.

3.   If such protective and preventive measures cannot be organized for lack of competent personnel in the undertaking and/or establishment, the employer shall enlist competent external services or persons.

4.   Where the employer enlists such services or persons, he shall inform them of the factors known to affect, or suspected of affecting, the safety and health of the workers and they must have access to the information referred to in Article 10 (2).

5.   In all cases:

–   the workers designated must have the necessary capabilities and the necessary means,

–   the external services or persons consulted must have the necessary aptitudes and the necessary personal and professional means, and

–   the workers designated and the external services or persons consulted must be sufficient in number

to deal with the organization of protective and preventive measures, taking into account the size of the undertaking and/or establishment and/or the hazards to which the workers are exposed and their distribution throughout the entire undertaking and/or establishment.

6. The protection from, and prevention of, the health and safety risks which form the subject of this Article shall be the responsibility of one or more workers, of one service or of separate services whether from inside or outside the undertaking and/or establishment.

The worker(s) and/or agency(ies) must work together whenever necessary.

7. Member States may define, in the light of the nature of the activities and size of the undertakings, the categories of undertakings in which the employer, provided he is competent, may himself take responsibility for the measures referred to in paragraph 1.

8. Member States shall define the necessary capabilities and aptitudes referred to in paragraph 5.

They may determine the sufficient number referred to in paragraph 5.

Article 8

FIRST AID, FIRE-FIGHTING AND EVACUATION OF WORKERS, SERIOUS AND IMMINENT DANGER

1. The employer shall:

–   take the necessary measures for first aid, fire-fighting and evacuation of workers, adapted to the nature of the activities and the size of the undertaking and/or establishment and taking into account other persons present,

–   arrange any necessary contacts with external services, particularly as regards first aid, emergency medical care, rescue work and fire-fighting.

2. Pursuant to paragraph 1, the employer shall, inter alia, for first aid, fire-fighting and the evacuation of workers, designate the workers required to implement such measures.

The number of such workers, their training and the equipment available to them shall be adequate, taking account of the size and/or specific hazards of the undertaking and/or establishment.

3. The employer shall:

(a) as soon as possible, inform all workers who are, or may be, exposed to serious and imminent danger of the risk involved and of the steps taken or to be taken as regards protection;

(b) take action and give instructions to enable workers in the event of serious, imminent and unavoidable danger to stop work and/or immediately to leave the work place and proceed to a place of safety;

(c) save in exceptional cases for reasons duly substantiated, refrain from asking workers to resume work in a working situation where there is still a serious and imminent danger.

4.   Workers who, in the event of serious, imminent and unavoidable danger, leave their workstation and/or a dangerous area may not be placed at any disadvantage because of their action and must be protected against any harmful and unjustified consequences, in accordance with national laws and/or practices.

5.   The employer shall ensure that all workers are able, in the event of serious and imminent danger to their own safety and/or that of other persons, and where the immediate superior responsible cannot be contacted, to take the appropriate steps in the light of their knowledge and the technical means at their disposal, to avoid the consequences of such danger.

Their actions shall not place them at any disadvantage, unless they acted carelessly or there was negligence on their part.

Article 9

VARIOUS OBLIGATIONS ON EMPLOYERS

1.   The employer shall:

(a) be in possession of an assessment of the risks to safety and health at work, including those facing groups of workers exposed to particular risks;

(b) decide on the protective measures to be taken and, if necessary, the protective equipment to be used;

(c) keep a list of occupational accidents resulting in a worker being unfit for work for more than three working days;

(d) draw up, for the responsible authorities and in accordance with national laws and/or practices, reports on occupational accidents suffered by his workers.

2.   Member States shall define, in the light of the nature of the activities and size of the undertakings, the obligations to be met by the different categories of undertakings in respect of the drawing-up of the documents provided for in paragraph 1 (a) and (b) and when preparing the documents provided for in paragraph 1 (c) and (d).

Article 10

WORKER INFORMATION

1.   The employer shall take appropriate measures so that workers and/or their representatives in the undertaking and/or establishment receive, in

accordance with national laws and/or practices which may take account, inter alia, of the size of the undertaking and/or establishment, all the necessary information concerning:

(a) the safety and health risks and protective and preventive measures and activities in respect of both the undertaking and/or establishment in general and each type of workstation and/or job;

(b) the measures taken pursuant to Article 8 (2).

2. The employer shall take appropriate measures so that employers of workers from any outside undertakings and/or establishments engaged in work in his undertaking and/or establishment receive, in accordance with national laws and/or practices, adequate information concerning the points referred to in paragraph 1 (a) and (b) which is to be provided to the workers in question.

3. The employer shall take appropriate measures so that workers with specific functions in protecting the safety and health of workers, or workers' representatives with specific responsibility for the safety and health of workers shall have access, to carry out their functions and in accordance with national laws and/or practices, to:

(a) the risk assessment and protective measures referred to in Article 9 (1) (a) and (b);

(b) the list and reports referred to in Article 9 (1) (c) and (d);

(c) the information yielded by protective and preventive measures, inspection agencies and bodies responsible for safety and health.

Article 11

CONSULTATION AND PARTICIPATION OF WORKERS

1. Employers shall consult workers and/or their representatives and allow them to take part in discussions on all questions relating to safety and health at work.

This presupposes:

– the consultation of workers,

– the right of workers and/or their representatives to make proposals,

– balanced participation in accordance with national laws and/or practices.

2. Workers or workers' representatives with specific responsibility for the safety and health of workers shall take part in a balanced way, in accordance with national laws and/or practices, or shall be consulted in advance and in good time by the employer with regard to:

(a) any measure which may substantially affect safety and health;

(b) the designation of workers referred to in Articles 7 (1) and 8 (2) and the activities referred to in Article 7 (1);

(c) the information referred to in Articles 9 (1) and 10;

(d) the enlistment, where appropriate, of the competent services or persons outside the undertaking and/or establishment, as referred to in Article 7 (3);

(e) the planning and organization of the training referred to in Article 12.

3. Workers' representatives with specific responsibility for the safety and health of workers shall have the right to ask the employer to take appropriate measures and to submit proposals to him to that end to mitigate hazards for workers and/or to remove sources of danger.

4. The workers referred to in paragraph 2 and the workers' representatives referred to in paragraphs 2 and 3 may not be placed at a disadvantage because of their respective activities referred to in paragraphs 2 and 3.

5. Employers must allow workers' representatives with specific responsibility for the safety and health of workers adequate time off work, without loss of pay, and provide them with the necessary means to enable such representatives to exercise their rights and functions deriving from this Directive.

6. Workers and/or their representatives are entitled to appeal, in accordance with national law and/or practice, to the authority responsible for safety and health protection at work if they consider that the measures taken and the means employed by the employer are inadequate for the purposes of ensuring safety and health at work.

Workers' representatives must be given the opportunity to submit their observations during inspection visits by the competent authority.

Article 12

TRAINING OF WORKERS

1. The employer shall ensure that each worker receives adequate safety and health training, in particular in the form of information and instructions specific to his workstation or job:

–   on recruitment,

–   in the event of a transfer or a change of job,

–   in the event of the introduction of new work equipment or a change in equipment,

– in the event of the introduction of any new technology.

The training shall be:

– adapted to take account of new or changed risks, and

– repeated periodically if necessary.

2.   The employer shall ensure that the workers from outside undertakings and/or establishments engaged in work in his undertaking and/or establishment have in fact received appropriate instructions regarding health and safety risks during their activities in his undertaking and/or establishment.

3.   Workers' representatives with a specific role in protecting the safety and health of workers shall be entitled to appropriate training.

4.   The training referred to in paragraphs 1 and 3 may not be at the workers' expense or at that of the workers' representatives.

The training referred to in paragraph 1 must take place during working hours.

The training referred to in paragraph 3 must take place during working hours or in accordance with national practice either within or outside the undertaking and/or the establishment.

SECTION III

Workers' obligations

Article 13

1.   It shall be the responsibility of each worker to take care as far as possible of his own safety and health and that of other persons affected by his acts or Commissions at work in accordance with his training and the instructions given by his employer.

2.   To this end, workers must in particular, in accordance with their training and the instructions given by their employer:

(a)   make correct use of machinery, apparatus, tools, dangerous substances, transport equipment and other means of production;

(b)   make correct use of the personal protective equipment supplied to them and, after use, return it to its proper place;

(c) refrain from disconnecting, changing or removing arbitrarily safety devices fitted, eg. to machinery, apparatus, tools, plant and buildings, and use such safety devices correctly;

(d) immediately inform the employer and/or the workers with specific responsibility for the safety and health of workers of any work situation they have reasonable grounds for considering represents a serious and immediate danger to safety and health and of any shortcomings in the protection arrangements;

(e) cooperate, in accordance with national practice, with the employer and/or workers with specific responsibility for the safety and health of workers, for as long as may be necessary to enable any tasks or requirements imposed by the competent authority to protect the safety and health of workers at work to be carried out;

(f) cooperate, in accordance with national practice, with the employer and/or workers with specific responsibility for the safety and health of workers, for as long as may be necessary to enable the employer to ensure that the working environment and working conditions are safe and pose no risk to safety and health within their field of activity.

SECTION IV

Miscellaneous provisions

Article 14

HEALTH SURVEILLANCE

1.   To ensure that workers receive health surveillance appropriate to the health and safety risks they incur at work, measures shall be introduced in accordance with national law and/or practices.

2.   The measures referred to in paragraph 1 shall be such that each worker, if he so wishes, may receive health surveillance at regular intervals.

3.   Health surveillance may be provided as part of a national health system.

Article 15

RISK GROUPS

Particularly sensitive risk groups must be protected against the dangers which specifically affect them.

Article 16

INDIVIDUAL DIRECTIVES – AMENDMENTS – GENERAL SCOPE
OF THIS DIRECTIVE

1.   The Council, acting on a proposal from the Commission based on
Article 118a of the Treaty, shall adopt individual Directives, inter alia, in
the areas listed in the Annex.

2.   This Directive and, without prejudice to the procedure referred to in
Article 17 concerning technical adjustments, the individual Directives may
be amended in accordance with the procedure provided for in Article 118a
of the Treaty.

3.   The provisions of this Directive shall apply in full to all the areas
covered by the individual Directives, without prejudice to more stringent
and/or specific provisions contained in these individual Directives.

Article 17

COMMITTEE

1.   For the purely technical adjustments to the individual Directives
provided for in Article 16 (1) to take account of:

–   the adoption of Directives in the field of technical harmonization and
    standardization, and/or

–   technical progress, changes in international regulations or specifica-
    tions, and new findings,

the Commission shall be assisted by a committee composed of the
representatives of the Member States and chaired by the representative of
the Commission.

2.   The representative of the Commission shall submit to the committee a
draft of the measures to be taken.

The committee shall deliver its opinion on the draft within a time limit
which the chairman may lay down according to the urgency of the matter.

The opinion shall be delivered by the majority laid down in Article 148 (2)
of the Treaty in the case of decisions which the Council is required to adopt
on a proposal from the Commission.

The votes of the representatives of the Member States within the committee
shall be weighted in the manner set out in that Article. The chairman shall
not vote.

3.   The Commission shall adopt the measures envisaged if they are in accordance with the opinion of the committee.

If the measures envisaged are not in accordance with the opinion of the committee, or if no opinion is delivered, the Commission shall, without delay, submit to the Council a proposal relating to the measures to be taken. The Council shall act by a qualified majority.

If, on the expiry of three months from the date of the referral to the Council, the Council has not acted, the proposed measures shall be adopted by the Commission.

Article 18

FINAL PROVISIONS

1.   Member States shall bring into force the laws, regulations and administrative provisions necessary to comply with this Directive by 31 December 1992.

They shall forthwith inform the Commission thereof.

2.   Member States shall communicate to the Commission the texts of the provisions of national law which they have already adopted or adopt in the field covered by this Directive.

3.   Member States shall report to the Commission every five years on the practical implementation of the provisions of this Directive, indicating the points of view of employers and workers.

The Commission shall inform the European Parliament, the Council, the Economic and Social Committee and the Advisory Committee on Safety, Hygiene and Health Protection at Work.

4.   The Commission shall submit periodically to the European Parliament, the Council and the Economic and Social Committee a report on the implementation of this Directive, taking into account paragraphs 1 to 3.

Article 19

This Directive is addressed to the Member States.

Done at Luxembourg, 12 June 1989.

For the Council
The President
M CHAVES GONZALES

ANNEX

List of areas referred to in Article 16 (1)

- – Work places
- – Work equipment
- – Personal protective equipment
- – Work with visual display units
- – Handling of heavy loads involving risk of back injury
- – Temporary or mobile work sites
- – Fisheries and agriculture

COUNCIL DIRECTIVE OF 30 NOVEMBER 1989
concerning the minimum safety and health requirements for the workplace (first individual directive within the meaning of Article 16 (1) of Directive 89/391/EEC) (89/654/EEC)

The Council of the European Communities,

Having regard to the Treaty establishing the European Economic Community, and in particular Article 118a thereof,

Having regard to the proposal from the Commission submitted after consulting the Advisory Committee on Safety, Hygiene and Health Protection at Work,

In cooperation with the European Parliament

Having regard to the opinion of the Economic and Social Committee,

Whereas Article 118a of the Treaty provides that the Council shall adopt, by means of directives, minimum requirements for encouraging improvements, especially in the working environment, to ensure a better level of protection of the safety and health of workers;

Whereas, under the terms of that Article, those directives are to avoid imposing administrative, financial and legal constraints in a way which would hold back the creation and development of small and medium-sized undertakings;

Whereas the communication from the Commission on its programme concerning safety, hygiene and health at work provides for the adoption of a directive designed to guarantee the safety and health of workers at the workplace;

Whereas, in its resolution of 21 December 1987 on safety, hygiene and health at work, the Council took note of the Commission's intention of submitting to the Council in the near future minimum requirements concerning the arrangement of the place of work;

Whereas compliance with the minimum requirements designed to guarantee a better standard of safety and health at work is essential to ensure the safety and health of workers;

Whereas this Directive is an individual directive within the meaning of Article 16 (1) of Council Directive 89/391 EEC of 12 June 1989 on the introduction of measures to encourage improvements in the safety and health of workers at work; whereas the provisions of the latter are therefore fully applicable to the workplace without prejudice to more stringent and/or specific provisions contained in the present Directive;

Whereas this Directive is a practical contribution towards creating the social dimension of the internal market;

Whereas, pursuant to Decision 74/325/EEC, as last amended by the 1985 Act of Accession, the Advisory Committee on Safety, Hygiene and Health Protection at Work is consulted by the Commission on the drafting of proposals in this field,

HAS ADOPTED THIS DIRECTIVE:

SECTION I

General provisions

Article 1

SUBJECT

1.   This Directive, which is the first individual directive within the meaning of Article 16 (1) of Directive 89/391/EEC, lays down minimum requirements for safety and health at the workplace, as defined in Article 2.

2.   This Directive shall not apply to:

(a)   means of transport used outside the undertaking and/or the establishment, or workplaces inside means of transport;

(b)   temporary or mobile work sites;

(c)   extractive industries;

(d)   fishing boats;

(e)   fields, woods and other land forming part of an agricultural or forestry undertaking but situated away from the undertaking's buildings.

3.   The provisions of Directive 89/391/EEC are fully applicable to the whole scope referred to in paragraph 1, without prejudice to more stringent and/or specific provisions contained in this Directive.

Article 2

DEFINITION

For the purposes of this Directive, 'workplace' means the place intended to house workstations on the premises of the undertaking and/or establishment and any other place within the area of the undertaking and/or establishment to which the worker has access in the course of his employment.

SECTION II

Employers' obligations

Article 3

WORKPLACES USED FOR THE FIRST TIME

Workplaces used for the first time after 31 December 1992 must satisfy the minimum safety and health requirements laid down in Annex 1.

Article 4

WORKPLACES ALREADY IN USE

Workplaces already in use before 1 January 1993 must satisfy the minimum safety and health requirements laid down in Annex II at the latest three years after that date.

However, as regards the Portuguese Republic, workplaces used before 1 January 1993 must satisfy, at the latest four years after that date, the minimum safety and health requirements appearing in Annex II.

Article 5

MODIFICATIONS TO WORKPLACES

When workplaces undergo modifications, extensions and/or conversions after 31 December 1992, the employer shall take the measures necessary to ensure that those modifications, extensions and/or conversions are in compliance with the corresponding minimum requirements laid down in Annex 1.

Article 6

GENERAL REQUIREMENTS

To safeguard the safety and health of workers, the employer shall see to it that:

- traffic routes to emergency exits and the exits themselves are kept clear at all times,

- technical maintenance of the workplace and of the equipment and devices, and in particular those referred to in Annexes I and II, is carried out and any faults found which are liable to affect the safety and health of workers are rectified as quickly as possible,

- the workplace and the equipment and devices, and in particular those referred to in Annex I, point 6 and Annex II, point 6 are regularly cleaned to an adequate level of hygiene,

- safety equipment and devices intended to prevent or eliminate hazards, and in particular those referred to in Annexes I and II, are regularly maintained and checked.

Article 7

INFORMATION OF WORKERS

Without prejudice to Article 10 of Directive 89/391/EEC, workers and/or their representatives shall be informed of all measures to be taken concerning safety and health at the workplace.

Article 8

CONSULTATION OF WORKERS AND WORKERS' PARTICIPATION

Consultation and participation of workers and/or of their representatives shall take place in accordance with Article 11 of Directive 89/391 EEC on the matters covered by this Directive, including the Annexes thereto.

SECTION III

Miscellaneous provisions

Article 9

AMENDMENTS TO THE ANNEXES

Strictly technical amendments to the Annexes as a result of:

- the adoption of Directives on technical harmonization and standardization of the design, manufacture or construction of parts of workplaces, and/or

- technical progress, changes in international regulations or specifications and knowledge with regard to workplaces, shall be adopted in accordance with the procedure laid down in Article 17 of Directive 89/391/EEC.

Article 10

FINAL PROVISIONS

1.   Member States shall bring into force the laws, regulations and administrative provisions necessary to comply with this Directive by 31 December 1992. They shall forthwith inform the Commission thereof.

However, the date applicable for the Hellenic Republic shall be 31 December 1994.

2.   Member States shall communicate to the Commission the texts of the provisions of national law which they have already adopted or adopt in the field governed by this Directive.

3.   Member States shall report to the Commission every five years on the practical implementation of the provisions of this Directive, indicating the points of view of employers and workers.

The Commission shall inform the European Parliament, the Council, the Economic and Social Committee and the Advisory Council on Safety, Hygiene and Health Protection at Work.

4.   The Commission shall submit periodically to the European Parliament, the Council and the Economic and Social Committee a report on the implementation of this Directive, taking into account paragraphs 1 to 3.

Article 11

This Directive is addressed to the Member States.

Done at Brussels, 30 November 1989.

FOR THE COUNCIL
THE PRESIDENT
J P SOISSON

ANNEX I: MINIMUM SAFETY AND HEALTH REQUIREMENTS FOR WORKPLACES USED FOR THE FIRST TIME, AS REFERRED TO IN ARTICLE 3 OF THE DIRECTIVE

1. Preliminary note

    The obligations laid down in this Annex apply whenever required by the features of the workplace, the activity, the circumstances or a hazard.

2. Stability and solidity

    Buildings which house workplaces must have a structure and solidity appropriate to the nature of their use.

3. Electrical installations

    Electrical installations must be designed and constructed so as not to present a fire or explosion hazard; persons must be adequately protected against the risk of accidents caused by direct or indirect contact.

    The design, construction and choice of material and protection devices must be appropriate to the voltage, external conditions and the competence of persons with access to parts of the installation.

4. Emergency routes and exits

4.1 Emergency routes and exits must remain clear and lead as directly as possible to the open air or to a safe area.

4.2 In the event of danger, it must be possible for workers to evacuate all workstations quickly and as safely as possible.

4.3 The number, distribution and dimensions of the emergency routes and exits depend on the use, equipment and dimensions of the workplaces and the maximum number of persons that may be present.

4.4 Emergency doors must open outwards.

    Sliding or revolving doors are not permitted if they are specifically intended as emergency exits.

    Emergency doors should not be locked or fastened that they cannot be easily and immediately opened by any person who may require to use them in an emergency.

4.5 Specific emergency routes and exits must be indicated by signs in accordance with the national regulations transposing Directive 77/576/EEC into law.

Such signs must be placed at appropriate points and be made to last.

4.6   Emergency doors must not be locked.

The emergency routes and exits, and the traffic routes and doors giving access to them, but be free from obstruction so that they can be used at any time without hindrance.

4.7   Emergency routes and exits requiring illumination must be provided with emergency lighting of adequate intensity in case the lighting fails.

5.   Fire detection and fire fighting

5.1   Depending on the dimensions and use of the buildings, the equipment they contain, the physical and chemical properties of the substances present and the maximum potential number of people present, workplaces must be equipped with appropriate fire-fighting equipment and, as necessary, with fire detectors and alarm systems.

5.2   Non-automatic fire-fighting equipment must be easily accessible and simple to use.

The equipment must be indicated by signs in accordance with the national regulations transposing Directive 77/576/EEC into law.

Such signs must be placed at appropriate points and be made to last.

6.   Ventilation of enclosed workplaces

6.1   Steps shall be taken to see to it that there is sufficient fresh air in enclosed workplaces, having regard to the working methods used and the physical demands placed on the workers.

If a forced ventilation system is used, it shall be maintained in working order.

Any breakdown must be indicated by a control system where this is necessary for workers' health.

6.2   If air-conditioning or mechanical ventilation installations are used, they must operate in such a way that workers are not exposed to draughts which cause discomfort.

Any deposit or dirt likely to create an immediate danger to the health of workers by polluting the atmosphere must be removed without delay.

7. Room temperature

7.1 During working hours, the temperature in rooms containing workstations must be adequate for human beings, having regard to the working methods being used and the physical demands placed on the workers.

7.2 The temperature in rest areas, rooms for duty staff, sanitary facilities, canteens and first aid rooms must be appropriate to the particular purpose of such areas.

7.3 Windows, skylights and glass partitions should allow excessive effects of sunlight in workplaces to be avoided, having regard to the nature of the work and of the workplace.

8. Natural and artificial room lighting

8.1 Workplaces must as far as possible receive sufficient natural light and be equipped with artificial lighting adequate for the protection of workers' safety and health.

8.2 Lighting installations in rooms containing workstations and in passageways must be placed in such a way that there is no risk of accident to workers as a result of the type of lighting fitted.

8.3 Workplaces in which workers are especially exposed to risks in the event of failure of artificial lighting must be provided with emergency lighting of adequate intensity.

9. Floors, walls, ceilings and roofs of rooms

9.1 The floors of rooms must have no dangerous bumps, holes or slopes and must be fixed, stable and not slippery.

Workplaces containing workstations must be adequately thermally insulated, bearing in mind the type of undertaking involved and the physical activity of the workers.

9.2 The surfaces of floors, walls and ceilings in rooms must be such that they can be cleaned or refurbished to an appropriate standard of hygiene.

9.3 Transparent or translucent walls, in particular all-glass partitions, in rooms or in the vicinity of workstations and traffic routes must be clearly indicated and made of safety material or be shielded from such places or traffic routes to prevent workers from coming into contract with walls or being injured should the walls shatter.

9.4   Access to roofs made of materials of insufficient strength must not be permitted unless equipment is provided to ensure that the work can be carried out in a safe manner.

10.   Windows and skylights

10.1   It must be possible for workers to open, close, adjust or secure windows, skylights and ventilators in a safe manner. When open, they must not be positioned so as to constitute a hazard to workers.

10.2   Windows and skylights must be designed in conjunction with equipment or otherwise fitted with devices allowing them to be cleaned without risk to the workers carrying out this work or to workers present in and around the building.

11.   Doors and gates

11.1   The position, number and dimensions of doors and gates, and the materials used in their construction, are determined by the nature and use of the rooms or areas.

11.2   Transparent doors must be appropriately marked at a conspicuous level.

11.3   Swing doors and gates must be transparent or have see-through panels.

11.4   If transparent or translucent surfaces in doors and gates are not made of safety material and if there is a danger that workers may be injured if a door or gate should shatter, the surfaces must be protected against breakage.

11.5   Sliding doors must be fitted with a safety device to prevent them from being derailed and falling over.

11.6   Doors and gates opening upwards must be fitted with a mechanism to secure them against falling back.

11.7   Doors along escape routes must be appropriately marked.

It must be possible to open them from the inside at any time without special assistance.

It must be possible to open the doors when the workplaces are occupied.

11.8   Doors for pedestrians must be provided in the immediate vicinity of any gates intended essentially for vehicle traffic, unless it is safe for pedestrians to pass through; such doors must be clearly marked and left permanently unobstructed.

11.9 Mechanical doors and gates must function in such a way that there is no risk of accident to workers.

They must be fitted with easily identifiable and accessible emergency shut-down devices, and, unless they open automatically in the event of a power failure, it must also be possible to open them manually.

12. Traffic routes – danger areas

12.1 Traffic routes, including stairs, fixed ladders and loading bays and ramps, must be located and dimensioned to ensure easy, safe and appropriate access for pedestrians or vehicles in such a way as not to endanger workers employed in the vicinity of these traffic routes.

12.2 Routes used for pedestrian traffic and/or goods traffic must be dimensioned in accordance with the number of potential users and the type of undertaking.

If means of transport are used on traffic routes, a sufficient safety clearance must be provided for pedestrians.

12.3 Sufficient clearance must be allowed between vehicle traffic routes and doors, gates, passages for pedestrians, corridors and staircases.

12.4 Where the use and equipment of rooms so requires for the protection of workers, traffic routes must be clearly identified.

12.5 If the workplaces contain danger areas in which, owing to the nature of the work, there is a risk of the worker or objects falling, the places must be equipped, as far as possible, with devices preventing unauthorized workers from entering those areas.

Appropriate measures must be taken to protect workers authorized to enter danger areas.

Danger areas must be clearly indicated.

13. Specific measures for escalators and travelators

Escalators and travelators must function safely.

They must be equipped with any necessary safety devices.

They must be fitted with easily identifiable and accessible emergency shut-down devices.

14.   Loading bays and ramps

14.1   Loading bays and ramps must be suitable for the dimensions of the loads to be transported.

14.2   Loading bays must have at least one exit point.

Where technically feasible, bays over a certain length must have an exit point at each end.

14.3   Loading ramps must as far as possible be safe enough to prevent workers from falling off.

15.   Room dimensions and air space in rooms – freedom of movement at the workstation

15.1   Workrooms must have sufficient surface area, height and air space to allow workers to perform their work without risk to their safety, health or well-being.

15.2   The dimensions of the free unoccupied area at the workstation must be calculated to allow workers sufficient freedom of movement to perform their work.

If this is not possible for reasons specific to the workstation, the worker must be provided with sufficient freedom of movement near his workstation.

16.   Rest rooms

16.1   Where the safety or health of workers, in particular because of the type of activity carried out or the presence of more than a certain number of employees, so require, workers must be provided with an easily accessible rest room.

This provision does not apply if the workers are employed in offices or similar workrooms providing equivalent relaxation during breaks.

16.2   Rest rooms must be large enough and equipped with an adequate number of tables and seats with backs for the number of workers.

16.3   In rest rooms appropriate measures must be introduced for the protection of non-smokers against discomfort caused by tobacco smoke.

16.4   If working hours are regularly and frequently interrupted and there is no rest room, other rooms must be provided in which workers can stay during such interruptions, wherever this is required for the safety or health of workers.

Appropriate measures should be taken for the protection of non-smokers against discomfort caused by tobacco smoke.

17.   Pregnant women and nursing mothers

Pregnant women and nursing mothers must be able to lie down to rest in appropriate conditions.

18.   Sanitary equipment

18.1   Changing rooms and lockers

18.1.1   Appropriate changing rooms must be provided for workers if they have to wear special work clothes and where, for reasons of health or propriety, they cannot be expected to change in another room.

Changing rooms must be easily accessible, be of sufficient capacity and be provided with seating.

18.1.2   Changing rooms must be sufficiently large and have facilities to enable each worker to lock away his clothes during working hours.

If circumstances so require (e.g. dangerous substances, humidity, dirt), lockers for work clothes must be separate from those for ordinary clothes.

18.1.3   Provision must be made for separate changing rooms or separate use of changing rooms for men and women.

18.1.4   If changing rooms are not required under 18.1.1, each worker must be provided with a place to store his clothes.

18.2   Showers and washbasins

18.2.1   Adequate and suitable showers must be provided for workers if required by the nature of the work or for health reasons.

Provision must be made for separate shower rooms or separate use of shower rooms for men and women.

18.2.2   The shower rooms must be sufficiently large to permit each worker to wash without hindrance in conditions of an appropriate standard of hygiene.

The showers must be equipped with hot and cold running water.

18.2.3   Where showers are not required under the first subparagraph of 18.2.1, adequate and suitable washbasins with running water (hot water if necessary) must be provided in the vicinity of the workstations and the changing rooms.

Such washbasins must be separate for, or used separately by, men and women when so required for reasons of propriety.

18.2.4   Where the rooms housing the showers or washbasins are separate from the changing rooms, there must be easy communication between the two.

18.3   Lavatories and washbasins

Separate facilities must be provided in the vicinity of workstations, rest rooms, changing rooms and rooms housing showers or washbasins, with an adequate number of lavatories and washbasins.

Provision must be made for separate lavatories or separate use of lavatories for men and women.

19.   First aid rooms

19.1   One or more first aid rooms must be provided where the size of the premises, type of activity being carried out and frequency of accidents so dictate.

19.2   First aid rooms must be fitted with essential first aid installations and equipment and be easily accessible to stretchers.

They must be signposted in accordance with the national regulations transposing Directive 77/576/EEC into law.

19.3   In addition, first aid equipment must be available in all places where working conditions require it.

This equipment must be suitably marked and easily accessible.

20.   Handicapped workers

Workplaces must be organized to take account of handicapped workers, if necessary.

This provision applies in particular to the doors, passageways, staircases, showers, washbasins, lavatories and workstations used or occupied directly by handicapped persons.

21.   Outdoor workplaces (special provisions)

21.1   Workstations, traffic routes and other areas or installations outdoors which are used or occupied by the workers in the course of their activity must be organized in such a way that pedestrians and vehicles can circulate safely.

Sections 12, 13 and 14 also apply to main traffic routes on the site of the undertaking (traffic routes leading to fixed workstations), to traffic routes used for the regular maintenance and supervision of the undertaking's installations and to loading bays.

Section 12 is also applicable to outdoor workplaces.

21.2 Workplaces outdoors must be adequately lit by artificial lighting if daylight is not adequate.

21.3 When workers are employed at workstations outdoors, such workstations must as far as possible be arranged so that workers:

(a) are protected against inclement weather conditions and if necessary against falling objects;

(b) are not exposed to harmful noise levels nor to harmful outdoor influences such as gases, vapours or dust;

(c) are able to leave their workstations swiftly in the event of danger or are able to be rapidly assisted;

(d) cannot slip or fall.

ANNEX II: MINIMUM HEALTH AND SAFETY REQUIREMENTS FOR WORKPLACES ALREADY IN USE, AS REFERRED TO IN ARTICLE 4 OF THE DIRECTIVE

1. Preliminary note

   The obligations laid down in this Annex apply wherever required by the features of the workplace, the activity, the circumstances or a hazard.

2. Stability and solidity

   Buildings which have workplaces must have a structure and solidity appropriate to the nature of their use.

3. Electrical installations

   Electrical installations must be designed and constructed so as not to present a fire or explosion hazard; persons must be adequately protected against the risk of accidents caused by direct or indirect contact.

Electrical installations and protection devices must be appropriate to the voltage, external conditions and the competence of persons with access to parts of the installation.

4.   Emergency routes and exits

4.1   Emergency routes and exits must remain clear and lead as directly as possible to the open air or to a safe area.

4.2   In the event of danger, it must be possible for workers to evacuate all workstations quickly and as safely as possible.

4.3   There must be an adequate number of escape routes and emergency exits.

4.4   Emergency exit doors must open outwards.

Sliding or revolving doors are not permitted if they are specifically intended as emergency exits.

Emergency doors should not be locked or fastened so that they cannot be easily and immediately opened by any person who may require to use them in an emergency.

4.5   Specific emergency routes and exits must be indicated by signs in accordance with the national regulations transposing Directive 77/576/EEC into law.

Such signs must be placed at appropriate points and be made to last.

4.6   Emergency doors must not be locked.

The emergency routes and exits, and the traffic routes and doors giving access to them, must be free from obstruction so that they can be used at any time without hindrance.

4.7   Emergency routes and exits requiring illumination must be provided with emergency lighting of adequate intensity in case the lighting fails.

5.   Fire detection and fire fighting

5.1   Depending on the dimensions and use of the buildings, the equipment they contain, the physical and chemical characteristics of the substances present and the maximum potential number of people present, workplaces must be equipped with appropriate fire-fighting equipment, and, as necessary, fire detectors and an alarm system.

5.2 Non-automatic fire-fighting equipment must be easily accessible and simple to use.

It must be indicated by signs in accordance with the national regulations transposing Directive 77/576/EEC into law.

Such signs must be placed at appropriate points and be made to last.

6. Ventilation of enclosed workplaces

Steps shall be taken to see to it that there is sufficient fresh air in enclosed workplaces, having regard to the working methods used and the physical demands placed on the workers.

If a forced ventilation system is used, it shall be maintained in working order.

Any breakdown must be indicated by a control system where this is necessary for the workers' health.

7. Room temperature

7.1 During working hours, the temperature in rooms containing workstations must be adequate for human beings, having regard to the working methods being used and the physical demands placed on the workers.

7.2 The temperature in rest areas, rooms for duty staff, sanitary facilities, canteens and first aid rooms must be appropriate to the particular purpose of such areas.

8. Natural and artificial room lighting

8.1 Workplaces must as far as possible receive sufficient natural light and be equipped with artificial lighting adequate for workers' safety and health.

8.2 Workplaces in which workers are especially exposed to risks in the event of failure of artificial lighting must be provided with emergency lighting of adequate intensity.

9. Doors and gates.

9.1 Transparent doors must be appropriately marked at a conspicuous level.

9.2 Swing doors and gates must be transparent or have see-through panels.

10.   Danger areas

If the workplaces contain danger areas in which, owing to the nature of the work, there is a risk of the worker or objects failing, the places must be equipped, as far as possible, with devices preventing unauthorized workers from entering those areas.

Appropriate measures must be taken to protect workers authorized to enter danger areas.

Danger areas must be clearly indicated.

11.   Rest rooms and rest areas

11.1   Where the safety or health of workers, in particular because of the type of activity carried out or the presence of more than a certain number of employees, so require, workers must be provided with an easily accessible rest room or appropriate rest area.

This provision does not apply if the workers are employed in offices or similar workrooms providing equivalent relaxation during breaks.

11.2   Rest rooms and rest areas must be equipped with tables and seats with backs.

11.3   In rest rooms and rest areas appropriate measures must be introduced for the protection of non-smokers against discomfort caused by tobacco smoke.

12.   Pregnant women and nursing mothers

Pregnant women and nursing mothers must be able to lie down to rest in appropriate conditions.

13.   Sanitary equipment

13.1   Changing rooms and lockers

13.1.1 Appropriate changing rooms must be provided for workers if they have to wear special work clothes and where, for reasons of health or propriety, they cannot be expected to change in another room.

Changing rooms must be easily accessible and of sufficient capacity.

13.1.2 Changing rooms must have facilities to enable each worker to lock away his clothes during working hours.

If circumstances so require (eg dangerous substances, humidity, dirt), lockers for work clothes must be separate from those for ordinary clothes.

13.1.3 Provision must be made for separate changing rooms or separate use of changing rooms for men and women.

13.2 Showers, lavatories and washbasins

13.2.1 Workplaces must be fitted out in such a way that workers have in the vicinity:

- showers, if required by the nature of their work,

- special facilities equipped with an adequate number of lavatories and washbasins.

13.2.2 The showers and washbasins must be equipped with running water (hot water if necessary).

13.2.3 Provision must be made for separate showers or separate use of showers for men and women.

Provision must be made for separate lavatories or separate use of lavatories for men and women.

14. First aid equipment

Workplaces must be fitted with first aid equipment.

The equipment must be suitably marked and easily accessible.

15. Handicapped workers

Workplaces must be organized to take account of handicapped workers, if necessary.

This provision applies in particular to the doors, passageways, staircases, showers, washbasins, lavatories and workstations used or occupied directly by handicapped persons.

16. Movement of pedestrians and vehicles

Outdoor and indoor workplaces must be organized in such a way that pedestrians and vehicles can circulate in a safe manner.

17. Outdoor workplaces (special provisions)

When workers are employed at workstations outdoors, such workstations must as far as possible be organized so that workers:

(a) are protected against inclement weather conditions and if necessary against falling objects;

(b) are not exposed to harmful noise levels nor to harmful outdoor influences such as gases, vapours or dust;

    (c) are able to leave their workstations swiftly in the event of danger or are able to be rapidly assisted;

    (d) cannot slip or fall.

COUNCIL DIRECTIVE OF 30 NOVEMBER 1989

concerning the minimum safety and health requirements for the use of work equipment by workers at work (second individual Directive within the meaning of Article 16 (1) of Directive 89/391/EEC) (89/655/EEC)

The Council of the European Communities,

Having regard to the Treaty establishing the European Economic Community, and in particular Article 118a thereof,

Having regard to the proposal from the Commission submitted after consulting the Advisory Committee on Safety, Hygiene and Health Protection at Work,

In cooperation with the European Parliament,

Having regard to the opinion of the Economic and Social Committee,

Whereas Article 118a of the Treaty provides that the Council shall adopt, by means of directives, minimum requirements for encouraging improvements, especially in the working environment, to guarantee a better level of protection of the safety and health of workers;

Whereas, pursuant to the said Article, such directives must avoid imposing administrative, financial and legal constraints in a way which would hold back the creation and development of small and medium-sized undertakings;

Whereas the communication from the Commission on its programme concerning safety, hygiene and health at work provides for the adoption of a directive on the use of work equipment at work;

Whereas, in its resolution of 21 December 1987 on safety, hygiene and health at work, the Council took notice of the Commission's intention of submitting to the Council in the near future minimum requirements concerning the organization of safety and health at work;

Whereas compliance with the minimum requirements designed to guarantee a better standard of safety and health in the use of work equipment is essential to ensure the safety and health of workers;

Whereas this Directive is an individual directive within the meaning of Article 16 (1) of Council Directive 89/391/EEC of 12 June 1989 on the introduction of measures to encourage improvements in the safety and health of workers at work; whereas, therefore, the provisions of the said Directive are fully applicable to the scope of the use of work equipment by workers at work without prejudice to more restrictive and/or specific provisions contained in this Directive;

Whereas this Directive constitutes a practical aspect of the realization of the social dimension of the internal market;

Whereas, pursuant to Directive 83/189/EEC, Member States are required to notify the Commission of any draft technical regulations relating to machines, equipment and installations;

Whereas, pursuant to Decision 74/325/EEC, as last amended by the 1985 Act of Accession, the Advisory Committee on Safety, Hygiene and Health Protection at Work is consulted by the Commission on the drafting of proposals in this field,

HAS ADOPTED THIS DIRECTIVE:

SECTION I

General provisions

Article 1

SUBJECT

1.   This Directive, which is the second individual directive within the meaning of Article 16 (1) of Directive 89/391/EEC, lays down minimum safety and health requirements for the use of work equipment by workers at work, as defined in Article 2.

2.   The provisions of Directive 89/391/EEC are fully applicable to the whole scope referred to in paragraph 1, without prejudice to more restrictive and/or specific provisions contained in this Directive.

Article 2

DEFINITIONS

For the purposes of this Directive, the following terms shall have the following meanings:

(a) 'work equipment': any machine, apparatus, tool or installation used at work;

(b) 'use of work equipment': any activity involving work equipment such as starting or stopping the equipment, its use, transport, repair, modification, maintenance and servicing, including, in particular, cleaning;

(c) 'danger zone': any zone within and/or around work equipment in which an exposed worker is subject to a risk to his health or safety;

(d) 'exposed worker': any worker wholly or partially in a danger zone;

(e) 'operator': the worker or workers given the task of using work equipment.

SECTION II

Employers' obligations

Article 3

GENERAL OBLIGATIONS

1. The employer shall take the measures necessary to ensure that the work equipment made available to workers in the undertaking and/or establishment is suitable for the work to be carried out or properly adapted for that purpose and may be used by workers without impairment to their safety or health.

In selecting the work equipment which he proposes to use, the employer shall pay attention to the specific working conditions and characteristics and to the hazards which exist in the undertaking and/or establishment, in particular at the workplace, for the safety and health of the workers, and/or any additional hazard posed by the use of work equipment in question.

2. Where it is not possible fully so to ensure that work equipment can be used by workers without risk to their safety or health, the employer shall take appropriate measures to minimize the risks.

Article 4

RULES CONCERNING WORK EQUIPMENT

1. Without prejudice to Article 3, the employer must obtain and/or use:

(a) work equipment which, if provided to workers in the undertaking and/ or establishment for the first time after 31 December 1992, complies with:

      (i)   the provisions of any relevant Community directive which is applicable;

     (ii)   the minimum requirements laid down in the Annex, to the extent that no other Community directive is applicable or is so only partially;

(b)   work equipment which, if already provided to workers in the undertaking and/or establishment by 31 December 1992, complies with the minimum requirements laid down in the Annex no later than four years after that date.

2.   The employer shall take the measures necessary to ensure that, throughout its working life, work equipment is kept, by means of adequate maintenance, at a level such that it complies with the provisions of paragraph 1 (a) or (b) as applicable.

Article 5

WORK EQUIPMENT INVOLVING SPECIFIC RISKS

When the use of work equipment is likely to involve a specific risk to the safety or health of workers, the employer shall take the measures necessary to ensure that:

–   the use of work equipment is restricted to those persons given the task of using it;

–   in the case of repairs, modifications, maintenance or servicing, the workers concerned are specifically designated to carry out such work.

Article 6

INFORMING WORKERS

1.   Without prejudice to Article 10 of Directive 89/391/EEC, the employer shall take the measures necessary to ensure that workers have at their disposal adequate information and, where appropriate, written instructions on the work equipment used at work.

2.   The information and the written instructions must contain at least adequate safety and health information concerning:

–   the conditions of use of work equipment,

–   foreseeable abnormal situations,

–   the conclusions to be drawn from experience, where appropriate, in using work equipment.

3. The information and the written instructions must be comprehensible to the workers concerned.

Article 7

TRAINING OF WORKERS

Without prejudice to Article 12 of Directive 89/391/EEC, the employer shall take the measures necessary to ensure that:

– workers given the task of using work equipment receive adequate training, including training on any risks which such use may entail,

– workers referred to in the second indent of Article 5 receive adequate specific training.

Article 8

Consultation of workers and workers' participation

Consultation and participation of workers and/or of their representatives shall take place in accordance with Article 11 of Directive 89/391/EEC on the matters covered by this Directive, including the Annexes thereto.

SECTION III

Miscellaneous provisions

Article 9

AMENDMENT TO THE ANNEX

1. Addition to the Annex of the supplementary minimum requirements applicable to specific work equipment referred to in point 3 thereof shall be adopted by the Council in accordance with the procedure laid down in Article 118a of the Treaty.

2. Strictly technical adaptations of the Annex as a result of:

– the adoption of directives on technical harmonization and standardization of work equipment, and/or

– technical progress, changes in international regulations or specifications or knowledge in the field of work equipment shall be adopted, in accordance with the procedure laid down in Article 17 of Directive 89/391/EEC.

Article 10

FINAL PROVISIONS

1.   Member States shall bring into force the laws, regulations and administrative provisions necessary to comply with this Directive by 31 December 1992. They shall forthwith inform the Commission thereof.

2.   Member States shall communicate to the Commission the texts of the provisions of national law which they have already adopted or adopt in the field governed by this Directive.

3.   Member States shall report to the Commission every five years on the practical implementation of the provisions of this Directive, indicating the points of view of employers and workers.

The Commission shall accordingly inform the European Parliament, the Council, the Economic and Social Committee, and the Advisory Committee on Safety, Hygiene and Health Protection at Work.

4.   The Commission shall submit periodically to the European Parliament, the Council and the Economic and Social Committee a report on the implementation of this Directive, taking into account paragraphs 1 to 3.

Article 11

This Directive is addressed to the Member States.

Done at Brussels, 30 November 1989

For the Council
The President
J P SOISSON

ANNEX:
MINIMUM REQUIREMENTS REFERRED TO IN ARTICLE 4 (1) (A) (II) AND (B)

1.   General comment

The obligations laid down in this Annex apply having regard to the provisions of the Directive and where the corresponding risk exists for the work equipment in question.

2.   General minimum requirements applicable to work equipment

2.1   Work equipment control devices which affect safety must be clearly visible and identifiable and appropriately marked where necessary.

Except where necessary for certain control devices, control devices must be located outside danger zones and in such a way that their operation cannot cause additional hazard. They must not give rise to any hazard as a result of any unintentional operation.

If necessary, from the main control position, the operator must be able to ensure that no person is present in the danger zones. If this is impossible, a safe system such as an audible and/or visible warning signal must be given automatically whenever the machinery is about to start. An exposed worker must have the time and/or the means quickly to avoid hazards caused by the starting and/or stopping of the work equipment.

Control systems must be safe. A breakdown in, or damage to, control systems must not result in a dangerous situation.

2.2   It must be possible to start work equipment only by deliberate action on a control provided for the purpose.

The same shall apply:

–   to restart it after a stoppage for whatever reason,

–   for the control of a significant change in the operating conditions (eg speed, pressure, etc),

unless such a restart or change does not subject exposed workers to any hazard.

This requirement does not apply to restarting or a change in operating conditions as a result of the normal operating cycle of an automatic device.

2.3   All work equipment must be fitted with a control to stop it completely and safely.

Each workstation must be fitted with a control to stop some or all of the work equipment, depending on the type of hazard, so that the equipment is in a safe state. The equipment's stop control must have priority over the start controls. When the work equipment or the dangerous parts of it have stopped, the energy supply of the actuators concerned must be switched off.

2.4   Where appropriate, and depending on the hazards the equipment present and its normal stopping time, work equipment must be fitted with an emergency stop device.

2.5   Work equipment presenting risk due to falling objects or projections must be fitted with appropriate safety devices corresponding to the risk.

Work equipment presenting hazards due to emissions of gas, vapour, liquid or dust must be fitted with appropriate containment and/or extraction devices near the sources of the hazard.

2.6   Work equipment and parts of such equipment must, where necessary for the safety and health of workers, be stabilized by clamping or some other means.

2.7   Where there is a risk of rupture or disintegration of parts of the work equipment, likely to pose significant danger to the safety and health of workers, appropriate protection measures must be taken.

2.8   Where there is a risk of mechanical contact with moving parts of work equipment which could lead to accidents, those parts must be provided with guards or devices to prevent access to danger zones or to halt movements of dangerous parts before the danger zones are reached.

The guards and protection devices must:

–   be of robust construction,

–   not give rise to any additional hazard,

–   not be easily removed or rendered inoperative,

–   be situated at sufficient distance from the danger zone,

–   not restrict more than necessary the view of the operating cycle of the equipment,

–   allow operations necessary to fit or replace parts and for maintenance work, restricting access only to the area where the work is to be carried out and, if possible, without removal of the guard or protection device.

2.9   Areas and points for working on, or maintenance of, work equipment must be suitably lit in line with the operation to be carried out.

2.10   Work equipment parts at high or very low temperature must, where appropriate, be protected to avoid the risk of workers coming into contact or coming too close.

2.11   Warning devices on work equipment must be unambiguous and easily perceived and understood.

2.12   Work equipment may be used only for operations and under conditions for which it is appropriate.

2.13   It must be possible to carry out maintenance operations when the equipment is shut down. If this is not possible, it must be possible to take appropriate protection measures for the carrying out of such operations or for such operations to be carried out outside the danger zones.

If any machine has a maintenance log, it must be kept up to date.

2.14   All work equipment must be fitted with clearly identifiable means to isolate it from all its energy sources.

Reconnection must be presumed to pose no risk to the workers concerned.

2.15   Work equipment must bear the warnings and markings essential to ensure the safety of workers.

2.16   Workers must have safe means of access to , and be able to remain safely in, all the areas necessary for production, adjustment and maintenance operations.

2.17   All work equipment must be appropriate for protecting workers against the risk of the work equipment catching fire or overheating, or of discharges of gas, dust, liquid, vapour or other substances produced, used or stored in the work equipment.

2.18   All work equipment must be appropriate for preventing the risk of explosion of the work equipment or of substances produced, used or stored in the work equipment.

2.19   All work equipment must be appropriate for protecting exposed workers against the risk of direct or indirect contact with electricity.

3.   Minimum additional requirements applicable to specific work equipment, as referred to in Article 9 (1) of the Directive.

COUNCIL DIRECTIVE OF 30 NOVEMBER 1989
on the minimum health and safety requirements for the use
by workers of personal protective equipment at the
workplace (third individual directive within the meaning
of Article 16 (1) of Directive 89/391/EEC) (89/656/EEC)

The Council of the European Communities,

Having regard to the Treaty establishing the European Economic
Community and in particular Article 118a thereof,

Having regard to the Commission proposal, submitted after consultation
with the Advisory Committee on Safety, Hygiene and Health Protection at
Work,

In cooperation with the European Parliament,

Having regard to the opinion of the Economic and Social Committee,

Whereas Article 118a of the Treaty provides that the Council shall adopt,
by means of directives, minimum requirements designed to encourage
improvements, especially in the working environment, to guarantee greater
protection of the health and safety of workers;

Whereas, under the said Article, such directives shall avoid imposing
administrative, financial and legal constraints in a way which would hold
back the creation and development of small and medium-sized undertakings;

Whereas the Commission communication on its programme concerning
safety, hygiene and health at work provides for the adoption of a directive
on the use of personal protective equipment at work;

Whereas the Council, in its resolution of 21 December 1987 concerning
safety, hygiene and health at work, noted the Commission's intention of
submitting to it in the near future minimum requirements concerning the
organization of the safety and health of workers at work;

Whereas compliance with the minimum requirements designed to
guarantee greater health and safety for the user of personal protective
equipment is essential to ensure the safety and health of workers;

Whereas this Directive is an individual directive within the meaning of
Article 16 (1) of Council Directive 89/391/EEC of 12 June 1989 on the
introduction of measures to encourage improvements in the safety and
health of workers at work; whereas, consequently, the provisions of the said
Directive apply fully to the use by workers of personal protective
equipment at the workplace, without prejudice to more stringent and/or
specific provisions contained in this Directive;

Whereas this Directive constitutes a practical step towards the achievement of the social dimension of the internal market;

Whereas collective means of protection shall be accorded priority over individual protective equipment; whereas the employer shall be required to provide safety equipment and take safety measures;

Whereas the requirements laid down in this Directive should not entail alterations to personal protective equipment whose design and manufacture complied with Community directives relating to safety and health at work;

Whereas provision should be made for descriptions which Member States may use when laying down general rules for the use of individual protective equipment;

Whereas, pursuant to Decision 74/325/EEC, as last amended by the 1985 Act of Accession, the Advisory Committee on Safety, Hygiene and Health Protection at Work is consulted by the Commission with a view to drawing up proposals in this field,

HAS ADOPTED THIS DIRECTIVE:

SECTION I

General provisions

Article 1

SUBJECT

1. This Directive, which is the third individual directive within the meaning of Article 16 (1) of Directive 89/391/EEC, lays down minimum requirements for personal protective equipment used by workers at work.

2. The provisions of Directive 89/391/EEC are fully applicable to the whole scope referred to in paragraph 1, without prejudice to more restrictive and/or specific provisions contained in this Directive.

Article 2

DEFINITION

1. For the purposes of this Directive, personal protective equipment shall mean all equipment designed to be worn or held by the worker to protect

him against one or more hazards likely to endanger his safety and health at work, and any addition or accessory designed to meet this objective.

2.   The definition in paragraph 1 excludes:

(a) ordinary working clothes and uniforms not specifically designed to protect the safety and health of the worker;

(b) equipment used by emergency and rescue services;

(c) personal protective equipment worn or used by the military, the police and other public order agencies;

(d) personal protective equipment for means of road transport;

(e) sports equipment;

(f)   self-defence or deterrent equipment;

(g) portable devices for detecting and signalling risks and nuisances.

Article 3

GENERAL RULE

Personal protective equipment shall be used when the risks cannot be avoided or sufficiently limited by technical means of collective protection or by measures, methods or procedures of work organization.

SECTION II

Employers' obligations

Article 4

GENERAL PROVISIONS

1.   Personal protective equipment must comply with the relevant Community provisions on design and manufacture with respect to safety and health.

All personal protective equipment must:

(a) be appropriate for the risks involved, without itself leading to any increased risk;

(b) correspond to existing conditions at the workplace;

(c) take account of ergonomic requirements and the worker's state of health;

(d) fit the wearer correctly after any necessary adjustment.

2. Where the presence of more than one risk makes it necessary for a worker to wear simultaneously more than one item of personal protective equipment, such equipment must be compatible and continue to be effective against the risk or risks in question.

3. The conditions of use of personal protective equipment, in particular the period for which it is worn, shall be determined on the basis of the seriousness of the risk, the frequency of exposure to the risk, the characteristics of the workstation of each worker and the performance of the personal protective equipment.

4. Personal protective equipment is, in principle, intended for personal use.

If the circumstances require personal protective equipment to be worn by more than one person, appropriate measures shall be taken to ensure that such use does not create any health or hygiene problem for the different users.

5. Adequate information on each item of personal protective equipment, required under paragraphs 1 and 2, shall be provided and made available within the undertaking and/or establishment.

6. Personal protective equipment shall be provided free of charge by the employer, who shall ensure its good working order and satisfactory hygienic condition by means of the necessary maintenance, repair and replacements.

However, Member States may provide, in accordance with their national practice, that the worker be asked to contribute towards the cost of certain personal protective equipment in circumstances where use of the equipment is not exclusive to the workplace.

7. The employer shall first inform the worker of the risks against which the wearing of the personal protective equipment protects him.

8. The employer shall arrange for training and shall, if appropriate, organize demonstrations in the wearing of personal protective equipment.

9. Personal protective equipment may be used only for the purposes specified, except in specific and exceptional circumstances.

It must be used in accordance with instructions.

Such instructions must be understandable to the workers.

Article 5

ASSESSMENT OF PERSONAL PROTECTIVE EQUIPMENT

1.   Before choosing personal protective equipment, the employer is required to assess whether the personal protective equipment he intends to use satisfies the requirements of Article 4 (1) and (2).

This assessment shall involve:

(a) an analysis and assessment of risks which cannot be avoided by other means;

(b) the definition of the characteristics which personal protective equipment must have in order to be effective against the risks referred to in (a), taking into account any risks which this equipment itself may create;

(c) comparison of the characteristics of the personal protective equipment available with the characteristics referred to in (b).

2.   The assessment provided for in paragraph 1 shall be reviewed if any changes are made to any of its elements.

Article 6

RULES FOR USE

1.   Without prejudice to Articles 3, 4 and 5, Member States shall ensure that general rules are established for the use of personal protective equipment and/or rules covering cases and situations where the employer must provide the personal protective equipment, taking account of Community legislation on the free movement of such equipment.

These rules shall indicate in particular the circumstances or the risk situations in which, without prejudice to the priority to be given to collective means of protection, the use of personal protective equipment is necessary.

Annexes I, II and III, which constitute a guide, contain useful information for establishing such rules.

2.   When Member States adapt the rules referred to in paragraph 1, they shall take account of any significant changes to the risk, collective means of protection and personal protective equipment brought about by technological developments.

3.   Member States shall consult the employers' and workers' organization on the rules referred to in paragraphs 1 and 2.

Article 7

INFORMATION FOR WORKERS

Without prejudice to Article 10 of Directive 89/391/EEC, workers and/or their representatives shall be informed of all measures to be taken with regard to the health and safety of workers when personal protective equipment is used by workers at work.

Article 8

CONSULTATION OF WORKERS AND WORKERS' PARTICIPATION

Consultation and participation of workers and/or of their representatives shall take place in accordance with Article 11 of Directive 89/391/EEC on the matters covered by this Directive, including the Annexes thereto.

SECTION III

Miscellaneous provisions

Article 9

ADJUSTMENT OF THE ANNEXES

Alterations of a strictly technical nature to Annexes I, II and III resulting from:

–   the adoption of technical harmonization and standardization directives relating to personal protective equipment, and/or

–   technical progress and changes in international regulations and specifications or knowledge in the field of personal protective equipment, shall be adopted in accordance with the procedure provided for in Article 17 of Directive 89/391/EEC.

Article 10

FINAL PROVISIONS

1.   Member States shall bring into force the laws, regulations and administrative provisions necessary to comply with this Directive not later than 31 December 1992. They shall immediately inform the Commission thereof.

2.   Member States shall communicate to the Commission the text of the provisions of national law which they adopt, as well as those already adopted, in the field covered by this Directive.

3.   Member States shall report to the Commission every five years on the practical implementation of the provisions of this Directive, indicating the points of view of employers and workers.

The Commission shall inform the European Parliament, the Council, the Economic and Social Committee, and the Advisory Committee on Safety, Hygiene and Health Protection at Work.

4.   The Commission shall report periodically to the European Parliament, the Council and the Economic and Social Committee on the implementation of the Directive in the light of paragraphs 1, 2 and 3.

Article 11

This Directive is addressed to the Member States.

Done at Brussels, 30 November 1989.

For the Council
The President
J P SOISSON

ANNEX I:
SPECIMEN RISK SURVEY TABLE FOR THE USE OF PERSONAL PROTECTIVE EQUIPMENT

ANNEX II:
NON-EXHAUSTIVE GUIDE LIST OF ITEMS OF
PERSONAL PROTECTIVE EQUIPMENT

HEAD PROTECTION

- Protective helmets for use in industry (mines, building sites, other industrial uses).

- Scalp protection (caps, bonnets, hairnets - with or without eye shade).

- Protective headgear (bonnets, caps, sou'westers, etc in fabric, fabric with proofing, etc).

HEARING PROTECTION

- Earplugs and similar devices.

- Full acoustic helmets.

- Earmuffs which can be fitted to industrial helmets.

- Ear defenders with receiver for LF induction loop.

- Ear protection with intercom equipment.

EYE AND FACE PROTECTION

- Spectacles.

- Goggles.

- X-ray goggles, laser beam goggles, ultra violet, infra-red, visible radiation goggles.

- Face shields.

- Arc-welding masks and helmets (hand masks, headband masks or masks which can be fitted to protective helmets).

RESPIRATORY PROTECTION

- Dust filters, gas filters and radioactive dust filters.

- Insulating appliances with an air supply.

- Respiratory devices including a removable welding mask.

- Diving equipment.

- Diving suits.

HAND AND ARM PROTECTION

- Gloves to provide protection:
    - from machinery (piercing, cuts, vibrations, etc),
    - from chemicals,
    - for electricians and from heat.
- Mittens.
- Finger stalls.
- Oversleeves.
- Wrist protection for heavy work.
- Fingerless gloves.
- Protective gloves.

FOOT AND LEG PROTECTION

- Low shoes, ankle boots, calf-length boots, safety boots.
- Shoes which can be unlaced or unhooked rapidly.
- Shoes with additional protective toe-cap.
- Shoes and overshoes with heat-resistant soles.
- Heat-resistant shoes, boots and overboots.
- Thermal shoes, boots and overboots.
- Vibration-resistant shoes, boots and overboots.
- Anti-static shoes, boots and overboots.
- Insulating shoes, boots and overboots.
- Protective boots for chain saw operators.
- Clogs.
- Kneepads.
- Removable instep protectors.
- Gaiters.
- Removable soles (heat-proof, pierce-proof, or sweat-proof).
- Removable spikes for ice, snow or slippery flooring.

SKIN PROTECTION

–   Barrier creams/ointments.

TRUNK AND ABDOMEN PROTECTION

–   Protective waistcoats, jackets and aprons to provide protection from machinery (piercing, cutting, molten metal splashes, etc).

–   Protective waistcoats, jackets and aprons to provide protection from chemicals.

–   Heated waistcoats.

–   Life jackets.

–   Protective X-ray aprons.

–   Body belts.

WHOLE BODY PROTECTION

–   Equipment designed to prevent falls

–   Fall-prevention equipment (full equipment with all necessary accessories).

–   Braking equipment to absorb kinetic energy (full equipment with all necessary accessories).

–   Body-holding devices (safety harness).

–   Protective clothing

–   'Safety' working clothing (two-piece and overalls).

–   Clothing to provide protection from machinery (piercing, cutting, etc).

–   Clothing to provide protection from chemicals.

–   Clothing to provide protection from molten metal splashes and infra-red radiation.

–   Heat-resistant clothing.

–   Thermal clothing.

–   Clothing to provide protection from radioactive contamination.

–   Dust-proof clothing.

– Gas-proof clothing.

– Fluorescent signalling, retro-reflecting clothing and accessories (armbands, gloves, etc).

– Protective coverings.

ANNEX III:
NON-EXHAUSTIVE GUIDE LIST OF ACTIVITIES AND SECTORS OF ACTIVITY WHICH MAY REQUIRE THE PROVISION OF PERSONAL PROTECTIVE EQUIPMENT

1.   HEAD PROTECTION (SKULL PROTECTION)

Protective helmets

– Building work, particularly work on, underneath or in the vicinity of scaffolding and elevated workplaces, erection and stripping of formwork, assembly and installation work, work on scaffolding and demolition work.

– Work on steel bridges, steel building construction, masts, towers, steel hydraulic structures, blast furnaces, steel works and rolling mills, large containers, large pipelines, boiler plants and power stations.

– Work in pits, trenches, shafts and tunnels.

– Earth and rock works.

– Work in underground workings, quarries, open diggings, coal stock removal.

– Work with bolt-driving tools.

– Blasting work.

– Work in the vicinity of lifts, lifting gear, cranes and conveyors.

– Work with blast furnaces, direct reduction plants, steelworks, rolling mills, metalworks, forging, drop forging and casting.

– Work with industrial furnaces, containers, machinery, silos, bunkers and pipelines.

– Shipbuilding.

– Railway shunting work.

– Slaughterhouses.

2. FOOT PROTECTION

Safety shoes with puncture-proof soles

– Carcase work, foundation work and roadworks.

– Scaffolding work.

– The demolition of carcase work.

– Work with concrete and prefabricated parts involving form-work erection and stripping.

– Work in contractors' yards and warehouses.

– Roof work.

Safety shoes without pierce-proof soles

– Work on steel bridges, steel building construction, masts, towers, lifts, steel hydraulic structures, blast furnaces, steel-works and rolling mills, large containers, large pipelines, cranes, boiler plants and power stations.

– Furnace construction, heating and ventilation installation and metal assembly work.

– Conversion and maintenance work.

– Work with blast furnaces, direct reduction plants, steelworks, rolling mills, metalworks, forging, drop forging, hot pressing and drawing plants.

– Work in quarries and open diggings, coal stock removal.

– Working and processing of rock.

– Flat glass products and container glassware manufacture, working and processing.

– Work with moulds in the ceramics industry.

– Lining of kilns in the ceramics industry.

– Moulding work in the ceramic ware and building materials industry.

– Transport and storage.

– Work with frozen meat blocks and preserved foods packaging.

– Shipbuilding.

– Railway shunting work.

Safety shoes with heels or wedges and pierce-proof soles

– Roof work.

Protective shoes with insulated soles

- Work with and on very hot or very cold materials.

Safety shoes which can easily be removed

- Where there is a risk of penetration by molten substances.

3.   EYE OR FACE PROTECTION

Protective goggles, face shields or screens

- Welding, grinding and separating work.

- Caulking and chiselling.

- Rock working and processing.

- Work with bolt-driving tools.

- Work on stock removing machines for small chippings.

- Drop forging.

- The removal and breaking up of fragments.

- Spraying of abrasive substances.

- Work with acids and caustic solutions, disinfectants and corrosive cleaning products.

- Work with liquid sprays.

- Work with and in the vicinity of molten substances.

- Work with radiant heat.

- Work with lasers.

4.   RESPIRATORY PROTECTION

Respirators/breathing apparatus

- Work in containers, restricted areas and gas-fired industrial furnaces where there may be gas or insufficient oxygen.

- Work in the vicinity of the blast furnace charge.

- Work in the vicinity of gas converters and blast furnace gas pipes.

- Work in the vicinity of blast furnace taps where there may be heavy metal fumes.

- Work on the lining of furnaces and ladles where there may be dust.

- Spray painting where dedusting is inadequate.
- Work in shafts, sewers and other underground areas connected with sewage.
- Work in refrigeration plants where there is a danger that the refrigerant may escape.

5.   HEARING PROTECTION

Ear protectors

- Work with metal presses.
- Work with pneumatic drills.
- The work of ground staff at airports.
- Pile-driving work.
- Wood and textile working.

6.   BODY, ARM AND HAND PROTECTION

Protective clothing

- Work with acids and caustic solutions, disinfectants and corrosive cleaning substances.
- Work with or in the vicinity of hot materials and where the effects of heat are felt.
- Work on flat glass products.
- Shot blasting.
- Work in deep-freeze rooms.

Fire-resistant protective clothing

- Welding in restricted areas.

Pierce-proof aprons

- Boning and cutting work.
- Work with hand knives involving drawing the knife towards the body.

Leather aprons

- Welding.
- Forging.
- Casting.

Forearm protection

– Boning and cutting.

Gloves

– Welding.

– Handling of sharp-edged objects, other than machines where there is a danger of the glove's being caught.

– Unprotected work with acids and caustic solutions.

Metal mesh gloves

– Boning and cutting.

– Regular cutting using a hand knife for production and slaughtering.

– Changing the knives of cutting machines.

7.   WEATHERPROOF CLOTHING

– Work in the open air in rain and cold weather.

8.   REFLECTIVE CLOTHING

– Work where the workers must be clearly visible.

9.   SAFETY HARNESSES

– Work on scaffolding.

– Assembly of prefabricated parts.

– Work on masts.

10.   SAFETY ROPES

– Work in high crane cabs.

– Work in high cabs of warehouse stacking and retrieval equipment.

– Work in high sections of drilling towers.

    – Work in shafts and sewers.

11.   **SKIN PROTECTION**

    – Processing of coating materials.

    – Tanning.

COUNCIL DIRECTIVE OF 29 MAY 1990
on the minimum health and safety requirements for
the manual handling of loads where there is a risk
particularly of back injury to workers (fourth individual
Directive within the meaning of Article 16 (1) of Directive
89/391/EEC) (90/269/EEC)

The Council of the European Communities,

Having regard to the Treaty establishing the European Economic
Community, and in particular Article 118a thereof

Having regard to the Commission proposal submitted after consultation
with the Advisory Committee on Safety, Hygiene and Health Protection at
Work,

In Cooperation with the European Parliament,

Having regard to the opinion of the Economic and Social Committee,

Whereas Article 118a of the Treaty provides that the Council shall adopt,
by means of Directives, minimum requirements for encouraging improvements, especially in the working environment, to guarantee a better level of
protection of the health and safety of workers;

Whereas, pursuant to that Article, such Directives must avoid imposing
administrative, financial and legal constraints in a way which would hold
back the creation and development of small and medium-sized undertakings;

Whereas the Commission communication on its programme concerning
safety, hygiene and health at work, provides for the adoption of
Directives designed to guarantee the health and safety of workers at the
workplace;

Whereas the Council, in its resolution of 21 December 1987 on safety,
hygiene and health at work, took note of the Commission's intention of
submitting to the Council in the near future a Directive on protection
against the risks resulting from the manual handling of heavy loads;

Whereas compliance with the minimum requirements designed to
guarantee a better standard of health and safety at the workplace is
essential to ensure the health and safety of workers;

Whereas this Directive is an individual Directive within the meaning of
Article 16 (1) of Council Directive 89/391/EEC of 12 June 1989 on the
introduction of measures to encourage improvements in the health and

safety of workers at work; whereas therefore the provisions of the said Directive are fully applicable to the field of the manual handling of loads where there is a risk particularly of back injury to workers, without prejudice to more stringent and/or specific provisions set out in this Directive;

Whereas this Directive constitutes a practical step towards the achievement of the social dimension of the internal market;

Whereas, pursuant to Decision 74/325/EEC, the Advisory Committee on Safety, Hygiene and Health Protection at Work shall be consulted by the Commission with a view to drawing up proposals in this field,

HAS ADOPTED THIS DIRECTIVE:

SECTION I

General provisions

Article 1

SUBJECT

1. This Directive, which is the fourth individual Directive within the meaning of Article 16 (1) of Directive 89/391/EEC, lays down minimum health and safety requirements for the manual handling of loads where there is a risk particularly of back injury to workers.

2. The provisions of Directive 89/391/EEC shall be fully applicable to the whole sphere referred to in paragraph 1, without prejudice to more restrictive and/or specific provisions contained in this Directive.

Article 2

DEFINITION

For the purposes of this Directive, 'manual handling of loads' means any transporting or supporting of a load, by one or more workers, including lifting, putting down, pushing, pulling, carrying or moving of a load, which, by reason of its characteristics or of unfavourable ergonomic conditions, involves a risk particularly of back injury to workers.

SECTION II

Employers' obligations

Article 3

GENERAL PROVISION

1.   The employer shall take appropriate organizational measures, or shall use the appropriate means, in particular mechanical equipment, in order to avoid the need for the manual handling of loads by workers.

2.   Where the need for the manual handling of loads by workers cannot be avoided, the employer shall take the appropriate organizational measures, use the appropriate means or provide workers with such means in order to reduce the risk involved in the manual handling of such loads, having regard to Annex 1.

Article 4

ORGANIZATION OF WORKSTATIONS

Wherever the need for manual handling of loads by workers cannot be avoided, the employer shall organize workstations in such a way as to make such handling as safe and healthy as possible and:

(a)   assess, in advance if possible, the health and safety conditions of the type of work involved, and in particular examine the characteristics of loads, taking account of Annex I;

(b)   take care to avoid or reduce the risk particularly of back injury to workers, by taking appropriate measures, considering in particular the characteristics of the working environment and the requirements of the activity, taking account of Annex I.

Article 5

REFERENCE TO ANNEX II

For the implementation of Article 6 (3) (b) and Articles 14 and 15 of Directive 89/391/EEC, account should be taken of Annex II.

Article 6

INFORMATION, FOR AND TRAINING OF, WORKERS

1.   Without prejudice to Article 10 of Directive 89/391/EEC, workers and/
or their representatives shall be informed of all measures to be
implemented, pursuant to this Directive, with regard to the protection of
safety and of health.

Employers must ensure that workers and/or their representatives receive
general indications and, where possible, precise information on:

- the weight of a load,
- the centre of gravity of the heaviest side when a package is
  eccentrically loaded.

2.   Without prejudice to Article 12 of Directive 83/391/EEC, employers
must ensure that workers receive in addition proper training and
information on how to handle loads correctly and the risks they might be
open to particularly if these tasks are not performed correctly, having
regard to Annexes I and II.

Article 7

CONSULTATION OF WORKERS AND WORKERS' PARTICIPATION

Consultation and participation of workers and/or of their representatives
shall take place in accordance with Article 11 of Directive 89/391/EEC on
matters covered by this Directive, including the Annexes thereto.

SECTION III

Miscellaneous provisions

Article 8

ADJUSTMENT OF THE ANNEXES

Alterations of a strictly technical nature to Annexes I and II resulting from
technical progress and changes in international regulations and specifications or knowledge in the field of the manual handling of loads shall be

adopted in accordance with the procedure provided for in Article 17 of Directive 89/391/EEC.

Article 9

FINAL PROVISIONS

1.   Member States shall bring into force the laws, regulations and administrative provisions needed to comply with this Directive not later than 31 December 1992.

They shall forthwith inform the Commission thereof.

2.   Member States shall communicate to the Commission the text of the provisions of national law which they adopt, or have adopted, in the field covered by this Directive.

3.   Member States shall report to the Commission every four years on the practical implementation of the provisions of this Directive, indicating the points of view of employers and workers.

The Commission shall inform the European Parliament, the Council, the Economic and Social Committee and the Advisory Committee on Safety, Hygiene and Health Protection at Work thereof.

4.   The Commission shall report periodically to the European Parliament, the Council and the Economic and Social Committee on the implementation of the Directive in the light of paragraphs 1, 2 and 3.

Article 10

This Directive is addressed to the Member States.

Done at Brussels, 29 May 1990.

For the Council
The President
B AHERN

ANNEX I:
REFERENCE FACTORS (ARTICLE 3 (2), ARTICLE 4 (a) AND (b) AND ARTICLE 6 (2))

1.   Characteristics of the load

The manual handling of a load may present a risk particularly of back injury if it is:

–   too heavy or too large,

–   unwieldy or difficult to grasp,

–   unstable or has contents likely to shift,

–   positioned in a manner requiring it to be held or manipulated at a distance from the trunk, or with a bending or twisting of the trunk,

–   likely, because of its contours and/or consistency, to result in injury to workers, particularly in the event of a collision.

2.   Physical effort required

A physical effort may present a risk particularly of back injury if it is:

–   too strenuous,

–   only achieved by a twisting movement of the trunk,

–   likely to result in a sudden movement of the load,

–   made with the body in an unstable posture.

3.   Characteristics of the working environment

The characteristics of the work environment may increase a risk particularly of back injury if:

–   there is not enough room, in particular vertically, to carry out the activity,

–   the floor is uneven, thus presenting tripping hazards, or is slippery in relation to the worker's footwear,

–   the place of work or the working environment prevents handling of loads at a safe height or with good posture by the worker,

–   there are variations in the level of the floor or the working surface, requiring the load to be manipulated on different levels,

- the floor or foot rest is unstable,
- the temperature, humidity or ventilation is unsuitable.

4.   Requirements of the activity

The activity may present a risk particularly of back injury if it entails one or more of the following requirements:

- over-frequent or over-prolonged physical effort involving in particular the spine,
- an insufficient bodily rest or recovery period,
- excessive lifting, lowering or carrying distances,
- a rate of work imposed by a process which cannot be altered by the worker.

ANNEX II:
INDIVIDUAL RISK FACTORS
(ARTICLES 5 AND 6 (2))

The worker may be at risk if he/she:

- is physically unsuited to carry out the task in question,
- is wearing unsuitable clothing, footwear or other personal effects,
- does not have adequate or appropriate knowledge or training.

COUNCIL DIRECTIVE OF 29 MAY 1990
on the minimum safety and health requirements for work with
display screen equipment (fifth individual Directive within the
meaning of Article 16 (1) of Directive 87/391/EEC)
(90/270/EEC)

The Council of the European Communities,

Having regard to the Treaty establishing the European Economic
Community, and in particular Article 118a thereof,

Having regard to the Commission proposal drawn up after consultation
with the Advisory Committee on Safety, Hygiene and Health Protection at
Work,

In cooperation with the European Parliament

Having regard to the opinion of the Economic and Social Committee,

Whereas Article 118a of the Treaty provides that the Council shall adopt,
by means of Directives, minimum requirements designed to encourage
improvements, especially in the working environment, to ensure a better
level of protection of workers' safety and health;

Whereas, under the terms of that Article, those Directives shall avoid
imposing administrative, financial and legal constraints, in a way which
would hold back the creation and development of small and medium-sized
undertakings;

Whereas the communication from the Commission on its programme
concerning safety, hygiene and health at work provides for the adoption of
measures in respect of new technologies; whereas the Council has taken
note thereof in its resolution of 21 December 1987 on safety, hygiene and
health at work;

Whereas compliance with the minimum requirements for ensuring a better
level of safety at workstations with display screens is essential for ensuring
the safety and health of workers;

Whereas this Directive is an individual Directive within the meaning of
Article 16 (1) of the Council Directive 89/391/EEC of 12 June 1989 on the
introduction of measures to encourage improvements in the safety and
health of workers at work; whereas the provisions of the latter are therefore
fully applicable to the use by workers of display screen equipment, without
prejudice to more stringent and/or specific provisions contained in the
present Directive;

Whereas employers are obliged to keep themselves informed of the latest advances in technology and scientific findings concerning workstation design so that they can make any changes necessary so as to be able to guarantee a better level of protection of workers' safety and health;

Whereas the ergonomic aspects are of particular importance for a workstation with display screen equipment;

Whereas this Directive is a practical contribution towards creating the social dimension of the internal market;

Whereas, pursuant to Decision 74/325/EEC, the Advisory Committee on Safety, Hygiene and Health Protection at Work shall be consulted by the Commission on the drawing-up of proposals in this field,

HAS ADOPTED THIS DIRECTIVE;

SECTION I

General provisions

Article 1

SUBJECT

1.   This Directive, which is the fifth individual Directive within the meaning of Article 16 (1) of Directive 89/391/EEC, lays down minimum safety and health requirements for work with display screen equipment as defined in Article 2.

2.   The provisions of Directive 89/391/EEC are fully applicable to the whole field referred to in paragraph 1, without prejudice to more stringent and/or specific provisions contained in the present Directive.

3.   This Directive shall not apply to:

(a)   drivers' cabs or control cabs for vehicles or machinery;

(b)   computer systems on board a means of transport;

(c)   computer systems mainly intended for public use;

(d)   'portable' systems not in prolonged use at a workstation;

(e) calculators, cash registers and any equipment having a small data or measurement display required for direct use of the equipment;

(f) typewriters of traditional design, of the type known as 'typewriter with window'.

Article 2

DEFINITIONS

For the purpose of this Directive, the following terms shall have the following meanings:

(a) display screen equipment: an alphanumeric or graphic display screen, regardless of the display process employed;

(b) workstation: an assembly comprising display screen equipment, which may be provided with a keyboard or input device and/or software determining the operator/machine interface, optional accessories, peripherals including the diskette drive, telephone, modem, printer, document holder, work chair and work desk or work surface, and the immediate work environment;

(c) worker: any worker as defined in Article 3 (a) of Directive 89/391/EEC who habitually uses display screen equipment as a significant part of his normal work.

SECTION II

Employers' obligations

Article 3

ANALYSIS OF WORKSTATIONS

1. Employers shall be obliged to perform an analysis of workstations in order to evaluate the safety and health conditions to which they give rise for their workers, particularly as regards possible risks to eyesight, physical problems and problems of mental stress.

2. Employers shall take appropriate measures to remedy the risks found, on the basis of the evaluation referred to in paragraph 1, taking account of the additional and/or combined effects of the risks so found.

Article 4

WORKSTATIONS PUT INTO SERVICE FOR THE FIRST TIME.

Employers must take the appropriate steps to ensure that workstations first put into service after 31 December 1992 meet the minimum requirements laid down in the Annex.

Article 5

WORKSTATIONS ALREADY PUT INTO SERVICE

Employers must take the appropriate steps to ensure that workstations already put into service on or before 31 December 1992 are adapted to comply with the minimum requirements laid down in the Annex not later than four years after that date.

Article 6

INFORMATION FOR, AND TRAINING OF, WORKERS.

1.   Without prejudice to Article 10 of Directive 89/391/EEC, workers shall receive information on all aspects of safety and health relating to their workstation, in particular information on such measures applicable to workstations as are implemented under Articles 3, 7 and 9.

In all cases, workers or their representatives shall be informed of any health and safety measure taken in compliance with this Directive.

2.   Without prejudice to Article 12 of Directive 89/391/EEC, every worker shall also receive training in use of the workstation before commencing this type of work and whenever the organization of the workstation is substantially modified.

Article 7

DAILY WORK ROUTINE

The employer must plan the worker's activities in such a way that daily work on a display screen is periodically interrupted by breaks or changes of activity reducing the workload at the display screen.

Article 8

WORKER CONSULTATION AND PARTICIPATION

Consultation and participation of workers and/or their representatives shall take place in accordance with Article 11 of Directive 89/391/EEC on the matters covered by this Directive, including its Annex.

Article 9

PROTECTION OF WORKERS' EYES AND EYESIGHT

1. Workers shall be entitled to an appropriate eye and eyesight test carried out by a person with the necessary capabilities:

– before commencing display screen work,

– at regular intervals thereafter, and

– if they experience visual difficulties which may be due to display screen work.

2. Workers shall be entitled to an ophthalmological examination if the results of the test referred to in paragraph 1 show that this is necessary.

3. If the results of the test referred to in paragraph 1 or of the examination referred to in paragraph 2 show that it is necessary and if normal corrective appliances cannot be used, workers must be provided with special corrective appliances appropriate for the work concerned.

4. Measures taken pursuant to this Article may in no circumstances involve workers in additional financial cost.

5. Protection of workers' eyes and eyesight may be provided as part of a national health system.

SECTION III

Miscellaneous provisions

Article 10

ADAPTATIONS TO THE ANNEX

The strictly technical adaptations to the Annex to take account of technical progress, developments in international regulations and specifications and knowledge in the field of display screen equipment shall be adopted in accordance with the procedure laid down in Article 17 of Directive 89/391/EEC.

Article 11

FINAL PROVISIONS

1. Member States shall bring into force the laws, regulations and administrative provisions necessary to comply with this Directive by 31 December 1992.

They shall forthwith inform the Commission thereof.

2.   Member States shall communicate to the Commission the texts of the provisions of national law which they adopt, or have already adopted, in the field covered by this Directive.

3.   Member States shall report to the Commission every four years on the practical implementation of the provisions of this Directive, indicating the points of view of employers and workers.

The Commission shall inform the European Parliament, the Council, the Economic and Social Committee and the Advisory Committee on Safety, Hygiene and Health Protection at Work.

4.   The Commission shall submit a report on the implementation of this Directive at regular intervals to the European Parliament, the Council and the Economic and Social Committee, taking into account paragraphs 1, 2 and 3.

Article 12

This Directive is addressed to the Member States.

Done at Brussels, 29 May 1990.

For the Council
The President
B. AHERN

ANNEX:
MINIMUM REQUIREMENTS
(ARTICLES 4 AND 5)

Preliminary remark

The obligations laid down in this Annex shall apply in order to achieve the objectives of this Directive and to the extent that, firstly, the components concerned are present at the workstation, and secondly, the inherent requirements or characteristics of the task do not preclude it.

1.   EQUIPMENT

   (a) **General comment**

        The use as such of the equipment must not be a source of risk for workers.

(b) Display screen

The characters on the screen shall be well-defined and clearly formed, of adequate size and with adequate spacing between the characters and lines.

The image on the screen should be stable, with no flickering or other forms of instability.

The brightness and/or the contrast between the characters and the background shall be easily adjustable by the operator, and also be easily adjustable to ambient conditions.

The screen must swivel and tilt easily and freely to suit the needs of the operator.

It shall be possible to use a separate base for the screen or an adjustable table.

The screen shall be free of reflective glare and reflections liable to cause discomfort to the user.

(c) Keyboard

The keyboard shall be tiltable and separate from the screen so as to allow the worker to find a comfortable working position avoiding fatigue in the arms or hands.

The space in front of the keyboard shall be sufficient to provide support for the hands and arms of the operator.

The keyboard shall have a matt surface to avoid reflective glare.

The arrangement of the keyboard and the characteristics of the keys shall be such as to facilitate the use of the keyboard.

The symbols on the keys shall be adequately contrasted and legible from the design working position.

(d) Work desk or work surface

The work desk or work surface shall have a sufficiently large, low-reflectance surface and allow a flexible arrangement of the screen, keyboard, documents and related equipment.

The document holder shall be stable and adjustable and shall be positioned so as to minimize the need for uncomfortable head and eye movements.

There shall be adequate space for workers to find a comfortable position.

(e) Work chair

The work chair shall be stable and allow the operator easy freedom of movement and a comfortable position.

The seat shall be adjustable in height.

The seat back shall be adjustable in both height and tilt.

A footrest shall be made available to any one who wishes for one.

2.   ENVIRONMENT

(a) Space requirements

The workstation shall be dimensioned and designed so as to provide sufficient space for the user to change position and vary movements.

(b) Lighting

Room lighting and/or spot lighting (work lamps) shall ensure satisfactory lighting conditions and an appropriate contrast between the screen and the background environment, taking into account the type of work and the user's vision requirements.

Possible disturbing glare and reflections on the screen or other equipment shall be prevented by coordinating workplace and workstation layout with the positioning and technical characteristics of the artificial light sources.

(c) Reflections and glare

Workstations shall be so designed that sources of light, such as windows and other openings, transparent or translucid walls, and brightly coloured fixtures or walls cause no direct glare and no distracting reflections on the screen.

Windows shall be fitted with a suitable system of adjustable covering to attenuate the daylight that falls on the work-station.

(d) Noise

Noise emitted by equipment belonging to workstation(s) shall be taken into account when a workstations is being equipped, in particular so as not to distract attention or disturb speech.

(e) Heat

Equipment belonging to workstation(s) shall not produce excess heat which could cause discomfort to workers.

(f) Radiation

All radiation with the exception of the visible part of the electromagnetic spectrum shall be reduced to negligible levels from the point of view of the protection of workers' safety and health.

(g) Humidity

An adequate level of humidity shall be established and maintained.

3. OPERATOR/COMPUTER INTERFACE

In designing, selecting, commissioning and modifying software, and in designing tasks using display screen equipment, the employer shall take into account the following principles:

(a) software must be suitable for the task;

(b) software must be easy to use and, where appropriate, adaptable to the operator's level of knowledge or experience; no quantitative or qualitative checking facility may be used without the knowledge of the workers;

(c) systems must provide feedback to workers on their performance;

(d) systems must display information in a format and at a pace which are adapted to operators;

(e) the principles of software ergonomics must be applied, in particular to human data processing.

COUNCIL DIRECTIVE OF 25 JUNE 1991
supplementing the measures to encourage improvements in the safety and health at work of workers with a fixed-duration employment relationship or a temporary employment relationship (91/383/EEC)

The Council of the European Communities,

Having regard to the Treaty establishing the European Economic Community, and in particular Article 118a thereof,

Having regard to the proposal from the Commission,

In cooperation with the European Parliament,

Having regard to the opinion of the Economic and Social Committee,

Whereas Article 118a of the Treaty provides that the Council shall adopt, by means of Directives, minimum requirements for encouraging improvements, especially in the working environment, to guarantee a better level of protection of the safety and health of workers;

Whereas, pursuant to the said Article, Directives must avoid imposing administrative, financial and legal constraints which would hold back the creation and development of small and medium-sized undertakings;

Whereas recourse to forms of employment such as fixed-duration employment and temporary employment has increased considerably;

Whereas research has shown that in general workers with a fixed-duration employment relationship or temporary employment relationship are, in certain sectors, more exposed to the risk of accidents at work and occupational diseases than other workers;

Whereas these additional risks in certain sectors are in part linked to certain particular modes of integrating new workers into the undertaking; whereas these risks can be reduced through adequate provision of information and training from the beginning of employment;

Whereas the Directives on health and safety at work, notably Council Directive 89/391/EEC of 12 June 1989 on the introduction of measures to encourage improvements in the safety and health of workers at work, contain provisions intended to improve the safety and health of workers in general;

Whereas the specific situation of workers with a fixed-duration employment relationship or a temporary employment relationship and the special nature of the risks they face in certain sectors calls for special additional rules, particularly as regards the provision of information, the training and the medical surveillance of the workers concerned;

Whereas this Directive constitutes a practical step within the framework of the attainment of the social dimension of the internal market,

HAS ADOPTED THIS DIRECTIVE:

SECTION I

Scope and object

Article 1

SCOPE

This Directive shall apply to:

1. employment relationships governed by a fixed-duration contract of employment concluded directly between the employer and the worker, where the end of the contract is established by objective conditions such as: reaching a specific date, completing a specific task or the occurrence of a specific event;

2. temporary employment relationships between a temporary employment business which is the employer and the worker, where the latter is assigned to work for and under the control of an undertaking and/or establishment making use of his services.

Article 2

OBJECT

1. The purpose of this Directive is to ensure that workers with an employment relationship as referred to in Article 1 are afforded, as regards safety and health at work, the same level of protection as that of other workers in the user undertaking and/or establishment.

2. The existence of an employment relationship as referred to in Article 1 shall not justify different treatment with respect to working conditions inasmuch as the protection of safety and health at work are involved, especially as regards access to personal protective equipment.

3.   Directive 89/391/EEC and the individual Directives within the meaning of Article 16 (1) thereof shall apply in full to workers with an employment relationship as referred to in Article 1, without prejudice to more binding and/or more specific provisions set out in this Directive.

SECTION II

General provisions

Article 3

PROVISION OF INFORMATION TO WORKERS

Without prejudice to Article 10 of Directive 89/391/EEC, Member States shall take the necessary steps to ensure that:

1.   before a worker with an employment relationship as referred to in Article 1 takes up any activity, he is informed by the undertaking and/or establishment making use of his services of the risks which he faces;

2.   such information:

–   covers, in particular, any special occupational qualifications or skills or special medical surveillance required, as defined in national legislation, and

–   states clearly any increased specific risks, as defined in national legislation, that the job may entail.

Article 4

WORKERS' TRAINING

Without prejudice to Article 12 of Directive 89/391/EEC, Member States shall take the necessary measures to ensure that, in the cases referred to in Article 3, each worker receives sufficient training appropriate to the particular characteristics of the job, account being taken of his qualifications and experience.

Article 5

USE OF WORKERS' SERVICES AND MEDICAL SURVEILLANCE
OF WORKERS

1.   Member States shall have the option of prohibiting workers with an employment relationship as referred to in Article 1 from being used for

certain work as defined in national legislation, which would be particularly dangerous to their safety or health, and in particular for certain work which requires special medical surveillance, as defined in national legislation.

2.   Where Member States do not avail themselves of the option referred to in paragraph 1, they shall, without prejudice to Article 14 of Directive 89/391/EEC, take the necessary measures to ensure that workers with an employment relationship as referred to in Article 1 who are used for work which requires special medical surveillance, as defined in national legislation, are provided with appropriate special medical surveillance.

3.   It shall be open to Member States to provide that the appropriate special medical surveillance referred to in paragraph 2 shall extend beyond the end of the employment relationship of the worker concerned.

Article 6

PROTECTION AND PREVENTION SERVICES

Member States shall take the necessary measures to ensure that workers, services or persons designated, in accordance with Article 7 of Directive 89/391/EEC, to carry out activities related to protection from and prevention of occupational risks are informed of the assignment of workers with an employment relationship as referred to in Article 1, to the extent necessary for the workers, services or persons designated to be able to carry out adequately their protection and prevention activities for all the workers in the undertaking and/or establishment.

SECTION III

Special provisions

Article 7

TEMPORARY EMPLOYMENT RELATIONSHIPS: INFORMATION

Without prejudice to Article 3, Member States shall take the necessary steps to ensure that:

1.   before workers with an employment relationship as referred to in Article 1 (2) are supplied, a user undertaking and/or establishment shall specify to the temporary employment business, inter alia, the occupational qualifications required and the specific features of the job to be filled;

2.   the temporary employment business shall bring all these facts to the attention of the workers concerned.

Member States may provide that the details to be given by the user undertaking and/or establishment to the temporary employment business in accordance with point 1 of the first subparagraph shall appear in a contract of assignment.

Article 8

TEMPORARY EMPLOYMENT RELATIONSHIPS: RESPONSIBILITY

Member States shall take the necessary steps to ensure that:

1.   without prejudice to the responsibility of the temporary employment business as laid down in national legislation, the user undertaking and/or establishment is/are responsible, for the duration of the assignment, for the conditions governing performance of the work;

2.   for the application of point 1, the conditions governing the performance of the work shall be limited to those connected with safety, hygiene and health at work.

SECTION IV

Miscellaneous provisions

Article 9

MORE FAVOURABLE PROVISIONS

This Directive shall be without prejudice to existing or future national or Community provisions which are more favourable to the safety and health protection of workers with an employment relationship referred to in Article 1.

Article 10

FINAL PROVISIONS

1.   Member States shall bring into force the laws, regulations and administrative provisions necessary to comply with this Directive by 31 December 1992 at the latest. They shall forthwith inform the Commission thereof.

When Member States adopt these measures, the latter shall contain a reference to this Directive or shall be accompanied by such reference on the occasion of their official publication. The methods of making such a reference shall be laid down by the Member States.

2. Member States shall forward to the Commission the texts of the provisions of national law which they have already adopted or adopt in the field covered by this Directive.

3. Member States shall report to the Commission every five years on the practical implementation of this Directive, setting out the points of view of workers and employers.

The Commission shall bring the report to the attention of the European Parliament, the Council, the Economic and Social Committee and the Advisory Committee on Safety, Hygiene and Health Protection at Work.

4. The Commission shall submit to the European Parliament, the Council and the Economic and Social Committee a regular report on the implementation of this Directive, due account being taken of paragraphs 1, 2 and 3.

Article 11

This Directive is addressed to the Member States.

Done at Luxembourg, 25 June 1991

For the Council
The President
J-C JUNCKER

Appendix 1

Management of Health and Safety at Work Regulations 1992

THE REGULATIONS

Regulation 1

Citation, commencement and interpretation

(1) These Regulations may be cited as the Management of Health and Safety at Work Regulations 1992 and shall come into force on 1st January 1993.

(2) In these Regulations –

"the assessment" means, in the case of an employer, the assessment made by him in accordance with regulation 3(1) and changed by him where necessary in accordance with regulation 3(3); and, in the case of a self-employed person, the assessment made by him in accordance with regulation 3(2) and changed by him where necessary in accordance with regulation 3(3);

"employment business" means a business (whether or not carried on with a view to profit and whether or not carried on in conjunction with any other business) which supplies persons (other than seafarers) who are employed in it to work for and under the control of other persons in any capacity;

"fixed-term contract of employment" means a contract of employment for a specific term which is fixed in advance or which can be ascertained in advance by reference to some relevant circumstance; and

"the preventive and protective measures" means the measures which have been identified by the employer or by the self-employed person in consequence of the assessment as the measures he needs to take to comply with the requirements and prohibitions imposed upon him by or under the relevant statutory provisions.

(3) Any reference in these Regulations to –

(a) a numbered regulation is a reference to the regulation in these Regulations so numbered; or

(b) a numbered paragraph is a reference to the paragraph so numbered in the regulation in which the reference appears.

Regulation 2

Disapplication of these Regulations

These Regulations shall not apply to or in relation to the master or crew of a sea-going ship or to the employer of such persons in respect of the normal ship-board activities of a ship's crew under the direction of the master.

Regulation 3 *(See p 214 for ACOP)*

Risk assessment

(1) Every employer shall make a suitable and sufficient assessment of –

(a) the risks to the health and safety of his employees to which they are exposed whilst they are at work; and
(b) the risks to the health and safety of persons not in his employment arising out of or in connection with the conduct by him of his undertaking,

for the purposes of identifying the measures he needs to take to comply with the requirements and prohibitions imposed upon him by or under the relevant statutory provisions.

(2) Every self-employed person shall make a suitable and sufficient assessment of –

(a) the risks to his own health and safety to which he is exposed whilst he is at work; and
(b) the risks to the health and safety of persons not in his employment arising out of or in connection with the conduct by him of his undertaking,

for the purpose of identifying the measures he needs to take to comply with the requirements and prohibitions imposed upon him by or under the relevant statutory provisions.

(3) Any assessment such as is referred to in paragraph (1) or (2) shall be reviewed by the employer or self-employed person who made it if –

(a) there is reason to suspect that it is no longer valid; or
(b) there has been a significant change in the matters to which it relates;

and where as a result of any such review changes to an assessment are required, the employer or self-employed person concerned shall make them.

(4) Where the employer employs five or more employees, he shall record –

(a) the significant findings of the assessment; and
(b) any group of his employees identified by it as being especially at risk.

Regulation 4 *(See p 221 for ACOP)*

Health and safety arrangements

(1) Every employer shall make and give effect to such arrangements as are appropriate, having regard to the nature of his activities and the size of his undertaking, for the effective planning, organisation, control, monitoring and review of the preventive and protective measures.

(2) Where the employer employs five or more employees, he shall record the arrangements referred to in paragraph (1).

Regulation 5 *(See p 221 for ACOP)*

Health surveillance

Every employer shall ensure that his employees are provided with such health surveillance as is appropriate having regard to the risks to their health and safety which are identified by the assessment.

Regulation 6 *(See p 222 for ACOP)*

Health and safety assistance

(1) Every employer shall, subject to paragraphs (6) and (7), appoint one or more competent persons to assist him in undertaking the measures he needs to take to comply with the requirements and prohibitions imposed upon him by or under the relevant statutory provisions.

(2) Where an employer appoints persons in accordance with paragraph (1), he shall make arrangements for ensuring adequate co-operation between them.

(3) The employer shall ensure that the number of persons appointed under paragraph (1), the time available for them to fulfil their functions and the means at their disposal are adequate having regard to the size of his undertaking, the risks to which his employees are exposed and the distribution of those risks throughout the undertaking.

(4) The employer shall ensure that –

(a) any person appointed by him in accordance with paragraph (1) who is not in his employment –
    (i) is informed of the factors known by him to affect, or suspected by him of affecting, the health and safety of any other person who may be affected by the conduct of his undertaking, and
    (ii) has access to the information referred to in regulation 8; and
(b) any person appointed by him in accordance with paragraph (1) is given such information about any person working in his undertaking who is –
    (i) employed by him under a fixed-term contract of employment, or
    (ii) employed in an employment business,
    as is necessary to enable that person properly to carry out the function specified in that paragraph.

(5) A person shall be regarded as competent for the purposes of paragraph (1) where he has sufficient training and experience or knowledge and other qualities to enable him properly to assist in undertaking the measures referred to in that paragraph.

(6) Paragraph (1) shall not apply to a self-employed employer who is not in partnership with any other person where he has sufficient training and experience or knowledge and other qualities properly to undertake the measures referred to in that paragraph himself.

(7) Paragraph (1) shall not apply to individuals who are employers and who are together carrying on business in partnership where at least one of the individuals concerned has sufficient training and experience or knowledge and other qualities –

(a) properly to undertake the measures he needs to take to comply with the requirements and prohibitions imposed upon him by or under the relevant statutory provisions; and
(b) properly to assist his fellow partners in undertaking the measures they need to take to comply with the requirements and prohibitions imposed upon them by or under the relevant statutory provisions.

Regulation 7 *(See p 224 for ACOP)*

Procedures for serious and imminent danger and for danger areas

(1) Every employer shall –

(a) establish and where necessary give effect to appropriate procedures to be followed in the event of serious and imminent danger to persons at work in his undertaking;
(b) nominate a sufficient number of competent persons to implement those procedures insofar as they relate to the evacuation from premises of persons at work in his undertaking; and
(c) ensure that none of his employees has access to any area occupied by him to which it is necessary to restrict access on grounds of health and safety unless the employee concerned has received adequate health and safety instruction.

(2) Without prejudice to the generality of paragraph (1)(a), the procedures referred to in that sub-paragraph shall –

(a) so far as is practicable, require any persons at work who are exposed to serious and imminent danger to be informed of the nature of the hazard and of the steps taken or to be taken to protect them from it;
(b) enable the persons concerned (if necessary by taking appropriate steps in the absence of guidance or instruction and in the light of their knowledge and the technical means at their disposal) to stop work and immediately proceed to a place of safety in the event of their being exposed to serious, imminent and unavoidable danger; and
(c) save in exceptional cases for reasons duly substantiated (which cases and reasons shall be specified in those procedures), require the persons

concerned to be prevented from resuming work in any situation where there is still a serious and imminent danger.

(3) A person shall be regarded as competent for the purposes of paragraph (1)(b) where he has sufficient training and experience or knowledge and other qualities to enable him properly to implement the evacuation procedures referred to in that sub-paragraph.

Regulation 8 *(See p 225 for ACOP)*

Information for employees

Every employer shall provide his employees with comprehensible and relevant information on –

(a) the risks to their health and safety identified by the assessment;
(b) the preventive and protective measures;
(c) the procedures referred to in regulation 7(1)(a);
(d) the identity of those persons nominated by him in accordance with regulation 7(1)(b); and
(e) the risks notified to him in accordance with regulation 9(1)(c).

Regulation 9 *(See p 226 for ACOP)*

Co-operation and co-ordination

(1) Where two or more employers share a workplace (whether on a temporary or a permanent basis) each such employer shall –

(a) co-operate with the other employers concerned so far as is necessary to enable them to comply with the requirements and prohibitions imposed upon them by or under the relevant statutory provisions;
(b) (taking into account the nature of his activities) take all reasonable steps to co-ordinate the measures he takes to comply with the requirements and prohibitions imposed upon him by or under the relevant statutory provisions with the measures the other employers concerned are taking to comply with the requirements and prohibitions imposed upon them by or under the relevant statutory provisions; and
(c) take all reasonable steps to inform the other employers concerned of the risks to their employees' health and safety arising out of or in connection with the conduct by him of his undertaking.

(2) Paragraph (1) shall apply to employers sharing a workplace with self-employed persons and to self-employed persons sharing a workplace with other self-employed persons as it applies to employers sharing a workplace with other employers; and the references in that paragraph to employers and the reference in the said paragraph to their employees shall be construed accordingly.

Regulation 10 *(See p 228 for ACOP)*

Persons working in host employers' or self-employed persons' undertaking

(1) Every employer and every self-employed person shall ensure that the employer of any employees from an outside undertaking who are working in his undertaking is provided with comprehensible information on –

(a) the risks to those employees' health and safety arising out of or in connection with the conduct by that first-mentioned employer or by that self-employed person of his undertaking; and

(b) the measures taken by that first-mentioned employer or by that self-employed person in compliance with the requirements and prohibitions imposed upon him by or under the relevant statutory provisions insofar as the said requirements and prohibitions relate to those employees.

(2) Paragraph (1) shall apply to a self-employed person who is working in the undertaking of an employer or a self-employed person as it applies to employees from an outside undertaking who are working therein; and the reference in that paragraph to the employer of any employees from an outside undertaking who are working in the undertaking of an employer or a self-employed person and the reference in the said paragraph to employees from an outside undertaking who are working in the undertaking of an employer or a self-employed person shall be construed accordingly.

(3) Every employer shall ensure that any person working in his undertaking who is not his employee and every self-employed person (not being an employer) shall ensure that any person working in his undertaking is provided with appropriate instructions and comprehensible information regarding any risks to that person's health and safety which arise out of the conduct by that employer or self-employed person of his undertaking.

(4) Every employer shall –

(a) ensure that the employer of any employees from an outside undertaking who are working in his undertaking is provided with sufficient information to enable that second-mentioned employer to identify any person nominated by that first-mentioned employer in accordance with regulation 7(1)(b) to implement evacuation procedures as far as those employees are concerned; and

(b) take all reasonable steps to ensure that any employees from an outside undertaking who are working in his undertaking receive sufficient information to enable them to identify any person nominated by him in accordance with regulation 7(1)(b) to implement evacuation procedures as far as they are concerned.

(5) Paragraph (4) shall apply to a self-employed person who is working in an employer's undertaking as it applies to employees from an outside undertaking who are working therein; and the reference in that paragraph to the employer of any employees from an outside undertaking who are

working in an employer's undertaking and the references in the said paragraph to employees from an outside undertaking who are working in an employer's undertaking shall be construed accordingly.

Regulation 11 *(See p 229 for ACOP)*

Capabilities and training

(1) Every employer shall, in entrusting tasks to his employees, take into account their capabilities as regards health and safety.

(2) Every employer shall ensure that his employees are provided with adequate health and safety training –

(a) on their being recruited into the employer's undertaking; and
(b) on their being exposed to new or increased risks because of –
    (i)   their being transferred or given a change of responsibilities within the employer's undertaking,
    (ii) the introduction of new work equipment into or a change respecting work equipment already in use within the employer's undertaking,
    (iii) the introduction of new technology into the employer's undertaking, or
    (iv) the introduction of a new system of work into or a change respecting a system of work already in use within the employer's undertaking.

(3) The training referred to in paragraph (2) shall –

(a) be repeated periodically where appropriate;
(b) be adapted to take account of any new or changed risks to the health and safety of the employees concerned; and
(c) take place during working hours.

Regulation 12 *(See p 230 for ACOP)*

Employees' duties

(1) Every employee shall use any machinery, equipment, dangerous substance, transport equipment, means of production or safety device provided to him by his employer in accordance both with any training in the use of the equipment concerned which has been received by him and the instructions respecting that use which have been provided to him by the said employer in compliance with the requirements and prohibitions imposed upon that employer by or under the relevant statutory provisions.

(2) Every employee shall inform his employer or any other employee of that employer with specific responsibility for the health and safety of his fellow employees –

(a) of any work situation which a person with the first-mentioned employee's training and instruction would reasonably consider represented a serious and immediate danger to health and safety; and

(b) of any matter which a person with the first-mentioned employee's training and instruction would reasonably consider represented a shortcoming in the employer's protection arrangements for health and safety,

insofar as that situation or matter either affects the health and safety of that first-mentioned employee or arises out of or in connection with his own activities at work, and has not previously been reported to his employer or to any other employee of that employer in accordance with this paragraph.

Regulation 13 *(See p 231 for ACOP)*

Temporary workers

(1) Every employer shall provide any person whom he has employed under a fixed-term contract of employment with comprehensible information on –

(a) any special occupational qualifications or skills required to be held by that employee if he is to carry out his work safely; and
(b) any health surveillance required to be provided to that employee by or under any of the relevant statutory provisions,

and shall provide the said information before the employee concerned commences his duties.

(2) Every employer and every self-employed person shall provide any person employed in an employment business who is to carry out work in his undertaking with comprehensible information on –

(a) any special occupational qualifications or skills required to be held by that employee if he is to carry out his work safely; and
(b) any health surveillance required to be provided to that employee by or under any of the relevant statutory provisions.

(3) Every employer and every self-employed person shall ensure that every person carrying on an employment business whose employees are to carry out work in his undertaking is provided with comprehensible information on –

(a) any special occupational qualifications or skills required to be held by those employees if they are to carry out their work safely; and
(b) the specific features of the jobs to be filled by those employees (insofar as those features are likely to affect their health and safety);

and the person carrying on the employment business concerned shall ensure that the information so provided is given to the said employees.

Regulation 14

Exemption certificates

(1) The Secretary of State for Defence may, in the interests of national security, by a certificate in writing exempt –

(a) any of the home forces, any visiting force or any headquarters from those requirements of these Regulations which impose obligations on employers; or

(b) any member of the home forces, any member of a visiting force or any member of a headquarters from the requirements imposed by regulation 12;

and any exemption such as is specified in sub-paragraph (a) or (b) of this paragraph may be granted subject to conditions and to a limit of time and may be revoked by the said Secretary of State by a further certificate in writing at any time.

(2) In this regulation –

(a) "the home forces" has the same meaning as in section 12(1) of the Visiting Forces Act 1952(a);

(b) "headquarters" has the same meaning as in article 3(2) of the Visiting Forces and International Headquarters (Application of Law) Order 1965(b);

(c) "member of a headquarters" has the same meaning as in paragraph 1(1) of the Schedule to the International Headquarters and Defence Organisations Act 1964(c); and

(d) "visiting force" has the same meaning as it does for the purposes of any provision of Part I of the Visiting Forces Act 1952.

Regulation 15

Exclusion of civil liability

Breach of a duty imposed by these Regulations shall not confer a right of action in any civil proceedings.

Regulation 16

Extension outside Great Britain

(1) These Regulations shall, subject to regulation 2, apply to and in relation to the premises and activities outside Great Britain to which sections 1 to 59 and 80 to 82 of the Health and Safety at Work etc Act 1974 apply by virtue of the Health and Safety at Work etc Act 1974 (Application Outside Great Britain) Order 1989(d) as they apply within Great Britain.

(2) For the purposes of Part I of the 1974 Act, the meaning of "at work" shall be extended so that an employee or a self-employed person shall be treated as being at work throughout the time that he is present at the premises to and in relation to which these Regulations apply by virtue of paragraph (1); and, in that connection, these Regulations shall have effect subject to the extension effected by this paragraph.

Regulation 17

Modification of instrument

The Safety Representatives and Safety Committees Regulations 1977(e) shall be modified to the extent specified in the Schedule to these Regulations.

The Schedule

The following regulation shall be inserted after regulation 4 of the Safety Representatives and Safety Committees Regulations 1977 –

"Employer's duty to consult and provide facilities and assistance
4A. (1) Without prejudice to the generality of section 2(6) of the Health and Safety at Work etc Act 1974, every employer shall consult safety representatives in good time with regard to –

(a) the introduction of any measure at the workplace which may substantially affect the health and safety of the employees the safety representatives concerned represent;
(b) his arrangements for appointing or, as the case may be, nominating persons in accordance with regulations 6(1) and 7(1)(b) of the Management of Health and Safety at Work Regulations 1992;
(c) any health and safety information he is required to provide to the employees the safety representatives concerned represent by or under the relevant statutory provisions;
(d) the planning and organisation of any health and safety training he is required to provide to the employees the safety representatives concerned represent by or under the relevant statutory provisions; and
(e) the health and safety consequences for the employees the safety representatives concerned represent of the introduction (including the planning thereof) of new technologies into the workplace.

(2) Without prejudice to regulations 5 and 6 of these Regulations, every employer shall provide such facilities and assistance as safety representatives may reasonably require for the purpose of carrying out their functions under section 2(4) of the 1974 Act and under these Regulations.".

THE APPROVED CODE OF PRACTICE

Introduction

1 The duties of the Management of Health and Safety at Work Regulations, because of their wide ranging general nature, overlap with many existing regulations. Where duties overlap, compliance with the duty in the more specific regulation will normally be sufficient to comply with the corresponding duty in the Management of Health and Safety at Work Regulations. For example, the Control of Substances Hazardous to Health Regulations (COSHH) require employers and the self-employed to assess the risks arising from exposure to substances hazardous to health. An assessment made for the purposes of the COSHH Regulations will not need to be repeated for the purposes of the Management of Health and Safety at Work Regulations. Other instances where overlap may occur include the appointment of personnel to carry out specific tasks or arrangements for emergencies. However, where the duties in the Management of Health and Safety at Work Regulations go beyond those in the more specific regulations, additional measures will be needed to comply fully with the Management of Health and Safety at Work Regulations.

2 Words or expressions which are defined in the Management of Health and Safety at Work Regulations or in the 1974 Act have the same meaning in this Code unless the context requires otherwise.

Regulation 3

Risk assessment

General principles of risk assessment

3 This Regulation requires all employers and self-employed persons to assess the risks to workers and any others who may be affected by their undertaking. Employers with five or more employees must also record the significant findings of that assessment.

4 Many employers already carry out *de facto* risk assessments on a day-to-day basis during the course of their work; they will note changes in working practice, they will recognise faults as they develop and they will take necessary corrective actions. This Regulation however requires that employers should undertake a systematic general examination of their work activity and that they should record the significant findings of that risk assessment.

5 A risk assessment should usually involve identifying the hazards present in any undertaking (whether arising from work activities or from other factors, eg the layout of the premises) and then evaluating the extent of the risks involved, taking into account whatever precautions are already being taken. In this Approved Code:

(a) a hazard is something with the potential to cause harm (this can include substances or machines, methods of work and other aspects of work organisation);

(b) risk expresses the likelihood that the harm from a particular hazard is realised;

(c) the extent of the risk covers the population which might be affected by a risk; ie the number of people who might be exposed and the consequences for them.

Risk therefore reflects both the likelihood that harm will occur and its severity.

6 In some cases, this detailed approach may not be necessary since all the hazards are known and the risks are readily apparent and can therefore be addressed directly.

Purpose of risk assessment in this Regulation

7 The purpose of the risk assessment is to help the employer or self-employed person to determine what measures should be taken to comply with the employer's or self-employed person's duties under the "relevant statutory provisions". This phrase covers the general duties in the Health and Safety at Work etc Act 1974 and the more specific duties in the various Acts and Regulations (including these Regulations) associated with the HSW Act.

8 Regulation 3 does not itself stipulate the measures to be taken as a result of the risk assessment. The measures in each workplace will derive from compliance with other health and safety duties as described above, taking carefully into account the risk assessment. In essence, the risk assessment guides the judgement of the employer or the self-employed person, as to the measures they ought to take to fulfil their statutory obligations.

Suitable and sufficient

9 A suitable and sufficient risk assessment:

(a) should identify the significant risks arising out of work.

This means focusing on those risks that are liable to arise because of the work activity.

Trivial risks can usually be ignored as can risks arising from routine activities associated with life in general, unless the work activity compounds those risks, or there is evidence of significant relevance to the particular work activity.

Employers and the self-employed are expected to take reasonable steps, eg by reading HSE guidance, the trade press, company or supplier manuals etc to familiarise themselves with the hazards and risks in their work.

(b) should enable the employer or the self-employed person to identify and prioritise the measures that need to be taken to comply with the relevant statutory provisions.

(c) should be appropriate to the nature of the work and such that it remains valid for a reasonable period of time.

This will enable the risk assessment and the significant findings to be used positively by management, eg to change working procedures or to introduce medium to long-term controls.

For relatively static operations, the risk assessment should be such that it is not necessary to repeat it every time someone is exposed to a hazard in comparable circumstances.

For more dynamic activities, ie where the detailed work activity may change fairly frequently or the workplace itself changes and develops (eg on a temporary work site[1] or where the work involves peripatetic workers moving from site to site) the risk assessment might have to concentrate more on the broad range of risks that might arise so that detailed planning and employee training can take account of those risks and enable them to be controlled as and when they arise.

Review and revision

10 The Regulation requires employers and the self-employed to review and, if necessary, modify their risk assessments, since assessment should not be a once-and-for-all activity. The nature of work changes; the appreciation of hazards and risks may develop. Monitoring under the arrangements required by Regulation 4 may reveal near misses or defects in plant. Adverse events may take place even if a suitable and sufficient risk assessment has been made and appropriate preventive and protective measures taken.

11 The employer or self-employed person needs to review the risk of assessment if there are developments that suggest that it may no longer be valid (or that it can be improved). In most cases, it is prudent to plan to review risk assessments at regular intervals – the time between reviews being dependent on the nature of the risks and the degree of change likely in the work activity. Such reviews should form part of standard management practice.

Risk assessment in practice

12 There are no fixed rules about how a risk assessment should be undertaken, although paragraph 16 sets out the general principles that should be followed. The assessment will depend on the nature of the undertaking and the type and extent of the hazards and risks. Above all the process needs to be practical and it should involve management, whether or not advisers or consultants assist with the detail. Employers should ensure that those involved take all reasonable care in carrying out the risk assessment although the assessment would not be expected to cover risks which were not reasonably foreseeable.

13 For small undertakings presenting few or simple hazards a suitable and sufficient risk assessment can be a very straightforward process based on judgement and requiring no specialist skills or complicated techniques.

---

1   Such as a construction site.

At the other extreme, in the case of, for example, complex chemical, large scale mineral extraction, or nuclear plant, it may need to be developed so far as to produce the basis for a complete safety case or report for the plant incorporating such techniques as quantified risk assessment.

14 In many intermediate cases it will not be possible to make a suitable and sufficient assessment without specialist advice in respect of unfamiliar risks, such as those requiring some knowledge of ergonomics or the more complex processes and techniques in the enterprise. And some risks cannot be properly evaluated without the application of modern techniques of measurement.

15 In some cases a single exercise covering all risks in a workplace or activity may be appropriate; in other cases separate assessment exercises for the risks arising from particular operations or groups of hazards may be more effective. But in all cases, it is important that the employer or self-employed person adopts a structured approach to risk assessment.

16 In particular a risk assessment should:

(a) ensure that all relevant risks or hazards are addressed;
  (i) the aim is to identify the significant risks in the workplace. Do not obscure those risks with an excess of information or by concentrating on trivial risks;
  (ii) in most cases, first identify the hazards, ie those aspects of work (eg substances or equipment used, work processes or work organisation) which have the potential to cause harm;
  (iii) if there are specific Acts or Regulations to be complied with, these may help to identify the hazards;
  (iv) assess the risks from the identified hazards; if there are no hazards, there are no risks. Some risks may already be controlled in some way, whether by deliberate measures or by the circumstances in which they are found. The effectiveness of those controls needs to be taken into account in assessing the residual risk;
  (v) be systematic in looking at hazards and risks. For example it may be necessary to look at hazards or risks in groups such as machinery, transport, substances, electrical etc. In other cases, an operation by operation approach may be needed, eg materials in production, dispatch, offices etc;
  (vi) ensure all aspects of the work activity are reviewed.
(b) address what actually happens in the workplace or during the work activity;
  (i) actual practice may differ from the works manual; indeed this is frequently a route whereby risks creep in unnoticed;
  (ii) think about the non-routine operations, eg maintenance of operations, loading and unloading, changes in production cycles;
  (iii) interruptions to the work activity are a frequent cause of accidents. Look at management of such incidents and the procedures to be followed;
(c) ensure that all groups of employees and others who might be affected are considered;

do not forget office staff, night cleaners, maintenance staff, security guards, visitors;

(d) identify groups of workers who might be particularly at risk;
for example young or inexperienced workers; those who work alone; any disabled staff;

(e) take account of existing preventive or precautionary measures;
they may already reduce the risk sufficiently in terms of what needs to be done to comply with relevant statutory provisions. But are they working properly? Does action need to be taken to ensure they are properly maintained?

17 The level of detail in a risk assessment should be broadly proportionate to the risk. The purpose is not to catalogue every trivial hazard; nor is the employer or self-employed person expected to be able to anticipate hazards beyond the limits of current knowledge. A suitable and sufficient risk assessment will reflect what it is reasonably practicable to expect employers to know about the hazards in their workplaces.

18 Where employees of different employers work in the same workplace their respective employers would have to consider risks to their own employees and to the other employer's employees and may have to co-operate to produce an overall risk assessment. Detailed requirements on co-operation and co-ordination are covered by Regulation 9.

19 In some cases employers may make a first rough assessment, to eliminate from consideration those risks on which no further action need be taken. This should also show where a fuller assessment is needed, if appropriate, using more sophisticated techniques. However, care should be taken not to exaggerate the level of sophistication needed. As mentioned above, the use of quantified risk assessment will be needed only in the most extreme cases, and most of those are already identified by specific Regulations.

20 Employers who control a number of similar workplaces containing similar activities may produce a basic 'model' risk assessment reflecting the core hazards and risks associated with these activities. 'Model' assessments may also be developed by trade associations, employers' bodies or other organisations concerned with a particular activity. Such 'model' assessments may be applied by employers or managers at each workplace, but only if they:

(a) satisfy themselves that the 'model' assessment is broadly appropriate to their type of work; and

(b) adapt the 'model' to the detail of their own actual work situations, including any extension necessary to cover hazards and risks not referred to in the 'model'.

Assessment under other Regulations

21 Other Regulations also contain requirements for risk assessment but which are addressed specifically to the hazards and risks that are covered

by those Regulations. An assessment made for the purpose of such Regulations will cover in part the obligation to make assessments under these Regulations. Where employers have already carried out assessments under other Regulations, they need not repeat those assessments so long as they remain valid; but they do need to ensure that all significant risks are covered.

22 Where an employer is assessing a work situation or activity for the first time, a first rough assessment may be particularly useful in identifying those aspects of the work where a more detailed risk assessment may be needed in accordance with other Regulations. The overall risk assessment under this Regulation might then consist of separate risk assessments covering particular duties under other Regulations plus a further risk assessment covering any aspects of the work not covered elsewhere.

Recording

23 While all employers and self-employed persons are required to make a risk assessment, the Regulation also provides that employers with five or more employees must record the significant findings of their risk assessment. This record should represent an effective statement of hazards and risks which then leads management to take the relevant actions to protect health and safety. It needs therefore to be a part of an employer's overall approach to health and safety records or documents such as the record of health and safety arrangements required by Regulation 4 and the written health and safety policy statement required by Section 2(3) of the Health and Safety at Work Act.

24 This record would normally be in writing; however, it could also be recorded by other means, eg electronically, so long as it is retrievable for use by management or for examination, eg by an inspector or a safety representative. The record will often refer to and rely on other documents and records describing procedures and safeguards. In cases of highly hazardous plant which is required by law to present a 'safety case', the safety case documents will frequently incorporate the risk assessment so far as the main processes are concerned, and will probably be referred to as an ancillary document.

25 The significant findings should include:

(a) the significant hazards identified in the assessment. That is, those hazards which might pose serious risk to workers or others who might be affected by the work activity if they were not properly controlled;

(b) the existing control measures in place and the extent to which they control the risks (this need not replicate details of measures more fully described in works manuals etc but could refer to them);

(c) the population which may be affected by these significant risks or hazards, including any groups of employees who are especially at risk.

26 In many cases, employers (or the self-employed) will need to record sufficient detail of the assessment itself, in addition to the significant

findings, so that they can demonstrate (eg to an inspector or to safety representatives) that they have undertaken a suitable and sufficient assessment and also so that if circumstances change the assessment can be readily reviewed and, if necessary, revised. Only in the most straightforward and obvious cases in which the risk assessment can be easily repeated and explained is a record totally unnecessary.

Preventive and protective measures

27 The preventive and protective measures that have to be taken following the risk assessment depend upon the relevant legislation – both the Health and Safety at Work Act and legislation covering particular hazards or sectors of work – and the risk assessment. In deciding upon the measures employers and self-employed should apply the following principles:

(a) it is always best *if possible to avoid a risk altogether*, eg by not using or stocking a particular dangerous substance or article if it is not essential to the business;

(b) *combat risks at source*, rather than by palliative measures. Thus, if the steps are slippery, treating or replacing them is better than providing a warning sign;

(c) *wherever possible, adapt work to the individual* especially as regards the design of workplaces, the choice of work equipment and the choice of working and production methods, with a view in particular to alleviating monotonous work and work at a predetermined work rate. This helps reduce possible adverse effects on health and safety;

(d) *take advantage of technological and technical progress*, which often offers opportunities for improving working methods and making them safer;

(e) risk prevention measures need to *form part of a coherent policy and approach* having the effect of progressively reducing those risks that cannot be prevented or avoided altogether, and which will take account of the way work is to be organised, working conditions, the working environment and any relevant social factors. Health and safety policies required under Section 2(3) of the Health and Safety at Work Act should be prepared and applied by reference to these principles;

(f) *give a priority to those measures which protect the whole workplace* and all those who work there, and so yield the greatest benefit; ie give collective protective measures priority over individual measures;

(g) workers, whether employees or self-employed *need to understand what they need to do*;

(h) the avoidance, prevention and reduction of risks at work needs to be an accepted part of the approach and attitudes at all levels of the organisation and to apply to all its activities, *ie the existence of an active health and safety culture affecting the organisation as a whole needs to be assured.*

Regulation 4

Health and safety arrangements

28 This Regulation in effect requires employers to have arrangements in place to cover health and safety. It should be integrated with the management system for all other purposes. The system in place will depend on the size and nature of the activities of the undertaking but generally will include the following elements which are typical of any other management function:

(a) *Planning*: Adopting a systematic approach which identifies priorities and sets objectives. Whenever possible, risks are eliminated by the careful selection and design of facilities, equipment and processes or minimised by the use of physical control measures.

(b) *Organisation*: Putting in place the necessary structure with the aim of ensuring that there is a progressive improvement in health and safety performance.

(c) *Control*: Ensuring that the decisions for ensuring and promoting health and safety are being implemented as planned.

(d) *Monitoring and review*: Like quality, progressive improvement in health and safety can only be achieved through the constant development of policies, approaches to implementation and techniques of risk control.

29 The Regulation also provides that undertakings with five or more employees should record their arrangements for health and safety. The arrangements recorded should include a list of those competent persons appointed under Regulation 6. As with the risk assessment, this record could form part of the same document containing the health and safety policy required under Section 2(3) of the Health and Safety at Work Act.

Regulation 5

Health surveillance

30 The risk assessment will identify circumstances in which health surveillance is required by specific health and safety regulations (eg COSHH, Asbestos). In addition, health surveillance should be introduced where the assessment shows the following criteria to apply:

(a) there is an identifiable disease or adverse health condition related to the work concerned;

(b) valid techniques are available to detect indications of the disease or condition;

(c) there is a reasonable likelihood that the disease or condition may occur under the particular conditions of work; and

(d) surveillance is likely to further the protection of the health of the employees to be covered.

31 The primary benefit, and therefore the objective, of health surveillance should be to detect adverse health effects at an early stage, thereby enabling

further harm to be prevented. In addition the results of health surveillance can provide a means of:

(a) checking the effectiveness of control measures;
(b) providing feedback on the accuracy of the risk assessment;
(c) identifying and protecting individuals at increased risk.

32 Once it is decided that health surveillance is appropriate, such health surveillance should be maintained during the employee's employment unless the risk to which the worker is exposed and associated health effects are short term. The minimum requirement for health surveillance is the keeping of an individual health record. Where it is appropriate, health surveillance may also involve one or more health surveillance procedures depending on their suitability in the circumstances. Such procedures can include:

(a) inspection of readily detectable conditions by a responsible person acting within the limits of their training and experience;
(b) enquiring about symptoms, inspection and examination by a qualified person such as an Occupational Health Nurse;
(c) medical surveillance, which may include clinical examination and measurements of physiological or psychological effects by an appropriately qualified practitioner;
(d) biological effect monitoring, ie the measurement and assessment of early biological effects such as diminished lung function in exposed workers;
(e) biological monitoring, ie the measurement and assessment of workplace agents or their metabolites either in tissue, secreta, excreta, expired air or any combination of these in exposed workers.

33 The frequency of the use of such methods should be determined either on the basis of suitable general guidance (eg as regards skin inspection for dermal effects) or on the advice of a qualified practitioner; the employees concerned should be given an opportunity to comment on the proposed frequency of such health surveillance procedures and should have access to an appropriately qualified practitioner for advice on surveillance.

Regulation 6

Health and safety assistance

34 Employers must have access to competent help in applying the provisions of health and safety law, including these Regulations and in particular in devising and applying protective measures unless they are competent to undertake the measures without assistance. Appointment of competent persons for this purpose should be included among the arrangements recorded under Regulation 4(2).

35 Employers may appoint one or more of their own employees to do all that is necessary or may enlist help or support from outside the organisation, or they may do both. Employers who are sole traders, or

are members of partnerships, may appoint themselves (or other partners) to carry out health and safety measures, so long as they are competent. Large employers may well appoint a whole department with specific health and safety responsibilities including specialists in such matters as occupational hygiene or safety engineering. In any case where external support is brought in, its activities must be co-ordinated by those appointed by the employer to manage the health and safety measures.

36 External services employed usually will be appointed in an advisory capacity only. They will often be specialists or general consultants on health and safety matters.

37 The appointment of such health and safety assistants, departments or advisers does not absolve the employer from responsibilities for health and safety under the Health and Safety at Work Act and other relevant statutory provisions. It can do no more than give added assurance that these responsibilities will be discharged adequately.

38 Employers are solely responsible for ensuring that those they appoint to assist them with health and safety measures are competent to carry out whatever tasks they are assigned and given adequate information and support. In making their decisions employers should take into account the need for:

(a) a knowledge and understanding of the work involved, the principles of risk assessment and prevention, and current health and safety applications;

(b) the capacity to apply this to the task required by the employer which might include identifying the health and safety problems, assessing the need for action, designing and developing strategies and plans, implementing these strategies and plans, evaluating their effectiveness and promoting and communicating health and safety and welfare advances and practices.

39 Competence in the sense it is used in these Regulations does not necessarily depend on the possession of particular skills or qualifications. Simple situations may require only the following:

(a) an understanding of relevant current best practice;

(b) awareness of the limitations of one's own experience and knowledge; and

(c) the willingness and ability to supplement existing experience and knowledge.

40 The provision of effective health and safety measures in more complex or highly technical situations will call for specific applied knowledge and skills which can be offered by appropriately qualified specialists. In the case of specific knowledge and skills in occupational health and safety, membership of a professional body or similar organisation at an appropriate level and in an appropriate part of health and safety, or possession of an appropriate qualification in health and safety, can help to guide employers. Competence based qualifications accredited by the National Council for Vocational Qualifications and SCOTVEC (the

Scottish Vocational Education Council), which are being developed for most occupations, may also provide a guide.

Regulation 7

Procedures for serious and imminent danger and for danger areas

41 Employers need to establish procedures to be followed by any worker if situations presenting serious and imminent danger were to arise. The aim has to be to set out clear guidance on when employees and others at work should stop work and how they should move to a place of safety. In some cases this will require full evacuation of the workplace. In other cases it might mean some or all of the workforce moving to a safer part of the workplace.

42 The risk assessment should identify the foreseeable events that need to be covered by these procedures. For some employers, fire (and possibly bomb) risks will be the only ones that need to be covered. But even in those cases the nature of the fire risk (eg in which parts of a building, the substances that might be involved etc) may need to be reflected in the detail of the procedures.

43 Many workplaces or work activities will pose additional risks. All employers should consider carefully in their risk assessment whether such additional risks might arise. Where such risks are identified, additional procedures will be needed and those procedures should be geared, as far as is practicable, to the nature of the serious and imminent danger that those risks might pose.

44 The procedures may need to take account of responsibilities of specific employees. Some employees, or groups of employees, may have specific tasks to perform in the event of emergencies (eg to shut down plant that might otherwise compound the danger); some employees may have had training so that they can seek to bring an emergency event under control. The circumstances in which such workers should stop work and move to a place of safety may well be different from those for other workers; the procedures should if necessary reflect these differences.

45 The procedures should set out the role and responsibilities of the competent persons nominated to implement the detailed actions. The procedures should also ensure that employees know who the relevant competent persons are and understand their role.

46 Some specific emergency situations will be covered by certain health and safety regulations. Employers' procedures should reflect any requirements laid on them by such regulations.

47 Procedures should cater for the fact that emergency events can occur and develop rapidly, thus requiring employees to act without waiting for further guidance. The procedures should specify when and how they are to be activated so that employees can proceed in good time to a place of safety. For example, it may be necessary to commence evacuation while attempts to control an emergency (eg a process in danger of running out of control) are still under way, in case those attempts fail.

48 Emergency procedures should normally be written down (eg under Regulation 4(2)), clearly setting out the limits of actions to be taken by employees. Information on the procedures should be made available to all employees (under Regulation 8), to any external health and safety personnel appointed under Regulation 6(1), and, if necessary, to other workers and/or their employers under Regulation 10. They should also form part of induction training under Regulation 11. It may be advisable to carry out exercises to familiarise employees with the procedures (eg the use of alarms etc to initiate action) and to test their effectiveness.

49 Work should not be resumed after an emergency if a serious danger remains. If there are any doubts expert assistance should be sought, eg from the emergency services and others. The occurrence of an emergency may also indicate the need for a review of the risk assessment (paragraphs 8-9). There may, for certain groups of workers, be exceptional circumstances when re-entry to areas of serious danger may be deemed necessary, eg the emergency services where human life is at risk. Where such exceptional circumstances can be anticipated, the procedures should set out the special protective measures to be taken (and the pre-training required) and the steps to be taken for authorisation of such actions.

50 Where different employers (or self-employed persons) share a workplace their separate emergency procedures should take account of others in the workplace and as far as is appropriate should be co-ordinated. Detailed requirements on co-operation and co-ordination are covered by Regulation 9.

Danger areas

51 A danger area is a work environment which must be entered by an employee where the level of risk is unacceptable without special precautions being taken. Such areas are not necessarily static in that minor alterations or an emergency may convert a normal work environment into a danger area. The hazard involved need not occupy the whole area, such as a toxic gas, but can be localised where an employee is likely to come into contact, such as bare live electrical conductors. The area must be restricted to prevent inadvertent access by other employees and other persons.

52 This Regulation does not specify the precautions that should be taken to ensure safe working in the danger area – this is covered by other legislation. However, once the employer has established suitable precautions the relevant employees must receive adequate instruction in those precautions prior to entry into any such danger area.

Regulation 8

Information for employees

53 The risk assessment will help identify information which has to be provided to employees under specific regulations, as well as any further information relevant to risks to employees' health and safety. Relevant

information on risks and on preventive and protective measures will be limited to what employees need to know to ensure their health and safety. The Regulation also requires information to be provided on the emergency arrangements established under Regulation 7, including the identity of staff nominated to assist in the event of evacuation.

54 To be comprehensible, information must be capable of being understood by the employees to whom it is addressed. This should take account of their level of training, knowledge and experience. Special consideration should be given to any employees with language difficulties or with disabilities which may impede their receipt of information. For employees with little or no understanding of English or who cannot read English, employers may need to make special arrangements. These could include providing translation, using interpreters, or in some cases replacing written notices with clearly understood symbols or diagrams.

55 Information can be provided in whatever form is most suitable in the circumstances, so long as it is comprehensible.

56 This Regulation applies to all employees, including trainees and those on fixed-duration contracts. Additional information requirements for employees on fixed-duration contracts are contained in Regulation 13.

Regulation 9

Co-operation and co-ordination

57 Employers and the self-employed have obligations under the Health and Safety at Work Act towards anyone who may be put at risk by their activities. Where the activities of different employers and self-employed people interact, for example where they share premises or workplaces, they may need to co-operate with each other to ensure that their respective obligations are met. This Regulation makes specific the duty to co-operate where employers and the self-employed share a workplace, ie where they have a physical presence on the same worksite.

58 The duties to co-operate and to co-ordinate measures relate to all statutory duties and therefore concern all people who may be at risk, both on and off-site. The specific duty to exchange information relates only to those employees and the self-employed who are at risk on-site, though co-operation on off-site risks may also involve exchanging information. A self-employed contractor carrying out work on an employer's or self-employed person's premises would be regarded as sharing the workplace for the purposes of Regulation 9.

59 Risk assessments under Regulation 3 and subsequent measures (in particular emergency procedures under Regulation 7) may need to cover the workplace as a whole to be fully effective, which will require some degree of co-ordination. The form of co-ordination adopted will depend on the circumstances, but all employers and self-employed involved will need to satisfy themselves that the arrangements adopted are adequate. Employers will also need to ensure that all their employees, but especially the competent persons appointed under Regulations 6 and 7, are aware of

and take full part in the arrangements. In some cases, specific co-ordination arrangements will be required by other regulations.[2]

60 Where a particular employer (eg the main employer) controls the worksite, other employers or self-employed sharing the site should assist the controlling employer in assessing the shared risks and co-ordinating any necessary measures, primarily by providing information. A controlling employer who has established site-wide arrangements will have to inform new minor employers or self-employed so that they can integrate themselves into the arrangements.

Appointment of health and safety co-ordinator

61 Where there is no controlling employer, the employers and self-employed persons present should agree such joint arrangements, such as appointing a health and safety co-ordinator, as are needed to meet the Regulations' requirements. In workplaces where management control is fragmented and employment is largely casual or short-term,[3] appointing a health and safety supervisor or co-ordinator is likely to be the most effective way of ensuring co-ordination and co-operation and the efficient exchange of information. The co-ordinator would be responsible for bringing together the efforts of individual employers and self-employed persons across the workplace. In worksites which are complex or contain significant hazards, the controlling employer or health and safety co-ordinator (on behalf of the employers etc present) may need to seek competent advice in making or assisting with the risk assessment and determining appropriate measures.

Persons in control

62 Even when the person in control of a multi-occupancy workplace is not an employer of persons working in that workplace or self-employed, such persons will nonetheless need to co-operate with those occupying the workplace under their control; for example, procedures for authorising or carrying out repairs and modifications will have to take account of the need for co-operation and exchanges of information. Such co-operation will be needed to carry out effectively the general duties placed on such persons under Section 4 of the Health and Safety at Work Act as well as as more specific duties under certain regulations (eg in offshore health and safety legislation or in relation to welfare facilities provided under the Workplace (Health, Safety and Welfare) Regulations 1992).

63 Where the circumstances in paragraph 59 apply, and there is also a person (who is not an employer on those premises or self-employed) in control of the workplace, then the joint arrangements (including, if

---

2 For example, under regulations which are likely to be made to implement the Temporary and Mobile Construction Sites Directive.
3 In construction, for example.

appropriate, the appointment of a health and safety co-ordinator) will need to be agreed with that person, as well as the employers (or self-employed) present.

64 Where any persons in control of premises make arrangements to co-ordinate health and safety activities, particularly for emergencies, this may be sufficient to enable employers and the self-employed who participate in those arrangements to comply with Regulation 9(1)(b).

65 This Regulation does not apply to multi-occupancy buildings or sites where each unit under the control of an individual tenant employer or self-employed person will be regarded as a separate workplace. In some cases, however, the common parts of such multi-occupancy sites may be shared workplaces (eg a common reception area in an office building) or may be under the control of a person to whom Section 4 of the HSW Act applies (see paragraph 60 above) and suitable arrangements may need to be put in place to cover these areas, including the appointment of a health and safety co-ordinator where appropriate.

Regulation 10

Persons working in host employers' or self-employed persons' undertakings

66 This Regulation applies where employees or self-employed persons carry out work in the undertaking (or business) of an employer other than their own or of another self-employed person. There will be some overlap with Regulation 9 (mainly in the case of some self-employed contractors), for which adequate arrangements established under Regulation 9 should suffice. However, this Regulation does not depend on workplaces being shared. Employers and the self-employed who are sole occupiers may also need to provide comprehensible information to other employers whose employees (or to other self-employed) carry out work, often for a short time, on behalf of the first employers or self-employed, at any place. Such employees would include:

(a) contractors' employees carrying out cleaning, repair, or maintenance under a service contract;

(b) employees in temporary employment businesses hired to work under the first employer's control (additional requirements for information to employment businesses are under Regulation 13).

67 The risk assessment under Regulation 3 will have identified risks to these people. The information provided must include those risks and the health and safety measures in place to address those risks and be sufficient to enable the other employers to identify any person that they (the first employer) have nominated to help with emergency evacuation. The first employer also has a duty to take reasonable steps to ensure that the employees of the second employer have indeed received the latter information.

68 People who visit another employer's premises to carry out work must be provided with appropriate information and instructions regarding

relevant risks to their health and safety. These visitors could be specialists who are better informed than the host employer of the risks normally associated with the tasks which they are to carry out. The host employer's instructions should be concerned with those risks which are peculiar to his activity or premises. The visitors may also introduce risks to the permanent workforce (eg from equipment or substances they may bring with them). Their employers should inform the host employer of such risks, under their general duty under Section 3 of the Health and Safety at Work Act. The risk assessment under Regulation 3(1)(b) should identify the necessary information.

69 The guidance on comprehensibility of information under Regulation 8 (paragraphs 51-54 of this Code) applies equally to information provided under Regulation 10.

Regulation 11

Capabilities and training

70 When allocating work to employees, employers should ensure that the demands of the job do not exceed the employees' ability to carry out the work without risk to themselves or others. Employers should take account of the employees' capabilities and the level of their training, knowledge and experience. If additional training is needed, it should be provided.

Training

71 Training is an important way of achieving competence and helps to convert information into safe working practices. It contributes to the organisation's health and safety culture and is needed at all levels, including top management. The risk assessment will help determine the level of training needed for each type of work as part of the preventive and protective measures. This can include basic skills training, specific on-the-job training and training in health and safety or emergency procedures.

72 Training needs are likely to be greatest on recruitment. New employees should receive basic induction training on health and safety, including arrangements for first-aid, fire and evacuation. Particular attention should be given to the needs of young workers. The risk assessment should indicate further specific training needs. In some cases, training may be required even though an employee already holds formal qualifications.

73 Changes in an employee's work environment may cause them to be exposed to new or increased risks, requiring further training. The need for further training should be considered when:

(a) employees transfer or take on new responsibilities. There may be a change in the work activity or in the work environment;

(b) there is a change in the work equipment or systems of work in use. A significant change is likely to need a review and re-assessment of risks, which may indicate additional training needs. If the change includes introducing completely new technology, it may bring with it new and unfamiliar risks. Competent outside advice may be needed.

Refresher training

74 An employee's competence will decline if skills (eg in emergency procedures) are not used regularly. Training therefore needs to be repeated periodically to ensure continued competence. Information from personal performance monitoring, health and safety checks, accident investigations and near miss incidents can help to establish a suitable period for re-training. Special attention should be given to employees who occasionally deputise for others. Their skills are likely to be under-developed and they may need more frequent refresher training.

Adaptation/working hours

75 Changes in risks may also require changes in the content of training, eg where new procedures have been introduced. Health and safety training should take place during working hours. If it is necessary to arrange training outside an employee's normal hours, this should be treated as an extension of time at work.

Regulation 12

Employees' duties

76 Employees have a duty under Section 7 of the Health and Safety at Work etc Act 1974 to take reasonable care for their own health and safety and of that of others who may be affected by their acts or omissions at work. Towards this end, employees should use correctly all work items provided by their employer, in accordance with their training and the instructions they receive to enable them to use the items safely.

77 Employees' duties under Section 7 also include co-operating with their employer to enable the employer to comply with statutory duties for health and safety. Employers or those they appoint (eg under Regulation 6) to assist them with health and safety matters therefore need to be informed without delay of any work situation which might present a serious and imminent danger. The danger could be to the employee concerned or, if it results from the employee's work, to others. Employees should also notify any shortcomings in the health and safety arrangements even when no immediate danger exists, so that employers in pursuit of their duties under the HSW Act and other statutory provisions can take such remedial action as may be needed.

78 The duties placed on employees do not reduce the responsibility of the employer to comply with duties under these Regulations and the other relevant statutory provisions. In particular, employers need to ensure that employees receive adequate instruction and training to enable them to comply with their duties under this Regulation.

Regulation 13

Temporary workers

79 This Regulation supplements previous regulations requiring the provision of information with additional requirements on temporary workers (ie those employed on fixed-duration contracts and those employed in employment businesses, but working under the control of a user company). The use of temporary workers will also have been notified to health and safety personnel under Regulation 6(6), where necessary for the personnel to be able to carry out their functions.

Fixed-duration contracts

80 Regulation 8 deals with the provisions of information by employers to their employees. This includes those on fixed-duration contracts. Under Regulation 13(1), employees on fixed-duration contracts also have to be informed of any special occupational qualifications or skills required to carry out the work safely and whether the job is subject to statutory health surveillance (the latter being in any case a protective measure covered in general by Regulation 8(b)).

Employment businesses

81 Regulation 10(4) deals with the provision of information by employers to other employers whose employees are working in the first employer's undertaking. This includes employees of persons carrying on an employment business. Under Regulation 13(3), employment businesses also have to be informed of any special occupational qualifications or skills required to carry out the work safely and the specific features of the job which might affect health and safety (eg work at heights).

82 Both the person carrying on the employment business and the user employer have duties to provide information to the employee. The person carrying on the employment business has a duty under Regulation 8 (as an employer) and a duty under Regulation 13(3) to ensure that the information provided by the user employer is given to the employee. The user employer has a duty under Regulation 10(4) to check that information provided to an employer (including someone carrying on an employment business) is received by the employee. In addition, Regulations 13(1) and (2) require information on qualifications, skills and health surveillance to be provided directly to employees in an employment business.

83 These duties overlap to ensure that the information needs of those working for, but not employed by, user employers are not overlooked. User employers and persons carrying on employment businesses should therefore make suitable arrangements to satisfy themselves that information is provided. In most cases, it may be sufficient for information to be provided directly to employees by user employers, who will know the risks and preventive measures in their workplaces. Those carrying on employment businesses will need to satisfy themselves that arrangements for this

are adequate. However, basic information on job demands and risks should be supplied to the employment business at an early stage to help select those most suitable to carry out the work (in accordance with Regulation 13(3)).

Self-employed

84 The self-employed have similar duties under Regulations 9(2) and 10 and Regulations 13(2) and 13(3) to inform employment businesses and the employees of employment businesses who carry out work in their undertakings. They may also need to agree arrangements with the employment business concerned. Self-employed workers hired through employment businesses are entitled to receive health and safety information from the employers or self-employed for whom they carry out work under Regulation 10(2).

Appendix 2

Workplace (Health, Safety and Welfare) Regulations 1992

THE REGULATIONS

Regulation 1 *(See p 250 for ACOP)*

Citation and commencement

(1) These Regulations may be cited as the Workplace (Health, Safety and Welfare) Regulations 1992.

(2) Subject to paragraph (3), these Regulations shall come into force on 1 January 1993.

(3) Regulations 5 to 27, and the Schedules shall come into force on 1 January 1996 with respect to any workplace or part of a workplace which is not –

(a) a new workplace; or
(b) a modification, an extension or a conversion.

Regulation 2 *(See p 250 for ACOP)*

Interpretation

(1) In these Regulations, unless the context otherwise requires –

'new workplace" means a workplace used for the first time as a workplace after 31 December 1992;

'public road" means (in England and Wales) a highway maintainable at public expense within the meaning of section 329 of the Highways Act 1980 and (in Scotland) a public road within the meaning assigned to that term by section 151 of the Roads (Scotland) Act 1984;

'traffic route" means a route for pedestrian traffic, vehicles or both and includes any stairs, staircase, fixed ladder, doorway, gateway, loading bay or ramp;

'workplace" means, subject to paragraphs (2) and (3), any premises or part of premises which are not domestic premises and are made available to any person as a place of work, and includes –

(a) any place within the premises to which such person has access while at work; and
(b) any room, lobby, corridor, staircase, road or other place used as a means of access to or egress from the workplace or where facilities are provided for use in connection with the workplace other than a public road.

(2) A modification, an extension or a conversion shall not be a workplace or form part of a workplace until the modification, extension or conversion is complete.

(3) Any reference in these Regulations to a modification, an extension or a conversion is a reference, as the case may be, to a modification, an extension or a conversion of a workplace started after 31 December 1992.

(4) Any requirement that anything done or provided in pursuance of these Regulations shall be suitable shall be construed to include a requirement that it is suitable for any person in respect of whom such thing is so done or provided.

(5) Any reference in these Regulations to –

(a) a numbered regulation or Schedule is a reference to the regulation or Schedule to these Regulations so numbered; and
(b) a numbered paragraph is a reference to the paragraph so numbered in the regulation in which the reference appears.

Regulation 3 *(See p 251 for ACOP)*

Application of these Regulations

(1) These Regulations apply to every workplace but shall not apply to –

(a) a workplace which is or is in or on a ship within the meaning assigned to that word by regulation 2(1) of the Docks Regulations 1988;
(b) a workplace where the only activities being undertaken are building operations or works of engineering construction within, in either case, section 176 of the Factories Act 1961 and activities for the purpose of or in connection with those activities;
(c) a workplace where the only activities being undertaken are the exploration for or extraction of mineral resources; or
(d) a workplace which is situated in the immediate vicinity of another workplace or intended workplace where exploration for or extraction of mineral resources is being or will be undertaken, and where the only activities being undertaken are activities preparatory to, for the purposes of, or in connection with such exploration for or extraction of mineral resources at that other workplace.

(2) In their application to temporary work sites, any requirement to ensure a workplace complies with any of regulations 20 to 25 shall have effect as a requirement to so ensure so far as is reasonably practicable.

(3) As respects any workplace which is or is in or on an aircraft, locomotive or rolling stock, trailer or semi-trailer used as a means of

transport or a vehicle for which a licence is in force under the Vehicles (Excise) Act 1971 or a vehicle exempted from duty under that Act –

(a) regulations 5 to 12 and 14 to 25 shall not apply to any such workplace; and

(b) regulation 13 shall apply to any such workplace only when the aircraft, locomotive or rolling stock, trailer or semi-trailer or vehicle is stationary inside a workplace and, in the case of a vehicle for which a licence is in force under the Vehicles (Excise) Act 1971, is not on a public road.

(4) As respects any workplace which is in fields, woods or other land forming part of an agricultural or forestry undertaking but which is not inside a building and is situated away from the undertaking's main buildings –

(a) regulations 5 to 19 and 23 to 25 shall not apply to any such workplace; and

(b) any requirement to ensure that any such workplace complies with any of regulations 20 to 22 shall have effect as a requirement to so ensure so far as is reasonably practicable.

Regulation 4 *(See p 252 for ACOP)*

Requirements under these Regulations

(1) Every employer shall ensure that every workplace, modification, extension or conversion which is under his control and where any of his employees work complies with any requirement of these Regulations which –

(a) applies to that workplace or, as the case may be, to the workplace which contains that modification, extension or conversion; and

(b) is in force in respect of the workplace, modification, extension or conversion.

(2) Subject to paragraph (4), every person who has, to any extent, control of a workplace, modification, an extension or a conversion shall ensure that such workplace, modification, extension or conversion complies with any requirement of these Regulations which –

(a) applies to that workplace or, as the case may be, to the workplace which contains that modification, extension or conversion;

(b) is in force in respect of the workplace, modification, extension, or conversion; and

(c) relates to matters within that person's control.

(3) Any reference in this regulation to a person having control of any workplace, modification, extension or conversion is a reference to a person having control of the workplace, modification, extension or conversion in connection with the carrying on by him of a trade, business or other undertaking (whether for profit or not).

(4) Paragraph (2) shall not impose any requirement upon a self-employed person in respect of his own work or the work of any partner of his in the undertaking.

(5) Every person who is deemed to be the occupier of a factory by virtue of section 175(5) of the Factories Act 1961 shall ensure that the premises which are so deemed to be a factory comply with these Regulations.

Regulation 5 *(See p 253 for ACOP)*

Maintenance of workplace, and of equipment, devices and systems

(1) The workplace and the equipment, devices and systems to which this regulation applies shall be maintained (including cleaned as appropriate) in an efficient state, in efficient working order and in good repair.

(2) Where appropriate, the equipment, devices and systems to which this regulation applies shall be subject to a suitable system of maintenance.

(3) The equipment, devices and systems to which this regulation applies are –

(a) equipment and devices a fault in which is liable to result in a failure to comply with any of these Regulations; and
(b) mechanical ventilation systems provided pursuant to regulation 6 (whether or not they include equipment or devices within sub-paragraph (a) of this paragraph).

Regulation 6 *(See p 254 for ACOP)*

Ventilation

(1) Effective and suitable provision shall be made to ensure that every enclosed workplace is ventilated by a sufficient quantity of fresh or purified air.

(2) Any plant used for the purpose of complying with paragraph (1) shall include an effective device to give visible or audible warning of any failure of the plant where necessary for reasons of health or safety.

(3) This regulation shall not apply to any enclosed workplace or part of a workplace which is subject to the provisions of –

(a) section 30 of the Factories Act 1961;
(b) regulations 49 to 52 of the Shipbuilding and Ship-Repairing Regulations 1960;
(c) regulation 21 of the Construction (General Provisions) Regulations 1961;
(d) regulation 18 of the Docks Regulations 1988.

Regulation 7 *(See p 256 for ACOP)*

Temperature in indoor workplaces

(1) During working hours, the temperature in all workplaces inside buildings shall be reasonable.

(2) A method of heating or cooling shall not be used which results in the escape into a workplace of fumes, gas or vapour of such character and to such extent that they are likely to be injurious or offensive to any person.

(3) A sufficient number of thermometers shall be provided to enable persons at work to determine the temperature in any workplace inside a building.

Regulation 8 *(See p 258 for ACOP)*

Lighting

(1) Every workplace shall have suitable and sufficient lighting.

(2) The lighting mentioned in paragraph (1) shall, so far as is reasonably practicable, be by natural light.

(3) Without prejudice to the generality of paragraph (1), suitable and sufficient emergency lighting shall be provided in any room in circumstances in which persons at work are specially exposed to danger in the event of failure of artificial lighting.

Regulation 9 *(See p 259 for ACOP)*

Cleanliness and waste materials

(1) Every workplace and the furniture, furnishings and fittings therein shall be kept sufficiently clean.

(2) The surfaces of the floor, wall and ceiling of all workplaces inside buildings shall be capable of being kept sufficiently clean.

(3) So far as is reasonably practicable, waste materials shall not be allowed to accumulate in a workplace except in suitable receptacles.

Regulation 10 *(See p 260 for ACOP)*

Room dimensions and space

(1) Every room where persons work shall have sufficient floor area, height and unoccupied space for purposes of health, safety and welfare.

(2) It shall be sufficient compliance with this regulation in a workplace which is not a new workplace, conversion or extension and which, immediately before this regulation came into force in respect of it, was subject to the provisions of the Factories Act 1961 if the workplace does not contravene Part I of Schedule 1.

Regulation 11 *(See p 261 for ACOP)*

Workstations and seating

(1) Every workstation shall be so arranged that it is suitable both for any person at work in the workplace who is likely to work at that workstation and for any work of the undertaking which is likely to be done there.

(2) Without prejudice to the generality of paragraph (1), every workstation outdoors shall be so arranged that –

(a) so far as is reasonably practicable, it provides protection from adverse weather;
(b) it enables any person at the workstation to leave it swiftly or, as appropriate, to be assisted in the event of an emergency; and
(c) it ensures that any person at the workstation is not likely to slip or fall.

(3) A suitable seat shall be provided for each person at work in the workplace whose work includes operations of a kind that the work (or a substantial part of it) can or must be done sitting.

(4) A seat shall not be suitable for the purposes of paragraph (3) unless –

(a) it is suitable for the person for whom it is provided as well as for the operations to be performed; and
(b) a suitable footrest is also provided where necessary.

Regulation 12 *(See p 262 for ACOP)*

Condition of floors and traffic routes

(1) Every floor in a workplace and the surface of every traffic route in a workplace shall be of a construction such that the floor or surface of the traffic route is suitable for the purpose for which it is used.

(2) Without prejudice to the generality of paragraph (1), the requirements in that paragraph shall include requirements that –

(a) the floor, or surface of the traffic route, shall have no hole or slope, or be uneven or slippery so as, in each case, to expose any person to a risk to his health or safety;
(b) every such floor shall have effective means of drainage where necessary.

(3) So far as is reasonably practicable, every floor in a workplace and the surface of every traffic route in a workplace shall be kept free from obstructions and from any article or substance which may cause a person to slip, trip or fall;

(4) In considering whether for the purposes of paragraph (2)(a) a hole or slope exposes any person to a risk to his health or safety –

(a) no account shall be taken of a hole where adequate measures have been taken to prevent a person falling;
(b) account shall be taken of any handrail provided in connection with any slope.

(5) Suitable and sufficient handrails and, if appropriate, guards shall be provided on all traffic routes which are staircases except in circumstances in which a handrail can not be provided without obstructing the traffic route.

Regulation 13 *(See p 264 for ACOP)*

Falls or falling objects

(1) So far as is reasonably practicable, suitable and effective measures shall be taken to prevent any event specified in paragraph (3).

(2) So far as is reasonably practicable, the measures required by paragraph (1) shall be measures other than the provision of personal protective equipment, information, instruction, training or supervision.

(3) The events mentioned in this paragraph are –

(a) any person falling a distance likely to cause personal injury;
(b) any person being struck by a falling object likely to cause personal injury.

(4) Any area where there is a risk to health or safety from any event mentioned in paragraph (3) shall be clearly indicated where appropriate.

(5) So far as is practicable, every tank, pit or structure where there is a risk of a person in the workplace falling into a dangerous substance in the tank, pit or structure, shall be securely covered or fenced.

(6) Every traffic route over, across or in an uncovered tank, pit or structure such as is mentioned in paragraph (5) shall be securely fenced.

(7) In this Regulation, "dangerous substance" means –

(a) any substance likely to scald or burn;
(b) any poisonous substance;
(c) any corrosive substance;
(d) any fume, gas or vapour likely to overcome a person; or
(e) any granular or free-flowing solid substance, or any viscous substance which, in any case, is of a nature or quantity which is likely to cause danger to any person.

Regulation 14 *(See p 269 for ACOP)*

Windows, and transparent or translucent doors, gates and walls

(1) Every window or other transparent or translucent surface in a wall or partition and every transparent or translucent surface in a door or gate shall, where necessary for reasons of health or safety –

(a) be of safety material or be protected against breakage of the transparent or translucent material; and
(b) be appropriately marked or incorporate features so as, in either case, to make it apparent.

Regulation 15 *(See p 270 for ACOP)*

Windows, skylights and ventilators

(1) No window, skylight or ventilator which is capable of being opened shall be likely to be opened, closed or adjusted in a manner which exposes any person performing such operation to a risk to his health or safety.

(2) No window, skylight or ventilator shall be in a position when open which is likely to expose any person in the workplace to a risk to his health or safety.

Regulation 16 *(See p 270 for ACOP)*

Ability to clean windows etc safely

(1) All windows and skylights in a workplace shall be of a design or be so constructed that they may be cleaned safely.

(2) In considering whether a window or skylight is of a design or so constructed as to comply with paragraph (1), account may be taken of equipment used in conjunction with the window or skylight or of devices fitted to the building.

Regulation 17 *(See p 271 for ACOP)*

Organisation etc of traffic routes

(1) Every workplace shall be organised in such a way that pedestrians and vehicles can circulate in a safe manner.

(2) Traffic routes in a workplace shall be suitable for the persons or vehicles using them, sufficient in number, in suitable positions and of sufficient size.

(3) Without prejudice to the generality of paragraph (2), traffic routes shall not satisfy the requirements of that paragraph unless suitable measures are taken to ensure that –

(a) pedestrians or, as the case may be, vehicles may use a traffic route without causing danger to the health or safety of persons at work near it; and

(b) there is sufficient separation of any traffic route for vehicles from doors or gates or from traffic routes for pedestrians which lead onto it;

(c) where vehicles and pedestrians use the same traffic route, there is sufficient separation between them.

(4) All traffic routes shall be suitably indicated where necessary for reasons of health or safety.

(5) Paragraph (2) shall apply so far as is reasonably practicable, to a workplace which is not a new workplace, a modification, an extension or a conversion.

Regulation 18 *(See p 274 for ACOP)*

Doors and gates

(1) Doors and gates shall be suitably constructed (including being fitted with any necessary safety devices).

(2) Without prejudice to the generality of paragraph (1), doors and gates shall not comply with that paragraph unless –

(a) any sliding door or gate has a device to prevent it coming off its track during use;
(b) any upward opening door or gate has a device to prevent it falling back;
(c) any powered door or gate has suitable and effective features to prevent it causing injury by trapping any person;
(d) where necessary for reasons of health or safety, any powered door or gate can be operated manually unless it opens automatically if the power fails; and
(e) any door or gate which is capable of opening by being pushed from either side is of such a construction as to provide, when closed, a clear view of the space close to both sides.

Regulation 19 *(See p 275 for ACOP)*

Escalators and moving walkways

(1) Escalators and moving walkways shall –

(a) function safely;
(b) be equipped with any necessary safety devices;
(c) be fitted with one or more emergency stop control which is easily identifiable and readily accessible.

Regulation 20

Sanitary conveniences

(1) Suitable and sufficient sanitary conveniences shall be provided at readily accessible places.

(2) Without prejudice to the generality of paragraph (1), sanitary conveniences shall not be suitable unless –

(a) the rooms containing them are adequately ventilated and lit;
(b) they and the rooms containing them are kept in a clean and orderly condition; and
(c) separate rooms containing conveniences are provided for men and women, except where and so far as each convenience is in a separate room the door of which is capable of being secured from inside.

(3) It shall be sufficient compliance with the requirement in paragraph (1) to provide sufficient sanitary conveniences in a workplace which is not a new workplace, an extension or a conversion and which, immediately before this regulation came into force in respect of it, was subject to the provisions of the Factories Act 1961 if sanitary conveniences are provided in accordance with Part II of Schedule 1.

Regulation 21 *(See p 275 for ACOP)*

Washing facilities

(1) Suitable and sufficient washing facilities, including showers if required by the nature of the work or for health reasons, shall be provided at readily accessible places.

(2) Without prejudice to the generality of paragraph (1), washing facilities shall not be suitable unless –

(a) they are provided in the immediate vicinity of every sanitary convenience, whether or not provided elsewhere as well;

(b) they are provided in the vicinity of any changing rooms required by these regulations, whether or not provided elsewhere as well;

(c) they include a supply of clean hot and cold, or warm, water (which shall be running water so far as is practicable);

(d) they include soap or other suitable means of cleaning;

(e) they include towels or other suitable means of drying;

(f) the rooms containing them are sufficiently ventilated and lit;

(g) they and the rooms containing them are kept in a clean and orderly condition; and

(h) separate facilities are provided for men and women, except where and so far as they are provided in a room the door of which is capable of being secured from inside and the facilities in each such room are intended to be used by one person at a time.

(3) Paragraph (2)(h) shall not apply to facilities which are provided for washing the hands, forearms and face only.

Regulation 22 *(See p 278 for ACOP)*

Drinking water

(1) An adequate supply of wholesome drinking water shall be provided for all persons at work in the workplace.

(2) Every supply of drinking water required by paragraph (1) shall –

(a) be readily accessible at suitable places; and

(b) be conspicuously marked by an appropriate sign where necessary for reasons of health or safety.

(3) Where a supply of drinking water is required by paragraph (1), there shall also be provided a sufficient number of suitable cups or other drinking vessels unless the supply of drinking water is in a jet from which persons can drink easily.

Regulation 23 *(See p 279 for ACOP)*

Accommodation for clothing

(1) Suitable and sufficient accommodation shall be provided –

(a) for any person at work's own clothing which is not worn during working hours; and
(b) for special clothing which is worn by any person at work but which is not taken home.

(2) Without prejudice to the generality of paragraph (1) the accommodation mentioned in that paragraph shall not be suitable unless –

(a) where facilities to change clothing are required by regulation 24, it provides suitable security for the clothing mentioned in paragraph (1)(a);
(b) where necessary to avoid risks to health or damage to the clothing, it includes separate accommodation for clothing worn at work and for other clothing;
(c) so far as is reasonably practicable, it allows or includes facilities for drying clothing; and
(d) it is in a suitable location.

Regulation 24 *(See p 279 for ACOP)*

Facilities for changing clothing

(1) Suitable and sufficient facilities shall be provided for any person at work in the workplace to change clothing in all cases where –

(a) the person has to wear special clothing for the purpose of work; and
(b) the person can not, for reasons of health or propriety, be expected to change in another room.

(2) Without prejudice to the generality of paragraph (1), the facilities mentioned in that paragraph shall not be suitable unless they include separate facilities for, or separate use of facilities by, men and women where necessary for reasons of propriety.

Regulation 25 *(See p 280 for ACOP)*

Facilities for rest and to eat meals

(1) Suitable and sufficient rest facilities shall be provided at readily accessible places.
(2) Rest facilities provided by virtue of paragraph (1) shall –

(a) where necessary for reasons of health or safety include, in the case of a new workplace, extension or conversion, rest facilities provided in one or more rest rooms, or, in other cases, in rest rooms or rest areas;
(b) include suitable facilities to eat meals where food eaten in the workplace would otherwise be likely to become contaminated.

(3) Rest rooms and rest areas shall include suitable arrangements to protect non-smokers from discomfort caused by tobacco smoke.
(4) Suitable facilities shall be provided for any person at work who is a pregnant woman or nursing mother to rest.

(5) Suitable and sufficient facilities shall be provided for persons at work to eat meals where meals are regularly eaten in the workplace.

Regulation 26

Exemption certificates

(1) The Secretary of State for Defence may, in the interests of national security, by a certificate in writing exempt any of the home forces, any visiting force or any headquarters from the requirements of these Regulations and any exemption may be granted subject to conditions and to a limit of time and may be revoked by the said Secretary of State by a further certificate in writing at any time.

(2) In this Regulation –

(a) "the home forces" has the same meaning as in section 12(1) of the Visiting Forces Act 1952;
(b) "headquarters" has the same meaning as in article 3(2) of the Visiting Forces and International Headquarters (Application of Law) Order 1965;
(c) "visiting force" has the same meaning as it does for the purposes of any provision of Part I of the Visiting Forces Act 1952.

Regulation 27

Repeals, saving and revocations

(1) The enactments mentioned in Part I of Schedule 2 are repealed to the extent specified in column 3 of that Part.

(2) Nothing in this regulation shall affect the operation of any provision of the Offices, Shops and Railway Premises Act 1963 as that provision has effect by virtue of section 90(4) of that Act.

(3) The instruments mentioned in Part II of Schedule 2 are revoked to the extent specified in column 3 of that Part.

Schedule 1

Regulations 10 and 20

Provisions applicable to factories which are not new workplaces, extensions or conversions

Part I – Space

1 No room in the workplace shall be so overcrowded as to cause risk to the health or safety of persons at work in it.

2 Without prejudice to the generality of paragraph 1 the number of persons employed at a time in any workroom shall not be such that the amount of cubic space allowed for each is less than 11 cubic metres.

3 In calculating, for the purposes of this Part, the amount of cubic space in any room no space more than 4.2 metres from the floor shall be taken into account and, where a room contains a gallery, the gallery shall be treated for the purposes of this Schedule as if it were part-itioned off from the remainder of the room and formed a separate room.

Part II – Number of sanitary conveniences

4 In workplaces where females work, there shall be at least one suitable water closet for use by females only for every 25 females.

5 In workplaces where males work, there shall be at least one suitable water closet for use by males only for every 25 males.

6 In calculating the number of males or females who work in any workplace for the purposes of this Part of this Schedule, any number not itself divisible by 25 without fraction or remainder shall be treated as the next number higher than it which is so divisible.

Schedule 2

Regulation 27

Repeals and revocations

Part I – Repeals

1 *Chapter*	2 *Short title*	3 *Extent of repeal*
1961 c.34	The Factories Act 1961	Sections 1 to 7, 18, 28, 29, 57 to 60 and 69
1963 c.41	The Offices. Shops and Railway Premises Act 1963	Sections 4 to 16
1956 c.49	The Agriculture (Safety, Health and Welfare Provisions) Act 1956	Sections 3 and 5 and, in section 25, sub-sections (3) and (6)

Part II – Revocations

(1) *Title*	(2) *Reference*	(3) *Extent of revocation*
The Flax and Tow Spinning and Weaving Regulations 1906	S.R. & O. 1906/177 amended by S.I. 1988/ 1657	Regulation 3 8, 10, 11 and 14

(1) Title	(2) Reference	(3) Extent of revocation
The Hemp Spinning and Weaving Regulations 1907	S.R. & O. 1907/660, amended by S.I. 1988/1657	Regulations 3 to 5 and 8
Order dated 5 October 1917 (the Tin or Terne Plates Manufacture Welfare Order 1917)	S.R. & O. 1917/1035	The whole Order
Order dated 15 May 1918 (the Glass Bottle, etc. Manufacture Welfare Order 1918)	S.R. & O. 1918/558	The whole Order
Order dated 15 August 1919 (the Fruit Preserving Welfare Order 1919)	S.R. & O. 1919/1136, amended by S.I. 1988/1657	The whole Order
Order dated 23 April 1920 (the Laundries Welfare Order 1920)	S.R. & O. 1920/654	The whole Order
Order dated 28 July 1920 (the Gut Scraping, Tripe Dressing, etc. Welfare Order 1920)	S.R. & O. 1920/1437	The whole Order
Order dated 9 September 1920 (the)Herring Curing (Norfolk and Suffolk) Welfare Order 1920)	S.R. & O. 1920/1662	The whole Order
Order dated 3 March 1921 (the Glass Bevelling Welfare Order 1921)	S.R. & O. 1921/288	The whole Order
The Herring Curing (Scotland) Welfare Order 1926	S.R. & O. 1926/535 (S.24)	The whole Order
The Herring Curing Welfare Order 1927	S.R. & O. 1927/813, amended by S.I. 1960/1690 and 917	The whole Order
The Sacks (Cleaning and Repairing) Welfare Order 1927	S.R. & O. 1927/860	The whole Order

(1) *Title*	(2) *Reference*	(3) *Extent of revocation*
The Horizontal Milling Machines Regulations 1928	S.R. & O. 1928/548	The whole Regulations
The Cotton Cloth Factories Regulations 1929	S.I. 1929/300	Regulations 5 to 10, 11 and 12
The Oil Cake Welfare Order 1929	S.R. & O. 1929/534	Articles 3 to 6
The Cement Works Welfare Order 1930	S.R. & O. 1930/94	The whole Order
The Tanning Welfare Order 1930	S.R.&O. 1930/312	The whole Order
The Kiers Regulations 1938	S.R. & O. 1938/106 amended by S.I. 1981/1152	Regulations 12 to 15
The Sanitary Accommodation Regulations 1938	S.R.& O. 1938/611	The whole Regulations
The Clay Works (Welfare) Special Regulations 1948	S.I. 1948/1547	Regulations 3, 4, 6, 8 and 9
The Jute (Safety, Health and Welfare) Regulations 1948	S.I. 1948/1696. amended by S.I. 1988/1657	Regulations 11, 13, 14 to 16 and 19 to 26
The Pottery (Health and Welfare) Special Regulations 1950	S.I. 1950/65, amended by S.I. 1963/879, 1973/36, 1980/1248. 1982/877, 1988/1657, 1989/2311 and 1990/305	Regulation 15
The Iron and Steel Foundries Regulations 1953	S.I. 1953/1464, amended by S.I. 1974/1681 and 1981/1332	The whole Regulations
The Washing Facilities (Running Water) Exemption Regulations 1960	S.I. 1960/1029	The whole Regulations
The Washing Facilities (Miscellaneous Industries) Regulations 1960	S.I. 1960/1214	The whole Regulations

(1) *Title*	(2) *Reference*	(3) *Extent of revocation*
The Factories (Cleanliness of Walls and Ceilings) Order 1960	S.I. 1960/1794, amended by S.I. 1974/427	The whole Order
The Non-ferrous Metals (Melting and Founding) Regulations 1962	S.I. 1962/1667. amended by S.I. 1974/1681, 1981/1332 and 1988/165	Regulations 5, 6 to 10. 14 to 17 and 20
The Offices, Shops and Railway Premises Act 1963 (Exemption No. 1) Order 1964	S.I. 1964/964	The whole Order
The Washing Facilities Regulations 1964	S.I. 1964/965	The whole Regulations
The Sanitary Conveniences Regulations 1964	S.I. 1964/966, amended by S.I. 1982/827	The whole Regulations
The Offices, Shops and Railway Premises Act 1963 (Exemption No. 7) Order 1968	S.I. 1968/1947, amended by S.I. 1982/827	The whole Order
The Abrasive Wheels Regulations 1970	S.I. 1970/535	Regulation 17
The Sanitary Accommodation (Amendment) Regulations 1974	S.I. 1974/426	The whole Regulations
The Factories (Cleanliness of Walls and Ceilings) (Amendment) Regulations 1974	S.I. 1974/427	The whole Regulations
The Woodworking Machines Regulations 1974	S.I. 1974/903, amended by S.I. 1978/1126	Regulations 10 to 12

(1) *Title*	(2) *Reference*	(3) *Extent of revocation*
The Offices, Shops and Railway Premises Act 1963 etc. (Metrication) Regulations 1982	S.I. 1982/827	The whole Regulations

THE APPROVED CODE OF PRACTICE

Regulation 1

Citation and commencement

1 The Regulations come into effect in two stages. Workplaces which are used for the first time after 31 December 1992, and modifications, extensions and conversions started after that date, should comply as soon as they are in use. In existing workplaces (apart from any modifications) the Regulations take effect on 1 January 1996 and the laws in Schedule 2 will continue to apply until that date.

Regulation 2

Interpretation

2 These Regulations apply to a very wide range of workplaces, not only factories, shops and offices but, for example, schools, hospitals, hotels and places of entertainment. The term workplace also includes the common parts of shared buildings, private roads and paths on industrial estates and business parks, and temporary work sites (but not construction sites).

3 'Workplace' is defined in regulation 2(1). Certain words in the definition are themselves defined in sections 52 and 53 of the Health and Safety at Work etc Act 1974. In brief:

'Work' means work as an employee or self-employed person, and also:

(a) work experience on certain training schemes (Health and Safety (Training for Employment) Regulations 1990 No 138 regulation 3);

(b) training which includes operations involving ionising radiations (Ionising Radiations Regulations 1985 No 1333 regulation 2(1));

(c) activities involving genetic manipulation (Genetic Manipulation Regulations 1989 No 1810 regulation 3); and

(d) work involving the keeping and handling of a listed pathogen (Health and Safety (Dangerous Pathogens) Regulations 1981, S.I. 1981 No 1011 regulation 9).

'Premises' means any place (including an outdoor place).

'Domestic Premises' means a private dwelling. These Regulations do not apply to domestic premises, and do not therefore cover homeworkers. They do, however, apply to hotels, nursing homes and the like, and to parts of workplaces where 'domestic' staff are employed such as the kitchens of hostels or sheltered accommodation.

4 These Regulations aim to ensure that workplaces meet the health, safety and welfare needs of each member of the workforce which may include people with disabilities. Several of the Regulations require things to be 'suitable' as defined in regulation 2(3) in a way which makes it clear that traffic routes, facilities and workstations which are used by people with disabilities should be suitable for them to use.

5 Building Regulations contain requirements which are intended to make new buildings accessible to people with limited mobility, or impaired sight

or hearing. There is also a British Standard on access to buildings for people with disabilities.

New workplaces

6 A 'new workplace' is one that is taken into use for the first time after 31 December 1992. Therefore if a building was a workplace at any time in the past it is not a new workplace (although it may be a conversion).

Modifications, extensions and conversions

7 Any modification or extension started after 31 December 1992 should comply with any relevant requirements of these Regulations as soon as it is in use. This applies only to the actual modification or extension. The rest of the workplace should comply as from 1 January 1996 and until that date the laws listed in Schedule 2 will continue to apply. A 'modification' includes any alteration but not a simple replacement.

8 The whole of any conversion started after 31 December 1992 should comply as soon as it is in use. 'Conversion' is not defined and is therefore any workplace which would ordinarily be considered to be a conversion. Examples of conversions include:

(a) a large building converted into smaller industrial units. Each unit is a 'conversion';

(b) a private house, or part of a house, converted into a workplace;

(c) workplaces which undergo a radical change of use involving structural alterations.

Note: certain modifications, extensions and conversions will also be subject to Building Regulations and may need planning consent. Advice can be obtained from the local authority.

Regulation 3

Application of these Regulations

Means of transport

9 All operational ships, boats, hovercraft, aircraft, trains and road vehicles are excluded from these Regulations, except that regulation 13 applies to aircraft, trains and road vehicles when stationary in a workplace (but not when on a public road). Non-operational means of transport used as, for example, restaurants or tourist attractions, are subject to these Regulations.

Extractive industries (mines, quarries etc)

10 These Regulations do not apply to mines, quarries or other mineral extraction sites, including those off-shore. Nor do they apply to any related workplace on the same site. Other legislation applies to this sector.

Construction sites

11 Construction sites (including site offices) are excluded from these Regulations. Where construction work is in progress within a workplace, it can be treated as a construction site and so excluded from these Regulations, if it is fenced off; otherwise, these Regulations and Construction Regulations will both apply.

Temporary work sites

12 At temporary work sites the requirements of these Regulations for sanitary conveniences, washing facilities, drinking water, clothing accommodation, changing facilities and facilities for rest and eating meals (regulations 20–25) apply 'so far as is reasonably practicable'. Temporary work sites include:

(a)   work sites used only infrequently or for short periods; and
(b)   fairs and other structures which occupy a site for a short period.

Farming and forestry

13 Agricultural or forestry workplaces which are outdoors and away from the undertaking's main buildings are excluded from these Regulations, except for the requirements on sanitary conveniences, washing facilities and drinking water (regulations 20-22) which apply 'so far as is reasonably practicable'.

Regulation 4

Requirements under these Regulations

14 Employers have a general duty under Section 2 of the Health and Safety at Work etc Act 1974 to ensure, so far as is reasonably practicable, the health, safety and welfare of their employees at work. Persons in control of non-domestic premises also have a duty under Section 4 of the Act towards people who are not their employees but use their premises. (These Sections are reproduced in Appendix 2.) These Regulations expand on these duties. They are intended to protect the health and safety of everyone in the workplace, and to ensure that adequate welfare facilities are provided for people at work.

15 Employers have a duty to ensure that workplaces under their control comply with these Regulations. Tenant employers are responsible for ensuring that the workplace which they control complies with the Regulations, and that the facilities required by the Regulations are provided, for example that sanitary conveniences are sufficient and suitable, adequately ventilated and lit and kept in a clean and orderly condition. Facilities should be readily accessible but it is not essential that they are within the employer's own workplace; arrangements can be made to use facilities provided by, for example, a landlord or a neighbouring business but the employer is responsible for ensuring that they comply with the Regulations.

16 People other than employers also have duties under these Regulations if they have control, to any extent, of a workplace. For example, owners and landlords (of business premises) should ensure that common parts,

common facilities, common services and means of access within their control, comply with the Regulations. Their duties are limited to matters which are within their control. For example, an owner who is responsible for the general condition of a lobby, staircase and landings, for shared toilets provided for tenants' use, and for maintaining ventilation plant, should ensure that those parts and plant comply with these Regulations. However, the owner is not responsible under these Regulations for matters outside his control, for example a spillage caused by a tenant or shortcomings in the day-to-day cleaning of sanitary facilities where this is the tenants' responsibility. Tenants should cooperate with each other, and with the landlord, to the extent necessary to ensure that the requirements of the Regulations are fully met.

17 In some cases, measures additional to those indicated in the Regulations and the Approved Code of Practice may be necessary in order to fully comply with general duties under the Health and Safety at Work etc Act. The Management of Health and Safety at Work Regulations 1992 require employers and self-employed people to assess risks; an associated Approved Code of Practice states that it is always best if possible to avoid a risk altogether, and that work should, where possible, be adapted to the individual. A risk assessment may show that the workplace or the work should be reorganised so that the need for people to work, for example, at an unguarded edge or to work in temperatures which may induce stress does not arise in the first place.

18 It is often useful to seek the views of workers before and after changes are introduced, for example on the design of workstations, the choice of work chairs, and traffic management systems such as one-way vehicle routes or traffic lights. As well as promoting good relations, consultation can result in better decisions and in some cases help employers avoid making expensive mistakes. The Management of Health and Safety at Work Regulations extend the law which requires employers to consult employees' safety representatives on matters affecting health and safety.

19 Where employees work at a workplace which is not under their employer's control, their employer has no duty under these Regulations, but should (as part of his or her general duties under the Health and Safety at Work etc Act 1974) take any steps necessary to ensure that sanitary conveniences and washing facilities will be available. It may be necessary to make arrangements for the use of facilities already provided on site, or to provide temporary facilities. This applies, for example, to those who employ seasonal agricultural workers to work on someone else's land.

Regulation 5

Maintenance of workplace, and of equipment, devices and systems

20 The workplace, and the equipment and devices mentioned in these Regulations, should be maintained in an efficient state, in efficient working order and in good repair. 'Efficient' in this context means efficient from the view of health, safety and welfare (not productivity or economy). If a potentially dangerous defect is discovered, the defect should be rectified

immediately or steps should be taken to protect anyone who might be put at risk, for example by preventing access until the work can be carried out or the equipment replaced. Where the defect does not pose a danger but makes the equipment unsuitable for use, for example a sanitary convenience with a defective flushing mechanism, it may be taken out of service until it is repaired or replaced, but if this would result in the number of facilities being less than that required by the Regulations the defect should be rectified without delay.

21 Steps should be taken to ensure that repair and maintenance work is carried out properly.

22 Regulation 5(2) requires a system of maintenance where appropriate, for certain equipment and devices and for ventilation systems. A suitable system of maintenance involves ensuring that:

(a) regular maintenance (including, as necessary, inspection, testing, adjustment, lubrication and cleaning) is carried out at suitable intervals;
(b) any potentially dangerous defects are remedied, and that access to defective equipment is prevented in the meantime;
(c) regular maintenance and remedial work is carried out properly; and
(d) a suitable record is kept to ensure that the system is properly implemented and to assist in validating maintenance programmes.

23 Examples of equipment and devices which require a system of maintenance include emergency lighting, fencing, fixed equipment used for window cleaning, anchorage points for safety harnesses, devices to limit the opening of windows, powered doors, escalators and moving walkways.

24 The frequency of regular maintenance, and precisely what it involves, will depend on the equipment or device concerned. The likelihood of defects developing, and the foreseeable consequences, are highly relevant. The age and condition of equipment, how it is used and how often it is used should also be taken into account. Sources of advice include published HSE guidance, British and EC standards and other authoritative guidance, manufacturers' information and instructions, and trade literature.

25 The Management of Health and Safety at Work Regulations 1992 include requirements on the competence of people whom employers appoint to assist them in matters affecting health and safety and on employees' duties to report serious dangers and shortcomings in health and safety precautions.

26 There are separate HSE publications covering maintenance of escalators and window access equipment.

27 Advice on systems of maintenance for buildings can be found in a British Standard and in publications by the Chartered Institution of Building Services Engineers (CIBSE). The maintenance of work equipment and personal protective equipment is addressed in other Regulations.

Regulation 6

Ventilation

28 Enclosed workplaces should be sufficiently well ventilated so that stale air, and air which is hot or humid because of the processes or equipment in the workplace, is replaced at a reasonable rate.

29 The air which is introduced should, as far as possible, be free of any impurity which is likely to be offensive or cause ill health. Air which is taken from the outside can normally be considered to be 'fresh', but air inlets for ventilation systems should not be sited where they may draw in excessively contaminated air (for example close to a flue, an exhaust ventilation system outlet, or an area in which vehicles manoeuvre). Where necessary the inlet air should be filtered to remove particulates.

30 In many cases, windows or other openings will provide sufficient ventilation in some or all parts of the workplace. Where necessary, mechanical ventilation systems should be provided for parts or all of the workplace, as appropriate.

31 Workers should not be subject to uncomfortable draughts. In the case of mechanical ventilation systems it may be necessary to control the direction or velocity of air flow. Workstations should be re-sited or screened if necessary.

32 In the case of mechanical ventilation systems which recirculate air, including air conditioning systems, recirculated air should be adequately filtered to remove impurities. To avoid air becoming unhealthy, purified air should have some fresh air added to it before being recirculated. Systems should therefore be designed with fresh air inlets which should be kept open.

33 Mechanical ventilation systems (including air conditioning systems) should be regularly and properly cleaned, tested and maintained to ensure that they are kept clean and free from anything which may contaminate the air.

34 The requirement of regulation 6(2) for a device to give warning of breakdowns applies only 'where necessary for reasons of health or safety'. It will not apply in most workplaces. It will, however, apply to 'dilution ventilation' systems used to reduce concentrations of dust or fumes in the atmosphere, and to any other situation where a breakdown in the ventilation system would be likely to result in harm to workers.

35 Regulation 6 covers general workplace ventilation, not local exhaust ventilation for controlling employees' exposure to asbestos, lead, ionising radiations or other substances hazardous to health. There are other health and safety regulations and approved codes of practice on the control of such substances.

36 It may not always be possible to remove smells coming in from outside, but reasonable steps should be taken to minimise them. Where livestock is kept, smells may be unavoidable, but they should be controlled by good ventilation and regular cleaning.

37 Where a close, humid atmosphere is necessary, for example in mushroom growing, workers should be allowed adequate breaks in a well-ventilated place.

38 The fresh air supply rate should not normally fall below 5 to 8 litres per second, per occupant. Factors to be considered include the floor area per person, the processes and equipment involved, and whether the work is strenuous.

39 More detailed guidance on ventilation is contained in HSE publications and in publications by the Chartered Institution of Building Services Engineers.

40 Guidance on the measures necessary to avoid legionnaires' disease, caused by bacteria which can grow in water cooling towers and elsewhere, is covered in separate HSE publications and in a CIBSE publication.

41 The legislation referred to in regulation 6(3) deals with what are known as 'confined spaces' where breathing apparatus may be necessary.

Regulation 7

Temperature in indoor workplaces

42 The temperature in workrooms should provide reasonable comfort without the need for special clothing. Where such a temperature is impractical because of hot or cold processes, all reasonable steps should be taken to achieve a temperature which is as close as possible to comfortable. 'Workroom' in paragraphs 43 to 49 means a room where people normally work for more than short periods.

43 The temperature in workrooms should normally be at least 16 degrees Celsius unless much of the work involves severe physical effort in which case the temperature should be at least 13 degrees Celsius. These temperatures may not, however, ensure reasonable comfort, depending on other factors such as air movement and relative humidity. These temperatures refer to readings taken using an ordinary dry bulb thermometer, close to workstations, at working height and away from windows.

44 Paragraph 43 does not apply to rooms or parts of rooms where it would be impractical to maintain those temperatures, for example in rooms which have to be open to the outside, or where food or other products have to be kept cold. In such cases the temperature should be as close to those mentioned in paragraph 43 as is practical. In rooms where food or other products have to be kept at low temperatures this will involve such measures as:

(a) enclosing or insulating the product
(b) pre-chilling the product
(c) keeping chilled areas as small as possible
(d) exposing the product to workroom temperatures as briefly as possible.

45 Paragraphs 43 and 44 do not apply to rooms where the lower maximum room temperatures are required in other laws, such as the Fresh Meat Export (Hygiene and Inspection) Regulations 1987. It should be noted however that general Food Hygiene Regulations do not specify maximum room temperatures.

46 Where the temperature in a workroom would otherwise be uncomfortably high, for example because of hot processes or the design of the building, all reasonable steps should be taken to achieve a reasonably comfortable temperature, for example by:

(a) insulating hot plants or pipes;
(b) providing air cooling plant;

(c) shading windows;

(d) siting workstations away from places subject to radiant heat.

47 Where a reasonably comfortable temperature cannot be achieved throughout a workroom, local heating or cooling (as appropriate) should be provided. In extremely hot weather fans and increased ventilation may be used instead of local cooling. Insulated duckboards or other floor coverings should be provided where workers have to stand for long periods on cold floors unless special footwear is provided which prevents discomfort. Draughts should be excluded and self-closing doors installed where such measures are practical and would reduce discomfort.

48 Where, despite the provision of local heating or cooling, workers are exposed to temperatures which do not give reasonable comfort, suitable protective clothing and rest facilities should be provided. Where practical there should be systems of work (for example, task rotation) to ensure that the length of time for which individual workers are exposed to uncomfortable temperatures is limited.

49 In parts of the workplace other than workrooms, such as sanitary facilities or rest facilities, the temperature should be reasonable in all the circumstances including the length of time people are likely to be there. Changing rooms and shower room should not be cold.

50 Where persons are required to work in normally unoccupied rooms such as storerooms, other than for short periods, temporary heating should be provided if necessary to avoid discomfort.

51 More detailed guidance on thermal comfort is expected to be published by HSE in 1993.

52 Care needs to be taken when siting temporary heaters so as to prevent burns from contact with hot surfaces. The Provision and Use of Work Equipment Regulations require protection from hot surfaces.

53 The Personal Protective Equipment at Work Regulations 1992 apply to the protective clothing provided for workers' use.

54 Information about Food Hygiene Regulations can be obtained from the Environmental Health Departments of local authorities.

55 Design data relevant to workplace temperatures are published by the Chartered Institution of Building Services Engineers.

Injurious or offensive fumes

56 Fixed heating systems should be installed and maintained in such a way that the products of combustion do not enter the workplace. Any heater which produces heat by combustion should have a sufficient air supply to ensure complete combustion. Care should be taken that portable paraffin and liquefied petroleum gas heaters do not produce fumes which will be harmful or offensive.

Thermometers

57 Thermometers should be available at a convenient distance from every part of the workplace to persons at work to enable temperatures to be

measured throughout the workplace, but need not be provided in each workroom.

Regulation 8

Lighting

58 Lighting should be sufficient to enable people to work, use facilities and move from place to place safely and without experiencing eye-strain. Stairs should be well lit in such a way that shadows are not cast over the main part of the treads. Where necessary, local lighting should be provided at individual workstations, and at places of particular risk such as pedestrian crossing points on vehicular traffic routes. Outdoor traffic routes used by pedestrians should be adequately lit after dark.

59 Dazzling lights and annoying glare should be avoided. Lights and light fitting should be of a type, and so positioned, that they do not cause a hazard (including electrical, fire, radiation or collision hazards). Light switches should be positioned so that they may be found and used easily and without risk.

60 Lights should not be allowed to become obscured, for example by stacked goods, in such a way that the level of light becomes insufficient. Lights should be replaced, repaired or cleaned, as necessary, before the level of lighting becomes insufficient. Fittings or lights should be replaced immediately if they become dangerous, electrically or otherwise.

61 More detailed guidance is given in a separate HSE publication. There are also a number of publications on lighting by the Chartered Institution of Building Services Engineers.

62 Requirements on lighting are also contained in the Dock Regulations 1988, the Provisions and Use of Work Equipment Regulations 1992 and the Health and Safety (Display Screen Equipment) Regulations 1992. The electrical safety of lighting installations is subject to the Electricity at Work Regulations 1989.

Natural lighting

63 Windows and skylights should where possible be cleaned regularly and kept free from unnecessary obstructions to admit maximum daylight. Where this would result in excessive heat or glare at a workstation, however, the workstation should be repositioned or the window or skylight should be shaded.

64 People generally prefer to work in natural rather than artificial light. In both new and existing workplaces workstations should be sited to take advantage of the available natural light. Natural lighting may not be feasible where windows have to be covered for security reasons or where process requirements necessitate particular lighting conditions.

Emergency lighting

65 The normal precautions required by these and other Regulations, for example on the prevention of falls and the fencing of dangerous parts of machinery, mean that workers are not in most cases 'specially exposed' to risk if normal lighting fails. Emergency lighting is not therefore essential in most cases. Emergency lighting should however be provided in workrooms where sudden loss of light would present a serious risk, for example if process plant needs to be shut down under manual control or a potentially hazardous process needs to be made safe, and this cannot be done safely without lighting.

66 Emergency lighting should be powered by a source independent from that of normal lighting. It should be immediately effective in the event of failure of the normal lighting, without need for action by anyone. It should provide sufficient light to enable persons at work to take any action necessary to ensure their, and others', health and safety.

67 Fire precautions legislation may require the lighting of escape routes. Advice can be obtained from local fire authorities.

Regulation 9

Cleanliness and waste materials

68 The standard of cleanliness required will depend on the use to which the workplace is put. For example, an area in which workers take meals would be expected to be cleaner than a factory floor, and a factory floor would be expected to be cleaner than an animal house. However, regulation 12(3) (avoidance of slipping, tripping and falling hazards) should be complied with in all cases.

69 Floors and indoor traffic routes should be cleaned at least once a week. In factories and other workplaces of a type where dirt and refuse accumulates, any dirt and refuse which is not in suitable receptacles should be removed at least daily. These tasks should be carried out more frequently where necessary to maintain a reasonable standard of cleanliness or to keep workplaces free of pests and decaying matter. This paragraph does not apply to parts of workplaces which are normally visited only for short periods, or to animal houses.

70 Interior walls, ceilings and work surfaces should be cleaned at suitable intervals. Except in parts which are normally visited only for short periods, or where any soiling is likely to be light, ceilings and interior walls should be painted, tiled or otherwise treated so that they can be kept clean, and the surface treatment should be renewed when it can no longer be cleaned properly. This paragraph does not apply to parts of workplaces which cannot be safely reached using a 5-metre ladder.

71 Apart from regular cleaning, cleaning should also be carried out when necessary in order to clear up spillages or to remove unexpected soiling of

surfaces. Workplaces should be kept free from offensive waste matter or discharges, for example, leaks from drains or sanitary conveniences.

72 Cleaning should be carried out by an effective and suitable method and without creating, or exposing anyone to, a health or safety risk.

73 Care should be taken that methods of cleaning do not expose anyone to substantial amounts of dust, including flammable or explosive concentrations of dusts, or to health or safety risks arising from the use of cleaning agents. The Control of Substances Hazardous to Health Regulations 1988 are relevant.

74 Absorbent floors, such as untreated concrete or timber, which are likely to be contaminated by oil or other substances which are difficult to remove, should preferably be sealed or coated, for example with a suitable non-slip floor paint. Carpet should also be avoided in such situations.

75 Washable surfaces, and high standards of cleanliness, may be essential for the purposes of infection control (as in the case of post-mortem rooms and pathology laboratories), for the control of exposure to substances hazardous to health or for the purposes of hygiene in the processing or handling of food. In such cases, steps should be taken to eliminate traps for dirt or germs by, for example, sealing joints between surfaces and fitting curved strips or coving along joins between walls and floors and between walls and work surfaces. Further information about food hygiene can be obtained from Environmental Health Departments of local authorities.

Regulation 10

Room dimensions and space

Minimum space

76 Workrooms should have enough free space to allow people to get to and from workstations and to move within the room, with ease. The number of people who may work in any particular room at any one time will depend not only on the size of the room, but on the space taken up by furniture, fittings, equipment, and on the layout of the room. Workrooms, except those where people only work for short periods, should be of sufficient height (from floor to ceiling) over most of the room to enable safe access to workstations. In older buildings with obstructions such as low beams the obstruction should be clearly marked.

77 The total volume of the room, when empty, divided by the number of people normally working in it should be at least 11 cubic metres. In making this calculation a room or part of a room which is more than 3.0 m high should be counted as 3.0 m high. The figure of 11 cubic metres per person is a minimum and may be insufficient if, for example, much of the room is taken up by furniture etc.

78 The figure of 11 cubic metres referred to in paragraph 77 does not apply to:

(a) Retails sales kiosks, attendants' shelters, machine control cabs or similar small structures, where space is necessarily limited; or

(b)   Rooms being used for lectures, meetings and similar purposes.

79   In a typical room, where the ceiling is 2.4 m high, a floor area of 4.6 m^2 (for example 2.0 x 2.3 m) will be needed to provide a space of 11 m^3. Where the ceiling is 3.0 m high or higher the minimum floor area will be 3.7 m^2 (for example 2.0 x 1.85 m). (These floor areas are only for illustrative purposes and are approximate.)

80   The floor space per person indicated in paragraph 77 and 79 will not always give sufficient unoccupied space, as required by the Regulation. Rooms may need to be larger, or to have fewer people working in them, than indicated in those paragraphs, depending on such factors as the contents and layout of the room and the nature of the work. Where space is limited careful planning of the workplace is particularly important.

Regulation 11

Workstations and seating

81   Workstations should be arranged so that each task can be carried out safely and comfortably. The worker should be at a suitable height in relation to the work surface. Work materials and frequently used equipment or controls should be within easy reach, without undue bending or stretching.

82   Workstations including seating, and access to workstations, should be suitable for any special needs of the individual worker, including workers with disabilities.

83   Each workstation should allow any person who is likely to work there adequate freedom of movement and the ability to stand upright. Spells of work which unavoidably have to be carried out in cramped conditions should be kept as short as possible and there should be sufficient space nearby to relieve discomfort.

84   There should be sufficient clear and unobstructed space at each workstation to enable the work to be done safely. This should allow for the manoeuvring and positioning of materials, for example lengths of timber.

85   Seating provided in accordance with regulation 11(3) should where possible provide adequate support for the lower back, and a footrest should be provided for any worker who cannot comfortably place his or her feet flat on the floor.

86   More detailed guidance on seating is given in an HSE publication. There are other HSE publications on visual display units and ergonomics.

87   Static and awkward posture at the workstation, the use of undesirable force and an uncomfortable hand grip, often coupled with continuous repetitive work without sufficient rest and recovery, may lead to chronic injury. Guidance is contained in an HSE publication.

88   This Regulation covers all workstations. Workstations where visual display units, process control screens, microfiche readers and similar display units are used are subject to the Health and Safety (Display Screen Equipment) Regulations 1992.

Regulation 12

Condition of floors and traffic routes

89 Floor and traffic routes should be of sound construction and should have adequate strength and stability taking account of the loads placed on them and the traffic passing over them. Floors should not be overloaded.

90 The surfaces of floors and traffic routes should be free from any hole, slope, or uneven or slippery surface which is likely to:

(a) cause a person to slip, trip or fall;
(b) cause a person to drop or lose control of anything being lifted or carried; or
(c) cause instability or loss of control of vehicles and/or their loads.

91 Holes, bumps or uneven areas resulting from damage or wear and tear, which may cause a person to trip or fall, should be made good. Until they can be made good, adequate precautions should be taken against accidents, for example by barriers or conspicuous marking. Temporary holes, for example an area where floor boards have been removed, should be adequately guarded. Account should be taken of people with impaired or no sight. Surfaces with small holes (for example metal gratings) are acceptable provided they are not likely to be a hazard. Deep holes into which people may fall are subject to regulation 13 and the relevant section of this Code.

92 Slopes should not be steeper than necessary. Moderate and steep slopes, and ramps used by people with disabilities, should be provided with a secure handrail where necessary.

93 Surfaces of floors and traffic routes which are likely to get wet or to be subject to spillages should be of a type which does not become unduly slippery. A slip-resistant coating should be applied where necessary. Floors near to machinery which could cause injury if anyone were to fall against it (for example a woodworking or grinding machine) should be slip-resistant and be kept free from slippery substances or loose materials.

94 Where possible, processes and plant which may discharge or leak liquids should be enclosed (for example by bunding), and leaks from taps or discharge points on pipes, drums and tanks should be caught or drained away. Stop valves should be fitted to filling points on tank filling lines. Where work involves carrying or handling liquids or slippery substances, as in food processing and preparation, the workplace and work surfaces should be arranged in such a way as to minimise the likelihood of spillages.

95 Where a leak or spillage occurs and is likely to be a slipping hazard, immediate steps should be taken to fence it off, mop it up, or cover it with absorbent granules.

96 Arrangements should be made to minimise risks from snow and ice. This may involve gritting, snow clearing and closure of some routes, particularly outside stairs, ladders and walkways on roofs.

97 Floors and traffic routes should be kept free of obstructions which may present a hazard or impede access. This is particularly important on or

near stairs, steps, escalators and moving walkways, on emergency routes, in or near doorways or gangways, and in any place where an obstruction is likely to cause an accident, for example near a corner or junction. Where a temporary obstruction is unavoidable and is likely to be a hazard, access should be prevented or steps should be taken to warn people or the drivers of vehicles of the obstruction by, for example, the use of hazard cones. Where furniture or equipment is being moved within a workplace, it should if possible be moved in a single operation and should not be left in a place where it is likely to be a hazard. Vehicles should not be parked where they are likely to be a hazard. Materials which fall onto traffic routes should be cleared as soon as possible.

98 Effective drainage should be provided where a floor is liable to get wet to the extent that the wet can be drained off. This is likely to be the case in, for example, laundries, textile manufacture (including dyeing, bleaching and finishing), work on hides and skins, potteries and food processing. Drains and channels should be positioned so as to minimise the area of wet floor, and the floor should slope slightly towards the drain. Where necessary to prevent tripping hazards, drains and channels should have covers which should be as near flush as possible with the floor surface.

99 Every open side of a staircase should be securely fenced. As a minimum the fencing should consist of an upper rail at 900 mm or higher and a lower rail.

100 A secure and substantial handrail should be provided and maintained on at least one side of every staircase, except at points where a handrail would obstruct access or egress, as in the case of steps in a theatre aisle. Handrails should be provided on both sides if there is a particular risk of falling, for example where stairs are heavily used, or are wide, or have narrow treads, or where they are liable to be subject to spillages. Additional handrails should be provided down the centre of particularly wide staircases where necessary.

101 Further guidance on slips, trips and falls, and on the containment of pesticides in storage, is contained in separate HSE publications.

102 Methods of draining and containing toxic, corrosive or highly flammable liquids should not result in the contamination of drains, sewers, watercourses, or groundwater supplies, or put people or the environment at risk. Maximum concentration levels are specified in the Environmental Protection (Prescribed Processes and Substances) Regulations 1991, and the Surface Waters (Dangerous Substances) (Classification) Regulations 1989 and 1992. Consent for discharges may be required under the Environmental Protection Act 1990, the Water Resources Act 1991 and the Water Industry Act 1991.

103 Consideration should be given to providing slip resistant footwear in workplaces where slipping hazards arise despite the precautions set out in paragraph 93.

104 Building Regulations also have requirements on floors and stairs. Advice may be obtained from the local authority. There is also a British Standard on the construction and maximum loading of floors.

105 Steep stairways are classed as fixed ladders and are dealt with under regulation 13.

Regulation 13

Falls or falling objects

106 The consequences of falling from heights or into dangerous substances are so serious that a high standard of protection is required. Secure fencing should normally be provided to prevent people falling from edges, and the fencing should also be adequate to prevent objects falling onto people. Where fencing cannot be provided or has to be removed temporarily, other measures should be taken to prevent falls. Dangerous substances in tanks, pits or other structures should be securely fenced or covered.

107 The guarding of temporary holes, such as an area where floorboards have been removed, is dealt with in paragraph 91 of this Code.

Provisions of fencing or covers

108 Secure fencing should be provided wherever possible at any place where a person might fall 2 metres or more. Secure fencing should also be provided where a person might fall less than 2 metres, where there are factors which increase the likelihood of a fall or the risk of serious injury; for example where a traffic route passes close to an edge, where large numbers of people are present, or where a person might fall onto a sharp or dangerous surface or into the path of a vehicle. Tanks, pits or similar structures may be securely covered instead of being fenced.

109 Fencing should be sufficiently high, and filled in sufficiently, to prevent falls (of people or objects) over or through the fencing. As a minimum, fencing should consist of two guard-rails (a top rail and a lower rail) at suitable heights. In the case of fencing installed after 1 January 1993 (but not repairs or partial replacement) the top of the fencing should be at least 1100 mm above the surface from which a person might fall except in cases where lower fencing has been approved by a local authority under Building Regulations.

110 Fencing should be of adequate strength and stability to restrain any person or object liable to fall on to or against it. Untensioned chains, ropes and other non-rigid materials should not be used.

111 Fencing should be designed to prevent objects falling from the edge including items used for cleaning or maintenance. Where necessary an adequate upstand or toeboard should be provided.

112 Covers should be capable of supporting all loads liable to be imposed upon them, and any traffic which is liable to pass over them. They should be of a type which cannot be readily detached and removed, and should not be capable of being easily displaced.

113 Paragraphs 108 to 111 do not apply to edges on roofs or to places to which there is no general access. Nevertheless, secure, adequate fencing

ould be provided wherever possible in such cases. Tanks, pits or similar
ructures containing dangerous substances should always be provided with
cure fencing or a secure cover.

114 Additional safeguards may be necessary in places where unauthor-
ed entry is foreseeable. A separate HSE publication gives guidance on
afeguards for effluent storage in farms.

115 Building Regulations also have requirements on fencing. Advice can
e obtained from local authorities. There is a British Standard on the
onstruction of fencing.

emporary removal of fencing or covers

16 When an opening or an edge is being used to transfer goods or
aterials from one level to another, it should be fenced as far as possible.
cure handholds should be provided where workers have to position
emselves at an unfenced opening or edge, such as a teagle opening or
milar doorway used for the purpose of hoisting or lowering goods. Where
e operation necessarily involves the use of an unguarded edge, as little
ncing or rail as possible should be removed, and should be replaced as
on as possible.

117 One method of fencing an opening or edge where articles are raised
lowered by means of a lift truck is to provide a special type of fence or
arrier which the worker can raise without having to approach the edge, for
ample by operating a lever, to give the lift truck access to the edge.

118 Covers should be kept securely in place except when they have to be
moved for inspection purposes or in order to gain access. Covers should
e replaced as soon as possible.

ixed ladders

9 Fixed ladders should not be provided in circumstances where it would
e practical to install a staircase (see paragraph 162 of this Code). Fixed
dders or other suitable means of access or egress should be provided in
ts, tanks and similar structures into which workers need to descend. In
is Code a 'fixed ladder' includes a steep stairway (a staircase which a
erson normally descends facing the treads or rungs).

120 Fixed ladders should be of sound construction, properly maintained
nd securely fixed. Rungs of a ladder should be horizontal, give adequate
othold and not depend solely upon nails, screws or similar fixings for
eir support.

121 Unless some other adequate handhold exists, the stiles of the ladder
ould extend at least 1100 mm above any landing served by the ladder or
e highest rung used to step or stand on except that in the case of chimneys
e stiles should not project into the gas stream.

122 Fixed ladders installed after 31 December 1992 with a vertical
stance of more than 6 m should normally have a landing or other
dequate resting place at every 6 m point. Each run should, where possible,
e out of line with the last run, to reduce the distance a person might fall.

Where it is not possible to provide such landings, for example on chimney, the ladders should only be used by specially trained and proficien people.

123 Where a ladder passes through a floor, the opening should be a small as possible. The opening should be fenced as far as possible, and gate should be provided where necessary to prevent falls.

124 Fixed ladders at an angle of less than 15 degrees to the vertical (pitch of more than 75 degrees) which are more than 2.5 m high shoul where possible be fitted with suitable safety hoops or permanently fixed fa arrest systems. Hoops should be at intervals of not more than 900 mr measured along the stiles, and should commence at a height of 2.5 m abov the base of the ladder. The top hoop should be in line with the top of th fencing on the platform served by the ladder. Where a ladder rises less tha 2.5 m, but is elevated so that it is possible to fall a distance of more tha 2 m, a single hoop should be provided in line with the top of the fencin; Where the top of a ladder passes through a fenced hole in a floor, a hoo need not be provided at that point.

125 Stairs are much safer than ladders, especially when loads are to b carried. A sloping ladder is generally easier and safer to use than a vertic; ladder (see Regulation 17 and paragraph 162 of the Code.)

126 British Standards deal with ladders for permanent access.

Roof work

127 Slips and trips which may be trivial at ground level may result in fat; accidents when on a roof. It is therefore vital that precautions are taker even when access is only occasional, for example for maintenance c cleaning.

128 As well as falling from the roof edge, there may be a risk of fallin through a fragile material. Care should be taken of old materials whic may have become fragile because of corrosion. The risks may be increase by moss, lichen, ice, etc. Surfaces may also be deceptive.

129 Where regular access is needed to roofs (including internal roofs, fc example a single storey office within a larger building) suitable permaner access should be provided and there should be fixed physical safeguards t prevent falls from edges and through fragile roofs. Where occasional acces is required, other safeguards should be provided, for example crawlin boards, temporary access equipment etc.

130 A fragile roof or surface is one which would be liable to fracture if person's weight were to be applied to it, whether by walking, falling on to or otherwise. All glazing and asbestos cement or similar sheeting should b treated as being fragile unless there is firm evidence to the contrary. Fragil roofs or surfaces should be clearly identified.

131 Construction Regulations contain specific requirements on roc work. An HSE publication gives more detailed advice on roof work. Ther is also a British Standard on imposed roof loads.

Falls into dangerous substances

132 The tanks, pits and structures mentioned in regulation 13(5) are referred to here as 'vessels' and include sumps, silos, vats, and kiers which persons could fall into. (Kiers are fixed vessels which are used for boiling textile materials in workplaces where the printing, bleaching or dyeing of textile materials or waste is carried out.)

133 Every vessel containing a dangerous substance should be adequately protected to prevent a person from falling into it. Vessels installed after 31 December 1992 should be securely covered, or fenced to a height of at least 1100 mm unless the sides extend to at least 1100 mm above the highest point from which people could fall into them. In the case of existing vessels the height should be at least 915 mm or, in the case of atmospheric or open kiers, 840 mm.

Changes of level

134 Changes of level, such as a step between floors, which are not obvious should be marked to make them conspicuous.

Stacking and racking

135 Materials and objects should be stored and stacked in such a way that they are not likely to fall and cause injury. Racking should be of adequate strength and stability having regard to the loads placed on it and its vulnerability to damage, for example by vehicles.

136 Appropriate precautions in stacking and storage include:

a) safe palletisation;
b) banding or wrapping to prevent individual articles falling out;
c) setting limits for the height of stacks to maintain stability;
d) regular inspection of stacks to detect and remedy any unsafe stacks; and
e) particular instruction and arrangements for irregularly shaped objects.

137 Further guidance on stacking materials is given in HSE publications.

Loading or unloading vehicles

138 The need for people to climb on top of vehicles or their loads should be avoided as far as possible. Where it is unavoidable, effective measures should be taken to prevent falls.

139 Where a tanker is loaded from a fixed gantry and access is required on to the top of the tanker, fencing should be provided where possible. The fencing may be collapsible fencing on top of the tanker or may form part of the gantry. In the latter case if varying designs of tankers are loaded the

fencing should be adjustable, where necessary. Similar fencing should also be provided wherever people regularly go on top of tankers at a particular location, for example for maintenance.

140 Where loaded lorries have to be sheeted before leaving a workplace suitable precautions should be taken against falls. Where sheeting is done frequently it should be carried out in designated parts of the workplace which are equipped for safe sheeting. Where reasonably practicable gantries should be provided which lorries can drive under or alongside, so that the load is sheeted from the gantry without any need to stand on the cargo. In other situations safety lines and harnesses should be provided for people on top of the vehicle.

Measures other than fencing, covers, etc

141 When fencing or covers cannot be provided, or have to be removed effective measures should be taken to prevent falls. Access should be limited to specified people and others should be kept out by, for example, barriers in high risk situations suitable formal written permit to work system should be adopted. A safe system of work should be operated which may include the provision and use of a fall arrest system, or safety lines and harnesses, and secure anchorage points. Safety lines should be short enough to prevent injury should a fall occur and the safety line operate. Adequate information, instruction, training and supervision should be given.

142 People should not be allowed into an area where, despite safeguards they would be in danger, for example from work going on overhead.

143 Systems which do not require disconnection and reconnection of safety harnesses from safety lines, when at risk of falling, should be used in preference to those that do. Where there is no need to approach the edge the length of the line and the position of the anchorage should be such as to prevent the edge being approached.

144 The provision and use of safety harnesses etc are also subject to the Personal Protective Equipment at Work Regulations 1992. There are also relevant British Standards.

Scaffolding

145 Scaffolding and other equipment used for temporary access may either follow the provisions of this code or the requirements of Construction Regulations.

Other Regulations

146 Other Regulations concerning shipyards, docks and agricultural workplaces also contain specific requirements for preventing injury from falls. Those specific requirements stand. Regulation 13 of these Regulation and relevant parts of this Code will also apply to such premises (subject to regulation 3(4) which partially excludes open farmland). However it is no

intended that regulation 13 or this Code should be interpreted as overriding or increasing those specific requirements of other Regulations.

Regulation 14

Windows, and transparent or translucent doors, gates and walls

147 Transparent or translucent surfaces in doors, gates, walls and partitions should be of a safety material or be adequately protected against breakage in the following cases:

(a) in doors and gates, and door and gate side panels, where any part of the transparent or translucent surface is at shoulder level or below;

(b) in windows, walls and partitions, where any part of the transparent or translucent surface is at waist level or below, except in glasshouses where people there will be likely to be aware of the presence of glazing and avoid contact.

This paragraph does not apply to narrow panes up to 250 mm wide measured between glazing beads.

148 'Safety materials' are:

(a) materials which are inherently robust, such as polycarbonates or glass blocks; or

(b) glass which, if it breaks, breaks safely; or

(c) ordinary annealed glass which meets the thickness criteria in the following table:

Nominal thickness	Maximum size
8 mm	1.10 m x 1.10 m
10 mm	2.25 m x 2.25 m
12 mm	3.00 m x 4.50 mm
15 mm	Any size

149 As an alternative to the use of safety materials, transparent or translucent surfaces may be adequately protected against breakage. This may be achieved by means of a screen or barrier which will prevent a person from coming into contact with the glass if he or she falls against it. If a person going through the glass would fall from a height, the screen or barrier should also be designed to be difficult to climb.

150 A transparent or translucent surface should be marked where necessary to make it apparent. The risk of collision is greatest in large uninterrupted surfaces where the floor is at a similar level on each side, so that people might reasonably think they can walk straight through. If features such as mullions, transoms, rails, door frames, large pull or push handles, or heavy tinting make the surface apparent, marking is not essential. Where it is needed, marking may take any form (for example coloured lines or patterns), provided it is conspicuous and at a conspicuous height.

151 The term 'safety glass' is used in a British Standard which is concerned with the breakage of flat glass or flat plastic sheet. Materials

meeting that Standard, for example laminated or toughened glass, will break in a way that does not result in large sharp pieces and will fulfil paragraph 148(b) above. 'Safety materials' as used in these Regulations includes safety glass, but also other materials as described in paragraphs 148(a) and (c) above. There is also a British Standard which contains a code of practice for the glazing for buildings.

152 Building Regulations also have similar requirements. Advice may be obtained from local authorities.

Regulation 15

Windows, skylights and ventilators

153 It should be possible to reach and operate the control of openable windows, skylights and ventilators in a safe manner. Where necessary, window poles or similar equipment should be kept available, or a stable platform or other safe means of access should be provided. Controls should be so placed that people are not likely to fall through or out of the window. Where there is a danger of falling from a height devices should be provided to prevent the window opening too far.

154 Open windows, skylights or ventilators should not project into an area where persons are likely to collide with them. The bottom edge of opening windows should normally be at least 800 mm above floor level, unless there is a barrier to prevent falls.

155 There is a British Standard on windows and skylights.

Regulation 16

Ability to clean windows etc safely

156 Suitable provision should be made so that windows and skylights can be cleaned safely if they cannot be cleaned from the ground or other suitable surface.

157 Suitable provision includes:

(a)   fitting windows which can be cleaned safely from the inside, for example windows which pivot so that the outer surface is turned inwards;

(b)   fitting access equipment such as suspended cradles, or travelling ladders with an attachment for a safety harness;

(c)   providing suitable conditions for the future use of mobile access equipment, including ladders up to 9 metres long. Suitable conditions are adequate access for the equipment, and a firm level surface in a safe place on which to stand it. Where a ladder over 6 metres long will be needed, suitable points for tying or fixing the ladder should be provided.

(d)   suitable and suitably placed anchorage points for safety harnesses.

158 Further guidance on safe window cleaning and access equipment is given in other HSE publications. There is also a relevant British Standard.

Regulation 17

Organisation etc of traffic routes

159 This section of the Code applies to both new and existing workplaces. In paragraphs 160, 165 and 171 special provision is made for traffic routes in existence before 1 January 1993. This is because it might, in a few cases, otherwise be difficult for existing routes to comply fully with the Code. These special provisions reflect regulation 17(5) which has the effect of requiring existing traffic routes to comply with Regulation 17(2) and 17(3) only to the extent that it is reasonably practicable. 'Traffic route' is defined in regulation 2 as 'a route for pedestrian traffic, vehicles or both and includes any stairs, staircase, fixed ladder, doorway, gateway, loading bay or ramp'.

160 There should be sufficient traffic routes, of sufficient width and headroom, to allow people on foot or in vehicles to circulate safely and without difficulty. Features which obstruct routes should be avoided. On traffic routes in existence before 1 January 1993, obstructions such as limited headroom are acceptable provided they are indicated by, for example, the use of conspicuous tape. Consideration should be given to the safety of people with impaired or no sight.

161 In some situations people in wheelchairs may be at greater risk than people on foot, and special consideration should be given to their safety. Traffic routes used by people in wheelchairs should be wide enough to allow unimpeded access, and ramps should be provided where necessary. Regulation 12(4) and paragraph 92 of this Code also deal with ramps.

162 Access between floors should not normally be by way of ladders or steep stairs. Fixed ladders or steep stairs may be used where a conventional staircase cannot be accommodated, provided they are only used by people who are capable of using them safely and any loads to be carried can be safely carried.

163 Routes should not be used by vehicles for which they are inadequate or unsuitable. Any necessary restrictions should be clearly indicated. Uneven or soft ground should be made smooth and firm if vehicles might otherwise overturn or shed their loads. Sharp or blind bends on vehicle routes should be avoided as far as possible; where they are unavoidable, measures such as one-way systems or the use of mirrors to improve vision should be considered. On vehicle routes, prominent warning should be given of any limited headroom, both in advance and at the obstruction itself. Any potentially dangerous obstructions such as overhead electric cables or pipes containing, for example, flammable or hazardous chemicals should be shielded. Screens should be provided where necessary to protect people who have to work at a place where they would be at risk from exhaust fumes, or to protect people from materials which are likely to fall from vehicles.

164 Sensible speed limits should be set and clearly displayed on vehicle routes except those used only by slow vehicles. Where necessary, suitable speed retarders such as road humps should be provided. These should always be preceded by a warning sign or a mark on the road. Arrangements

should be made where necessary to avoid fork lift trucks having to pass over road humps unless the truck is of a type which can negotiate them safely.

165 Traffic routes used by vehicles should be wide enough to allow vehicles to pass oncoming or parked vehicles without leaving the route. One-way systems or restrictions on parking should be introduced as necessary. On traffic routes in existence before 1 January 1993, where it is not practical to make the route wide enough, passing places or traffic management systems should be provided as necessary.

166 Traffic routes used by vehicles should not pass close to any edge, or to anything that is likely to collapse or be left in a dangerous state if hit (such as hollow cast–iron columns and storage racking), unless the edge or thing is fenced or adequately protected.

167 The need for vehicles with poor rear visibility to reverse should be eliminated as far as possible, for example by the use of one-way systems.

168 Where large vehicles have to reverse, measures for reducing risks to pedestrians and any people in wheelchairs should be considered, such as:

(a) restricting reversing to places where it can be carried out safely;

(b) keeping people on foot or in wheelchairs away;

(c) providing suitable high visibility clothing for people who are permitted in the area;

(d) fitting reversing alarms to alert, or with a detection device to warn the driver of an obstruction or apply the brakes automatically; and

(e) employing banksmen to supervise the safe movement of vehicles.

Whatever measures are adopted, a safe system of work should operate at all times. Account should be taken of people with impaired sight or hearing.

169 If crowds of people are likely to overflow on to roadways, for example at the end of a shift, consideration should be given to stopping vehicles from using the routes at such times.

170 Where a load has to be tipped into a hopper, waste pit, or similar place, and the vehicle is liable to fall into it, substantial barriers or portable wheel stops should be provided at the end of the traffic route to prevent this type of occurrence.

Separation of people and vehicles

171 Any traffic route which is used by both pedestrians and vehicles should be wide enough to enable any vehicle likely to use the route to pass pedestrians safely. On traffic routes in existence before 1 January 1993, where it is not practical to make the route wide enough, passing places or traffic management systems should be provided as necessary. In buildings, lines should be drawn on the floor to indicate routes followed by vehicles such as fork lift trucks.

172 On routes used by automatic, driverless vehicles which are also used by pedestrians, steps should be taken to ensure that pedestrians do not

become trapped by vehicles. The vehicles should be fitted with safeguards to minimise the risk of injury, sufficient clearance should be provided between the vehicles and pedestrians, and care should be taken that fixtures along the route do not create trapping hazards.

173 In doorways, gateways, tunnels, bridges, or other enclosed routes, vehicles should be separated from pedestrians by a kerb or barrier. Where necessary, for safety, separate routes through should be provided and pedestrians should be guided to use the correct route by clear marking. Such routes should be kept unobstructed. Similar measures should be taken where the speed or volume of vehicles would put pedestrians at risk.

174 Workstations should be adequately separated or shielded from vehicles.

Crossings

175 Where pedestrian and vehicle routes cross, appropriate crossing points should be provided and used. Where necessary, barriers or rails should be provided to prevent pedestrians crossing at particularly dangerous points and to guide them to designated crossing places. At crossing places where volumes of traffic are particularly heavy, the provision of suitable bridges or subways should be considered.

176 At crossing points there should be adequate visibility and open space for the pedestrian where the pedestrian route joins the vehicle route. For example, where an enclosed pedestrian route, or a doorway or staircase, joins a vehicle route there should be an open space of at least one metre from which pedestrians can see along the vehicle route in both directions (or in the case of a one-way route, in the direction of on-coming traffic). Where such a space cannot be provided barriers or rails should be provided to prevent pedestrians walking directly onto the vehicular route.

Loading bays

177 Loading bays should be provided with at least one exit point from the lower level. Wide loading bays should be provided with at least two exit points, one being at each end. Alternatively, a refuge should be provided which can be used to avoid being struck or crushed by a vehicle.

Signs

178 Potential hazards on traffic routes used by vehicles should be indicated by suitable warning signs. Such hazards may include: sharp bends, junctions, crossings, blind corners, steep gradients or roadworks.

179 Suitable road markings and signs should also be used to alert drivers to any restrictions which apply to the use of a traffic route. Adequate directions should also be provided to relevant parts of a workplace. Buildings, departments, entrances, etc should be clearly marked, where necessary, so that unplanned manoeuvres are avoided.

180 Any signs used in connection with traffic should comply with the Traffic Signs Regulations and General Directions 1981 (SI 1981 No 859) and the Highway Code for use on the public highway.

181 Further guidance on workplace transport is given in separate HSE publications.

182 There are also separate Regulations on dock work which have requirements on traffic routes.

Regulation 18

Doors and gates

183 Doors and gates which swing in both directions should have a transparent panel except if they are low enough to see over. Conventionally hinged doors on main traffic routes should also be fitted with such panels. Panels should be positioned to enable a person in a wheelchair to be seen from the other side.

184 Sliding doors should have a stop or other effective means to prevent the door coming off the end of the track. They should also have a retaining rail to prevent the door falling should the suspension system fail or the rollers leave the track.

185 Upward opening doors should be fitted with an effective device such as a counter balance or ratchet mechanism to prevent them falling back in a manner likely to cause injury.

186 Power operated doors and gates should have safety features to prevent people being injured as a result of being struck or trapped. Safety features include:

(a) a sensitive edge, or other suitable detector, and associated trip device to stop, or reverse, the motion of the door or gate when obstructed;

(b) a device to limit the closing force so that it is insufficient to cause injury;

(c) an operating control which must be held in position during the whole of the closing motion. This will only be suitable where the risk of injury is low and the speed of closure is slow. Such a control, when released, should cause the door to stop or reopen immediately and should be positioned so that the operator has a clear view of the door throughout its movement.

187 Where necessary, power operated doors and gates should have a readily identifiable and accessible control switch or device so that they can be stopped quickly in an emergency. Normal on/off controls may be sufficient.

188 It should be possible to open a power operated door or gate if the power supply fails, unless it opens automatically in such circumstances, or there is an alternative way through. This does not apply to lift doors and other doors and gates which are there to prevent falls or access to areas of potential danger.

189 Where tools are necessary for manual opening they should be readily available at all times. If the power supply is restored while the door is being opened manually, the person opening it should not be put at risk.

190 The fire resistance of doors is dealt with in Building Regulations and in fire precaution legislation. Advice can be obtained from local authorities and fire authorities.

Regulation 19

Escalators and moving walkways

191 There are HSE publications on the safe use and periodic thorough examination of escalators. There is also a relevant British Standard.

Regulation 21

Washing facilities

192 In paragraphs 193–211 'facilities' means sanitary and washing facilities, 'sanitary accommodation' means a room containing one or more sanitary conveniences and 'washing station' means a wash-basin or a section of a trough or fountain sufficient for one person.

193 Sufficient facilities should be provided to enable everyone at work to use them without undue delay. Minimum numbers of facilities are given in paragraphs 201–205 but more may be necessary if, for example, breaks are taken at set times or workers finish work together and need to wash before leaving.

194 Special provision should be made if necessary for any worker with a disability to have access to facilities which are suitable for his or her use.

195 The facilities do not have to be within the workplace, but they should if possible be within the building. Where arrangements are made for the use of facilities provided by someone else, for example the owner of the building, the facilities should still meet the provisions of this Code and they should be available at all material times. The use of public facilities is only acceptable as a last resort, where no other arrangement is possible.

196 Facilities should provide adequate protection from the weather.

197 Water closets should be connected to a suitable drainage system and be provided with an effective means for flushing with water. Toilet paper in a holder or dispenser and a coat hook should be provided. In the case of water closets used by women, suitable means should be provided for the disposal of sanitary dressings.

198 Washing stations should have running hot and cold, or warm water, and be large enough to enable effective washing of face, hands and forearms. Showers or baths should also be provided where the work is:

(a) particularly strenuous;
(b) dirty; or

(c)   results in contamination of the skin by harmful or offensive materials.

This includes, for example, work with molten metal in foundries and the manufacture of oil cake.

199 Showers which are fed by both hot and cold water should be fitted with a device such as a thermostatic mixer valve to prevent users being scalded.

200 The facilities should be arranged to ensure adequate privacy for the user. In particular:

(a)   each water closet should be situated in a separate room or cubicle, with a door which can be secured from the inside;
(b)   it should not be possible to see urinals, or into communal shower or bathing areas, from outside the facilities when any entrance or exit door opens;
(c)   windows to sanitary accommodation, shower or bathrooms should be obscured by means of frosted glass, blinds or curtains unless it is not possible to see into them from outside; and
(d)   the facilities should be fitted with doors at entrances and exits unless other measures are taken to ensure an equivalent degree of privacy.

Minimum numbers of facilities

201 Table 1 shows the minimum number of sanitary conveniences and washing stations which should be provided. The number of people at work shown in column 1 refers to the maximum number likely to be in the workplace at any one time. Where separate sanitary accommodation is provided for a group of workers, for example men, women, office workers or manual workers, a separate calculation should be made for each group.

Table 1

1 Number of people at work	2 Number of water closets	3 Number of washstations
1 to 5	1	1
6 to 25	2	2
26 to 50	3	3
51 to 75	4	4
76 to 100	5	5

202 In the case of sanitary accommodation used only by men, Table 2 may be followed if desired, as an alternative to column 2 of Table 1. A urinal may either be an individual urinal or a section of urinal space which is at least 600 mm long.

Table 2

1 Number of men at work	2 Number of water closets	3 Number of urinals
1 to 15	1	1
16 to 30	2	1
31 to 45	2	2
46 to 60	3	2
61 to 75	3	3
76 to 90	4	3
91 to 100	4	4

203 An additional water closet, and one additional washing station, should be provided for every 25 people above 100 (or fraction of 25). In the case of water closets used only by men, an additional water closet for every 50 men (or fraction of 50) above 100 is sufficient provided at least an equal number of additional urinals are provided.

204 Where work activities result in heavy soiling of face, hands and forearms, the number of washing stations should be increased to one for every 10 people at work (or fraction of 10) up to 50 people; and one extra for every additional 20 people (or fraction of 20).

205 Where facilities provided for workers are also used by members of the public the number of conveniences and washing stations specified above should be increased as necessary to ensure that workers can use the facilities without undue delay.

Remote workplaces and temporary work sites

206 In the case of remote workplaces without running water or a nearby sewer, sufficient water in containers for washing, or other means of maintaining personal hygiene, and sufficient chemical closets should be provided. Chemical closets which have to be emptied manually should be avoided as far as possible. If they have to be used a suitable deodorising agent should be provided and they should be emptied and recharged at suitable intervals.

207 In the case of temporary work sites, which are referred to in paragraph 12 of this document, regulation 3(2) requires that suitable and sufficient sanitary conveniences and washing facilities should be provided so far as is reasonably practicable. As far as possible, water closets and washing stations which satisfy this Code should be provided. In other cases, mobile facilities should be provided wherever possible. These should if possible include flushing sanitary conveniences and running water for washing and meet the other requirements of this Code.

Ventilation, cleanliness and lighting

208 Any room containing a sanitary convenience should be well ventilated, so that offensive odours do not linger. Measures should also be taken to prevent odours entering other rooms. This may be achieved by, for example, providing a ventilated area between the room containing the convenience and the other room. Alternatively it may be possible to achieve it by mechanical ventilation or, if the room containing the convenience is well sealed from the workroom and has a door with an automatic closer, by good natural ventilation. However, no room containing a sanitary convenience should communicate directly with a room where food is processed, prepared or eaten.

209 Arrangements should be made to ensure that rooms containing sanitary conveniences or washing facilities are kept clean. The frequency and thoroughness of cleaning should be adequate for this purpose. The surfaces of the internal walls and floors of the facilities should normally have a surface which permits wet cleaning, for example ceramic tiling or a plastic coated surface. The rooms should be well lit; this will also facilitate cleaning to the necessary standard and give workers confidence in the cleanliness of the facilities. Responsibility for cleaning should be clearly established, particularly where facilities are shared by more than one workplace.

Other Regulations and publications

210 Legionnaires' disease is caused by bacteria which may be found where water stands for long periods at lukewarm or warm temperatures in, for example, tanks or little used pipes. Separate HSE publications are available.

211 Other Regulations and Approved Codes of Practice on the control of substances hazardous to health also deal with washing facilities. Information about the requirements of food hygiene legislation can be obtained from the Environmental Health Department of local authorities.

Regulation 22

Drinking water

212 Drinking water should normally be obtained from a public or private water supply by means of a tap on a pipe connected directly to the water main. Alternatively, drinking water may be derived from a tap on a pipe connected directly to a storage cistern which complies with the requirements of the UK Water Bye-laws. In particular, any cistern, tank or vessel used as a supply should be well covered, kept clean and tested and disinfected as necessary. Water should only be provided in refillable containers where it cannot be obtained directly from a mains supply. Such containers should be suitably enclosed to prevent contamination and should be refilled at least daily.

213 Drinking water taps should not be installed in places where contamination is likely, for example in a workshop where lead is handled or

processed. As far as is reasonably practicable they should also not be installed in sanitary accommodation.

214 Drinking cups or beakers should be provided unless the supply is by means of a drinking fountain. In the case of non-disposable cups a facility for washing them should be provided nearby.

215 Drinking water supplies should be marked as such if people may otherwise drink from supplies which are not meant for drinking. Marking is not necessary if non-drinkable cold water supplies are clearly marked as such.

216 Any cold water supplies which are likely to be grossly contaminated, as in the case of supplies meant for process use only, should be clearly marked by a suitable sign.

Regulation 23

Accommodation for clothing

217 Special work clothing includes all clothing which is only worn at work such as overalls, uniforms, thermal clothing and hats worn for food hygiene purposes.

218 Accommodation for work clothing and workers' own personal clothing should enable it to hang in a clean, warm, dry, well-ventilated place where it can dry out during the course of a working day if necessary. If the workroom is unsuitable for this purpose then accommodation should be provided in another convenient place. The accommodation should consist of, as a minimum, a separate hook or peg for each worker.

219 Where facilities to change clothing are required by regulation 24, effective measures should be taken to ensure the security of clothing. This may be achieved, for example, by providing a lockable locker for each worker.

220 Where work clothing (including personal protective equipment) which is not taken home becomes dirty, damp or contaminated due to the work it should be accommodated separately from the worker's own clothing. Where work clothing becomes wet, the facilities should enable it to be dried by the beginning of the following work period unless other dry clothing is provided.

221 Separate Regulations deal with personal protective equipment at work in greater detail.

222 Other Regulations and Approved Codes of Practice on the control of substances hazardous to health also deal with accommodation for clothing. Information about the requirements for food hygiene legislation can be obtained from the Environmental Health Department of local authorities.

Regulation 24

Facilities for changing clothing

223 A changing room or rooms should be provided for workers who change into special work clothing (see paragraph 217) and where they remove more than outer clothing. Changing rooms should also be provided

where necessary to prevent workers' own clothing being contaminated by a harmful substance.

224 Changing facilities should be readily accessible from workrooms and eating facilities, if provided. They should be provided with adequate seating and should contain, or communicate directly with, clothing accommodation and showers or baths if provided. They should be constructed and arranged to ensure the privacy of the user.

225 The facilities should be large enough to enable the maximum number of persons at work expected to use them at any one time, to do so without overcrowding or unreasonable delay. Account should be taken of starting and finishing times of work and the time available to use the facilities.

226 Other Regulations and Approved Codes of Practice on the control of substances hazardous to health also deal with changing facilities.

Regulation 25

Facilities for rest and to eat meals

227 For workers who have to stand to carry out their work, suitable seats should be provided for their use if the type of work gives them an opportunity to sit from time to time.

228 Suitable seats should be provided for workers to use during breaks. These should be in a suitable place where personal protective equipment (for example respirators or hearing protection) need not be worn. In offices and other reasonably clean workplaces, work seats or other seats in the work area will be sufficient, provided workers are not subject to excessive disturbance during breaks, for example, by contact with the public. In other cases one or more separate rest areas should be provided (which in the case of new work-places, extensions and conversions should include a separate rest room).

229 Rest areas or rooms provided in accordance with regulation 25(2) should be large enough, and have sufficient seats with backrests and tables, for the number of workers likely to use them at any one time.

230 If workers frequently have to leave their work area, and to wait until they can return, there should be a suitable rest area where they can wait.

231 Where workers regularly eat meals at work suitable and sufficient facilities should be provided for the purpose. Such facilities should also be provided where food would otherwise be likely to be contaminated, including by dust or water, for example:

(a) cement works, clay works, foundries, potteries, tanneries, and laundries;
(b) the manufacture of glass bottles and pressed glass articles, sugar, oil cake, jute, and tin or terne plates; and
(c) glass bevelling, fruit preserving, gut scraping, tripe dressing, herring curing, and the cleaning and repairing of sacks.

232 Seats in work areas can be counted as eating facilities provided they are in a sufficiently clean place and there is a suitable surface on which to place food. Eating facilities should include a facility for preparing or obtaining a hot drink, such as an electric kettle, a vending machine or a canteen. Workers who work during hours or at places where hot food cannot be obtained in, or reasonably near to, the workplace should be provided with the means for heating their own food.

233 Eating facilities should be kept clean to a suitable hygiene standard. Responsibility for cleaning should be clearly allocated. Steps should be taken where necessary to ensure that the facilities do not become contaminated by substances brought in on footwear or clothing. If necessary, adequate washing and changing facilities should be provided in a conveniently accessible place.

234 Canteens or restaurants may be used as rest facilities, provided that there is no obligation to purchase food in order to use them.

235 Good hygiene standards should be maintained in those parts of rest facilities used for eating or preparing food and drinks.

236 The subject of eating in the workplace is also dealt with in other Regulations concerning asbestos, lead, and ionising radiations, and in Approved Codes of Practice on the control of substances hazardous to health and on work in potteries.

Facilities for pregnant women and nursing mothers

237 Facilities for pregnant women and nursing mothers to rest should be conveniently situated in relation to sanitary facilities and, where necessary, include the facility to lie down.

238 There is an HSE guidance sheet on health aspects of pregnancy.

Prevention of discomfort caused by tobacco smoke

239 Rest areas and rest rooms should be arranged to enable employees to use them without experiencing discomfort from tobacco smoke. Methods of achieving this include:

(a) the provision of separate areas or rooms for smokers and non-smokers; or

(b) the prohibition of smoking in rest areas and rest rooms.

240 Passive smoking in the workplace is dealt with in a separate HSE publication.

Appendix 1

References

This appendix is not reproduced in this book.

Appendix 2

Extracts from relevant health and safety legislation

Health and Safety at Work etc Act 1974 – Section 2

"(1) It shall be the duty of every employer to ensure, so far as is reasonably practicable, the health, safety and welfare at work of all his employees.

(2) Without prejudice to the generality of an employer's duty under the preceding subsection, the matters to which that duty extends include in particular –

(a) the provision and maintenance of plant and systems of work that are, so far as is reasonably practicable, safe and without risks to health;

(b) arrangements for ensuring, so far as is reasonably practicable, safety and absence of risks to health in connection with the use, handling, storage and transport of articles and substances;

(c) the provision of such information, instruction, training and supervision as is necessary to ensure, so far as is reasonably practicable, the health and safety at work of his employees;

(d) so far as is reasonably practicable as regards any place of work under the employer's control, the maintenance of it in a condition that is safe and without risks to health and the provision and maintenance of means of access to and egress from it that are safe and without such risks;

(e) the provision and maintenance of a working environment for his employees that is, so far as is reasonably practicable, safe, without risks to health, and adequate as regards facilities and arrangements for their welfare at work."

Health and Safety at Work etc Act 1974 – Section 4

"(1) This section has effect for imposing on persons duties in relation to those who –

(a) are not their employees; but

(b) use non-domestic premises made available to them as a place of work or as a place where they may use plant or substances provided for their use there,

and applies to premises so made available and other non-domestic premises used in connection with them.

(2) It shall be the duty of each person who has, to any extent, control of premises to which this section applies or of the means of access thereto or egress therefrom or of any plant or substance in such measures as it is reasonable for a person in his position to take to ensure, so far as is reasonably practicable, that the premises, all means of access thereto or egress therefrom available for use by persons using the premises, and any plant or substance in the premises or, as the case may be, provided for use there, is or are safe and without risks to health.

(3) Where a person has, by virtue of any contract or tenancy, an obligation of any extent in relation to –

(a) the maintenance or repair of any premises to which this section applies or any means of access thereto or egress therefrom; or
(b) the safety of or the absence of risks to health arising from plant or substances in any such premises;

that person shall be treated, for the purposes of subsection (2) above, as being a person who has control of the matters to which his obligations extends.

(4) Any reference in this section to a person having control of any premises or matter is a reference to a person having control of the premises or matter in connection with the carrying on by him of a trade, business or other undertaking (whether for profit or not)."

Factories Act 1961 – Section 175(5)

"Any workplace in which, with the permission of or under agreement with the owner or occupier, two or more persons carry on any work which would constitute a factory if the persons working therein were in the employment of the owner or occupier, shall be deemed to be a factory for the purposes of this Act, and, in the case of any such workplace not being a tenement factory or part of a tenement factory, the provisions of this Act shall apply as if the owner or occupier of the workplace were the occupier of the factory and the persons working therein were persons employed in the factory."

Appendix 3

Provision and Use of Work Equipment Regulations 1992

THE REGULATIONS

Regulation 1 *(See p 303 for Guidance notes)*

Citation and commencement

(1) These Regulations may be cited as the Provision and Use of Work Equipment Regulations 1992.

(2) Subject to paragraph (3), these Regulations shall come into force on 1st January 1993.

(3) Regulations 11 to 24 and 27 and Schedule 2 in so far as they apply to work equipment first provided for use in the premises or undertaking before 1st January 1993 shall come into force on 1st January 1997.

Regulation 2 *(See p 305 for Guidance notes)*

Interpretation

(1) In these Regulations, unless the context otherwise requires –

"use" in relation to work equipment means any activity involving work equipment and includes starting, stopping, programming, setting, transporting, repairing, modifying, maintaining, servicing and cleaning, and related expressions shall be construed accordingly;

"work equipment" means any machinery, appliance, apparatus or tool and any assembly of components which, in order to achieve a common end, are arranged and controlled so that they function as a whole.

(2) Any reference in these Regulations to –

(a) a numbered regulation or Schedule is a reference to the regulation or Schedule in these Regulations so numbered; and

(b) a numbered paragraph is a reference to the paragraph so numbered in the regulation in which the reference appears.

Regulation 3 *(See p 307 for Guidance notes)*

Disapplication of these Regulations

These Regulations shall not apply to or in relation to the master or crew of a sea-going ship or to the employer of such persons, in respect of the normal ship-board activities of a ship's crew under the direction of the master.

Regulation 4 *(See p 307 for Guidance notes)*

Application of requirements under these Regulations

(1) The requirements imposed by these Regulations on an employer shall apply in respect of work equipment provided for use or used by any of his employees who is at work or who is on an offshore installation within the meaning assigned to that term by section 1(4) of the Offshore Safety Act 1992.

(2) The requirements imposed by these Regulations on an employer shall also apply –

(a) to a self-employed person, in respect of work equipment he uses at work;

(b) to any person who has control, to any extent, of non-domestic premises made available to persons as a place of work, in respect of work equipment used in such premises by such persons and to the extent of his control; and

(c) to any person to whom the provisions of the Factories Act 1961(b) apply by virtue of section 175(5) of that Act as if he were the occupier of a factory, in respect of work equipment used in the premises deemed to be a factory by that section.

(3) Any reference in paragraph (2)(b) to a person having control of any premises or matter is a reference to the person having control of the premises or matter in connection with the carrying on by him of a trade, business or other undertaking (whether for profit or not).

Regulation 5 *(See p 309 for Guidance notes)*

Suitability of work equipment

(1) Every employer shall ensure that work equipment is so constructed or adapted as to be suitable for the purpose for which it is used or provided.

(2) In selecting work equipment, every employer shall have regard to the working conditions and to the risks to the health and safety of persons which exist in the premises or undertaking in which that work equipment is to be used and any additional risk posed by the use of that work equipment.

(3) Every employer shall ensure that work equipment is used only for operations for which, and under conditions for which, it is suitable.

(4) In this regulation "suitable" means suitable in any respect which it is reasonably foreseeable will affect the health or safety of any person.

Regulation 6 *(See p 311 for Guidance notes)*

Maintenance

(1) Every employer shall ensure that work equipment is maintained in an efficient state, in efficient working order and in good repair.

(2) Every employer shall ensure that where any machinery has a maintenance log, the log is kept up to date.

Regulation 7 *(See p 312 for Guidance notes)*

Specific risks

(1) Where the use of work equipment is likely to involve a specific risk to health or safety, every employer shall ensure that –

(a) the use of that work equipment is restricted to those persons given the task of using it; and

(b) repairs, modifications, maintenance or servicing of that work equipment is restricted to those persons who have been specifically designated to perform operations of that description (whether or not also authorised to perform other operations).

(2) The employer shall ensure that the persons designated for the purposes of sub-paragraph (b) of paragraph (1) have received adequate training related to any operations in respect of which they have been so designated.

Regulation 8 *(See p 313 for Guidance notes)*

Information and instructions

(1) Every employer shall ensure that all persons who use work equipment have available to them adequate health and safety information and, where appropriate, written instructions pertaining to the use of the work equipment.

(2) Every employer shall ensure that any of his employees who supervises or manages the use of work equipment has available to him adequate health and safety information and, where appropriate, written instructions pertaining to the use of the work equipment.

(3) Without prejudice to the generality of paragraphs (1) or (2), the information and instructions required by either of those paragraphs shall include information and, where appropriate, written instructions on –

(a) the conditions in which and the methods by which the work equipment may be used;

(b) foreseeable abnormal situations and the action to be taken if such a situation were to occur; and

(c) any conclusions to be drawn from experience in using the work equipment.

(4) Information and instructions required by this regulation shall be readily comprehensible to those concerned.

Regulation 9 *(See p 314 for Guidance notes)*

Training

(1) Every employer shall ensure that all persons who use work equipment have received adequate training for purposes of health and safety, including training in the methods which may be adopted when using the work equipment, any risks which such use may entail and precautions to be taken.

(2) Every employer shall ensure that any of his employees who supervises or manages the use of work equipment has received adequate training for purposes of health and safety, including training in the methods which may be adopted when using the work equipment, any risks which such use may entail and precautions to be taken.

Regulation 10 *(See p 315 for Guidance notes)*

Conformity with Community requirements

(1) Every employer shall ensure that any item of work equipment provided for use in the premises or undertaking of the employer complies with any enactment (whether in an Act or instrument) which implements in Great Britain any of the relevant Community Directives listed in Schedule 1 which is applicable to that item of work equipment.

(2) Where it is shown that an item of work equipment complies with an enactment (whether in an Act or instrument) to which it is subject by virtue of paragraph (1), the requirements of regulations 11 to 24 shall apply in respect of that item of work equipment only to the extent that the relevant Community directive implemented by that enactment is not applicable to that item of work equipment.

(3) This regulation applies to items of work equipment provided for use in the premises or undertaking of the employer for the first time after 31st December 1992.

Regulation 11 *(See pp 317 and 344 for Guidance notes)*

Dangerous parts of machinery

(1) Every employer shall ensure that measures are taken in accordance with paragraph (2) which are effective –

(a) to prevent access to any dangerous part of machinery or to any rotating stock-bar; or

(b) to stop the movement of any dangerous part of machinery or rotating stock-bar before any part of a person enters a danger zone.

(2) The measures required by paragraph (1) shall consist of –

(a) the provision of fixed guards enclosing every dangerous part or rotating stock-bar where and to the extent that it is practicable to do so, but where or to the extent that it is not, then

(b) the provision of other guards or protection devices where and to the extent that it is practicable to do so, but where or to the extent that it is not, then

(c) the provision of jigs, holders, push-sticks or similar protection appliances used in conjunction with the machinery where and to the extent that it is practicable to do so, but where or to the extent that it is not, then

(d) the provision of information, instruction, training and supervision.

(3) All guards and protection devices provided under sub-paragraphs (a) or (b) of paragraph (2) shall –

(a) be suitable for the purpose for which they are provided;

(b) be of good construction, sound material and adequate strength;

(c) be maintained in an efficient state, in efficient working order and in good repair;

(d) not give rise to any increased risk to health or safety;

(e) not be easily bypassed or disabled;

(f) be situated at sufficient distance from the danger zone;

(g) not unduly restrict the view of the operating cycle of the machinery, where such a view is necessary;

(h) be so constructed or adapted that they allow operations necessary to fit or replace parts and for maintenance work, restricting access so that it is allowed only to the area where the work is to be carried out and, if possible, without having to dismantle the guard or protection device.

(4) All protection appliances provided under sub-paragraph (c) of paragraph (2) shall comply with sub-paragraphs (a) to (d) and (g) of paragraph (3).

(5) In this regulation –

"danger zone" means any zone in or around machinery in which a person is exposed to a risk to health or safety from contact with a dangerous part of machinery or a rotating stock-bar;

"stock-bar" means any part of a stock-bar which projects beyond the head-stock of a lathe.

Regulation 12 *(See p 319 for Guidance notes)*

Protection against specific hazards

(1) Every employer shall take measures to ensure that the exposure of a person using work equipment to any risk to his health or safety from any

hazard specified in paragraph (3) is either prevented, or, where that is not reasonably practicable, adequately controlled.

(2) The measures required by paragraph (1) shall –

(a) be measures other than the provision of personal protective equipment or of information, instruction, training and supervision, so far as is reasonably practicable; and
(b) include, where appropriate, measures to minimise the effects of the hazard as well as to reduce the likelihood of the hazard occurring.

(3) The hazards referred to in paragraph (1) are –

(a) any article or substance falling or being ejected from work equipment;
(b) rupture or disintegration of parts of work equipment;
(c) work equipment catching fire or overheating;
(d) the unintended or premature discharge of any article or of any gas, dust, liquid, vapour or other substance which, in each case, is produced, used or stored in the work equipment;
(e) the unintended or premature explosion of the work equipment or any article or substance produced, used or stored in it.

(4) For the purposes of this regulation "adequate" means adequate having regard only to the nature of the hazard and the nature and degree of exposure to the risk, and "adequately" shall be construed accordingly.

(5) This regulation shall not apply where any of the following Regulations apply in respect of any risk to a person's health or safety for which such Regulations require measures to be taken to prevent or control such risk, namely –

(a) the Control of Lead at Work Regulations 1980;
(b) the Ionising Radiations Regulations 1985;
(c) the Control of Asbestos at Work Regulations 1987;
(d) the Control of Substances Hazardous to Health Regulations 1988;
(e) the Noise at Work Regulations 1989;
(f) the Construction (Head Protection) Regulations 1989.

Regulation 13 *(See p 322 for Guidance notes)*

High or very low temperature

Every employer shall ensure that work equipment, parts of work equipment and any article or substance produced, used or stored in work equipment which, in each case, is at a high or very low temperature shall have protection where appropriate so as to prevent injury to any person by burn, scald or sear.

Regulation 14 *(See p 323 for Guidance notes)*

Controls for starting or making a significant change in operating conditions

(1) Every employer shall ensure that, where appropriate, work equipment is provided with one or more controls for the purposes of –

(a) starting the work equipment (including re-starting after a stoppage for any reason); or

(b) controlling any change in the speed, pressure or other operating conditions of the work equipment where such conditions after the change result in risk to health and safety which is greater than or of a different nature from such risks before the change.

(2) Subject to paragraph (3), every employer shall ensure that where a control is required by paragraph (1), it shall not be possible to perform any operation mentioned in sub-paragraph (a) or (b) of that paragraph except by a deliberate action on such control.

(3) Paragraph (1) shall not apply to re-starting or changing operating conditions as a result of the normal operating cycle of an automatic device.

Regulation 15 *(See p 325 for Guidance notes)*

Stop controls

(1) Every employer shall ensure that, where appropriate, work equipment is provided with one or more readily accessible controls the operation of which will bring the work equipment to a safe condition in a safe manner.

(2) Any control required by paragraph (1) shall bring the work equipment to a complete stop where necessary for reasons of health and safety.

(3) Any control required by paragraph (1) shall, if necessary for reasons of health and safety, switch off all sources of energy after stopping the functioning of the work equipment.

(4) Any control required by paragraph (1) shall operate in priority to any control which starts or changes the operating conditions of the work equipment.

Regulation 16 *(See p 326 for Guidance notes)*

Emergency stop controls

(1) Every employer shall ensure that, where appropriate, work equip-ment is provided with one or more readily accessible emergency stop controls unless it is not necessary by reason of the nature of the haz-ards and the time taken for the work equipment to come to a complete stop as a result of the action of any control provided by virtue of regul-ation 15(1).

(2) Any control required by paragraph (1) shall operate in priority to any control required by regulation 15(1).

Regulation 17 *(See p 326 for Guidance notes)*

Controls

(1) Every employer shall ensure that all controls for work equipment shall be clearly visible and identifiable, including by appropriate marking where necessary.

(2) Except where necessary, the employer shall ensure that no control for work equipment is in a position where any person operating the control is exposed to a risk to his health or safety.

(3) Every employer shall ensure where appropriate –

(a) that, so far as is reasonably practicable, the operator of any control is able to ensure from the position of that control that no person is in a place where he would be exposed to any risk to his health or safety as a result of the operation of that control, but where or to the extent that it is not reasonably practicable;

(b) that, so far as is reasonably practicable, systems of work are effective to ensure that, when work equipment is about to start, no person is in a place where he would be exposed to a risk to his health or safety as a result of the work equipment starting, but where neither of these is reasonably practicable;

(c) that an audible, visible or other suitable warning is given by virtue of regulation 24 whenever work equipment is about to start.

(4) Every employer shall take appropriate measures to ensure that any person who is in a place where he would be exposed to a risk to his health or safety as a result of the starting or stopping of work equipment has sufficient time and suitable means to avoid that risk.

Regulation 18 *(See p 329 for Guidance notes)*

Control systems

(1) Every employer shall ensure, so far as is reasonably practicable, that all control systems of work equipment are safe.

(2) Without prejudice to the generality of paragraph (1), a control system shall not be safe unless –

(a) its operation does not create any increased risk to health or safety;

(b) it ensures, so far as is reasonably practicable, that any fault in or damage to any part of the control system or the loss of supply of any source of energy used by the work equipment cannot result in additional or increased risk to health or safety;

(c) it does not impede the operation of any control required by regulation 15 or 16.

Regulation 19 *(See p 329 for Guidance notes)*

Isolation from sources of energy

(1) Every employer shall ensure that where appropriate work equipment is provided with suitable means to isolate it from all its sources of energy.

(2) Without prejudice to the generality of paragraph (1), the means mentioned in that paragraph shall not be suitable unless they are clearly identifiable and readily accessible.

(3) Every employer shall take appropriate measures to ensure that reconnection of any energy source to work equipment does not expose

any person using the work equipment to any risk to his health or safety.

Regulation 20 *(See p 331 for Guidance notes)*

Stability

Every employer shall ensure that work equipment or any part of work equipment is stabilised by clamping or otherwise where necessary for purposes of health and safety.

Regulation 21 *(See p 332 for Guidance notes)*

Lighting

Every employer shall ensure that suitable and sufficient lighting, which takes account of the operations to be carried out, is provided at any place where a person uses work equipment.

Regulation 22 *(See p 332 for Guidance notes)*

Maintenance operations

Every employer shall take appropriate measures to ensure that work equipment is so constructed or adapted that, so far as is reasonably practicable, maintenance operations which involve a risk to health or safety can be carried out while the work equipment is shut down or, in other cases –

(a) maintenance operations can be carried out without exposing the person carrying them out to a risk to his health or safety; or

(b) appropriate measures can be taken for the protection of any person carrying out maintenance operations which involve a risk to his health or safety.

Regulation 23 *(See p 333 for Guidance notes)*

Markings

Every employer shall ensure that work equipment is marked in a clearly visible manner with any marking appropriate for reasons of health and safety.

Regulation 24 *(See p 334 for Guidance notes)*

Warnings

(1) Every employer shall ensure that work equipment incorporates any warnings or warning devices which are appropriate for reasons of health and safety.

(2) Without prejudice to the generality of paragraph (1), warnings given by warning devices on work equipment shall not be appropriate unless they are unambiguous, easily perceived and easily understood.

egulation 25

xemption certificates

) The Secretary of State for Defence may, in the interests of national
:curity, by a certificate in writing exempt any of the home forces, any visiting
rce or any headquarters from any of the requirements of these Regulations
nd any such exemption may be granted subject to conditions and to a limit of
me and may be revoked by the said Secretary of State by a further certificate
writing at any time.

(2) In this regulation –

) "the home forces" has the same meaning as in section 12(1) of the
Visiting Forces Act 1952;

)) "headquarters" has the same meaning as in article 3(2) of the Visiting
Forces and International Headquarters (Application of Law) Order
1965;

:) "visiting force" has the same meaning as it does for the purposes of
any provision of Part I of the Visiting Forces Act 1952.

egulation 26 *(See p 335 for Guidance notes)*

xtension outside Great Britain

hese Regulations shall, subject to regulation 3, apply to and in relation to
e premises and activities outside Great Britain to which sections 1 to 59
nd 80 to 82 of the 1974 Act apply by virtue of the Health and Safety at
Vork etc. Act 1974 (Application outside Great Britain) Order 1989 as they
pply within Great Britain.

egulation 27 *(See p 335 for Guidance notes)*

.epeals, saving and revocations

) Subject to paragraph (2) the enactments mentioned in Part I of Schedule
are repealed to the extent specified in column 3 of that Part.

(2) Nothing in this regulation shall affect the operation of any provision
f the Offices, Shops and Railway Premises Act 1963 as that provision has
ffect by virtue of section 90(4) of that Act.

(3) The instruments mentioned in Part II of Schedule 2 are revoked to the
xtent specified in column 3 of that Part.

chedule 1 *(See p 336 for Guidance notes)*

.elevant Community Directives

egulation 10

Council Directive 73/23/EEC on the harmonization of the laws of
Member States relating to electrical equipment designed for use within
certain voltage limits (OJ No. L77, 26.3.1973, p.29)

2   Council Directive of 79/113/EEC on the approximation of the law of the Member States relating to the determination of the nois emission of construction plant and equipment (OJ No. L33, 8.2.197. p.15)

3   Council Directive 81/1051/EEC amending Directive 79/113/EEC o the approximation of the laws of the Member States relating to th determination of the noise emission of construction plant an equipment (OJ No. L376, 30.12.1981, p.49)

4   Council Directive 84/532/EEC on the approximation of the laws of th Member States relating to common provisions for con-struction plan and equipment (OJ No. L300, 19.11.1984, p.111)

5   Council Directive 84/533/EEC on the approximation of the laws of th Member States relating to the permissible sound power level c compressors (OJ No. L300, 19.11.1984, p.123)

6   Council Directive 84/534/EEC on the approximation of the laws of th Member States relating to the permissible sound power level of towe cranes (OJ No. L300, 19.11.1984, p.130)

7   Council Directive 84/535/EEC on the approximation of the laws of th Member States relating to the permissible sound power level o welding generators (OJ No. L300, 19.11.1984, p.142)

8   Council Directive 84/536/EEC on the approximation of the laws of th Member States relating to the permissible sound power level of powe generators (OJ No. L300, 19.11.1984, p.149)

9   Council Directive 84/537/EEC on the approximation of the laws of th Member States relating to the permissible sound power level o powered hand-held concrete-breakers and picks (OJ No. L30C 19.11.1984, p.156)

10   Council Directive 84/538/EEC on the approximation of the laws of th Member States relating to the permissible sound power level o lawnmowers (OJ No. L300, 19.11.1984, p.171)

11   Commission Directive 84/405/EEC adapting to technical progres Council Directive 791/113/EEC on the approximation of the laws o the Member States relating to the determination of the noise emissio of construction plant and equipment (OJ No. L233, 30.8.1985, p.9)

12   Commission Directive 85/406/EEC adapting to technical progres Council Directive 84/533/EEC on the approximation of the laws of th Member States relating to the permissible sound power level o compressors (OJ No. L233, 30.8.1985, p.11)

13 Commission Directive 85/407/EEC adapting to technical progress Council Directive 84/535/EEC on the approximation of the laws of the Member States relating to the permissible sound power level of welding generators (OJ No. L233, 30.8.1985, p.16)

14 Commission Directive 85/408/EEC adapting to technical progress Council Directive 84/536/EEC on the approximation of the laws of the Member States relating to the permissible sound power level of power generators (OJ No. L233, 30.8.1985, p.18)

15 Commission Directive 85/409/EEC adapting to technical progress Council Directive 84/537/EEC on the approximation of the laws of the Member States relating to the permissible sound power level of powered hand-held concrete-breakers and picks (OJ No. L233, 30.8.1985, p.20)

16 Commission Directive 87/252/EEC adapting to technical progress Council Directive 84/538/EEC on the approximation of the laws of the Member States relating to the permissible sound power level of lawn mowers (OJ No. L117, 5.5.1987, p.22 with corrigenda at OJ No. L158, 18.6.1987, p.31)

17 Council Directive 87/405/EEC amending Directive 84/534/EEC on the laws of the Member States relating to the permissible sound power level of tower cranes (OJ No. L220, 8.8.1987, p.60)

18 Council Directive 88/180/EEC amending Directive 84/538/EEC on the app-roximation of the laws of the Member States relating to the permissible sound power level of lawnmowers (OJ No. L81, 26.3.1988, p.69)

19 Council Directive 88/181/EEC amending Directive 84/538/EEC on the approximation of the laws of the Member States relating to the permissible sound power level of lawnmowers (OJ No. L81, 26.3.1988, p.71)

20 Council Directive 84/539/EEC on the approximation of the laws of the Member States relating to electro-medical equipment used in human or veterinary medicine (OJ No. L300, 19.11.1984, p.179)

21 Council Directive 86/295/EEC on the approximation of the laws of the Member States relating to roll-over protective structures (ROPS) for certain construction plant (OJ No. L186, 8.7.1986, p.1)

22 Council Directive 86/296/EEC on the approximation of the laws of the Member States relating to falling-object protective structures (FOPS) for certain construction plant (OJ No. L186, 8.7.1986, p.10)

23 Council Directive 86/662/EEC on the limitation of noise emitted by hydraulic excavators, rope-operated excavators, dozers, loaders and excavator-loaders (OJ No. L384, 31.12.1986, p.1)

24 Council Directive 86/663/EEC on the approximation of the laws of the Member States relating to self-propelled industrial trucks (OJ No. L384, 31.12.1986, p.12)

25 Council Directive 87/404/EEC on the harmonization of the laws of the Member States relating to simple pressure vessels (OJ No. L220, 8.8.1987, p.48)

26 Council Directive 89/106/EEC on the approximation of laws, regulations and administrative provisions of the Member States relating to construction products (OJ No. L40, 11.2.1989, p.12)

27 Commission Directive 89/240/EEC adapting to technical progress Council Directive 86/663/EEC on the approximation of the laws of the Member States relating to self-propelled industrial trucks (OJ No. L100, 12.4.1989, p.1)

28 Council Directive 89/336/EEC on the approximation of the laws of the Member States relating to electromagnetic compatibility (OJ No. L139, 23.5.1989, p.19)

29 Council Directive 89/392/EEC on the approximation of the laws of the Member States relating to machinery (OJ No. L183, 29.6.1989, p.9)

30 Commission Directive 89/514/EEC adapting to technical progress Council Directive 86/662/EEC on the limitation of noise emitted by hydraulic excavators, rope-operated excavators, dozers, loaders and excavator-loaders (OJ No. L253, 30.8.1989, p.35)

31 Council Directive 89/686/EEC on the approximation of the laws of the Member States relating to personal protective equipment (OJ No. L399, 30.12.1989, p.18)

32 Council Directive 90/385/EEC on the approximation of the laws of the Member States relating to active implantable medical devices (OJ No. L189, 20.7.1990, p.17)

33 Council Directive 90/396/EEC on the approximation of the laws of the Member States relating to appliances burning gaseous fuels (OJ No. L196, 26.7.1990, p.15)

34 Council Directive 91/368/EEC amending Directive 89/392/EEC on the approximation of the laws of the Member States relating to machinery (OJ No. L198, 22.7.1991, p.16)

35 Council Directive 92/31/EEC amending Directive 89/336/EEC on the approximation of the laws of the Member States relating to electromagnetic compatibility (OJ No. L126, 12.5.92, p.11)

Schedule 2

Repeals and revocations

Regulation 27

PART I
REPEALS

(1) *Chapter*	(2) *Short title*	(3) *Extent of repeal*
1954 c.70.	The Mines and Quarries Act 1954.	Sections 81(1) and 82.
1961 c.34.	The Factories Act 1961.	Sections 12 to 16, 17 and 19.
1963 c.41.	The Offices, Shops and Railway Premises Act 1963.	Section 17.

PART II
REVOCATIONS

(1) *Title*	(2) *Reference*	(3) *Extent of repeal*
Regulations dated 17th October 1905 (The Spinning by Self-Acting Mules Regulations 1905).	S.R. & O. 1905/1103, amended by the Employment Act 1989 (c.38), section 29(5), Schedule 8.	The whole Regulations.
The Aerated Water Regulations 1921.	S.R. & O. 1921/1932, amended by S. I. 1981/686.	Regulations 1, 2 and 8.
The Horizontal Milling Machines Regulations 1928.	S.R. & O. 1928/548, amended by S.R. & O. 1934/207.	The exemptions and regulations 2 to 7.
The Operations at Unfenced Machinery Regulations 1938.	S.R. & O. 1938/641, amended by S.R. & O. 1946/156 and S. I. 1976/955.	The whole Regulations.

(1) *Title*	(2) *Reference*	(3) *Extent of repeal*
The Jute (Safety, Health and Welfare) Regulations 1948.	S. I. 1948/1696, to which there are amendments not relevant to these Regulations.	Regulations 15, 27 and 28 and the First Schedule.
The Iron and Steel Foundries Regulations 1953.	S. I. 1953/1464, amended by S. I. 1974/1681 and S. I. 1981/1332.	Regulation 5.
The Agriculture (Power Take-Off) Regulations 1957.	S. I. 1957/1386, amended by S. I. 1976/1247, S. I. 1981/1414 and S. I. 1991/1913.	The whole Regulations.
The Agriculture (Circular Saws) Regulations 1959.	S. I. 1959/427, amended by S. I. 1981/1414.	(i) In regulation 1, in sub-paragraph (b), from the beginning to *and* where it first occurs: and sub-paragraph (c): (ii) regulations 3 and 4: (iii) in regulation 5(1), the words from *unless* to *or*: and (iv) Schedule 1.
The Agriculture (Stationary Machinery) Regulations 1959.	S. I. 1959/1216, amended by S. I. 1976/1247 and S. I. 1981/1414.	The whole Regulations.
The Agriculture (Threshers and Balers) Regulations 1960.	S. I. 1960/1199, amended by S. I. 1976/1247 and S. I. 1981/1414.	In the Schedule, paragraphs 2, 3, 6, 7, 8, 9, 10, 11, 12, 16 and 17.
The Shipbuilding and Ship-Repairing Regulations 1960.	S. I. 1960/1932, to which there are amendments not relevant to these Regulations.	Regulation 67.
The Construction (General Provisions) Regulations 1961.	S. I. 1961/1580, to which there are amendments not relevant to these Regulations.	Regulations 42, 43 and 57.
The Agriculture (Field Machinery) Regulations 1962.	S. I. 1962/1472, amended by S. I. 1976/1247 and S. I. 1981/1414.	In the Schedule, paragraphs 2 to 6 and 15 to 19.

(1) *Title*	(2) *Reference*	(3) *Extent of repeal*
The Abrasive Wheels Regulations 1970.	S. I. 1970/535.	In regulation 3, paragraphs (2), (3) and (4); and regulations 4, 6 to 8, 10 to 16, 18 and 19.
The Woodworking Machines Regulations 1974.	S. I. 1974/903, amended by S. I. 1978/1126.	In regulation 1, paragraphs (2) and (3); in regulation 2, the definitions of *cutters, machine table, narrow band sawing machine, sawmill* and *squared stock*; in regulation 3, paragraph (2); regulations 5 to 9, 14 to 19, 21 to 38, and 40 to 43.
The Offshore Installations (Operational Safety, Health and Welfare) Regulations 1976.	S. I. 1976/1019, which has effect as an existing statutory provision under the 1974 Act by virtue of section 1(1) of the Offshore Safety Act 1992 (c.15).	Regulations 10 and 12.
The Agriculture (Power Take-off) (Amendment) Regulations 1991.	S. I. 1991/1913.	The whole Regulations.

GUIDANCE NOTES

Introduction

1–6 . . .

Background

7–9

Relationship with existing health and safety legislation

10 PUWER amplifies and makes more explicit the general duties on employers, the self-employed and persons in control to provide safe plant and equipment. Virtually all the requirements already exist somewhere in the law or constitute good practice. PUWER brings together these requirements and applies them across all industrial, commercial and service sectors.

11 This means that employers with well chosen and well maintained equipment should need to do little more than before. Some older equipment may need to be up-graded to meet the requirements, and there is until 1 January 1997 to do the necessary work. Much old legislation – 17 codes of Regulations, seven sections of the Factories Act 1961, one section of the Offices, Shops and Railway Premises Act 1963 and two sections of the Mines and Quarries Act 1954 – is being replaced, in full or in part, by PUWER although most will continue to apply to existing equipment until 1 January 1997 when the transitional period ends.

12 PUWER will overlap many existing requirements but where this occurs compliance with the existing requirements should normally be sufficient to comply with PUWER. For example, the requirement concerning isolation from source of energy (regulation 19) is, so far as electricity is concerned, dealt with by the Electricity at Work Regulations 1989. Another example is that scaffolds which have been properly maintained under the Construction (Working Places) Regulations 1966 will also meet the requirements for maintenance under PUWER.

Relationship with other new health and safety legislation

13 In addition to the Provisions and Use of Work Equipment Regulations, the following Regulations (which also stem from recent European Directives) are also due to come into force in 1993:

The Management of Health and Safety at Work Regulations 1992
The Personal Protective Equipment at Work Regulations 1992
The Workplace (Health, Safety and Welfare) Regulations 1992

The Manual Handling Operations Regulations 1992
The Health and Safety (Display Screen Equipment) Regulations 1992

14 These new Regulations will operate alongside the HSW Act and Regulations made under the HSW Act, for example, the Electricity at Work Regulations 1989, the Noise at Work Regulations 1989, the Control of Substances Hazardous to Health Regulations 1988.

15 Therefore, PUWER cannot be considered in isolation. In particular, they need to be looked at together with the Management of Health and Safety at Work Regulations 1992 (MHSWR).

16 Regulation 3(1) of MHSWR requires all employers and the self-employed to assess the risks to the health and safety of workers and any others who may be affected by the work carried out, for the purpose of identifying the measures needed to be taken to comply with other legislation. Carrying out this assessment will help to identify all the protective and preventative measures that have to be taken to comply with these Regulations, particularly for regulation 5 – selection of suitable work equipment, regulation 11 – safeguarding dangerous parts of machinery and also regulations 12 to 24.

17 Further guidance on the procedure for risk assessment is to be found in the Approved Code of Practice on the MHSWR which includes advice on the selection of preventative and protective measures.

18 A common sense approach needs to be adopted to risk assessment, the most important part of which is to decide whether or not the requirements of these Regulations are already being complied with and if not, what additional measures need to be taken.

19 Most employers will be capable of making the risk assessment themselves using expertise within their own organisations to identify the measures which need to be taken concerning their work equipment. In a few cases, for example where there are complex hazards or equipment, it may need to be done in conjunction with the help of external health and safety advisors, appointed under regulation 6 of MHSWR.

20 For many items of work equipment, particularly machinery, the user will know from previous experience what measures need to be taken to comply with previous legal requirements. Generally those measures will ensure compliance with these Regulations. Where this is not the case there is usually a straightforward method of identifying the measures that need to be taken, because these are described in either general or industry specific or machine specific guidance. However, the user will need to decide whether these are appropriate.

21 Where guidance does not exist, or is not appropriate, the main factors that need to be taken into account are the severity of any likely injury or ill health likely to result from any hazard present, the likelihood of that happening and the numbers exposed, to identify the measures that need to be taken to eliminate or reduce the risk to an acceptable level.

22 There are complementary training requirements in PUWER and MHSWR. Regulation 11 of MHSWR is a general requirement dealing with when health and safety training should be provided, eg on recruitment or

on being exposed to new or increased risks, such as with the introduction of new technology or systems of work, or the introduction or change of work equipment. Regulation 9 of PUWER is concerned more specifically with what training should consist of, ie the precautions to be taken during the use of work equipment. MHSWR also amends the Safety Representatives and Safety Committees Regulations 1977. Safety representatives appointed under those Regulations will also have a role to play in the operation of PUWER, eg in the selection process of suitable work equipment and in its subsequent maintenance procedures.

23 There are limited areas of overlap between PUWER, the Workplace (Health, Safety and Welfare) Regulations 1992 and the Health and Safety (Display Screen Equipment) Regulations 1992 (eg on lighting) and the Personal Protective Equipment at Work Regulations 1992 (eg on maintenance). The guiding principle will be that where duties overlap, compliance with the more specific Regulation will normally be sufficient to comply with a general requirement.

Duties on manufacturers and suppliers

24 Manufacturers and suppliers of work equipment also have general legal duties under existing law and this too is being changed as a result of European Directives. These Directives, concerning products, are an essential part of the 'Single Market' which is due to be completed by 31 December 1992. In simple terms, the 'Single Market' means that manufacturers will be able to market their products without barriers to trade anywhere in the European Community providing these products meet essential health and safety requirements which have been agreed by Member States. In this context the most important 'product directive' is the Machinery Directive (89/392/EEC as amended by 91/368/EEC).

25 The Machinery Directive is concerned with health and safety through the design and construction of new machines and so corresponds most directly to the requirements of section 6 of the HSW Act. In common with other 'New Approach' Directives it sets out in general terms the essential health and safety requirements which must be met before new machinery is placed on the market. European harmonised standards will fill in the detail of these general requirements. The Directive will be implemented in the UK by Regulations made by the Department of Trade and Industry, due to take effect from 1 January 1993.

26 Equipment which satisfies these 'product' Directives will be exempt from many of the specific requirements contained in PUWER, ie regulations 11 to 24 (see guidance to regulation 10).

Duties on employees

27 The prime duty for ensuring health and safety rests with employers but employees have legal duties too, particularly under Sections 7 and 8 of the HSW Act. They include:

(a) taking reasonable care for their own health and safety and that of others who may be affected by what they do or don't do;
(b) co-operating with their employer on health and safety;
(c) not interfering with or misusing anything provided for their health, safety and welfare.

These duties have been supplemented by regulation 12 of MHSWR. One of the new requirements is that employees should use correctly all work items provided by their employer in accordance with their training and the instructions they receive to enable them to use the items safely.

28 This is very relevant to employees using work equipment. It means that employees who have received the necessary and appropriate instructions and training are required to use their work equipment correctly. They should not use portable electric drilling machines in the rain (unless they have been designed and constructed for use in such conditions), move mobile tower scaffolds except from the ground, use tractors with unguarded power take-off shafts, use welding equipment in confined spaces with inadequate ventilation, or bypass safety devices (unless expressly authorised and additional precautions are taken). On machines, where particular care is needed, eg woodworking machines, they should adjust guards in line with the work to be carried out and correctly use push sticks, jigs, holders, etc.

Regulation 1

Citation and commencement

29 The Regulations come into force on 1 January 1993, subject to the exceptions in regulation 1(3). Some of the Regulations do not apply to certain categories of work equipment until 1 January 1997. The date of application will depend on whether the equipment is new, existing, second-hand, hired or leased; this is set out in the following paragraphs.

New work equipment

30 All the Regulations come into force on 1 January 1993. Items of work equipment provided for use from that date ('new equipment') will need to meet these requirements.

Existing work equipment

31 Regulations 1 to 10 come into force on 1 January 1993. Regulations 11 to 24, 27 and Schedule 2 do not come into force until 1 January 1997 for work equipment first provided for use in a particular premises or undertaking before 1 January 1993 ('existing equipment'). This means that existing equipment will be exempt from the specific requirements in regulations 11 to 24, but will continue to be subject to the existing legislation (listed in Schedule 2) during this period. The provisions of

regulations 11 to 24 are generally specific 'hardware' provisions, ie they prescribe features that relate to the equipment itself. Employers with well chosen and well maintained existing equipment should need to do little more than at present. Some older equipment may need to be up-graded to meet the requirements, but there is time to do any necessary work until 1 January 1997.

Second-hand work equipment

32 When existing work equipment is sold by one company to another and brought into use by the second company from 1 January 1993 onwards, it becomes 'new equipment' in the sense of paragraph 30, even though it is second-hand. This means that the purchasing company will need to ascertain that the equipment meets the specific hardware provisions of regulations 11 to 24 before putting it into use. However, it will not have to comply with the 'essential safety requirements' of Article 100A Directives (see paragraph 99) as these are not retrospective.

Hired and leased equipment

33 Hired and leased equipment is treated in the same way as second-hand equipment. This means that existing equipment hired or leased to another company from 1 January 1993 is treated as 'new equipment' in the sense of paragraph 30. Therefore, companies hiring or leasing an existing item of work equipment from 1 January 1993 onwards will need to check that it meets the specific hardware provisions of regulations 11 to 24 before putting it into use. However, it will not have to comply with the 'essential safety requirements' of Article 100A Directives (see paragraph 99) as these are not retrospective.

First provided for use

34 The phrase 'first provided for use' refers to the date on which work equipment is first supplied in the premises or undertaking. This is not the same as first brought into use. Provided for use does not necessarily mean that it has actually been put to use. For example, equipment delivered to one of a company's premises before 1 January 1993 would be considered to be 'existing equipment', even though it might remain in store and not be put into use until after that date. (This is also relevant in the context of regulation 10.)

Premises or undertaking

35 Section 53 of the HSW Act defines premises in very wide terms to include any place and would cover individual plants, establishments, buildings, office blocks, shops, mines, offshore installations.

36 Some premises will be the sole premises owned by that employer. Others will be part of a larger undertaking with many separate premises,

for example a chain of shops or tyre stockists, a university with buildings scattered throughout a city, a company with plants throughout Great Britain, or a plant-hire company with many depots. Some employees may not have a fixed place of work, eg peripatetic workers such as foresters, contract gardeners, service engineers, but the work equipment that they use is part of the employer's undertaking.

37 Work equipment which was first provided for use before 1 January 1993 at one premises belonging to an undertaking, and moved to other premises of the same undertaking on or after 1 January 1993 will be treated as existing equipment, and will have until 1 January 1997 to conform with the specific hardware provisions of these Regulations (regulations 11 to 24).

Examples

38 Examples of equipment remaining within the same undertaking are:

(a) an engineering company which owns an existing lathe moves it from its plant in Cheshire to another one in Northumberland;

(b) a leased radiation gauge is transferred from a paper mill in southern England to a mill in Scotland owned by the same undertaking;

(c) a plant-hire company moves a crane or lift-truck from a depot it owns in Leeds to one in Swansea.

In all cases, the specific hardware requirements of the Regulations would not apply until 1 January 1997, providing the equipment is used by the same undertaking.

39 But if on or after 1 January 1993 the lathe is obtained by another separate undertaking or company second-hand, the radiation gauge is leased by a different company, or the crane or lift-truck is hired to a contractor on a construction site, the equipment would have been provided for use as if it were 'new equipment', and the Regulations would so apply when the equipment was used in the second undertaking.

Regulation 2

Interpretation

40 The definition of 'use' is wide and includes all activities involving the work equipment such as stopping or starting the equipment, repair, modification, maintenance and servicing. In addition to operations normally considered as use, cleaning and transport of the equipment are also included. In this context 'transport' means, for example, using a lift truck to carry goods around a warehouse.

41 The scope of 'work equipment' is also extremely wide. Work equipment includes single machines such as a power press, guillotine, circular saw bench, photocopier or a combine harvester, tools such as a portable drill or a hammer, and apparatus such as laboratory apparatus (bunsen burners etc). In addition to individual items of work equipment,

any assembly arranged and controlled to function as a whole is included, for example a bottling plant.

42 Motor vehicles which are not privately owned fall within the scope of the Regulations. However, the more specific road traffic legislation will take precedence when these vehicles are used on public roads. When such vehicles are used off the public highway these Regulations and the HSW Act would normally take precedence.

43 By way of example, the following is a non-exhaustive list of work equipment subject to these Regulations:

Work equipment

dumper truck	ladder
portable drill	combine harvester
mobile access platform	scalpel
X-ray baggage detector	car ramp
soldering iron	check-out machine
trench sheets	hammer
air compressor	laboratory apparatus
meat cleaver	lawn-mower
potato grading line	butcher's knife
automatic car wash	fire engine turntable
drill bit	computer
resuscitator	socket set
crane	detonator
hand saw	power press
microbiological safety cabinet	scaffolder's podger
road tanker	photoelectric device
tractor	lifting sling
lift truck	power harrow
vehicle hoist	overhead projector
dry cleaning unit	robot line
drilling equipment for use on an offshore installation	blast furnace
	pit winding gear
automatic storage and retrieval equipment	reactor solvent degreasing bath
scaffolding	LPG filling plant
cooling tower	quarry crushing plant
pressure vessel	nickel plating line
installed plant (eg for electricity generation)	linear accelerator

Not work equipment

livestock, substances (eg acids, alkalis, slurry, cement, water), structural items (walls, stairs, roof), private car.

Regulation 3

Disapplication of these Regulations

44 The Regulations have general application and apart from the exemption defined in this Regulation, apply wherever the HSW Act applies, ie to all industrial sectors, including offshore oil and gas installations, service occupations, hospitals, universities etc. The HSW Act applies throughout Great Britain and has effect wherever work is done by the employed or the self-employed other than domestic work in a private household. The HSW Act also applies to non-domestic premises made available as places of work.

Sea-going ships

45 Sea-going ships are subject to separate Merchant Shipping legislation administered by the Department of Transport. The Provision and Use of Work Equipment Regulations 1992 do not apply to the normal shipboard activities of a ship's crew under the direction of the master. However, the Regulations may apply to other activities aboard a ship, for example where a shore-based contractor carries out the work, provided the ship is within territorial waters. The Regulations also apply to certain activities carried out offshore – see regulation 26.

Regulation 4

Application of requirements under these Regulations

46 Employers have a general duty under Section 2 of the Health and Safety at Work etc Act 1974 to provide and maintain, so far as is reasonably practicable, machinery, equipment and other plant that is safe. They must also ensure that, so far as is reasonably practicable, the systems of work are safe. Persons in control of non-domestic premises also have a duty under Section 4 of the Act towards those who are not their employees but use their premises. These Regulations build on those duties.

47 Employers (whether individuals, partnerships or companies) have a duty to ensure that items of work equipment provided to their employees and the self-employed working for them complies with these Regulations. The self-employed must comply with the same duties in respect of work equipment they use at work. Persons in control of non-domestic premises who provide items of work equipment which is used by other people at work must also comply with the Regulations. For example, the owner of a multi-occupied building has a legal responsibility to ensure that a lift complies with the Regulations, and the main contractor of a construction site would be responsible for a scaffold.

48 The Regulations cover not only the normal situation where employers provide work equipment for their employees, but also cover the situation where employers choose to allow their employees to provide their own work equipment.

49 There are no separate duties on employees in these Regulations. These are covered in other legislation, in particular in Section 7 of the HSW Act and regulation 12 of the MHSWR (see also paragraphs 27 to 28).

50 The Regulations place duties on all employers providing work equipment to ensure that it is suitable, properly maintained etc. On multi-occupancy or multi-contractor sites where more than one employer uses the same piece of equipment, these duties can be discharged by the employers making arrangements among themselves whereby one of them takes responsibility for the measures necessary to discharge the duties in respect of that piece of equipment, provided that the arrangements are adequate and that they work effectively. Regulation 9 of the MHSWR and its supporting Approved Code of Practice is relevant here. It requires employers and the self-employed who share a workplace to coordinate their activities, cooperate with each other and share information to ensure that each complies with their responsibilities under health and safety legislation. The following paragraphs examine such situations in detail in the construction and offshore sectors. Similar principles should apply in other sectors.

Application to the construction industry

51 In the construction industry items of work equipment on sites are often used by a number of different contractors. Regulation 4 places a duty on each individual contractor to ensure that any work equipment used by their employees (or themselves in the case of self-employed contractors) conforms to, and is used in accordance with, these Regulations. It is recognised that it may sometimes be difficult to fully comply with this requirement. For example, a contractor who occasionally uses an item of machinery provided by another contractor may have little control over maintenance arrangements. Effective coordination between the parties involved is therefore essential.

52 The arrangements required by regulation 9 of the MHSWR would be strengthened by the proposed Construction (Design and Management) Regulations which are due to come into force on 31 December 1993.

53 These proposals would require the appointment of a single person or firm ('the principal contractor') who would be responsible for coordinating the activities of all the contractors on site and ensuring that work is carried out safely. The principal contractor would have a duty to ensure that all contractors cooperated.

54 Where work equipment is shared by a number of contractors the principal contractor would be required to coordinate its provision and use. Depending on the type of equipment, the nature of the project and the contractual arrangements, the principal contractor would have the option of either taking action themselves to achieve compliance with the Regulations on behalf of the common users or directing another contractor or group of contractors to do so. Cooperation and exchanging information is vital in such circumstances to ensure that faults or changes in conditions of use are reported to the coordinator for the equipment and that instructions or limitations on use are passed on to the common users.

55 Although the proposed Regulations are not due to come into force until 31 December 1993, the principle of a single coordinator for the provision and use of shared work equipment has advantages and it is recommended that it be followed in the meantime. However, it should be noted that the establishment of such arrangements, either on an informal basis or following the introduction of the Construction (Design and Management) Regulations, does not relieve the individual contractors from their duties under regulation 4. If a breach of the law should occur as a result of a failure in the common arrangements, the balance of blameworthiness between the various parties involved would be judged on the facts of the case.

Application to the offshore industry

56 Similar considerations apply in respect of the offshore industry, where owners of installations may provide equipment for use by contractors. Owners and contractors will need to make effective arrangements for coordination and communication to ensure that the duties of regulation 4 are met.

57 These matters will also be considered in the context of the Offshore Installation (Safety Case) Regulations 1992 (expected to come into force during 1993), which will place a duty on owners or operators to demonstrate in their Safety Case that their management system is adequate to ensure that relevant statutory provisions in respect of the installation and connected activities will be complied with.

58 Effective arrangements for cooperation and coordination will also be needed to cover maintenance arrangements, to take account of the responsibilities on individual employers under these Regulations, and on owners of offshore installations and offshore installation managers under the Offshore Installations (Operational Safety, Health and Welfare) Regulations 1976 (SI 1976/1019).

59 Equipment for use on offshore installations has to be certified as fit for purpose by independent certifying authorities under the Offshore Installations (Construction and Survey) Regulations 1974 (SI 1974/289). The Provision and Use of Work Equipment Regulations do not relieve individual employers of their duties under these Regulations.

Regulation 5

Suitability of work equipment

60 This Regulation lies at the heart of this set of Regulations. It addresses the safety of work equipment from three aspects:

(a) its initial integrity;
(b) the place where it will be used; and
(c) the purpose for which it will be used.

61 The selection of suitable work equipment for particular tasks and processes makes it possible to reduce or eliminate many risks to the health and safety of people at the workplace. This applies both to the normal use of the equipment as well as to other operations such as maintenance.

62 The risk assessment carried out under regulation 3(1) of the Management of Health and Safety at Work Regulations 1992 will help employers to select work equipment and assess its suitability for particular tasks.

Regulation 5(1)

63 Equipment must be suitable, by design, construction or adaptation, for the actual work it is provided to do. This should mean in practice that when employers provide equipment they should ensure that it has been produced for the work to be undertaken and that it is used in accordance with the manufacturer's specifications and instructions. If employers choose to adapt equipment then they must ensure that it is still suitable for its intended purpose.

64 This requirement provides the focal point for the other Regulations – for example compliance with regulation 10 should ensure the initial integrity of equipment in many cases, and compliance as appropriate with the specific requirements of regulations 11 to 24 should help the employer to meet the duties under this Regulation. For example, regulation 11(3)(h) deals with aspects of the integrity of guards and protection devices, and regulation 22 with the design and putting into use of work equipment that can be safely maintained.

Regulation 5(2)

65 This requires employers to assess the location in which the work equipment is to be used and to take account of any risks that may arise from the particular circumstances – for example, is the equipment to be used in a wet environment, or in a flammable atmosphere? Such factors can invalidate the use of equipment in a particular location which would be perfectly adequate to do the work in other locations. This would be the case for electrically powered equipment in wet or flammable atmospheres. In such circumstances the employer should consider the selection of pneumatically or hydraulically powered equipment or electrical equipment designed for use under such conditions.

66 Employers should also take into account the fact that work equipment itself can sometimes cause risks to health and safety in particular locations which would otherwise be safe, for example, a petrol generator discharging exhaust fumes into an enclosed space.

Regulation 5(3)

67 This requirement concerns each particular process for which the work equipment is to be used and the conditions under which it will be used. The

employer must ensure that the equipment is suitable for the process and conditions of use.

68 A crane already in use would not be suitable for any particular operation where the load to be lifted exceeded its rated load. Similarly, a circular saw is generally not suitable for cutting a rebate whereas a spindle moulding machine would be because it can be guarded to a high standard; knives with unprotected blades are often used for cutting operations where scissors or other cutting tools could be used with risk of less serious injury.

Regulation 6

Maintenance

69 This Regulation, which builds on the more general duty in the HSW Act, deals with the obligation to maintain equipment, not the need for such maintenance to be carried out safely. The latter is however a requirement of Section 2 of the HSW Act. The design of the equipment so that maintenance can be carried out without risk to health or safety is the subject of regulation 22 for existing work equipment and regulation 10 for new equipment.

70 In regulation 6, 'efficient' relates to how the condition of the equipment might affect health and safety; it is not concerned with productivity. Some parts of equipment such as guards, ventilation equipment, emergency shutdown systems and pressure relief devices clearly have to be maintained to do their job at all times. The necessity to maintain other parts may not be as obvious, but as an example failure to lubricate bearings or replace clogged filters might lead to danger because of seized parts or overheating.

71 It is important that equipment is maintained so that its performance does not deteriorate to the extent that it puts people at risk. The extent and complexity of maintenance will vary enormously, from simple checks on hand-held tools (for example to identify loose heads on hammers or splayed mushroom heads on chisels) to a substantial integrated programme for a complex process plant.

72 Equipment may need to be checked frequently to ensure that safety-related features are functioning correctly. A fault which affects production is normally apparent within a short time, however a fault in a safety critical system could remain undetected unless maintenance procedures provide adequate inspection or testing. The frequency at which equipment needs to be checked is dependent on the equipment itself and the risk involved; it could be each day, every three months, or even longer.

73 Any maintenance work should only be done by those who have received adequate information, instructions and training relating to that work; these should cover the reasons for the maintenance activities as well as the procedures and techniques which are applied; see also regulations 8 and 9.

74 In addition to any requirement to carry out maintenance under this regulation, other legislation may set out minimum requirements for

maintenance or for inspection or test. Examples are specific requirements for hoists, lifts, scaffolds and control measures such as ventilation plant. However, although minimum requirements may have been set, there is still a need for the equipment to be effectively maintained at all times.

Routine maintenance

75 This includes periodic lubrication, inspection and testing, based on the recommendations of the equipment manufacturer; it should also take account of any specific legal requirements as indicated in paragraph 74. However, while in most cases it would be expected that the combination of the manufacturer's instructions and legal requirements would allow adequate maintenance, in particularly arduous conditions, for example, further measures may be required.

76 Components which are found to have failed or are likely to fail before the next periodic check should be repaired or replaced. In some cases, faults may have occurred which are not immediately apparent.

Planned preventive maintenance

77 When inadequate maintenance could cause the equipment, guards or other protection devices to fail in a dangerous way, a formal system of planned preventive maintenance may be necessary.

78 Although all maintenance is preventive in some respect, the primary aim of planned preventive maintenance is to prevent failures occurring while the equipment is in use.

79 This is achieved through a system of written instructions which are used to initiate inspection, testing and, perhaps more importantly, the periodic replacement or refurbishing of components or equipment before they reach the end of their useful life. The instructions could be based as appropriate on the manufacturer's recommendations or experience from previous service and condition monitoring.

Maintenance log

80 There is no requirement for a maintenance log. However, it is recommended that a record of maintenance is kept. A maintenance log should provide information for future planning and inform maintenance personnel and others of previous action taken. This may be of value in complying with the requirements of regulation 8(3).

81 If there is a log, it should be kept up-to-date. Other legislation for particular types of equipment may require records of maintenance to be provided in a specified way, especially when this includes testing.

Regulation 7

Specific risks

82 This Regulation implements a requirement of the Directive. HSE takes the view that no additional measures, other than those required by existing

legislation, need to be taken by industry to comply with this Regulation. Those responsible for enforcement (HSE inspectors and local authority inspectors) are aware of this.

Regulation 8

Information and instructions

83 This Regulation builds on the general duty in the HSW Act to provide employees with such information and instruction as is necessary to ensure, so far as is reasonably practicable, their health and safety. In addition, it complements the general requirement in the Management of Health and Safety at Work Regulations 1992 to provide information to employees relating to their health and safety. It places a duty on employers to make available all relevant health and safety information and written instructions on the use of work equipment to their workforce. This means that the workforce should have easy access to such information and instructions and be able to understand them.

84 Information can be in writing or verbal where this is considered to be sufficient. It is the employer's responsibility to decide, given the individual circumstances, which is appropriate. Where there are more complicated or unusual situations the information should be in writing. The employer will need to take into account such matters as the degree of skill of the employees involved, their experience and training, the degree of supervision and the complexity and length of the particular job.

85 Written instructions refer primarily to the information provided by manufacturers or suppliers such as instruction sheets or manuals, instruction placards, warning labels and training manuals. There are duties on manufacturers and suppliers to provide sufficient information, including drawings, to make possible the correct installation, safe operation and maintenance of the work equipment. Employers should ask or check that they are provided. The Regulation requires employers to ensure that such written instructions are available to those directly using the work equipment; they should not be gathering dust in the purchasing department. Maintenance instructions should be made available/passed on to those involved in the maintenance of work equipment.

86 The information and written instructions should also be available to supervisors and managers. The amount of very detailed health and safety information they will need to have immediately available for day-to-day running of production lines or research laboratories will vary but it is important that they know what information is available and where it can be found.

87 The information and written instructions should cover all the health and safety aspects of use that will arise and any limitations on these uses together with any foreseeable difficulties that could arise and the methods to deal with them. Any conclusions drawn from experience in the use of the equipment should be acted upon and either recorded or steps taken to ensure that all appropriate members of the workforce are aware of them.

88 To be readily comprehensible all information and written instructions should be presented clearly in English, and/or other languages where necessary, and be in a logical sequence with good illustrations when appropriate. Standard symbols should be used. Account should be taken of the workforce's level of training, knowledge and experience. Special consideration should be given to any employees with language difficulties or with disabilities which may impede their receipt of information. For employees with little or no understanding of English or with reading difficulties, employers may need to make special arrangements.

Regulation 9

Training

89 An employer's obligation to train extends not only to those who use work equipment but also to those supervising or managing them. The training should be adequate for the circumstances.

90 It is impossible to lay down detailed requirements as to what constitutes 'adequate training' in all circumstances. In considering the extent of training which will be necessary in a particular case, the shortfall between the employee's existing competence and that necessary to use, supervise or manage the use of the work equipment with due regard to health and safety, will need to be evaluated and made up. Account should be taken of the circumstances in which the employee is to work (eg alone, under close supervision of a competent person, in a supervisory or management capacity.)

91 The development of specific statements of what the employee needs to do and to what level (ie statements of competence) will assist the employer to evaluate the extent of any shortfall in the employee's competence.

92 Statements of competence may be embodied in qualifications accredited by the National Council for Vocational Qualifications (NCVQ) and the Scottish Vocational Education Council (SCOTVEC).

Training requirements in other legislation

93 Training and instruction is a central requirement of both the HSW Act and of many specific Regulations. Regulation 11 of the Management of Health and Safety at Work Regulations 1992 requires employers to provide their employees with general health and safety training. This should be supplemented as necessary with more specific training on the use of work equipment. The detailed training requirements in, for example, the Woodworking Machines Regulations 1974 and the Abrasive Wheels Regulations 1970 are not replaced by these Regulations and will continue to apply.

Additional requirements for young people

94 Training, coupled with proper supervision, is particularly important for all young people because of their relative immaturity and unfamiliarity with

the working environment. Induction training is of particular importance. In addition, there are specific training requirements in current legislation that will continue to apply to young people using certain machines, including Section 21 of the Factories Act 1961, Section 19 of the Offices, Shops and Railway Premises Act 1963, and regulation 13 of the Woodworking Machines Regulations 1974.

Regulation 10

Conformity with Community requirements

95 This Regulation aims to ensure that when work equipment is first provided for use in the workplace after 31 December 1992 it meets certain health and safety requirements. It places a duty on employers that complements those on manufacturers and suppliers in other legislation regarding the initial integrity of equipment.

96 There are legal requirements covering all those involved in the chain of supply of work equipment which are designed to ensure that new work equipment is safe. For example, Section 6 of the HSW Act, which will remain in force, places general duties on designers, manufacturers, importers and suppliers to ensure this so far as is reasonably practicable.

97 Existing national legislation on the manufacture and supply of new work equipment is increasingly being supplemented by new and more detailed Regulations implementing EC Directives made under Article 100A of the Treaty of Rome. These new Regulations place duties on the manufacturer and supplier of new work equipment. (Further background to the Article 100A Directives is set out in paragraphs 102 to 106.)

Regulation 10(1)

98 Regulation 10(1) places a new duty on employers as users of work equipment. When first providing work equipment for use in the workplace they should ensure that it has been made to the requirements of the legislation implementing any product Directive which is relevant to the equipment. (For interpretation of 'first provided for use' see the guidance on regulation 1.) In practice this may mean that whereas previously employers would have specified to the supplier that work equipment should comply with current health and safety legislation, they would in future also specify that it should comply with the legislation implementing any relevant EC Directive. Where appropriate the employer can check to see that the equipment bears a CE mark and ask for a copy of the EC Declaration of Conformity.

99 The position is complicated because at present not all work equipment is covered by a product Directive. Nor are product Directives retrospective. If an employer provides second-hand equipment for the first time in the workplace it does not need to be modified to meet the 'essential safety requirements' of the relevant product Directive, but it must comply immediately with regulations 11 to 24 of PUWER. (Second-hand equipment imported from outside the European Community has to

comply immediately with the 'essential safety requirements' of the relevant product Directive.)

100 One of the most significant relevant Directives is the Machinery Directive, for which the Department of Trade and Industry has lead responsibility. This applies to machinery that is first placed on the market from 1/1/93 (but not to second-hand machinery unless it is being imported from outside the European Community). This will be implemented in this country by the proposed Machinery (Safety) Regulations. There is a transitional period from 1 January 1993 to 1 January 1995, where the manufacturer has the choice of either placing machinery on the market in accordance with the 'essential safety requirements' of those Directives and CE marked or of continuing to comply with the national legislation in force on 31 December 1992.

Regulation 10(2)

101 Regulation 10(2) means that if the work equipment complies with the implementing legislation of the relevant product Directive, then any corresponding requirements in regulations 11 to 24 will not apply (see Appendix 1).

Article 100A Directives

102 The aim of this group of Directives is to achieve the free movement of goods in the Community Single Market by eliminating differing national controls and harmonising essential technical requirements. Many of these Directives have been made within a common structure which was set out in a resolution of the Council of Ministers in 1985. These Directives are often called 'New Approach' Directives. Examples important to safety at work include the Machinery Directive, the Personal Protective Equipment Directive and the Simple Pressure Vessels Directive. Others are still in negotiation (eg a 2nd Amendment to the Machinery Directive and a Directive on Pressure Equipment).

103 These New Approach Directives set out 'essential safety requirements' which must be met before products may be sold in the Community. Products which comply with the Directives must be given free circulation within the Community. These Directives also apply to equipment made and put into service in-house. Suppliers must ensure that their products when placed on the market comply with the legal requirements implementing the Directives applicable to their product. It is a common feature of these Directives that compliance is claimed by the manufacturer affixing a mark – the 'CE Mark' – to the equipment. (At present the CE Mark has slightly different meanings depending on the Directive concerned; negotiations are underway to ensure that the mark has the same meaning across the range of 'New Approach' Directives.)

104 One way of demonstrating compliance with the 'essential safety requirements' applicable to a product will be by designing and manufacturing to harmonised standards. These are standards made by

the European Standardisation Bodies – CEN and CENELEC – under a mandate from the Commission of the European Communities to which a reference has been published in the Official Journal of the European Communities. When developed these harmonised standards will be transposed in the UK by the British Standards Institution and will bear a common number (ie EN XXXX will be BS EN XXXX here). In practice it is expected that most manufacturers will design and construct products according to these standards – although their use is voluntary.

105 Once these Directives are fully in force only products which conform and bear the 'CE Mark' may be placed on the market in the UK.

106 A list of relevant Directives in Schedule 1 of the Regulations and this includes a number of EC product Directives which pre-date the 'New Approach' Directives but which also specify the requirements which must be met before the products are placed on the market.

Regulation 11

Dangerous parts of machinery

107 This Regulation covers risks arising from most mechanical hazards, and replaces most of the existing legal requirements for the guarding of machinery. Unlike the old laws, the Regulation applies across all industrial and service sectors. For information on the time and circumstances when these Regulations take the place of the old laws, see the guidance to regulation 1 and 27.

108 Regulation 11(1) sets out the principal duty, to take effective measures to prevent contact with dangerous parts of machinery. The measures must either prevent access to the dangerous part, or stop the movement of the dangerous part before any part of a person can reach it. Regulation 11(2) lays down a hierarchy of preventive measures. Regulation 11(3) lists essential features of guards and protection devices. Regulation 11(4) indicates which of these features should also apply to protection appliances. Regulation 11(5) defines two terms used in this Regulation.

Regulation 11(1) – Principal duty

109 The term 'dangerous part of machinery' is well established in health and safety law. The safeguarding measures which were effective to comply with earlier law will continue to be appropriate under this Regulation, which maintains the emphasis of that law. The serious risks associated with dangerous parts of machinery have long been recognised. The technical aspects of assessing and removing these risks is a large and important subject, and full coverage is beyond the scope of this publication. Many HSC, HSE and industry-specific or machine-specific publications exist which illustrate the measures that can be taken to protect against risks associated with dangerous parts. Current national and international standards may also be used for guidance. European harmonised standards will carry forward present standards and should be used as appropriate.

Appendix 3 gives more detailed information about the available methods of safeguarding and the features they need to have in order to conform with regulation 11.

110 A risk assessment carried out under regulation 3 of the MHSWR should identify hazards presented by machinery. The types of hazard presented by machinery are described in detail in some standards (BS 5304, BS EN 292-1) and in other publications dealing with machinery safety. If the hazard could present a reasonably foreseeable risk to a person, the part of the machinery generating that hazard is a 'dangerous part'. The hazard generally results in a risk when the part of the machine is in motion. The risk assessment should evaluate the nature of the injury, its severity and likelihood of occurrence. The risk to be overcome is contact of part of the body or clothing with the dangerous part of the machine.

111 As well as parts of a machine, the Regulation also applies to contact with a rotating stock-bar which projects beyond the headstock of a lathe. This continues the protection afforded by sub-section 14(5) of the Factories Act 1961 and extends it to premises not subject to that Act.

112 Protection against other hazards associated with machinery, such as ejected particles and heat, is dealt with in other Regulations (eg 12 and 13). However, the measures used to conform with this Regulation may also be partly or fully effective in protecting against those other hazards.

Regulation 11(2) – Hierarchy of measures

113 The measures that may be taken are put into a hierarchy of four levels. The four levels are:

(a) fixed enclosing guards;
(b) other guards or protection devices;
(c) protection appliances (jigs, holders, push sticks etc); and
(d) the provision of information, instruction, training and supervision.

An explanation of the guarding and protection terms used is given in Appendix 3.

114 The hazard or hazards from machinery will be identified as part of the risk assessment. The assessment will then go on to identify measures that can be taken to overcome the risks that the hazard(s) present. In selecting measures, it is necessary to consider each level of the hierarchy in turn from the top, and use measures from that level as far as it is practicable to do so, provided they contribute to the reduction of risk. This will often result in a combination of measures being selected. The selection process continues down the hierarchy until the combined measures are effective in overcoming the risks and meeting the requirements of regulation 11(1).

115 The selection of the appropriate combination will need to take account of the requirements of the work, the evaluation of the risks, and the technical features of possible safeguarding. Further guidance is given in Appendix 3.

116 Most machines will present more than one mechanical hazard, and the risks associated with all of these need to be dealt with. Therefore at belt

conveyors there is a risk of entanglement with the rotating shafts and of being trapped by the intake between drum and moving belt and appropriate safety measures should be adopted.

117 Any risk assessment carried out under regulation 3 of the MHSWR should not just deal with the machine in its normal operating mode, but must also cover activities such as setting, maintenance, cleaning or repair. The assessment may indicate that these activities require a different combination of measures from those appropriate to the machine doing its normal work. In particular, parts of machinery that are not dangerous in normal use because they are not then accessible may become accessible and therefore dangerous while this type of work is being done.

118 Certain setting or adjustment operations which may have to be done with the machine running may require a greater reliance on provision of information, instruction, training and supervision than is the case for normal use. A permit-to-work system may be needed to prevent those doing the work being put at risk by others. See also the guidance to regulation 22.

119 To be effective, measures provided in accordance with regulation 11(2)(b) to (d) may need to be used in particular ways (defined by training, information and instruction), and not abused. Regulation 12(1) of the MHSWR requires employees to use such measures appropriately.

Regulation 11(3) – Features of guards and protective devices and Regulation 11(4) – Features of protection appliances

120 Regulation 11(3) sets out various requirements for guards and protection devices. These are largely common sense, and in large part are detailed in relevant national and international standards. Ways of achieving satisfactory guarding and other protection are discussed in more detail in the standards and in other guidance. These requirements are explained in detail in Appendix 3. Regulation 11(4) similarly sets out requirements for protection appliances.

Regulation 12

Protection against specific hazards

121 This Regulation covers risks arising from certain listed hazards during the use of equipment. Examples of the hazards that the Regulation addresses are:

(a) material falling from equipment, for example a loose board falling from scaffolding, a straw bale falling from a tractor foreloader, or molten metal spilling from a ladle;

(b) material held in the equipment being unexpectedly thrown out, for example swarf ejected from a machine tool;

(c) parts of the equipment breaking off and being thrown out, for example an abrasive wheel bursting;

(d) part of the equipment coming apart, for example collapse of scaffolding or falsework;

(e) overheating or fire due for example to friction (bearings running hot, conveyor belt on jammed roller), electric motor burning out, ignition by welding torch, thermostat failing, cooling system failure;

(f) explosion of the equipment due to pressure build-up, perhaps due to the failure of a pressure-relief device or the unexpected blockage or sealing off of pipework;

(g) explosion of substance in the equipment, due for example to exothermic chemical reaction or unplanned ignition of a flammable gas or vapour of finely divided organic material (eg flour, coal dust), or welding work on a container with flammable residues.

122 A risk assessment carried out under regulation 3 of the Management of Health and Safety at Work Regulations 1992 should identify these hazards, and assess the risks associated with them. The assessment will need to consider the likelihood of such events occurring and the consequent danger if they do occur, in order to identify measures to be taken to comply with this Regulation.

123 Regulation 12(1) sets the primary aim, which is to prevent any of the events in regulation 12(3) arising, if that event exposes a person to risk. Where possible, the equipment should be designed so that events presenting a risk cannot occur. If this is not reasonably practicable, steps should be taken to reduce the risk. Examples of measures that may be taken are the monitoring of solvent concentrations at evaporating ovens to detect the build-up of explosive atmospheres, or the use of inert gas systems to control and suppress dust explosions.

124 Regulation 12(1) permits the discharge or ejection of material as an intentional or unavoidable part of the process (eg grit-blasting of castings, sawdust from woodworking), but any risks to people must be controlled. The Regulation also allows the use of equipment designed to make use of explosive forces in a controlled manner (eg an internal combustion engine or a rail detonator signal).

125 Equipment may have been designed before manufacture to eliminate or reduce the likelihood of the type of event listed in regulation 12(3). But equipment suppliers cannot control the materials used in equipment, or the environment in which it is used, and it is up to employers to ensure that the equipment is suitable for their application, as required by regulation 5(2). Therefore a factor such as high temperature, vibration or a flammable atmosphere may generate a hazard, and exposure to risk from this must be controlled.

126 Regulation 12(2)(b) requires that in addition to reducing the likelihood of the event occurring, measures must be taken to mitigate the effect of any event which does occur. An example is the use of pressure relief panels. If failure would lead to risk of injury, containment measures are needed as a back-up. An example might be a blast wall; or where there is a risk from a pressure relief panel or vent bursting, ensuring that any gases or liquids discharged are directed to a safe place, contained, or made safe as appropriate.

127 Regulation 12(2)(a) requires that risk controlling measures should be provided as part of the equipment, so far as is reasonably practicable. Personal protective equipment may be appropriate where a risk remains that cannot otherwise be eliminated.

128 Training, supervision and provision of information will often have an important role to play. First, they can help to ensure that equipment is operated in the correct way to prevent dangers occurring. Secondly, they can help to ensure that the appropriate safeguards are taken to prevent personal injury in the event of a hazard materialising.

129 Regulation 12(1) of the MHSWR requires employees to use equipment in accordance with any appropriate training and instructions they receive from employers.

130 Guidance on accepted measures to control the risks covered by this Regulation is available in publications prepared by HSC, HSE and other bodies.

Abrasive wheels

131 One particular example of the application of these principles is the use of abrasive wheels. These Regulations replace many of the provisions of the Abrasive Wheels Regulations 1970. To minimise the risk of bursting, wheels should always be run within the specified maximum rotation speed: if they are large enough this will be marked on the wheel (in accordance with regulation 23); smaller wheels should have a notice fixed in the workroom giving the individual or class maximum permissible rotation speed. The power-driven spindle should be governed so that its rotation speed does not exceed this. Furthermore, guarding must be provided to contain fragments of the wheel that might fly off if it did burst, so as to prevent them injuring anyone in the workplace. The guarding has an additional role in helping to meet the requirements of regulation 11; it should be designed, constructed and maintained to fulfil both functions. Providing information and training of workers in the correct handling and mounting of abrasive wheels (including pre-mounting and storing procedures) is also necessary to reduce the risk of bursting.

Relationship with other legislation

132 As well as presenting risks to mechanical safety, some possible emissions or discharges may present a health hazard. Other Regulations deal with this aspect in many workplaces; they are listed in regulation 12(5). Regulation 12 does not apply where and to the extent that those other Regulations do. This means the Control of Substances Hazardous to Health Regulations (COSHH) 1988 would apply to leakage of a toxic substance, whereas regulation 12 would apply to leakage of steam or cooling water from the same equipment. Similarly, COSHH would apply to the discharge of coolant mist from a machine tool, but regulation 12 would apply in the case of ejected swarf.

133 There is other legislation which is relevant to some of the hazards dealt with in this Regulation. For general guidance on how such legislation

relates to these Regulations, see paragraphs 10 to 12. Some of the most relevant legislation is listed in the following paragraphs.

134 For fire or explosion hazards, Section 31 of the Factories Act 1961 and the Highly Flammable Liquids and Liquefied Petroleum Gases Regulations 1972 apply, although only in premises subject to the Factories Act 1961. Risks from electricity include fire, arcing or igniting an explosion: these risks are covered by the Electricity at Work Regulations 1989.

135 The use of vessels and systems under pressure is subject to the Pressure Systems and Transportable Gas Containers Regulations 1989.

Regulation 13

High or very low temperature

136 Regulation 13 deals with the risk of injury from contact with hot or very cold work equipment, parts of work equipment or articles/substances in the work equipment. It does not cover any related risk such as radiant heat or glare.

137 Accessible surfaces of equipment or machinery, when hot or very cold, represent sources of risk of burn or other injury such as frostbite. Examples of relevant equipment might include a flat-iron, liquid nitrogen tank, gas cooker, blast furnace, snow making machine, cold store, steam pipe, etc.

138 Touching such surfaces may take place intentionally, eg to operate a handle of the equipment, or unintentionally, when someone is near the equipment. Certain work equipment is necessarily hot as part of the process and employees may have to work close to the equipment eg, foundry equipment, drop forging, hot pressing.

139 The risk from contact with hot surfaces should be reduced by engineering methods, ie reduction of surface temperature, insulation, shielding, barricading and guarding. The risk from hot process materials – contact, splashing, spilling, etc – should likewise be reduced by limiting maximum temperature, limiting liquor level, indirect steam heating methods, provision of doors, lids or covers, temperature interlocking of doors or lids and deflection systems for hot liquor (catch pan, spillway etc).

140 In many cases surfaces of equipment or devices have to be hot and accessible to operate, eg cooker hot plates, soldering iron bit, heated rolls. In such cases no engineering protective measures can be taken. In cases in which engineering protective measures can be applied, eg by reducing surface temperatures, these should be adopted in preference to personal protective measures. The choice of protective measures will need to be decided in each particular case and according to the particular circumstances.

141 While engineering measures should always be applied where appropriate, alternative or complementary forms of protection may also be necessary, eg the use of personal protective equipment (see the Personal Protective Equipment at Work Regulations 1992) and/or organisational measures such as warning signs (warning signals, visual and noise alarm signals) instructions, training, supervision, technical documentation, operating instructions, instructions for use.

Regulations 14 to 18: Controls and control systems

142 Regulations 14 to 18 require the provision of controls and certain arrangements 'where appropriate'. This qualification relates both to the features and functioning of the work equipment itself and to whether there is a risk associated with its use.

143 Start, stop and emergency stop controls are not generally appropriate where work equipment has no moving parts. Similarly they are not appropriate where the risk of injury is negligible, for example battery-powered clocks or solar-powered calculators.

144 Some types of work equipment are powered by human effort and although their use involves risk of injury, their physical characteristics and the fact that they are under close human control makes the provision of controls inappropriate; examples include the following when they use only human power: guillotines, hand-drills and lawn-mowers.

145 Other types of human-powered work equipment may not need start controls, but it may be appropriate to provide other types of control, particularly stop controls, where the work equipment does not necessarily come to a halt when the human effort stops, for example luggage trolleys.

146 It is usually appropriate to provide all of the controls required by regulations 14 to 18 where work equipment is powered by means other than human effort. The decision should be based on the risk assessment carried out as required by regulation 3 of the MHSWR (see paragraph 16 for further details).

147 The Regulations on controls and control systems do not only apply to equipment with moving parts (machinery); they may also apply to other equipment which might generate a risk, such as ovens, X-ray generators, and lasers.

148 A control is the manual actuator that the operator touches, eg a button, foot-pedal, knob, or lever. It may operate directly, but is more often a part of a control device such as a brake, clutch, switch, or relay. The control and control device are parts of the control system which may be considered as all the components which act together to monitor and control the functions of the work equipment. Control systems may operate using mechanical linkages, electricity, pneumatics, hydraulics etc, or combinations of these.

149 In practice, most individual items of equipment are likely to be provided with appropriate controls when supplied. But for complex items of equipment, or installations or assemblies comprising several different items of equipment, it may be necessary to carry out a more detailed assessment of the risks and make special provisions to ensure that controls are provided that comply fully with these Regulations.

Regulation 14

Controls for starting or making a significant change in operating conditions

150 One or more controls must be provided, where appropriate, to start work equipment. Starting should only be possible by using a control.

Operating the control need not immediately start the equipment – control systems may require certain conditions (relating to operation or protection devices) to be met before starting can be achieved.

151 Restarting after any sort of stoppage is subject to the same requirement. The stop may have been deliberate, or may have happened, for example by the activation of a protection device. Restarting of the equipment should not be possible by the re-setting of a protection device such as an interlock, or a person's withdrawal from an area covered by a sensing device; operation of the start control should also be needed.

152 Any change in the operating conditions should only be possible by the use of a control, except if the change does not increase risk to health or safety. Examples of operating conditions include speed, pressure, temperature and power.

153 The purpose of regulation 14(1)(b), together with 14(2), is to ensure that users or other people are not caught unawares by any changes in the operating conditions or modes of the equipment in use. For example, certain multi-functional machines are used in the metal-working industry for punching or shearing metal via different tools located on different parts of the machines. Safety in the use of these machines is achieved by means of a combination of safe systems of work and physical safeguards which match the characteristics of the workpiece. It is essential that the function of the machine (eg punching or shearing) is changed by means of a conscious, positive action by the operator and that unused parts of the machine cannot start up unintentionally. Another example of this type of machine is multi-functional combination machines used in woodworking. Similarly, unexpected increases in speed, pressure etc could expose operators to risk, for example when using power drills.

154 Regulation 14(3) acknowledges that in the case of automatic machinery, for example those controlled by programmable electronic systems, it is not appropriate to require separate controls for changing operating conditions when such changes are part of the normal operating cycle. (Nevertheless these machines should be safeguarded as required by regulations 11 and 12). However, where interventions have to be made outside the normal sequence, such as clearing blockages, setting, or cleaning, controls should be provided in accordance with regulations 14(1) and (2).

155 The start control can be separate or combined with operating conditions controls, or more than one of each type of control can be provided. The controls do not have to be provided solely for the purpose of each Regulation and can be combined with other function controls such as stop controls required by regulation 15, although not with an emergency stop control provided in accordance with regulation 16. 'Hold-to-run' devices are examples of combined stop and start controls. These should be designed so that the stop function has priority, following the release of the control.

156 The controls provided should be designed and positioned so as to prevent, so far as possible, inadvertent or accidental operation. Buttons and levers should be of appropriate design, for example including a shrouding or locking facility. It should not be possible for the control to 'operate itself', such as due to the effects of gravity, vibration, or failure of

spring mechanism. Starting initiated from a keyboard or other multi-function device should require a confirmatory input in addition to the start command. Furthermore, the results of the actuation should be displayed.

Regulation 15

Stop controls

157 The primary requirement of this Regulation is that the action of the control should bring the equipment to a safe condition in a safe manner. This acknowledges that it is not always desirable to bring all items of work equipment immediately to a complete stop; for example, it would be unsafe to bring a self-contained hydraulic machine to a complete stop if doing so would cause it to collapse. Similarly, stopping the mixing mechanism of a reactor during certain chemical reactions could lead to a dangerous exothermic reaction.

158 Regulation 15(2) is qualified by 'where necessary for reasons of health and safety'. Therefore accessible dangerous parts must be rendered stationary. However, parts of equipment which do not present a risk, such as suitably guarded cooling fans, do not need to be positively stopped and may be allowed to idle.

159 The stop control does not have to be instantaneous in its action and can bring the equipment to rest in sequence or at the end of an operating cycle if this is required for safety. This may be necessary in some processes, for example to prevent the unsafe build-up of heat or pressure, to allow a controlled run-down of large rotating parts with high inertia.

160 Regulation 15(3) requires that the control should switch off all sources of energy from the equipment, after it has stopped, if this is necessary to prevent or minimise risk to health or safety. As the requirement is to minimise risk, the control should be arranged to switch off all energy sources unless this would actually increase the risk. That could be the case where materials are held by a magnetic clutch or grab, or where power is needed for restraint to prevent collapse or other uncontrolled movement. In such cases, power should be retained so as to ensure safety, and if necessary an appropriate system of work should be employed subsequently to isolate the equipment from its power source. Where it is necessary to retain power for production reasons and a hazard could arise due to unexpected movement giving rise to risk of injury, control systems should be designed so as to immediately remove the power should such an event occur.

161 Where internally stored energy could lead to risk, it should be cut off by the action of the stop control. For example, horizontal plastic injection moulding machines may store hydraulic energy in internal hydraulic reservoirs which, under certain fault conditions, may cause uncovenanted movements which could cause injury. In this case, the stop control should effectively isolate or dissipate the stored energy so as to ensure safety.

162 The stop control should override the effect of any operating or start control. Where possible it should not require anything other than a short

manual action to activate it, even though the stop and disconnection sequence so initiated may take some time to complete.

163 Further information on the categories of stop functions can be found in BS EN 60204-1. Although this standard applies to new machinery, it gives guidance which may be useful for any equipment.

Regulation 16

Emergency stop controls

164 An emergency stop control should be provided where the other safeguards are not adequate to prevent risk when some irregular event occurs. However, an emergency stop control should not be considered as a substitute for necessary safeguarding. Examples of such situations include: a person becoming exposed to a hazard; or the failure or malfunction of a machine generating additional hazards (eg overspeeding, failure to stop). However, if such an event can happen very quickly, (eg failure of the protection system at a hand-fed power-operated guillotine), it is unlikely that an emergency stop would be of benefit since people would have no time to react; it would not then be appropriate to provide an emergency stop control.

165 When it is appropriate to have one, an emergency stop should be provided at every control point and at other appropriate locations around the equipment so that action can be taken quickly. The location of emergency stop controls should be determined as a follow-up to the risk assessment.

166 Although it is desirable that emergency stops rapidly bring work equipment to a halt, this must be achieved under control so as not to create an additional hazard.

167 Emergency stops are intended to effect a rapid response to potentially dangerous situations and they should not be used as functional stops during normal operation.

168 Emergency stop controls should be easily reached and actuated. Common types are mushroom-headed buttons, bars, levers, kick-plates, or pressure-sensitive cables. Guidance on specific features of emergency stops is given in national and international standards (BS EN 292, BS 5304, prEN 418, BS EN 60204-1).

Regulation 17

Controls

Regulation 17(1)

169 It should be possible to identify easily what each control does and on which equipment it takes effect. Both the controls and their marking should be clearly visible. As well as having legible wording or symbols, factors such as the colour, shape and position of controls are important; a combination of these can often be used to reduce ambiguity. Some controls may need to be distinguishable by touch, for example inching buttons or

printing machines. Few controls will be adequately identifiable without marking of some sort.

170 The marking and form of many controls is covered by national and international standards (BS 3641, prEN 50099). However, additional marking may often be desirable.

Regulation 17(2)

171 Controls used in the normal running of the equipment should not be placed where anybody using them might be exposed to risk. However, controls used for setting-up and fault-finding procedures may have to be positioned where people are at some risk, for example on a robot-teaching pendant. In such cases particular precautions should be employed to ensure safety; examples include using hold-to-run controls, enabling controls, emergency stop controls. Further precautions include the selection of reduced/limited capability of the work equipment during such operations.

Regulation 17(3)(a)

172 The provisions of regulation 17(3)(a) apply where physical safeguarding methods employed in accordance with regulation 11(2)(a) and (b) do not completely prevent access to dangerous parts of work equipment, or where people are at risk from other aspects of the operation, eg noise, or harmful radiation. The preferred aim is to position controls so that operators of equipment are able to see from the control position that no-one is at risk from anything they set going. To be able to do this, operators need to have a view of any part of the equipment that may put anyone at risk. A direct view is best, but supplementing by mirrors or more sophisticated visual or sensing facilities may be necessary.

173 There will normally be little difficulty in meeting this requirement in the case of small and compact equipment. With larger equipment there is normally some latitude in the positioning of controls, and the safety aspect should be considered in deciding their location; this would apply for example on large process plant such as newspaper printing machinery or chemical plant.

174 Where people are at risk from dangerous parts of machinery, normal safeguarding procedures should restrict the need for surveillance to vulnerable areas; an example would be on large newspaper printing machines. However, where regular intervention is necessary which involves entry into, removal of, or opening of safeguards, (eg for maintenance purposes), interlocks or similar devices should be employed to prevent start-up while people are at risk. It may be necessary to employ additional measures to ensure that people do not remain inside safeguards at start-up. Similarly, where sensing devices are employed to aid surveillance, they may be interlocked with the controls so as to prevent start-up when people are at risk.

175 If anyone other than the operator also attend the equipment, they may have permissive start controls located at a position of safety from

where they can ascertain that no-one is at risk. Such controls can indicate to the operator that everyone is clear and permit a start.

176 Where the risk is from hazards other than dangerous parts of machinery (eg noise, radiation), people at some distance from the work equipment may be at risk. In such circumstances the means of compliance with regulation 17(3) should depend upon the nature and extent of the risk. It may not always be reasonably practicable for operators to have sight of all parts of the workplace that may be affected by such 'widespread risks'; so it may be necessary in such cases to employ systems of work or warning devices. In the latter case warning devices should be selected critically depending on the risk; for example, it would not be acceptable to rely on audible or visible alarms where the risk is of an imminent potentially fatal dose of ionising radiation, but they may be adequate where the risk is from noisy plant.

Regulation 17(3)(b)

177 If the nature of the installation is such that it is not reasonably practicable for the operator at the control position to ensure that no-one is at risk, then a system of work must be devised and used to achieve that aim. This should set out procedures to eliminate or reduce the probability of any workers being at risk as a result of starting-up. An example is the use of systems using signallers; these are often used to assist crane drivers, or tractor drivers setting a manned harvester in motion. As far as possible, the system of work should lay down procedures to be followed by those concerned with the use of the equipment, rather than placing responsibilities on others peripherally involved, such as people walking through the area.

Regulation 17(3)(c)

178 The warning should comply with regulation 24, ie it should be unambiguous, easily perceived and easily understood.

179 Circumstances will affect the type of warning chosen. Some general comments about warnings are made under regulation 24. Signals which are not audible and visual may be suitable (eg tactile signals). Often a combination of signals affecting different senses may be appropriate.

Regulation 17(4)

180 Warnings given in accordance with regulation 17(3)(c), should be given sufficiently in advance of the equipment actually starting to give those at risk time to get clear. As well as time, suitable means of avoiding the risk should be provided. This may take the form of a device by means of which the person at risk can prevent start-up or warn the operator of his/her presence. Otherwise there must be adequate provision to enable people at risk to withdraw, eg sufficient space or exits.

181 The provisions of regulation 17 do not preclude people from remaining in positions where they are at risk. Their aim is to prevent an operator

unintentionally placing people at risk. Regulation 11, in its hierarchical approach to safeguarding, recognises that in exceptional circumstances people may have to approach dangerous parts of machinery, such as for maintenance purposes. Access to such positions should only be allowed under strictly controlled conditions and in accordance with regulation 11.

Regulation 18

Control systems

182 A more complete definition of a control system than that given in paragraph 148 is:

> a control system is a system or device which responds to input signals and generates an output signal which causes the equipment under control to operate in a particular manner.

183 The input signals may be from an operator via a manual control, or from the equipment itself, for example from automatic sensors or protection devices (photo-electric guards, guard interlock devices, speed limiters, etc). Signals from the equipment may also include information (feedback) on the condition of the equipment and its response (eg position, whether running, speed).

184 Failure of any part of the control system or its power supply should lead to a 'fail-safe' condition (more correctly and realistically called 'minimised failure to danger'), and not impede the operation of the 'stop' or 'emergency stop' controls. The measures which should be taken in the design and application of a control system to mitigate against the effects of its failure will need to be balanced against the consequences of any failure. The greater the risk, the more resistant the control system should be to the effects of failure.

185 There are national and international standards both current and in preparation (BS 5304, BS EN 60204-1, BS 6491) which provide guidance on design of control systems so as to achieve high levels of performance related to safety.

Regulation 19

Isolation from sources of energy

186 Isolation means establishing a break in the energy supply in a secure manner, ie by ensuring that inadvertent reconnection is not possible. The possibilities and risks of reconnection should be identified as part of the risk assessment, which should then establish how security can be achieved. For some equipment, this can be achieved by simply removing the plug from the electrical supply socket. For other equipment, an isolating switch or valve may have to be locked in the off or closed position to avoid unsafe reconnection. The closed position is not always the safe position: for example, drain or vent outlets may need to be secured in the open position.

If work on isolated equipment is being done by more than one person, it may be necessary to provide a locking device with multiple locks and keys; each will have their own lock or key, and all locks have to be taken off before the isolating device can be removed.

187 The main aim of this Regulation is to allow equipment to be made safe under particular circumstances, such as when maintenance is to be carried out, when an unsafe condition develops (failure of a component, overheating, or pressure build-up), or where a temporary adverse environment would render the equipment unsafe, for example electrical equipment in wet conditions or in a flammable or explosive atmosphere.

188 There may be some circumstances in which, for particular safety reasons, stopping equipment does not remove all sources of energy, ie the power supply is helping to keep the equipment safe. In such cases, isolation could lead to consequent danger, so it will be necessary to take appropriate measures to overcome that risk before attempting to isolate the equipment.

189 It is appropriate to provide means of isolation where the work equipment is dependent upon external energy sources such as electricity, pressure (hydraulic or pneumatic) or heat. Internal energy which is an inherent part of the materials from which the equipment is made, such as its potential energy, chemical or radiological energy, similarly cannot be isolated from the equipment; nevertheless there should be means of preventing such energy adversely affecting workers, by restraint, barrier or shielding.

190 Electrical isolation of electrical equipment for work on or near conductors is dealt with by regulation 12 of the Electricity at Work Regulations 1989. Guidance to those Regulations expands on the means of isolating electrical equipment. Note that those Regulations are only concerned with electrical danger (electric shock or burn, arcing and fire or explosion caused by electricity), and do not deal with other hazards (such as mechanical) that may arise from failure to isolate electrical equipment.

191 Heat energy may be supplied by circulation of pre-heated fluid such as water or steam. In such cases, isolating valves should be fitted to the supply pipework. Similar provision should be made for energy supplies in the form of liquids or gases under pressure. The performance of such valves may deteriorate over time, and their effectiveness often cannot be judged visually. A planned preventive maintenance programme should therefore be instigated which assures effective means of isolation.

192 The energy source of some equipment is held in the substances contained within it. Examples are the use of gases or liquids as fuel, electrical accumulators (batteries) and radionuclides. In such cases, isolation may mean removing the energy-containing material, although this may not always be necessary.

193 Also, it is clearly not appropriate to isolate the terminals of a battery from the chemical cells within it, since that could not be done without destroying the whole unit.

194 Some equipment makes use of natural sources of energy such as light or flowing water. In such cases suitable means of isolation include screening from light, and the means of diverting water flow respectively. Another

atural energy source, wind power, is less easily diverted, so sail
echanisms should be designed and constructed so as to permit minimal
nergy transfer when necessary.

195 Regulation 19(3) requires precautions to ensure that people are not
ut at risk following reconnection of the energy source. So, reconnection of
he energy source should not put people at risk by itself initiating
ovement or other hazard. Measures are also required to ensure that
uards and other protection devices are functioning correctly before
peration begins.

egulation 20

tability

96 There are many types of work equipment that might fall over, collapse
r overturn unless suitable precautions are taken to fix them to the ground,
tabilise them, tie, fasten or clamp them in some way.

ixed work equipment

97 Most machines used in a fixed position should be bolted or otherwise
astened down so that they do not move or rock during use. It has long
een recognised that woodworking and other machines (except those
pecifically designed for portable use) should be bolted to the floor or
milarly secured to prevent unexpected movement.

198 The measures can be by fastening the equipment to an appropriate
oundation or supporting structure. Other means could include lashing or
ing to a support structure or platform.

199 Where the stability of work equipment is not inherent in its design or
peration or where it is mounted in a position where its stability could be
ompromised, eg by severe weather conditions, then additional measures
hould be taken to ensure its stability. Scaffolds are vulnerable to strong
inds and therefore sheeting and additional ties will be needed.

200 Ladders should be at the correct angle height and tied or footed.
1obile tower scaffolds should not be so high that they become unstable
nd should be tied to the building and be anchored or have the base
ppropriately extended by fitting outriggers.

obile work equipment

01 Some types of work equipment may need counterbalance weights to
alance loads at either the front or the rear (eg tractors). Mobile cranes are
tted with a wide range of devices to increase stability.

202 Additional measures may be needed for particular applications.
Vherever lift trucks are used the type selected should be suitable for the
rrain over which it may travel.

203 Certain types of mobile equipment, for example mobile cranes or
ccess platforms, while inherently stable when not lifting, can have their

stability increased during use by means of outriggers or similar device
While this equipment cannot be 'clamped' or 'fixed' steps must be taken t
ensure that the equipment is always used within the limits of its stability a
any given time.

Regulation 21

Lighting

204 Any place where a person uses work equipment should be suitably an
sufficiently lit. If the ambient lighting provided in the workplace is suitabl
and sufficient for the tasks involved in the use of the equipment then specia
lighting need not be provided. But if the task involves the perception c
detail, for example precision measurements, then additional lighting wou
need to be provided to comply with the Regulation. The lighting should b
adequate for the needs of the task.

205 Local lighting on the machine for the illumination of the work are
should be provided when the construction of the machine and/or its guarc
render the normal lighting inadequate for the safe and efficient operation c
the machine, eg on sewing machines. Local lighting may be needed to giv
sufficient view of a dangerous process or to reduce visual fatigue.

206 Additional lighting should also be provided in areas not covered b
general lighting when work, such as maintenance or repairs, for example,
carried out in them. The arrangements for the provision of lighting could b
temporary, by means of hand or other portable lights, eg miners' lamps, c
by fixed lighting inside enclosures, such as lift shafts. The standard c
lighting required will be related to the purpose for which the wor
equipment is used or to the work being carried out.

207 Where access is foreseeable on an intermittent but regular basis, cor
sideration should always be given to the provision of permanent lighting

208 This Regulation complements the requirement for sufficient an
suitable workplace lighting in the Workplace (Health, Safety and Welfare
Regulations 1992. Practical advice is contained in HSE guidance HS(G)3:

Regulation 22

Maintenance operations

209 Regulation 6 requires that equipment is maintained. Regulation 2
requires that equipment is constructed or adapted in a way that take
account of the risks associated with carrying out maintenance work, such a
routine and planned preventive maintenance, as described in the guidanc
to regulation 6. Compliance with this Regulation will help to ensure tha
when maintenance work is carried out, it is possible to do it safely an
without risk to health, as required by Section 2 of the HSW Act; it will als
help to comply with regulation 5(1), since 'used' includes maintaine
Regulation 11(3)(h) contains a requirement linked to regulation 22, b
focusing on the narrower aspect of the design of guards for such wor
Many accidents have occurred during maintenance work, often as a resu
of failure to adapt the equipment to reduce the risk.

210 In some cases the need for safe maintenance will have been considered at the design stage and attended to by the manufacturer, and the user will need to do little other than review the measures provided. In other cases, particularly when a range of interconnecting components may be put together, eg in a research laboratory or a production line, users of the equipment will need to consider when carrying out their risk assessment (paragraph 16) whether any extra features need to be incorporated so that maintenance can be done safely and without risks to health.

211 Ideally there is no risk associated with the maintenance operation. For example, lubrication points on machines may be designed so that they can be used safely even while the machine is in motion, or adjustment points positioned so that they can be used without opening guards.

212 If, however, the maintenance work might involve a risk, this Regulation requires that the installation should be designed so that the work can, so far as is reasonably practicable, be carried out with the equipment stopped or inactive. This will probably be the case for most equipment.

213 If equipment will have to be running or working during a maintenance operation and this presents risks, measures should be taken to enable the operation of the equipment in a way that reduces the risk. These measures include further safeguards or functions designed into the equipment, such as limiting the power, speed or range of movement that is available to dangerous parts during maintenance operations. Examples are:

(a)   providing temporary guards;
(b)   limited movement controls;
(c)   crawl speed operated by hold-to-run controls;
(d)   using a second low-powered visible laser beam to align a powerful invisible one.

214 Other measures that can be taken to protect against any residual risk include wearing personal protective equipment and provision of instruction and supervision. Although the actual use of these measures falls outside the scope of this Regulation, the work equipment should as far as possible be installed to be compatible with their use.

215 The design of equipment in relation to maintenance work on it may also be affected by other legislation. In particular, electrically powered equipment is subject to the Electricity at Work Regulations 1989 as regards risks of injury from electric shock or burn, or from explosion or ignition initiated by electricity. Guidance on those Regulations includes details of relevant equipment requirements.

Regulation 23

Markings

216 This Regulation is closely related to the following one which deals with warnings; some markings may also serve as the warning required by regulation 24. There are many circumstances in which marking of equipment is appropriate for health and safety reasons. Stop and start

controls for equipment need to be identified. The maximum rotation speed of an abrasive wheel should be marked upon it. The maximum safe working load should be marked on lifting beams. Gas cylinders should indicate (normally by colour) the gas in them. Storage and feed vessels containing hazardous substances should generally be marked to show their contents, and any hazard associated with them.

217 Some legislation lays down specific circumstances in which markings are needed, and what form they should take. Examples of Regulations requiring particular markings are Ionising Radiation Regulations 1985, and the Highly Flammable Liquids Regulations 1972 (regulations 6 to 7). Pressure vessels are subject to various Regulations, which include requirements for marking the vessel with specific information.

218 Employers should consider any other marking that might be appropriate for their own purposes, eg numbering machines to aid identification, particularly if the controls or isolators for the machines are not directly attached to them and there could otherwise be confusion.

219 Markings may use words, letters, numbers, or symbols, and the use of colour or shape may be significant. There are nationally or internationally agreed markings relating to some hazards, eg the international symbols for radiation and lasers. Markings should as far as possible conform to such published standards as BS 5378 or as required by any appropriate legislation such as the Safety Signs Regulations 1980.

Regulation 24

Warnings

220 Warnings or warning devices may be appropriate where risks to health or safety remain after other hardware measures have been taken. They may be incorporated into systems of work (including permit-to-work systems), and can reinforce measures of information, instruction and training. A warning is normally in the form of a notice or similar. Examples are positive instructions ('hard hats must be worn'), prohibitions ('not to be operated by people under 18 years'), restrictions ('do not heat above $60\frac{1}{2}$C'). A warning device is an active unit giving a signal; the signal may typically be visible or audible, and is often connected into equipment so that it is active only when a hazard exists.

221 In some cases, warnings and warning devices will be specified in other legislation, for example automatic safe load indicators on mobile cranes on construction sites, or 'X-rays on' lights.

Warnings

222 Warnings can be permanent printed ones; these may be attached to or incorporated into the equipment or positioned close to it. There may also be a need for portable warnings to be posted during temporary operations such as maintenance; these may form part of a permit-to-work system.

223 In some cases words can be augmented or replaced by appropriate graphical signs. So as to be readily understood, such signs will normally need to be from a nationally or internationally agreed standard set. The Safety Signs Regulations 1980 are relevant here.

Warning devices

224 Warning devices can be audible (eg reversing alarms on construction vehicles) or visible (eg a light on a control panel that a fan on a microbiological cabinet has broken down or a blockage has occurred on a particular machine). They may indicate imminent danger (eg machine about to start), development of a fault condition (eg pump failure or conveyor blockage indicator on a control panel) or the continued presence of a potential hazard (eg hot-plate or laser on). A particular warning may use both types of device simultaneously, for example some automatic safe load indicators on mobile cranes.

225 They must be easily perceived and understood, and unambiguous. It is important to consider factors which affect people's perception of such devices, especially for warnings of imminent danger. Visual warnings will be effective only if a person frequently looks in a particular direction, and therefore may not be as widely applicable as audible signals. Appropriate choice of colour and flashing can catch attention, and also reinforce the warning nature of a visual signal. The sound given by an audible signal should be of such a type that people unambiguously perceive it as a warning. This means that it must be possible to distinguish between the warnings given by separate warning devices and between the warnings and any other, unrelated, signal which may be in operation at the time. It may not be possible to rely on audible signals in a noisy environment, nor in circumstances where many such signals are expected to be active at one time.

Regulation 26

Extension outside Great Britain

226 The Regulations apply to offshore activities covered by the 1989 Order on or associated with oil and gas installations, including mobile installations, diving support vessels, heavy lift barges and pipe-lay barges.

Regulation 27

Repeals, saving and revocations

227 The Regulations replace many existing laws, particularly on machinery guarding, by repealing and revoking old and in many cases obsolescent legislation.

228 Existing legislation listed in Schedule 2 for repeal or revocation will continue to operate alongside the new Regulations until 1 January 1977, and will apply as explained in the guidance to regulation 1.

Schedule 1

Relevant Community Directives

Regulation 10

229 Listed below are the implementing Regulations for each relevant Community Directive. The Regulations are listed in the same order as the Directives.

1 The Low Voltage Electrical Equipment (Safety) Regulations 1989 (SI 1989/728)
   HMSO ISBN 0 11 096728 3

2 The Construction Plant and Equipment (Harmonisation of Noise Emission Standards) Regulations 1985 (SI 1985/1968)
   HMSO ISBN 0 11 057968 2
   The Construction Plant and Equipment (Harmonisation of Noise Emission Standards) Regulations 1988 (SI 1988/361)
   HMSO ISBN 0 11 086361 5
   The Falling-object Protective Structures for Construction Plant (EEC Requirements) Regulations 1988 (SI 1988/362)
   HMSO ISBN 0 11 086362 3
   The Roll-over Protective Structures for Construction Plant (EEC Requirements) Regulations 1988 (SI 1988/363
   HMSO ISBN 0 11 086363 1
   The Construction Plant and Equipment (Harmonisation of Noise Emission Standards) (Amendment) Regulations 1989 (SI 1989/1127)
   HMSO ISBN 0 11 097127 2
   The Construction Plant and Equipment (Harmonisation of Noise Emission Standards) (Amendment) Regulations 1992 (SI 1992/488)
   HMSO ISBN 0 11 023488 X

3 As No 2

4 As No 2

5 The Construction Plant and Equipment (Harmonisation of Noise Emission Standards) Regulations 1985 (SI 1985/1968)
   HMSO ISBN 0 11 057968 2

6 The Construction Plant and Equipment (Harmonisation of Noise Emission Standards) Regulations 1985 (SI 1985/1968)
   HMSO ISBN 0 11 057968 2
   and The Construction Plant and Equipment (Harmonisation of Noise Emission Standards) (Amendment) Regulations 1989 (SI 1989/1127)
   HMSO ISBN 0 11 097127 2

7 The Construction Plant and Equipment (Harmonisation of Noise
   Emission Standards) Regulations 1985 (SI 1985/1968)
   HMSO ISBN 0 11 057968 2

8 The Construction Plant and Equipment (Harmonisation of Noise
   Emission Standards) Regulations 1985 (SI 1985/1968)
   HMSO ISBN 0 11 057968 2

9 The Construction Plant and Equipment (Harmonisation of Noise
   Emission Standards) Regulations 1985 (SI 1985/1968)
   HMSO ISBN 0 11 057968 2

10 The Lawnmowers (Harmonisation of Noise Emission Standards)
   Regulations 1986 (SI 1986/1795)
   HMSO ISBN 0 11 067795 1

11 As No 2

12 The Construction Plant and Equipment (Harmonisation of Noise
   Emission Standards) Regulations 1985 (SI 1985/1968)
   HMSO ISBN 0 11 057968 2

13 The Construction Plant and Equipment (Harmonisation of Noise
   Emission Standards) Regulations 1985 (SI 1985/1968)
   HMSO ISBN 0 11 057968 2

14 The Construction Plant and Equipment (Harmonisation of Noise
   Emission Standards) Regulations 1985 (SI 1985/1968)
   HMSO ISBN 0 11 057968 2

15 The Construction Plant and Equipment (Harmonisation of Noise
   Emission Standards) Regulations 1985 (SI 1985/1968)
   HMSO ISBN 0 11 057968 2

16 The Lawnmowers (Harmonisation of Noise Emission Standards)
   (Amendment) Regulations 1987 (SI 1987/876)
   HMSO ISBN 0 11 076876 0

17 As No 6

18 The Lawnmowers (Harmonisation of Noise Emission Standards)
   Regulations 1992 (SI 1992/168)
   HMSO ISBN 0 11 023168 6

19 The Lawnmowers (Harmonisation of Noise Emission Standards)
   Regulations 1992 (SI 1992/168)
   HMSO ISBN 0 11 023168 6

20 The Electro-Medical Equipment (EEC Requirements) Regulations
   1988 (SI 1988/1586)
   HMSO ISBN 0 11 087586 9

21 The Roll-over Protective Structures for Construction Plant (EEC
   Requirements) Regulations 1988 (SI 1988/363)
   HMSO ISBN 0 11 086363 1

22   The Falling-object Protective Structures for Construction Plant (EEC Requirements) Regulations 1988 (SI 1988/362)
HMSO ISBN 0 11 086362 3

23   The Construction Plant and Equipment (Harmonisation of Noise Emission Standards) Regulations 1988 (SI 1988/361)
HMSO ISBN 0 11 086361 5
and The Construction Plant and Equipment (Harmonisation of Noise Emission Standards) (Amendment) Regulations 1992 (SI 1992/488)
HMSO ISBN 0 11 023488 X

24   The Self-Propelled Industrial Trucks (EEC) Requirements Regulations 1988 (SI 1988/1736)
HMSO ISBN 0 11 087736 5
as amended by SI 1989/1035
ISBN 0 11 097035 7

25   The Simple Pressure Vessels (Safety) Regulations 1991 (SI 1991/2749)
HMSO ISBN 0 11 015902 0

26   The Construction Products Regulations 1991 (SI 1991/1620)
HMSO ISBN 0 11 014620 4

27   As No 24

28   The Electromagnetic Compatibility Regulations 1992 (SI 1992/2372)
HMSO ISBN 0 11 025372 8

29   The proposed Machinery (Safety) Regulations 1992 (SI not yet known)

30   The Construction Plant and Equipment (Harmonisation of Noise Emission Standards) Regulations 1988 (SI 1988/361)
HMSO ISBN 0 11 086361 5
and The Construction Plant and Equipment (Harmon-isation of Noise Emission Standards) (Amendment) Regulations 1992 (SI 1992/488)
HMSO ISBN 0 11 023488 X

31   The proposed Personal Protective Equipment (Safety) Regulations 1992 (SI not yet known)

32   The proposed Active Implantable Medical Devices Regulations 1992 (SI not yet known)

33   The Gas Appliances (Safety) Regulations 1992 (SI 1992/711)
HMSO ISBN 0 11 025711 0

34   As No 29

35   As No 28

Appendix 1

Employers' duties from 1 January 1993

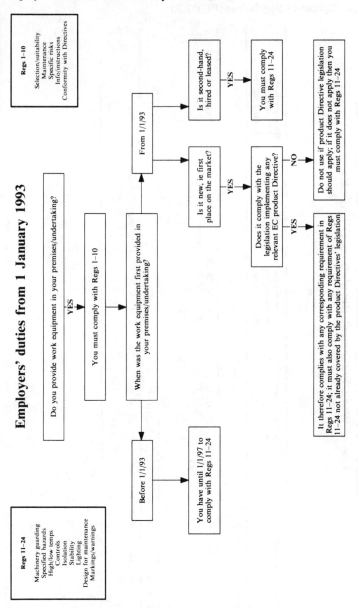

Employers' duties from 1 January 1993

Regs 11–24
Machinery guarding
Specified hazards
High/low temps
Controls
Isolation
Stability
Lighting
Design for maintenance
Markings/warnings

Do you provide work equipment in your premises/undertaking?

YES

You must comply with Regs 1–10

When was the work equipment first provided in your premises/undertaking?

Before 1/1/93

You have until 1/1/97 to comply with Regs 11–24

From 1/1/93

Is it second-hand, hired or leased?

YES

You must comply with Regs 11–24

Is it new, ie first place on the market?

YES

Does it comply with the legislation implementing any relevant EC product Directive?

NO

Do not use if product Directive legislation should apply; if it does not apply then you must comply with Regs 11–24

YES

It therefore complies with any corresponding requirement in Regs 11–24; it must also comply with any requirement of Regs 11–24 not already covered by the product Directives' legislation

Regs 1–10
Selection/suitability
Maintenance
Specific risks
Info/instructions
Conformity with Directives

Appendix 2

Non-exhaustive list of existing legislation relevant to the Provision and Use of Work Equipment Regulations (PUWER)

Non-exhaustive list of existing legislation relevant to the Provision and Use of Work Equipment Regulations (PUWER)

Existing legislation	Key provisions to be replaced by PUWER*	Key provisions to be replaced by other legislation	Notes	What provisions of PUWER are particularly relevant?
The Health and Safety at Work etc Act 1974				ALL
The Factories Act 1961	12, 13, 14, 15 16, 17, 19	1–7, 18, 24, 28, 29 57–60, 69, 72	20, 21 (young persons) and 22, 23, 25–27 (lifting equipment) will remain	ALL
The Mines and Quarries Act 1954	81(1), 82	93		ALL
The Offices, Shops and Railway Premises Act 1963	17	4–16, 23	18 (young persons) and 19 (training) will remain	ALL

* See guidance under Regulations 1 and 27 for details of the timetable for the repeal/revocation of these provisions

Existing legislation	Key provisions to be replaced by PUWER*	Key provisions to be replaced by other legislation	Notes	What provisions of PUWER are particularly relevant?
The Abrasive Wheels Regulations 1970	3(2), (3) and (4), 4, 6–8, 10–16, 18–19	17	9 (Training) and the Schedule will remain	ALL
The Aerated Waters Regulations 1921	1, 2, 8	3–5, 7, 9	All provisions will be revoked	5, 12
The Agriculture (Circular Saws) Regulations 1959	3, 4 Schedule 1			5, 6, 8, 11, 12, 21
The Agriculture (Power Take-off) Regulations 1957 (as amended)	All			11
The Agriculture (Stationary Machinery) Regulations 1959	All			5, 6, 11, 15, 16 17, 21
The Agriculture (Threshers and Balers) Regulations 1960	In the Schedule paras 2, 3, 6, 7, 8, 9, 10 11, 12, 16 and 17			5, 6, 11, 15, 16 17, 21
The Agriculture (Field Machinery) Regulations 1962	In the Schedule Paras 2–6, 15–19			5, 6, 11, 15, 16
The Agriculture (Tractor Cabs) Regulations 1974				5
The Construction (General Provisions) Regulations 1961	42, 43, 57	55		5, 6, 11, 12, 21
The Construction (Lifting Operations) Regulations 1961				5, 6, 9, 14, 20 23, 24

* See guidance under Regulations 1 and 27 for details of the timetable for the repeal/revocation of these provisions

Existing legislation	Key provisions to be replaced by PUWER*	Key provisions to be replaced by other legislation	Notes	What provisions of PUWER are particularly relevant?
The Construction (Working Places) Regulations 1966				5, 6, 9, 20
The Docks Regulations 1988				ALL
The Electricity at Work Regulations 1989				ALL
The Health and Safety (Display Screen Equipment) Regulations 1992			Implements Article 118A Directive	ALL
The Horizontal Milling Machines Regulations 1928	The Exemptions, 2–7	1	All provisions will be revoked	5, 6, 10, 11, 14, 15, 17, 21
The Iron and Steel Foundries Regulations 1953	5	4, 6, 8, 9	All provisions will be revoked	6, 13
The Jute (Safety, Health and Welfare) Regulations 1948	15, 27, 28 1st Schedule	11, 13, 14–16, 19–26		5, 6, 8, 9, 11, 12, 13, 21, 22
The Management of Health and Safety at Work Regulations 1992			Implements Article 118A Directive	ALL
The Manual Handling Operations Regulations 1992			Implements Article 118A Directive	ALL
The Offshore Installations (Operational Safety, Health and Welfare) Regulations 1976	10, 12			5, 6, 20, 23, 24

* See guidance under Regulations 1 and 27 for details of the timetable for the repeal/revocation of these provisions

Existing legislation	Key provisions to be replaced by PUWER*	Key provisions to be replaced by other legislation	Notes	What provisions of PUWER are particularly relevant?
The Offshore Installations (Construction and Survey) Regulations 1974				5, 11, 14, 20, 21
The Operations at Unfenced Machinery Regulations 1938	All			11
The Personal Protective Equipment at Work Regulations 1992			Implements Article 118A Directive	ALL
The Power Presses Regulations 1965				5, 6, 8, 9, 10, 11, 12, 23, 24
The Pressure Systems and Transportable Gas Containers Regulations 1989				5, 6, 10, 12, 13, 23, 24
The Shipbuilding and Ship-Repairing Regulations 1960	67	73, 74		5, 11, 12
The Spinning by Self-Acting Mules Regulations 1905	All			5, 8, 9, 10, 11
The Factories (Testing of Aircraft Engines and Accessories) Regulations 1952				5, 12, 14–17
The Workplace (Health, Safety and Welfare) Regulations 1992			Implements Article 118A Directive	ALL, especially 6, 21
The Woodworking Machines Regulations 1974	1(2) + (3), 3(2), 5–9, 14–19, 21–38, 40–43	10–12	13 (Training), 20, 39 and Schedule 1 will remain	ALL

* See guidance under Regulations 1 and 27 for details of the timetable for the repeal/revocation of these provisions

Appendix 3

Further guidance on regulation 11 – dangerous parts of machinery

Explanation of safeguarding terms, regulation 11(2)

1 Guards are physical barriers which prevent access to the danger zone. Fixed guards have no moving parts and are fastened in a constant position relative to the danger zone. They will normally need tools to undo the fasteners and remove them. If by themselves, or in conjunction with the structure of the equipment, they enclose the dangerous parts, fixed guards meet the requirements of the first level of the hierarchy. Note that it is permitted to have openings in fixed enclosing guards, and other types of guard, provided that they comply with appropriate safe reach distances (see EN 294).

2 Other guards in regulation 11(2)(b) include movable guards, adjustable guards, automatic guards and fixed guards that are not fully enclosing. Movable guards are likely to have interlocking. A control guard is a particular type of interlocked guard which should be used only in certain situations (see BS 5304). These allow limited access through openings, gates etc for feeding materials, making adjustments, cleaning, etc.

3 Protection devices are devices which do not prevent access to the danger zone but stop the movement of the dangerous part before contact is made. Typical examples are mechanical trip devices, photoelectric devices, pressure-sensitive mats and two-hand controls.

4 Protection appliances are used to hold or manipulate in a way which allows operators to control and feed a loose workpiece at a machine while keeping their body clear of the danger zone. They are commonly used in conjunction with woodworking machines and some other machines such as handsaws for cutting meat. These appliances will normally be used in addition to guards.

5 Adequate information, instruction, training and supervision is always important, even if the hazard is protected by hardware measures. But they are especially important when the risk cannot be adequately eliminated by the hardware measures in regulation 11(2)(a) to (c). It may be necessary to lay down procedures to define what information, instruction, training and supervision must be given, and to restrict use of the equipment to those who have received it.

Selection of measures

6 The guidance outlines how the hierarchy in regulation 11(2) should be applied in selecting safeguarding measures. Within each level of the hierarchy, there may be some choice available. In particular, the second level in the hierarchy allows a choice from among a number of different types of guard or protection device.

7 Regulation 11(2)(b) requires that when it is not practicable to use fixed enclosing guards, either at all or to the extent required for adequate protection, other guards and/or protection devices shall be used as far as

practicable. One example is where the need for frequent access prevents the use of a fixed guard. In this situation it may be necessary to choose between an interlocked movable guard or a protection device. The foreseeable probability and severity of injury will influence the choice of measures from among the range of guards and protection devices that are available. Regulation 11(3)(a) requires that guards must be suitable for their purpose. It is likely that some fixed guards will be practicable, and necessary to ensure that access can only be made through the movable opening guard or protection device. The use of movable guards which are interlocked is well established. Protection devices need to be carefully applied, taking into account the particular circumstances and the consequences of their failing to act as required.

8 Fixed distance guards, adjustable guards and other guards which do not completely enclose the dangerous parts should only be used in situations where it is not practicable to use fixed enclosing guards or protection devices which would give a greater level of protection.

Features of guards and protection devices, regulation 11(3)

Regulation 11(3)(a)

9 All guards and protection devices provided must be suitable for their purpose. In deciding what is suitable, employers should be guided by published national and international standards, guidance from HSC, HSE and industry associations, normal industrial practice and their own knowledge of the particular circumstances in which the machine is to be used.

10 A protection device or an interlocking system should be designed so that it will only operate as intended. Furthermore, if a component deteriorates or fails, the device or system should as far as possible fail in a safe manner by inhibiting the dangerous action of the machine. The force of this requirement depends on the combination of probability of failure and severity of the injury should the system fail. If the overall risk is high, then there should be adequate provision to counteract the effects of failure. Guidance on appropriate levels of protection is given in the publications referred to in paragraph 9.

Regulation 11(3)(b)

11 Guards and protection devices must be of good construction, sound material and adequate strength. They must be capable of doing the job they are intended to do. Several factors can be considered:

(a)   material of construction (metal, plastic, glass, etc);
(b)   form of the material (sheet, open mesh, bars, etc);
(c)   method of fixing.

12 Good construction involves design and layout as well as the mechanical nature and quality of the construction. Foreseeable use and misuse should be taken into account.

Regulation 11(3)(c)

13 Guards and protection devices must be maintained in an efficient state, in efficient working order and in good repair. This is an important requirement as many accidents have occurred when guards have not been maintained. It is a particular example of the general requirement under regulation 6 to maintain equipment. Compliance can be achieved by the use of an effective inspection or checking procedure for guards and protection devices, together with any necessary follow-up action. In the case of protection devices or interlocks, some form of recorded functional check or text is desirable.

14 In the case of certain types of guards and protection devices, for example power press guarding in a factory, employers are required to comply with other legislation relating to testing and examination of the guards and protection devices and to keep records. Compliance with such additional legislation will not necessarily guarantee compliance with the duty to ensure guards and protection devices are maintained within the terms of this Regulation. Risk assessment will determine extra steps that are needed to ensure continuing integrity.

Regulation 11(3)(d)

15 Guards and protection devices must not themselves give rise to any increased risk to health or safety. One effect of this sub-paragraph is to prevent use of inherently hazardous measures for guarding.

16 A second effect is that guards must be constructed so that they are not themselves dangerous parts. If a guard is power operated or assisted, the closing or opening action might create a potentially dangerous trap which needs secondary protection, for example a leading-edge trip bar or pressure-sensitive trip.

17 The main concern is the overall effect on risk. The fact that a guard may itself present a minor risk should not rule out its use if it can protect against the risk of major injury, but their use in guarding against more serious risks is justified.

Regulation 11(3)(e)

18 Guards and protection devices must be designed and installed so that they cannot easily be bypassed or disabled. This refers to accidental or deliberate action that removes the protection offered. By regulation 11(3)(a), guards must be suitable for their purpose, and one consequence of this is that simple mechanical bypassing or disabling should not be possible.

19 Movable panels in guards giving access to dangerous parts or movable guards themselves will often need to be fitted with an interlocking device. This device must be designed and installed so that it is difficult or impossible to bypass or defeat. Guidance on the selection and design of interlocking devices is available from the sources listed in paragraph 9.

20 In some cases, bypassing is needed for a particular purpose such as maintenance. The risks arising in such circumstances must be carefully

ssessed. As far as possible, the risks should be reduced or eliminated by ppropriate design of the machinery – see regulation 22.

Regulation 11(3)(f)

21 Guards and protection devices must be situated at a sufficient distance rom the danger zone they are protecting. In the case of solid fixed nclosing guards, there is no minimum distance between guard and danger one, except that required for good engineering design. However, the gap etween a fence type guard or protection device and machine should ormally be sufficiently small to prevent anybody remaining in it without eing detected; alternatively, the space between guard or protection device nd machine should be monitored by a suitable presence sensing device.

22 Where guarding is provided with holes or gaps (for visibility, entilation or weight reduction for example), or is not fully enclosing, the oles must be positioned or sized so that it prevents foreseeable access to he danger zone. Published national and international standards give uidance on suitable distances and opening sizes in different circumstances.

23 The positioning of protection devices which stop the dangerous part efore access can be gained to its danger zone will be affected by both the haracteristics of the device itself (response time) and those of the machine o which it is fitted (time needed to stop). In these circumstances the device nust be positioned so that it meets published criteria for the performance f such a system. Refer to the relevant standards and guidance.

24 Safeguarding is normally attached to the machine, but the Regulation oes not preclude the use of free-standing guards or protection devices. In uch cases, the guards or protection devices must be fixed in an appropriate osition relative to the machine.

Regulation 11(3)(g)

25 Guards and protection devices must not unduly restrict the view of the perating cycle of the machinery, where such a view is necessary. It is not sually necessary to be able to see all the machine; the part that needs to be een is normally that which is acting directly on material or a workpiece.

26 Operations for which it is necessary to provide a view include those where the operator controls and feeds a loose workpiece at a machine. Examples include woodworking machines, and food slicers. Many of these perations involve the use of protection appliances.

27 If the machine process needs to be seen, but cannot be, there is a emptation for the operator to remove or disable guards or interlocks. In uch cases, some view of the work may be considered necessary. Examples re a hopper feeding a screw conveyor, milling machines, and power presses.

28 In other cases it may be convenient but not absolutely necessary to see he entire operating cycle. The Regulation does not prohibit providing a view in these cases, but does not require it; an example is an industrial tumble drier.

29 Where an operation protected by guards needs to be seen, the guard should be provided with viewing slits or properly constructed panels perhaps backed up by internal lighting, enabling the operator to see the operation. The arrangements to ensure visibility should not prevent the guarding from carrying out is proper function; but any restriction of view should be the minimum compatible with that. An example of a guard providing necessary vision is viewing slits provided in the top guard of a circular saw.

Regulation 11(3)(h)

30 Guards and protection devices must be constructed or adapted so that they allow operations necessary to fit or replace parts and for maintenance work, restricting access so that it is allowed only to the area where the work is to be carried out and, if possible, without having to dismantle the guard or protection device.

31 This Regulation applies to the design of guards or protection device so as to reduce risks arising from some particular operations. Regulation 22 applies to the design of equipment as a whole so that maintenance and similar operations can be carried out safely; this Regulation is restricted to machine safeguards.

32 The aim is to design the safeguards so that operations like fitting or changing parts or maintenance can be done with minimal risk. If risk assessment shows this is not already the case, it may be possible to adapt the safeguarding appropriately.

33 Ideally, the machine is designed so that operations can be done in an area without risk, for example by using remote adjustment or maintenance points. If the work has to be done in the enclosed or protected area, then the safeguarding should be designed to restrict access just to that part where the work is to be carried out. This may mean using a series of guards.

34 If possible, the guard or protection device should not have to be dismantled. This is because of the possibility that after re-assembly, the guard or device may not work to its original performance standard.

Regulation 11(4)

35 Protection appliances also need to be suitable for their application. Factors for consideration come under the same headings as those for guards and protection devices as in regulation 11(3). Many of these are commonsense matters. Their design, material, manufacture and maintenance should all be adequate for the job they do. They should allow the person to use them without having to get too close to the danger zone, and they should not block the view of the workpiece.

References and further information

This section is not reproduced in this book.

Appendix 4

Personal Protective Equipment at Work Regulations 1992

THE REGULATIONS

Regulation 1

Citation and commencement

These Regulations may be cited as the Personal Protective Equipment at Work Regulations 1992 and shall come into force on 1st January 1993.

Regulation 2

Interpretation

(1) In these Regulations, unless the context otherwise requires, 'personal protective equipment' means all equipment (including clothing affording protection against the weather) which is intended to be worn or held by a person at work and which protects him against one or more risks to his health or safety, and any addition or accessory designed to meet that objective;

(2) Any reference in these Regulations to –

(a) a numbered regulation or Schedule is a reference to the regulation or Schedule in these Regulations so numbered; and
(b) a numbered paragraph is a reference to the paragraph so numbered in the regulation in which the reference appears.

Regulation 3 *(See p 362 for Guidance notes)*

Disapplication of these Regulations

(1) These Regulations shall not apply to or in relation to the master or crew of a sea-going ship or to the employer of such persons in respect of the normal ship-board activities of a ship's crew under the direction of the master.

(2) Regulations 4 to 12 shall not apply in respect of personal protective equipment which is –

(a) ordinary working clothes and uniforms which do not specifically protect the health and safety of the wearer;
(b) an offensive weapon within the meaning of section 1(4) of the Prevention of Crime Act 1953 used as self-defence or as deterrent equipment;
(c) portable devices for detecting and signalling risks and nuisances;
(d) personal protective equipment used for protection while travelling on a road within the meaning (in England and Wales) of section 192(1) of the Road Traffic Act 1988, and (in Scotland) of section 151 of the Roads (Scotland) Act 1984;
(e) equipment used during the playing of competitive sports.

(3) Regulations 4 and 6 to 12 shall not apply where any of the following Regulations apply and in respect of any risk to a person's health or safety for which any of them require the provision or use of personal protective equipment, namely –

(a) the Control of Lead at Work Regulations 1980;
(b) the Ionising Radiations Regulations 1985;
(c) the Control of Asbestos at Work Regulations 1987;
(d) the Control of Substances Hazardous to Health Regulations 1988;
(e) the Noise at Work Regulations 1989;
(f) the Construction (Head Protection) Regulations 1989.

Regulation 4 *(See p 365 for Guidance notes)*

Provision of personal protective equipment

(1) Every employer shall ensure that suitable personal protective equipment is provided to his employees who may be exposed to a risk to their health or safety while at work except where and to the extent that such risk has been adequately controlled by other means which are equally or more effective.

(2) Every self-employed person shall ensure that he is provided with suitable personal protective equipment where he may be exposed to a risk to his health or safety while at work except where and to the extent that such risk has been adequately controlled by other means which are equally or more effective.

(3) Without prejudice to the generality of paragraphs (1) and (2), personal protective equipment shall not be suitable unless –

(a) it is appropriate for the risk or risks involved and the conditions at the place where exposure to the risk may occur;
(b) it takes account of ergonomic requirements and the state of health of the person or persons who may wear it;
(c) it is capable of fitting the wearer correctly, if necessary, after adjustments within the range for which it is designed;
(d) so far as is practicable, it is effective to prevent or adequately control the risk or risks involved without increasing overall risk;

(e) it complies with any enactment (whether in an Act or instrument) which implements in Great Britain any provision on design or manufacture with respect to health or safety in any of the relevant Community directives listed in Schedule 1 which is applicable to that item of personal protective equipment.

Regulation 5 *(See p 368 for Guidance notes)*

Compatibility of personal protective equipment

(1) Every employer shall ensure that where the presence of more than one risk to health or safety makes it necessary for his employee to wear or use simultaneously more than one item of personal protective equipment, such equipment is compatible and continues to be effective against the risk or risks in question.

(2) Every self-employed person shall ensure that where the presence of more than one risk to health or safety makes it necessary for him to wear or use simultaneously more than one item of personal protective equipment, such equipment is compatible and continues to be effective against the risk or risks in question.

Regulation 6 *(See p 368 for Guidance notes)*

Assessment of personal protective equipment

(1) Before choosing any personal protective equipment which by virtue of regulation 4 he is required to ensure is provided, an employer or self-employed person shall ensure that an assessment is made to determine whether the personal protective equipment he intends will be provided is suitable.

(2) The assessment required by paragraph (1) shall include –

(a) an assessment of any risk or risks to health or safety which have not been avoided by other means;
(b) the definition of the characteristics which personal protective equipment must have in order to be effective against the risks referred to in sub-paragraph (a) of this paragraph, taking into account any risks which the equipment itself may create;
(c) comparison of the characteristics of the personal protective equipment available with the characteristics referred to in sub-paragraph (b) of this paragraph.

(3) Every employer or self-employed person who is required by paragraph (1) to ensure that any assessment is made shall ensure that any such assessment is reviewed if –

(a) there is reason to suspect that it is no longer valid; or
(b) there has been a significant change in the matters to which it relates,

and where as a result of any such review changes in the assessment are required, the relevant employer or self-employed person shall ensure that they are made.

Regulation 7 *(See p 369 for Guidance notes)*

Maintenance and replacement of personal protective equipment

(1) Every employer shall ensure that any personal protective equipment provided to his employees is maintained (including replaced or cleaned as appropriate) in an efficient state, in efficient working order and in good repair.

(2) Every self-employed person shall ensure that any personal protective equipment provided to him is maintained (including replaced or cleaned as appropriate) in an efficient state, in efficient working order and in good repair.

Regulation 8 *(See p 370 for Guidance notes)*

Accommodation for personal protective equipment

Where an employer or self-employed person is required, by virtue of regulation 4, to ensure personal protective equipment is provided, he shall also ensure that appropriate accommodation is provided for that personal protective equipment when it is not being used.

Regulation 9 *(See p 371 for Guidance notes)*

Information, instruction and training

(1) Where an employer is required to ensure that personal protective equipment is provided to an employee, the employer shall also ensure that the employee is provided with such information, instruction and training as is adequate and appropriate to enable the employee to know –

(a) the risk or risks which the personal protective equipment will avoid or limit;

(b) the purpose for which and the manner in which personal protective equipment is to be used; and

(c) any action to be taken by the employee to ensure that the personal protective equipment remains in an efficient state, in efficient working order and in good repair as required by regulation 7(1).

(2) Without prejudice to the generality of paragraph (1), the information and instruction provided by virtue of that paragraph shall not be adequate and appropriate unless it is comprehensible to the persons to whom it is provided.

Regulation 10 *(See p 372 for Guidance notes)*

Use of personal protective equipment

(1) Every employer shall take all reasonable steps to ensure that any personal protective equipment provided to his employees by virtue of regulation 4(1) is properly used.

(2) Every employee shall use any personal protective equipment provided to him by virtue of these Regulations in accordance both with any training in the use of the personal protective equipment concerned which has been received by him and the instructions respecting that use which have been provided to him by virtue of regulation 9.

(3) Every self-employed person shall make full and proper use of any personal protective equipment provided to him by virtue of regulation 4(2).

(4) Every employee and self-employed person who has been provided with personal protective equipment by virtue of regulation 4 shall take all reasonable steps to ensure that it is returned to the accommodation provided for it after use.

Regulation 11 *(See p 373 for Guidance notes)*

Reporting loss or defect

Every employee who has been provided with personal protective equipment by virtue of regulation 4(1) shall forthwith report to his employer any loss of or obvious defect in that personal protective equipment.

Regulation 12

Exemption certificates

(1) The Secretary of State for Defence may, in the interests of national security, by a certificate in writing exempt –

a) any of the home forces, any visiting force or any headquarters from those requirements of these Regulations which impose obligations on employers; or

b) any member of the home forces, any member of a visiting force or any member of a headquarters from the requirements imposed by regulations 10 or 11;

and any exemption such as is specified in sub-paragraph (a) or (b) of this paragraph may be granted subject to conditions and to a limit of time and may be revoked by the said Secretary of State by a further certificate in writing at any time.

(2) In this regulation –

a) 'the home forces' has the same meaning as in section 12(1) of the Visiting Forces Act 1952;

b) 'headquarters' has the same meaning as in article 3(2) of the Visiting Forces and International Headquarters (Application of Law) Order 1965;

c) 'member of a headquarters' has the same meaning as in paragraph 1(1) of the Schedule to the International Headquarters and Defence Organisations Act 1964; and

d) 'visiting force' has the same meaning as it does for the purposes of any provision of Part I of the Visiting Forces Act 1952.

Regulation 13 *(See p 373 for Guidance notes)*

Extension outside Great Britain

These Regulations shall apply to and in relation to the premises and activities outside Great Britain to which sections 1 to 59 and 80 to 82 of the Health and Safety at Work etc. Act 1974 apply by virtue of the Health and Safety at Work etc. Act 1974 (Application Outside Great Britain) Order 1989 as they apply within Great Britain.

Regulation 14 *(See p 373 for Guidance notes)*

Modifications, repeal and revocations

(1) The Act and Regulations specified in Schedule 2 shall be modified to the extent specified in the corresponding Part of that Schedule.

(2) Section 65 of the Factories Act 1961 is repealed.

(3) The instruments specified in column 1 of Schedule 2 are revoked to the extent specified in column 3 of that Schedule.

Schedule 1

Regulation 4(3)(e)

Relevant Community Directive

Council Directive of 21 December 1989 on the approximation of the law of the Member States relating to personal protective equipment (89/686 EEC)

Schedule 2

Regulation 14(1)

Modifications

Part I – The Factories Act 1961

1. In section 30(6), for "breathing apparatus of a type approved by the chief inspector", substitute "suitable breathing apparatus".

Part II – The Coal and Other Mines (Fire and Rescue) Order 1956

2. In Schedule 1, in regulation 23(a), for "breathing apparatus of a type approved by the Minister", substitute "suitable breathing apparatus".

3. In Schedule 1, in regulation 23(b), for "smoke helmets or other apparatus serving the same purpose, being helmets or apparatus of a type approved by the Minister,", substitute "suitable smoke helmets or other suitable apparatus serving the same purpose".

4. In Schedule 1, in regulation 24(a), for "smoke helmet or other apparatus serving the same purpose, being a helmet or apparatus of a type

approved by the Minister,", substitute "suitable smoke helmet or other suitable apparatus serving the same purpose".

Part III – The Shipbuilding and Ship-repairing Regulations 1960

5. In each of regulations 50, 51(1) and 60(1), for "breathing apparatus of a type approved for the purpose of this Regulation", substitute "suitable breathing apparatus".

Part IV – The Coal Mines (Respirable Dust) Regulations 1975

6. In regulation 10(a), for "dust respirators of a type approved by the Executive for the purpose of this Regulation", substitute "suitable dust respirators".

Part V – The Control of Lead at Work Regulations 1980

7. In regulation 7 –

(a) after "respiratory protective equipment", insert "which complies with regulation 8A or, where the requirements of that regulation do not apply, which is"; and
(b) after "as will", insert ", in either case,".

8. In regulation 8, for "adequate protective clothing", substitute "protective clothing which complies with regulation 8A or, where no requirement is imposed by virtue of that regulation, is adequate".

9. After regulation 8, insert the following new regulations –

"Compliance with relevant Community directives
8A. Any respiratory protective equipment or protective clothing shall comply with any enactment (whether in an Act or instrument) which implements any provision on design or manufacture with respect to health or safety in any relevant Community directive listed in Schedule 1 to the Personal Protective Equipment at Work Regulations 1992 which is applicable to that item of respiratory protective equipment or protective clothing.

Assessment of respiratory protective equipment or protective clothing
8B.–(1) Before choosing respiratory protective equipment or protective clothing, an employer shall make an assessment to determine whether it will satisfy regulation 7 or 8, as appropriate.
(2) The assessment required by paragraph (1) shall involve –

(a) definition of the characteristics necessary to comply with regulation 7 or, as the case may be, 8, and
(b) comparison of the characteristics or respiratory protective equipment or protective clothing available with the characteristics referred to in sub-paragraph (a) of this paragraph.

(3) The assessment required by paragraph (10 shall be revised if –

(a)   there is reason to suspect that it is no longer valid; or
(b)   there has been a significant change in the work to which it relates,

and, where, as a result of the review, changes in the assessment are required, the employer shall make them.".

10. In regulation 9, for sub-paragraph (b), substitute the following sub-paragraph –

"(b) where he is required under regulations 7 or 8 to provide respiratory protective equipment or protective clothing, adequate changing facilities and adequate facilities for the storage of –
(i)   the respiratory protective equipment or protective clothing, and
(ii)   personal clothing not worn during working hours.".

11. At the end of regulation 13, add the following new paragraph –

"(3) Every employee shall take all reasonable steps to ensure that any respiratory protective equipment provided to him pursuant to regulation 7 and protective clothing provided to him pursuant to regulation 8 is returned to the accommodation provided for it after use."

12. In regulation 18(2), omit the full stop and add "and that any provision imposed by the European Communities in respect of the encouragement of improvements in the safety and health of workers at work will be satisfied."

Part VI – The Ionising Radiations Regulations 1985

13. In regulation 23(1), after "that respiratory protective equipment", insert "complies with paragraph (1A) or, where no requirement is imposed by that paragraph,".

14. After regulation 23(1), insert the following paragraphs –

"(1A) For the purposes of paragraph (1), personal protective equipment complies with this paragraph if it complies with any enactment (whether in an Act or instrument) which implements in Great Britain any provision on design or manufacture with respect to health or safety in any relevant Community directive listed in Schedule 1 to the Personal Protective Equipment at Work Regulations 1992 which is applicable to that item of personal protective equipment.

(1B) Before choosing personal protective equipment, an employer shall make an assessment to determine whether it will satisfy regulation 6(3).

(1C) The assessment required by paragraph (1B) shall involve –

(a)   definition of the characteristics necessary to comply with regulation 6(3), and

(b) comparison of the characteristics of available personal protective equipment with the characteristics referred to in sub-paragraph (a) of this paragraph.

(1D) The assessment required by paragraph (1B) shall be reviewed if –

(a) there is reason to suspect that it is no longer valid; or
(b) there has been a significant change in the work to which it relates,

and where, as a result of the review, changes in the assessment are required, the employer shall make them.".

15. Add at the end of regulation 23 the following additional paragraphs –

"(2A) Every employer shall ensure that appropriate accommodation is provided for personal protective equipment when it is not being worn.

(2B) Every employee shall take all reasonable steps to ensure that personal protective equipment provided to him is returned to the accommodation provided for it after use.".

Part VII – The Control of Asbestos at Work Regulations 1987

16. In regulation 8(3), after "shall" the first time that word appears, insert "comply with paragraph (3A) or, where no requirement is imposed by that paragraph, shall".

17. Insert the following new paragraph after regulation 8(3) –

"(3A) Any respiratory protective equipment provided in pursuance of paragraph (2) or protective clothing provided in pursuance of regulation 11(1) shall comply with this paragraph if it complies with any enactment (whether in an Act or instrument) which implements in Great Britain any provision on design or manufacture with respect to health or safety in any relevant Community directive listed in Schedule 1 to the Personal Protective Equipment at Work Regulations 1992 which is applicable to that item of respiratory protective equipment or protective clothing.".

18. In regulation 20(2), omit the fullstop and add "and that any provision imposed by the European Communities in respect of the encouragement of improvements in the safety and health of workers at work will be satisfied.".

Part VIII – The Control of Substances Hazardous to Health Regulations 1988

19. In regulation 7, after paragraph (3), insert the following new paragraph –

"(3A) Any personal protective equipment provided by an employer in pursuance of this regulation shall comply with any enactment (whether in an Act or instrument) which implements in Great Britain any provision on design or manufacture with respect to health or safety in any relevant Community directive listed in Schedule 1 to the Personal Protective Equipment at Work Regulations 1992 which is applicable to that item of personal protective equipment.".

20. In regulation 7, in paragraph (6)(b), insert at the beginning "complies with paragraph (3A) or, where no requirement is imposed by virtue of that paragraph,".

21. In regulation 8(2), after "these regulations", insert "and shall take all reasonable steps to ensure it is returned after use to any accommodation provided for it".

Part IX – The Noise at Work Regulations 1989

22. Add the following new paragraph at the end of regulation 8 –

"(3) Any personal ear protectors provided by virtue of this regulation shall comply with any enactment (whether in an Act or instrument) which implements in Great Britain any provision on design or manufacture with respect to health or safety in any relevant Community directive listed in Schedule 1 to the Personal Protective Equipment at Work Regulations 1992 which is applicable to those ear protectors.".

Part X – The Construction (Head Protection) Regulations 1989

23. Add the following paragraphs at the end of regulation 3 –

"(3) Any head protection provided by virtue of this regulation shall comply with any enactment (whether in an Act or instrument) which implements any provision on design or manufacture with respect to health or safety in any relevant Community directive listed in Schedule 1 to the personal Protective Equipment at Work Regulations 1992 which is applicable to that head protection.

(4) Before choosing head protection, an employer or self-employed person shall make an assessment or determine whether it is suitable.

(5) The assessment required by paragraph (4) of this regulation shall involve –

(a) the definition of the characteristics which head protection must have in order to be suitable;

(b) comparison of the characteristics of the protection available with the characteristics referred to in sub-paragraph (a) of this paragraph.

(6) The assessment required by paragraph (4) shall be reviewed if –

(a) there is reason to suspect that it is no longer valid; or

(b) there has been a significant change in the work to which it relates, and where as a result of the review changes in the assessment are required, the relevant employer or self-employed person shall make them.

(7) Every employer and every self-employed person shall ensure that appropriate accommodation is available for head protection by or under these Regulation when it is not being used.".

24. For regulation 6(4), substitute the following paragraph –

"(4) Every employee or self-employed person who is required to wear suitable head protection by or under these Regulations shall –

(a) make full and proper use of it; and
(b) take all reasonable steps to return it to the accommodation provided for it after use.".

25. In regulation 9(2), omit the full stop and add "and that any provision imposed by the European Communities in respect of the encouragement of improvements in the safety and health of workers at work will be satisfied.".

Schedule 3

Regulation 14(3)

Revocations

(1) *Title*	*(2)* *Reference*	*(3)* *Extent of Revocation*
Regulations dated 26th February 1906 in respect of the processes of spinning and weaving of flax and tow and the processes incidental thereto (the Flax and Tow-Spinning and Weaving Regulations 1906).	S.R. & O. 1906/177, amended by S.I. 1988/1657.	In regulation 9, the words "unless waterproof skirts, and bibs of suitable material, are provided by the occupier and worn by the workers". Regulation 13.
Order dated 5th October 1917 (the Tin or Terne Plates Manufacture Welfare Order 1917).	S.R. & O. 1917/1035.	Paragraph 1.

(1) Title	(2) Reference	(3) Extent of Revocation
Order dated 15th August 1919 (the Fruit Preserving Welfare Order 1919).	S.R. & O. 1919/1136, amended by S.I. 1988/1657.	Paragraph 1.
Order dated 23rd April 1920 (the Laundries Welfare Order 1920).	S.R. & O. 1920/654.	Paragraph 1.
Order dated 28th July 1920 (the Gut-Scrapping, Tripe Dressing, etc. Welfare Order 1920).	S.R. & O. 1920/1437.	Paragraph 1.
Order dated 3rd March 1921 (the Glass Bevelling Welfare Order 1921).	S.R. & O. 1921/288.	Paragraph 1.
The Aerated Water Regulations 1921.	S.R. & O. 1921/1932; amended by S.I. 1981/686.	The whole Regulations.
The Sacks (Cleaning and Repairing) Welfare Order 1927.	S.R. & O. 1927/860.	Paragraph 1.
The Oil Cake Welfare Order 1929.	S.R. & O. 1929/534.	Paragraph 1.
The Cement Works Welfare Order 1930	S.R. & O. 1930/94.	Paragraph 1.
The Tanning Welfare Order 1930.	S.R. & O. 1930/312.	Paragraph 1 and the Schedule.

(1) *Title*	*(2)* *Reference*	*(3)* *Extent of Revocation*
The Magnesium (Grinding of Castings and Other Articles) Special Regulations 1946.	S.R. & O. 1946/2107.	Regulation 12.
The Clay Works (Welfare) Special Regulations 1948.	S.I. 1948/1547.	Regulation 5.
The Iron and Steel Foundries Regulations 1953.	S.I. 1953/1464; amended by S.I. 1974/1681 and S.I. 1981/1332.	Regulation 8.
The Shipbuilding and Ship-Repairing Regulations 1960.	S.I. 1960/1932; amended by S.I. 1974/1681.	Regulations 73 and 74.
The Non-Ferrous Metals (Melting and Founding) Regulations 1962.	S.I. 1962/1667; amended by S.I. 1974/1681.	Regulation 13.
The Abstract of Special Regulations (Aerated Water) Order 1963.	S.I. 1963/2058.	The whole Order.
The Construction (Health and Welfare) Regulations 1966.	S.I. 1966/95; to which there are amendments not relevant to these Regulations.	Regulation 15.
The Foundries (Protective Footwear and Gaiters) Regulations 1971.	S.I. 1971/476.	The whole Regulations.
The Protection of Eyes Regulations 1974.	S.I. 1974/1681; amended by S.I. 1975/303.	The whole Regulations.
The Aerated Water Regulations (Metrication) Regulations 1981.	S.I. 1981/686.	The whole Regulations.

GUIDANCE NOTES

Introduction

1–6 . . .

Part 1

Guidance on the Personal Protective Equipment at Work Regulations 1992

Regulation 3

Disapplication of these Regulations

7 Personal protective equipment (PPE) includes both the following, when they are worn for protection of health and safety:

(a) protective clothing such as aprons, protective clothing for adverse weather conditions, gloves, safety footwear, safety helmets, high visibility waistcoats etc; and

(b) protective equipment such as eye protectors, life-jackets, respirators, underwater breathing apparatus and safety harnesses.

8 In practice, however, these Regulations will not apply to ear protectors, most respiratory protective equipment and some other types of PPE used at work. These types of PPE are specifically excluded from the scope of the PPE at Work Regulations because they are covered by existing Regulations such as the Noise at Work Regulations 1989 (see Table 1 and paragraph 16). Even if the PPE at Work Regulations do not apply, the advice given in this guidance may still be applicable, as the general principles of selecting and maintaining suitable PPE and training employees in its use are common to all Regulations which refer to PPE.

Table 1 – Provisions on the use of personal protective equipment

Where there are existing comprehensive Regulations which require PPE.	The PPE at Work Regulations will not apply.	For example: The Control of Substances Hazardous to Health Regulations 1988 require respirators to be used in certain circumstances.
Where there are no current Regulations dealing with PPE.	The PPE at Work Regulations will apply.	For example: The PPE at Work Regulations will require that chainsaw operators are provided with and wear the appropriate PPE.

Where there are existing but not comprehensive Regulations requiring the use of PPE.	The PPE at Work Regulations will apply, and will complement the requirements of the existing Regulations.	For example: regulation 19 of the Docks Regulations 1988 requires the provision of high visibility clothing when an employee is working in specific areas of a dock. The PPE at Work Regulations complement this duty by laying down duties about the accommodation of PPE, training of employees in its use etc, and may also require the use of high visibility clothing in any other part of the dock where there is a risk from vehicle movements.

9 Items such as uniforms provided for the primary purpose of presenting a corporate image, and ordinary working clothes, are not subject to these Regulations. Likewise the Regulations will not apply to 'protective clothing' provided in the food industry primarily for food hygiene purposes. However where any uniform or clothing protects against a specific risk to health and safety, for example high visibility clothing worn by emergency services, it will be subject to the Regulations. Waterproof, weatherproof or insulated clothing is subject to the Regulations if it is worn to protect employees against risks to their health or safety, but not otherwise.

10 The Regulations do not cover the use of PPE such as cycle helmets, crash helmets or motorcycle leathers worn by employees on the public highway. Motor cycle crash helmets remain legally required for motorcyclists under road traffic legislation, and Section 2 of the Health and Safety at Work etc Act 1974 (HSW Act 1974) – requiring employers to ensure the health and safety of employees, so far as is reasonably practicable – will still apply. The Regulations do apply to the use of such equipment at work elsewhere if there is a risk to health and safety, for example, farm workers riding motorcycles or 'all-terrain' vehicles should use crash helmets.

11 The Regulations do not require professional sports people to use PPE such as shin guards or head protection during competition. However, they do apply to sports equipment used in other circumstances, for example, lifejackets worn by professional canoeing instructors, riding helmets worn by stable staff, or climbing helmets worn by steeplejacks.

12 The Regulations do not require employers to provide equipment for self defence or deterrent purposes, for example personal sirens/alarms or truncheons used by security staff. However, they do apply to PPE (such as

helmets or body armour) provided where staff are at risk from physical violence.

13 The Regulations do not cover personal gas detectors or radiation dosimeters. Although this equipment would come within the broad definition of PPE, the specific disapplication is included as many of the Regulations would not be appropriate to it (for example, the fitting and ergonomic requirements of regulation 4). However, employers will have a duty to provide such equipment under Section 2 of the HSW Act 1974 if its use is necessary to ensure the health and safety of employees.

Application to merchant shipping

14 Sea-going ships are subject to separate merchant shipping legislation, administered by the Department of Transport, which gives protection to people on board. Regulation 3(1) disapplies the Regulations from these ships in respect of the normal ship-board activities of a ship's crew under the direction of the master. But it does not disapply them in respect of other work activities, for example, where a shore-based contractor goes on board to carry out work on the ship, that person's activities will be subject to the Regulations within territorial waters as provided for under regulation 14. This partial exemption applies to sea-going ships only. Therefore the Regulations will apply to PPE used on ships that only operate on inland waters.

Aircraft

15 Aircraft are subject to these Regulations while on the ground and in airspace for which the United Kingdom has jurisdiction.

Application of other Regulations

16 The sets of Regulations listed in regulation 3(3) require the provision and use of certain PPE against particular hazards, and the PPE at Work Regulations will not apply where these Regulations remain in force. For example, a person working with asbestos would, where necessary, have to use respiratory protective equipment and protective clothing under the Control of Asbestos at Work Regulations 1987, rather than the PPE at Work Regulations.

17 Most older legislation on PPE has been revoked, for example the Protection of Eyes Regulations 1974; a complete list is in Schedule 3 to the Regulations. However, because they provide for the particular circumstances of the relevant industry or risk, it is necessary to retain some provisions apart from those in regulation 3(3) (for example in the Diving Operations at Work Regulations 1981 and the Docks Regulations 1988). The more comprehensive PPE at Work Regulations will apply in addition to these Regulations (see Table 1). Where necessary, therefore, employers (and others with duties under the Regulations) will have to comply with

both the specific Regulations and the PPE at Work Regulations. A list of these specific Regulations is at Appendix 2.

18 Where appropriate, PPE provided by virtue of the Regulations listed in regulation 3(3) of the PPE at Work Regulations will have to comply with the requirements of the Personal Protective Equipment (Safety) Regulations 1992 implementing the Personal Protective Equipment Product Directive and be 'CE' marked; as will PPE provided under these Regulations (see paragraphs 33 to 35). Personal protective equipment obtained before the Personal Protective Equipment (Safety) Regulations came fully into force can continue to be used without being 'CE' marked for as long as it remains suitable for the use to which it is being put.

Application to non-employees

19 These Regulations do not apply to people who are not employees, for example voluntary workers, or school children while in school. However Section 3 of the HSW Act 1974, which requires that 'It shall be the duty of every employer to conduct his undertaking in such a way as to ensure, so far as is reasonably practicable, that persons not in his employment who may be affected thereby are not exposed to risks to their health and safety', will still apply. If an employer needs to provide PPE to comply with this duty, then by following the requirements of these Regulations he will fully satisfy this duty. These Regulations do apply to trainees and children on work experience programmes.

Regulation 4

Provision of personal protective equipment

PPE as a 'last resort'

20 The Management of Health and Safety at Work Regulations (MHSWR) 1992 require employers to identify and assess the risks to health and safety present in the workplace, so enabling the most appropriate means of reducing those risks to an acceptable level to be determined. There is in effect a hierarchy of control measures, and PPE should always be regarded as the 'last resort' to protect against risks to safety and health; engineering controls and safe systems of work should always be considered first. It may be possible to do the job by another method which will not require the use of PPE or, if that is not possible, adopt other more effective safeguards: for example, fixed screens could be provided rather than individual eye protection to protect against swarf thrown off a lathe. Employers' duties in this respect are contained in much of the legislation under the HSW Act 1974, including MHSWR. The practical guidance to MHSWR given in its Approved Code of Practice is also particularly relevant. However in some circumstances PPE will still be needed to control the risk adequately, and the PPE at Work Regulations will then take effect.

21 There are a number of reasons for this approach. Firstly, PPE protects only the person wearing it, whereas measures controlling the risk at source

can protect everyone at the workplace. Secondly, theoretical maximum levels of protection are seldom achieved with PPE in practice, and the actual level of protection is difficult to assess. Effective protection is only achieved by suitable PPE, correctly fitted and maintained and properly used. Thirdly, PPE may restrict the wearer to some extent by limiting mobility or visibility, or by requiring additional weight to be carried. Other means of protection should therefore be used whenever reasonably practicable.

22 Employers should, therefore, provide appropriate PPE and training in its usage to their employees wherever there is a risk to health and safety that cannot be adequately controlled by other means.

Providing personal protective equipment

23 In order to provide PPE for their employees, employers must do more than simply have the equipment on the premises. The employees must have the equipment readily available, or at the very least have clear instructions on where they can obtain it. Most PPE is provided on a personal basis, but in certain circumstances items of PPE may be shared by employees, for example where they are only required for limited periods – see the guidance on regulation 7 (maintenance).

24 By virtue of Section 9 of the HSW Act 1974, no charge can be made to the worker for the provision of PPE which is used only at work.

25 Section 9 of the HSW Act 1974 states: 'No employer shall levy or permit to be levied on any employee of his any charge in respect of anything done or provided in pursuance of any specific requirement of the relevant statutory provisions'. Section 9 applies to these Regulations because they impose a 'specific requirement' – ie, to provide PPE.

26 Regulation 4 requires PPE to be provided where risks have not been adequately controlled by other means. Where risks are sufficiently low that they can be considered in effect to be adequately controlled, then PPE need not be provided. For example, in most workplaces there will be some risk of people dropping objects onto their feet, but it is only when there is manual handling of objects of sufficient weight that the risk will be sufficient to require the provision of safety footwear.

27 Adequate control of the risk is also in general the standard of protection which the PPE provided should achieve. However there may be some circumstances where no PPE will provide adequate control of the risk (for example fire fighters' protective clothing can give only limited protection from radiant heat and flames). In these cases, the employer is required only to provide PPE offering the best protection practicable in the circumstances. Use of PPE must not increase the overall level of risk, ie PPE must not be worn if the risk caused by wearing it is greater than the risk against which it is meant to protect.

28 Regulation 4(3)(a) to (e) lists other factors which determine whether PPE is suitable. Further guidance on the suitability of PPE is given in paragraphs 29 to 35.

Ergonomic and other factors

29 When selecting PPE to be used while doing a job, the nature of the job and the demands it places on the worker should be taken into account. This will involve considering the physical effort required to do the job, the methods of work, how long the PPE needs to be worn, and requirements for visibility and communication. Those who do the job are usually best placed to know what is involved, and they should be consulted. Other factors may also influence selection: for example, PPE used in the food industry may need to be cleaned easily. The aim should always be to choose PPE which will give minimum discomfort to the wearer, as uncomfortable equipment is unlikely to be worn properly.

30 There will be considerable differences in the physical dimensions of different workers and therefore more than one type or size of PPE may be needed. The required range may not be available from a single supplier. Those having to use PPE should be consulted and involved in the selection and specification of the equipment as there is a better chance of PPE being used effectively if it is accepted by each wearer.

31 All PPE which is approved by HSE or bears the 'CE' mark must pass basic performance requirements. These have usually been set following medical advice, and the use of such PPE should cause no problems to average healthy adults. Where problems occur, employers should seek medical advice as to whether the individual can tolerate wearing the PPE. Employers are able to take into account only those medical conditions of which they have been informed.

32 In some industries, particularly those where peripatetic workers (such as contract maintenance workers or building workers) are employed, the site operator will be better placed to provide the appropriate PPE than the peripatetic worker's employer. Although under these circumstances the employer does not have to repeat the provision of suitable PPE, it is still the employer's responsibility to ensure that suitable PPE is provided. Likewise, the site operator may in practice take the action necessary to meet the requirements of the Regulations which follow, but the employer still remains responsible for ensuring that this has been done.

The quality of personal protective equipment

33 Employers must ensure that any PPE they purchase complies with the United Kingdom legislation implementing Community Directives concerning the design or manufacture of PPE with regard to health and safety, listed in Schedule 1 of the Regulations, where that legislation is applicable. Currently (1 January 1993) the only provision listed in Schedule 1 is the PPE Product Directive, implemented by the Personal Protective Equipment (Safety) Regulations 1992. There are a few types of PPE such as escape equipment on aircraft which are not currently within the scope of this Directive. Regulation 4(3)(e) does not apply to this type of equipment, nor to any other type of PPE bought before this Directive is implemented fully.

34 The PPE (Safety) Regulations require that almost all PPE supplied for use at work must be certified by an independent inspection body which will, if the PPE meets the basic safety requirements, issue a certificate of conformity. For a few types of simple PPE protecting against low risks (eg gardening gloves) the manufacturer can himself certify that the PPE meets the basic safety requirements. The manufacturer is then able to display the 'CE' mark on the product. It will be illegal for suppliers to sell PPE unless it is 'CE' marked when the PPE (Safety) Regulations are fully in force.

35 In many cases, PPE will be made to harmonised European Standards or 'Norms' (ENs) which will systematically replace existing British Standards. These standards are published in the Official Journal of the European Communities and equipment conforming with these standards will be considered to comply with the basic safety requirements of the PPE Product Directive. Part 2 and Appendix 3 refer to some of these standards, but many ENs on PPE are still in preparation.

Regulation 5

Compatibility of personal protective equipment

36 If more than one item of PPE is being worn, the different items of PPE must be compatible with each other. For example, certain types of respirators will not fit properly and give adequate protection if a safety helmet is worn. In such cases when selecting PPE it should be ensured that both items when used together will adequately control the risks against which they are provided to protect.

Regulation 6

Assessment of personal protective equipment

Assessment

37 The purpose of the assessment provision in regulation 6 is to ensure that the employer who needs to provide PPE chooses PPE which is correct for the particular risks involved and for the circumstances of its use. It follows on from, but does not duplicate, the risk assessment requirement of the Management of Health and Safety at Work Regulations (MHSWR) 1992, which involves identifying the hazards present in any undertaking and then evaluating the extent of the risks involved. Regulation 6(2) lays down the steps the employer should take to identify appropriate PPE.

38 Whatever PPE is chosen, it should be remembered that, although some types of equipment do provide very high levels of protection, none provides 100%. Some indication is needed of the level of risk so that the performance required of the PPE can be estimated. This information may have been gathered as part of the overall risk assessment required under MHSWR (described above), or more generalised data may be available from sources such as HSE guidance.

39 In the simplest and most obvious cases which can easily be repeated and explained at any time, the assessment to identify suitable PPE need not be recorded. In more complex cases, however, the assessment will need to be recorded and kept readily accessible to those who need to know the results.

Selection of suitable PPE

40 Once potential hazards are known there may be several types of PPE that would be suitable. The risks at the workplace and the parts of the body endangered are the two key elements to consider. A specimen risk survey table is produced as Appendix 1 and is designed to help define the areas in which workers are at risk. Part 2 identifies types of PPE that may be suitable once the risks have been assessed.

41 For example, when assessing the need for eye protection, employers should first identify the types of hazard present, such as airborne dust, liquid splashes or projectiles, and then assess the degree of risk – for example the likely size and velocity of the projectiles. They can then select a suitable type of PPE from the range of 'CE' marked equipment available. In this case, eye protection is designed for dust or chemical protection, and to different levels of impact resistance.

42 Once a type of 'CE' marked PPE has been selected for a given application, further advice and information may be necessary to ensure that the equipment can provide the protection needed. Manufacturers and suppliers have duties under the PPE (Safety) Regulations 1992 and under Section 6 of the Health and Safety at Work etc Act 1974 to provide information of this type.

43 When selecting PPE to be used while doing a job, the nature of the job and the demands it places on the worker should be taken into account as explained in paragraphs 29 to 32. This will involve considering the physical effort required to do the job, the method of work, how long the PPE needs to be worn, and requirements for visibility and communication.

44 Selection should be seen as only the first stage in a continuing programme which is also concerned with the proper use and maintenance of the equipment, and the training and supervision of employees.

Regulation 7

Maintenance and replacement of personal protective equipment

45 An effective system of maintenance of PPE is essential to make sure the equipment continues to provide the degree of protection for which it was designed. Maintenance is required under the Regulations and includes, where appropriate, cleaning, disinfection, examination, replacement, repair and testing. The responsibility for carrying out maintenance should be laid down, together with the details of the procedures to be followed and their frequency. Where appropriate, records of tests and examinations should also be kept. The maintenance programme will vary with the type of equipment and the use to which it is put. For example, mechanical fall-

arrestors will require a regular planned preventive maintenance programme which will include examination, testing and overhaul. However, gloves may only require periodic inspection by the user, depending on what they are being used to protect against.

46 In general, PPE should be examined to ensure that it is in good working order, before being issued to the wearer. PPE should also be examined before it is put on and should not be worn if it is found to be defective or has not been cleaned. Such examinations should be carried out by properly trained staff in accordance with the manufacturer's instructions. While most PPE will be provided on a personal basis, some may be used by a number of people. There should therefore be arrangements for cleaning and disinfecting if necessary before PPE is reissued.

47 A sufficient stock of spare parts, when appropriate, should be available to wearers. Only proper spare parts should be used in maintaining PPE, or the equipment may not provide the required degree of protection. The use of different parts may also be prohibited under regulation 4(3)(e) – some new PPE components also have to be 'CE' marked.

48 Manufacturers' maintenance schedules and instructions (including recommended replacement periods and shelf lives) should normally be followed: any significant departure from them should be discussed beforehand with the manufacturers or their authorised agent. Some British or European Standards on PPE (many of which are listed in Part 2 and in Appendix 3) also contain useful information on maintenance.

49 Simple maintenance can be carried out by the trained wearer, but more intricate repairs should only be done by specialist personnel. With complex equipment, a high standard of training will be required. As an alternative to in-house maintenance, contract maintenance services are available from both manufacturers and suppliers of equipment and specialist maintenance firms.

50 In certain circumstances it may be more appropriate, instead of instituting a special maintenance procedure, to provide a supply of disposable PPE (eg single use coveralls) which can simply be discarded after use. If disposable PPE is used, it is important that users know when it should be discarded and replaced.

Regulation 8

Accommodation for personal protective equipment

51 The employer needs to ensure that accommodation is provided for PPE so that it can be safely stored or kept when it is not in use. Accommodation may be simple, for example, pegs for weatherproof clothing or safety helmets. It need not be fixed, for example, safety spectacles could be kept by the user in a suitable carrying case, and PPE used by mobile workers can be stored in suitable containers in their vehicle. The storage should be adequate to protect the PPE from contamination, loss, or damage by (for example) harmful substances, damp or sunlight. Where PPE becomes contaminated during use, the accommodation should be separate from any

provided for ordinary clothing (accommodation for ordinary work clothing is dealt with in the Workplace (Health, Safety and Welfare) Regulations 1992), and where necessary be suitably labelled. If the PPE itself contains hazardous materials, for example asbestos, it may need special storage arrangements.

52 Where quantities of PPE are stored, equipment which is ready for use should be clearly segregated from that which is awaiting repair or maintenance.

Regulation 9

Information, instruction and training

53 The Regulations require employers to provide suitable information, instruction and training for their employees, to enable them to make effective use of the PPE provided to protect them against workplace hazards to their health and safety. A systematic approach to training is needed; this means that everyone who is involved in the use or maintenance of PPE should be trained appropriately.

54 Users must be trained in the proper use of PPE, how to correctly fit and wear it, and what its limitations are. Managers and supervisors must also be aware of why PPE is being used and how it is used properly. People involved in maintaining, repairing and testing the equipment and in its selection for use will also need training. Training should include elements of theory as well as practice in using the equipment, and should be carried out in accordance with the recommendations and instructions supplied by the PPE manufacturer.

55 The extent of the instruction and training will vary with the complexity and performance of the equipment. For PPE which is simple to use and maintain, safety helmets for example, some basic instructions to the users may be all that is required. On the other hand, the safe use of anti-static footwear or laser eye protection will depend on an adequate understanding of the principles behind them, and in the case of the former, regular maintenance and testing. The instruction and training should include:

Theoretical training

(a) an explanation of the risks present and why PPE is needed;
(b) the operation, performance and limitations of the equipment;
(c) instructions on the selection, use and storage of PPE related to the intended use. Written operating procedures such as permits to work involving PPE should be explained;
(d) factors which can affect the protection provided by the PPE such as: other protective equipment; personal factors; working conditions; inadequate fitting; and defects, damage and wear;
(e) recognising defects in PPE and arrangements for reporting loss or defects.

Practical training

(a) practice in putting on, wearing and removing the equipment;
(b) practice and instruction in inspection and, where appropriate, testing of the PPE before use;
(c) practice and instruction in the maintenance which can be done by the user, such as cleaning and the replacement of certain components;
(d) instruction in the safe storage of equipment.

Duration and frequency of training

56 The extent of the training that is required will depend on the type of equipment, how frequently it is used and the needs of the people being trained. Many manufacturers of PPE run training courses for users of their equipment and these courses may be of particular benefit to small users who do not have training facilities.

57 In addition to initial training, users of PPE and others involved with the equipment may need refresher training from time to time. Records of training details should be kept, to assist in the efficient administration of the training programme.

58 Employers must ensure not only that their employees undergo the appropriate training but that they understand what they are being taught. Employers may have difficulty in understanding their training for a number of reasons. For example, the risks (and precautions) may be of a particularly complex nature, making it difficult for employees to understand the precise nature of the protective measures they must take. English may not be the first language of some employees, and in this case the instruction and training may have to be undertaken in the employee's mother tongue to ensure comprehensibility.

Regulation 10

Use of personal protective equipment

59 PPE should be used in accordance with the employer's instructions, which should in turn be based on the manufacturer's instructions for use. PPE should be used only after adequate training has been given to the user, and adequate levels of supervision should be provided to ensure that the training and instructions are being followed.

60 The self-employed user should ensure that he has been adequately trained to use PPE competently, to avoid creating risks to himself and others.

61 Most PPE should be returned after use to the storage place provided under regulation 8. However, there may be instances where the employee may take PPE away from the workplace, for example, some types of protective footwear or overalls. Equipment that is used or worn intermittently, welding visors for example, need only be returned at the end of the working period, shift or assignment.

Regulation 11

Reporting loss or defect

62 Employers should make arrangements to ensure that their employees can report to them (or their representative) the loss of or defects in PPE. These arrangements should also ensure that defective PPE is repaired or replaced before the employee concerned re-starts work.

63 Employees must take reasonable care of PPE provided and report to their employer any loss or obvious defect as soon as possible. If employees have any concerns about the serviceability of the PPE, they should immediately consult their employer or the employer's representative.

Regulation 13

Extension outside Great Britain

64 The Regulations apply to all work activities carried out in British territorial waters and on offshore installations on the Continental Shelf, with the exception of those activities which are exempted by virtue of the 1989 Order and regulation 3(1). The 1989 Order identifies those work activities taking place at sea (within British jurisdiction) that will be subject to the Health and Safety at Work Act 1974.

65 These Regulations will therefore apply to those activities associated with oil and gas installation, including mobile installations, diving support vessels, heavy lift barges and pipe-lay barges.

Regulation 14

Modifications, repeal and revocations

66 The Regulations specified in Schedule 2 have been amended to ensure that they are consistent with the requirements of the PPE at Work Regulations, particularly with regard to the assessment and provision of suitable PPE, and accommodation for PPE.

Part 2

Selection, use and maintenance of personal protective equipment

67 This part aims to help employers to comply with their duties to select suitable PPE and maintain it. It contains information about the main types of PPE which are widely used in industry, but does not cover more specialised and less frequently used items (for example, safety harnesses). More detailed information about particular items of PPE can be obtained from suppliers. It is also wise to involve those who will wear the PPE in its selection. Where possible, more than one model satisfying the appropriate safe performance and other criteria of suitability should be made available.

Head protection

Types of protection

68 There are four widely used types of head protection:

(a) crash helmets, cycling helmets, riding helmets and climbing helmets which are intended to protect the user in falls;

(b) industrial safety helmets which can protect against falling objects or impact with fixed objects;

(c) industrial scalp protectors (bump caps) which can protect against striking fixed obstacles, scalping or entanglement; and

(d) caps, hairnets etc which can protect against scalping/entanglement.

69 The following guidance deals only with industrial safety helmets, scalp protectors and climbing helmets (ie it excludes caps and hairnets).

Processes and activities

70 The following are examples of activities and processes involving risks of falling objects or impacts, which may require the provision of head protection; it is not an exhaustive list. Some of these activities will also be subject to the Construction (Head Protection) Regulations 1989:

(a) Building work, particularly work on, underneath or in the vicinity of scaffolding and elevated workplaces, erection and stripping of formwork, assembly and installation work, work on scaffolding and demolition work.

(b) Construction work on bridges, buildings, masts, towers, hydraulic structures, blast furnaces, steel works and rolling mills, large containers, pipelines and other large plants, boiler plants and power stations.

(c) Work in pits, trenches, shafts and tunnels. Underground workings, quarries, opencast mining, minerals preparation and stocking.

(d) Work with bolt-driving tools.

(e) Blasting work.

(f) Work near hoists, lifting plant, cranes and conveyors.

(g) Work with blast furnaces, direct reduction plants, steelworks, rolling mills, metalworks, forging, drop forging and casting.

(h) Work with industrial furnaces, containers, machinery, silos, storage bunkers and pipelines.

(i) Building or repairing ships and offshore platforms.

(j) Railway shunting work, and other transport activities involving a risk of falling material.

(k) Slaughterhouses.

(l) Tree-felling and tree surgery.

(m) Work from suspended access systems, bosun's chairs etc.

71 Some relevant British European standards:

– BS 5240 Part I:1987 Industrial safety helmets – specification for construction and performance (To be replaced by BS EN 397)

- BS 4033:1966 (1978) Specification for industrial scalp protectors (light duty) (To be replaced by BS EN 812)
- BS 3864:1989 Specification for protective helmets for firefighters (To be replaced by BS EN 443)

Note: Many British Standards will be replaced by harmonised European Standards, for example BS 3864:1989 will be replaced by the European Standard EN 443. When the European Standard is introduced it will be prefixed by 'BS' so EN 443 will become BS EN 443 in the United Kingdom. Those with the prefix 'pr' are provisional at the time of going to print. See Appendix 3 for a more comprehensive list of appropriate standards.

The selection of suitable head protection

72 To fit, head protection should:

(a) be of an appropriate shell size for the wearer; and
(b) have an easily adjustable headband, nape and chin strap.

The range of size adjustment should be large enough to accommodate thermal liners used in cold weather.

73 Head protection should be as comfortable as possible. Comfort is improved by the following:

(a) a flexible headband of adequate width and contoured both vertically and horizontally to fit the forehead;
(b) an absorbent, easily cleanable or replaceable sweat-band;
(c) textile cradle straps;
(d) chin straps (when fitted) which:
    (i) do not cross the ears,
    (ii) are compatible with any other PPE needed,
    (iii) are fitted with smooth, quick-release buckles which do not dig into the skin,
    (iv) are made from non-irritant materials,
    (v) can be stowed on the helmet when not in use.

Compatibility with the work to be done

74 Whenever possible, the head protection should not hinder the work being done. For example, an industrial safety helmet with little or no peak is useful for a surveyor taking measurements using a theodolite or to allow unrestricted upward vision for a scaffold erector. If a job involves work in windy conditions, especially at heights, or repeated bending or constantly looking upwards, a secure retention system is required. Flexible headbands and Y-shaped chin straps can help to secure the helmet. Head protection worn in the food industry may need to be easily cleaned or compatible with other hygiene requirements.

75 If other PPE such as ear defenders or eye protectors are required, the design must allow them to be worn safely and in comfort. Check manufacturer's instructions regarding the compatibility of head protection with other types of PPE.

Maintenance

76 Head protection must be maintained in good condition. It should:

(a) be stored, when not in use, in a safe place, for example, on a peg or in a cupboard. It should not be stored in direct sunlight or in excessively hot, humid conditions;

(b) be visually inspected regularly for signs of damage or deterioration;

(c) have defective harness components replaced (if the design or make allows this). Harnesses from one design or make of helmet cannot normally be interchanged with those from another;

(d) have the sweat-band regularly cleaned or replaced.

77 Before head protection is reissued to another person, it should be inspected to ensure it is serviceable and thoroughly cleaned in accordance with the manufacturer's instructions, eg using soap and water. The sweat-band should always be cleaned or replaced.

Damage to shell

78 Damage to the shell of a helmet can occur when:

(a) objects fall onto it;

(b) it strikes against a fixed object;

(c) it is dropped or thrown.

Deterioration in shock absorption or penetration resistance

79 Deterioration in shock absorption or penetration resistance of the shell can occur from:

(a) exposure to certain chemical agents;

(b) exposure to heat or sunlight;

(c) ageing due to heat, humidity, sunlight and rain.

80 Chemical agents which should be avoided include paint, adhesives or chemical cleaning agents. Where names or other markings need to be applied using adhesives, advice on how to do this safely should be sought from the helmet manufacturer.

81 Exposure to heat or sunlight can make the shell go brittle. Head protection should never be stored therefore near a window, eg the rear window of a motor vehicle, because excessive heat may build up.

Replacement

82 The head protection should normally be replaced at intervals recommended by the manufacturer. It will also need replacing when the harness is damaged and cannot be replaced, or when the shell is damaged or it is suspected that its shock absorption or penetration resistance has deteriorated – for example when:

(a) the shell has received a severe impact;
(b) deep scratches occur;
(c) the shell has any cracks visible to the naked eye.

Eye protection

Types of eye protection

83 Eye protection serves to guard against the hazards of impact, splashes from chemicals or molten metal, liquid droplets (chemical mists and sprays), dust, gases, welding arcs, non-ionising radiation and the light from lasers. Eye protectors include safety spectacles, eyeshields, goggles, welding filters, face-shields and hoods. Safety spectacles can be fitted with prescription lenses if required. Some types of eye protection can be worn over ordinary spectacles if necessary.

Processes and activities

84 The following are examples of activities and processes involving a risk to the face and eyes for which eye protectors should be used. It is not an exhaustive list.

(a) handling or coming into contact with acids, alkalis and corrosive or irritant substances;
(b) working with power-driven tools where chippings are likely to fly or abrasive materials be propelled;
(c) working with molten metal or other molten substances;
(d) during any welding operations where intense light or other optical radiation is emitted at levels liable to cause risk of injury;
(e) working on any process using instruments that produce light amplification or radiation; and
(f) using any gas or vapour under pressure.

Eye protectors must be provided both for persons directly involved in the work and also for others not directly involved or employed but who may come into contact with the process and be at risk from the hazards.

85 Some relevant British and European Standards:

- BS 6967:1988 Glossary of terms for personal eye protection (To be replaced by BS EN 165)
- BS 2092:1987 Specification for eye protectors for industrial and non-industrial uses (To be replaced by BS EN 166, 167 and 168)
- BS 7028:1988 Guide for selection, use and maintenance of eye-protection for industrial and other uses
- BS 1542:1982 Specification for equipment for eye, face and neck protection against non-ionising radiation arising during welding and similar operations

Note: Many British Standards will be replaced by harmonised European Standards, for example BS 3864:1989 will be replaced by the European

Standard EN 443. When the European Standard is introduced it will be prefixed by 'BS' so EN 443 will become BS EN 443 in the United Kingdom. Those with the prefix 'pr' are provisional at the time of going to print. See Appendix 3 for a more comprehensive list of appropriate standards.

Selecting suitable eye protection

86 The selection of eye protection depends primarily on the hazard. However, comfort, style and durability should also be considered.

(a) *Safety spectacles* are similar in appearance to prescription spectacles but may incorporate optional sideshields to give lateral protection to the eyes. To protect against impact, the lenses are made from tough optical quality plastic such as polycarbonate. Safety spectacles are generally light in weight and are available in several styles with either plastic or metal frames. Most manufacturers offer a range of prescription safety spectacles which are individually matched to the wearer.

(b) *Eyeshields* are like safety spectacles but are heavier and designed with a frameless one-piece moulded lens. Vision correction is not possible as the lenses cannot be interchanged. Some eyeshields may be worn over prescription spectacles.

(c) *Safety goggles* are heavier and less convenient to use than spectacles or eyeshields. They are made with a flexible plastic frame and one-piece lens and have an elastic headband. They afford the eyes total protection from all angles as the whole periphery of the goggle is in contact with the face. Goggles may have toughened glass lenses or have wide vision plastic lenses. The lenses are usually replaceable. Safety goggles are more prone to misting than spectacles. Double glazed goggles or those treated with an anti-mist coating may be more effective where misting is a problem. Where strenuous work is done in hot conditions, 'direct ventilation' goggles may be more suitable. However these are unsuitable for protection against chemicals, gases and dust. 'Indirect ventilation' goggles are not perforated, but are fitted with baffled ventilators to prevent liquids and dust from entering. Indirect ventilation goggles will not protect against gas or vapour.

(d) *Faceshields* are heavier and bulkier than other types of eye protector but are comfortable if fitted with an adjustable head harness. Faceshields protect the face but do not fully enclose the eyes and therefore do not protect against dusts, mist or gases. Visors on browguards or helmets are replaceable. They may be worn over standard prescription spectacles and are generally not prone to misting. Face shields with reflective metal screens permit good visibility while effectively deflecting heat and are useful in blast and open-hearth furnaces and other work involving radiant heat.

Maintenance

87 The lenses of eye protectors must be kept clean as dirty lenses restrict vision, which can cause eye fatigue and lead to accidents. There are two

methods for cleaning eye protectors. Glass, polycarbonate and other plastic lenses can be cleaned by thoroughly wetting both sides of the lenses and drying them with a wet strength absorbent paper. Anti-static and anti-fog lens cleaning fluids may be used, daily if necessary, if static or misting is a problem. Alternatively lenses can be 'dry' cleaned by removing grit with a brush and using a silicone treated non-woven cloth. However plastic or polycarbonate lenses should not be 'dry' cleaned as the cloth used in this method can scratch them.

88 Eye protectors should be issued on a personal basis and used only by the person they are issued to. If eye protectors are re-issued they should be thoroughly cleaned and disinfected. Eye protectors should be protected by being placed in suitable cases when not in use. Eye protector headbands should be replaced when worn out or damaged.

89 Lenses that are scratched or pitted must be replaced as they may impair vision and their resistance to impact may be impaired. Transparent face shields must be replaced when warped, scratched or have become brittle with age.

Foot protection

Types of safety footwear

90 The following are examples of types of safety footwear:

(a) *The safety boot or shoe* is the most common type of safety footwear. These normally have steel toe-caps. They may also have other safety features including slip resistant soles, steel midsoles and insulation against extremes of heat and cold.

(b) *Clogs* may also be used as safety footwear. They are traditionally made from beech wood which provides a good insulation against heat and absorbs shock. Clogs may be fitted with steel toe-caps and thin rubber soles for quieter tread and protection against slippage or chemicals.

(c) *Foundry boots* have steel toe-caps, are heat resistant and designed to keep out molten metal. They are without external features such as laces to avoid trapping molten metal blobs and should have velcro fasteners or elasticated sides for quick release.

(d) *Wellington boots* protect against water and wet conditions and can be useful in jobs where the footwear needs to be washed and disinfected for hygienic reasons, such as in the food industry. They are usually made from rubber but are available in polyurethane and PVC which are both warmer and have greater chemical resistance. Wellington boots can be obtained with corrosion resistant steel toe-caps, rot-proof insoles, steel midsoles, ankle bone padding and cotton linings. They range from ankle boots to chest-high waders.

(e) *Anti-static footwear* prevents the build up of static electricity on the wearer. It reduces the danger of igniting a flammable atmosphere and gives some protection against electric shock.

(f) *Conductive footwear* also prevents the build up of static electricity. It is particularly suitable for handling sensitive components or substances (eg explosive detonators). It gives no protection against electric shock.

Processes and activities

91 The following are examples of activities and processes involving risks to the feet. It is not an exhaustive list.

(a) *Construction:* Work on building and demolition sites will usually require safety footwear to protect the feet against a variety of hazards, particularly objects falling on them, or sharp objects (eg nails) on the ground piercing the shoe and injuring the sole of the foot.

(b) *Mechanical and manual handling:* There may be a risk of objects falling on or crushing the front of the foot. There may be a risk of a fall through slipping which could result in damage to the heel on impact. There is also a danger of treading on pointed or sharp objects which can penetrate the shoe and injure the sole of the foot.

(c) *Electrical:* People who work where there are flammable atmospheres should wear anti-static footwear to help prevent ignitions due to static electricity. Such footwear is similar to conventional footwear in that the soles are sufficiently insulated to give some measure of protection against electric shock.

(d) *Thermal:* Working in cold conditions requires footwear with thermal insulation. Work in hot conditions requires footwear with heat-resistant and insulating soles.

(e) *Chemical:* Footwear provided when working with hazardous chemicals should be both impermeable and resistant to attack by chemicals.

(f) *Forestry:* Forestry chain-saw boots are water-resistant and are part lined with Kevlar which strands on contact with the chain causing it to stop.

(g) *Molten substances:* Foundry boots that are easily removed should be provided where there is a danger of splashing by molten substances.

92 Some relevant British and European Standards:

– BS 1870:Part 1:1988 Specification for safety footwear other than all rubber and all plastic moulded compounds
– BS 1870:Part 2:1986 Specification for lined rubber safety boots
– BS 1870:Part 3:1981 Specification for PVC moulded safety footwear
– BS 4676:1983 Specification for gaiters and footwear for protection against burns and impact risks in foundries
– BS 4972:1973 Specification for women's protective footwear
– BS 5145:1989 Specification for lined industrial vulcanised rubber boots
– BS 5462: Footwear with midsole protection:
– BS 5462:Part 1:1984 Specification for lined vulcanised rubber footwear with penetration resistant midsoles
– BS 5462:Part 2:1984 Specification for lined or unlined polyvinyl chloride (PVC) footwear with penetration resistant midsoles
– BS 6159: Polyvinyl chloride boots:

- BS 6159:Part 1:1987 Specification for general and industrial lined or unlined boots

Note: Many British Standards will be replaced by harmonised European Standards, for example BS 3864:1989 will be replaced by the European Standard EN 443. When the European Standard is introduced it will be prefixed by 'BS' so EN 443 will become BS EN 443 in the United Kingdom. Those with the prefix 'pr' are provisional at the time of going to print. See Appendix 3 for a more comprehensive list of appropriate standards.

Selecting suitable foot protection

93 The selection of foot protection depends primarily on the hazard. However, comfort, style and durability should also be considered. The choice should be made on the basis of suitability for protection, compatibility with the work and the requirements of the user.

94 Generally, safety footwear should be flexible, wet resistant and absorb perspiration. Inflexible or unnecessarily bulky footwear will result in tired feet and legs. Boots and not shoes are required where ankles need protection. You should consider the ability of the footwear to resist corrosion, abrasion and industrial wear and tear. Always follow the manufacturer's instructions and markings for appropriate use and level of protection.

(a) *Soles:* Work shoes and boots should have treaded soles for slip-resistance. Soles can be heat and oil resistant, slip resistant, shock resistant, anti-static or conductive. Footwear intended to protect against oils, solvents or liquids need soles that are moulded or bonded to the upper. Soles that are stitched or glued may separate and expose the foot to hazard. Footwear with steel midsoles should be used where there is a risk that the sole could be pierced by nails or similar objects.

(b) *Steel toe-caps:* They should be capable of resisting a heavy sharp object falling from a considerable height. Footwear complying with BS 4676 will offer this resistance.

(c) *Heat resistance:* Leather or other heat resistant materials can be used in safety footwear to offer protection against heat, sparks and molten metal.

(d) *Waterproofing:* People working in wet places should wear safety footwear impervious to water. Rubber and PVC are suitable inexpensive water-proofing materials for footwear but they are not permeable. There are 'breathable materials' which are water resistant, but which also allow air to get through and perspiration to get out, and may therefore be more comfortable and more hygienic. However, footwear manufactured from this type of material tends to be more expensive.

95 Electrical hazards: The following provide protection against electrical hazards.

(a) *Anti-static footwear:* Anti-static footwear offers suitable protection against the hazard of static electricity and will give some protection against mains electric shock. Anti-static footwear must be worn where there is both a hazard from static build up and the possibility of contact with mains electricity. The soles must have a resistance low enough to allow static electricity to leak slowly away while maintaining enough resistance to protect against a 240 volt mains electricity shock.

(b) *Conductive footwear* offers greater protection against static electricity and is used where the wearer handles very sensitive components or materials. It must not be worn where there is a danger of electric shock. The soles of conductive footwear must have an electrical resistance low enough to enable static electricity to be taken quickly away from the body to the earth.

96 Leg protection: The following are examples of leg protection.

(a) People working around molten metal need protection for their lower legs. For example this can be achieved by the use of foundry boots and gaiters, or a high foundry boot worn inside molten metal protective trousers.

(b) Hard fibre or metal guards should be used to protect shins against impact. The top of the foot up to the ankle can be protected by added-on metatarsal guards.

Maintenance

97 Safety footwear should be maintained in good condition, checked regularly and discarded if worn or deteriorated. Laces should be checked and replaced if necessary. Materials lodged into the tread should be removed. The stitching should be checked for loose, worn or cut seams. Spraying the upper layers of new footwear with a silicone spray or applying a protective wax will give extra protection against wet conditions.

Hand and arm protection

Types of hand protection

98 Gloves of various designs provide protection against a range of industrial hazards, including:

(a) cuts and abrasions;
(b) extremes of temperature, hot and cold;
(c) skin irritation and dermatitis;
(d) contact with toxic or corrosive liquids.

99 The type and degree of protection depends on the glove material and the way in which it is constructed. Barrier creams may sometimes be used as an aid to skin hygiene in situations where gloves cannot be used. Experience shows, however, that barrier creams are less reliable than suitable gloves as a means of chemical protection.

Processes and activities

100 The following processes and activities involve risk of injury to the hands or hazards for which hand protection may be necessary. It is not an exhaustive list.

(a) *Manual handling:* Hands maybe pierced by abrasive, sharp or pointed objects or damaged by impact when handling goods. However, gloves should not be worn when working near moving equipment and machinery parts as the glove may get caught in the equipment and draw the hand and arm of the worker into the moving machinery.

(b) *Vibration:* Gloves are essential to keep hands warm in cold weather when operating machines that cause vibrations such as pneumatic drills and chain-saws. Vibration White Finger occurs more frequently and more severely when the hands and fingers are cold as the blood supply to the fingers is reduced by the body in an attempt to conserve heat.

(c) *Construction and outdoor work:* Keeping the hands warm and supple in cold weather is important when working on a building site handling scaffolding, bricks and timber. Manual dexterity is lost when the hands are cold, which can lead to accidents if articles are dropped. Gloves protect against hazards in site clearance such as previous contamination of soil which may contain disease spores that may seriously infect small cuts and abrasions.

(d) *Hot and cold materials:* Gloves will also protect against hazards from handling hot or cold materials and work involving contact with naked flames or welding.

(e) *Electricity:* Danger from electric shock.

(f) *Chemical:* There are many tasks where the hands may come into contact with toxic or corrosive substances. Examples include maintenance of machinery, cleaning up chemical spillages and mixing and dispensing pesticide formulations. If correctly selected and used, gloves provide a barrier between the wearer's skin and the harmful substance, preventing local damage, or in some cases absorption through the skin.

(g) *Radioactivity:* Danger from contamination when handling radioactive materials

101 Some relevant British and European Standards:

– BS 1651:1986 Specification for industrial gloves
– BS 697:1986 Specification for rubber gloves for electrical purposes

Note: Many British Standards will be replaced by harmonised European Standards, for example BS 3864:1989 will be replaced by the European Standard EN 443. When the European Standard is introduced it will be prefixed by 'BS' so EN 443 will become BS EN 443 in the United Kingdom. Those with the prefix 'pr' are provisional at the time of going to print. See Appendix 3 for a more comprehensive list of appropriate standards.

Selecting suitable hand protection

102 Gloves or other hand protection should be capable of giving protection from hazards, be comfortable and fit the wearer. The choice should be made on the basis of suitability for protection, compatibility with the work and the requirements of the user. You should consider the ability of protective gloves to resist abrasion and other industrial wear and tear. Always follow the manufacturer's instructions and markings for appropriate use and level of protection. When selecting gloves for chemical protection, reference should be made to chemical permeation and resistance data provided by manufacturers.

(a) *Penetration and abrasion:* Gloves made from chain-mail or leather protect against penetration and abrasion. Gloves made from knitted Kevlar will provide protection against cuts and gloves manufactured from Kevlar needlefelt gives good puncture resistance.

(b) *Thermal protection:* Depending upon their weight and construction, terrycloth gloves will provide protection against heat and cold. Gloves made from neoprene are good for handling oils in low temperatures. Gloves manufactured from other materials such as Kevlar, glass fibre and leather can be used to provide protection at high temperatures.

(c) *Fire resistance:* Chromed leather gloves are fire retardant.

(d) *Chemicals protection:* Chemical protective gloves are available in a range of materials including natural rubber, neoprene, nitrile, butyl, PVA, PVC and viton. The degree of protection against chemical permeation depends on the glove material, its thickness and method of construction. As a general rule, gloves for use in handling toxic liquids should be chosen on the basis of breakthrough time. This means that the duration of use should not exceed the breakthrough time quoted by the manufacturer of the glove for the chemical substance concerned. Laboratory testing may be required in order to establish adequacy in some applications. When handling dry powders, any chemically resistant glove may be used. The durability of the gloves in the workplace should also be considered. Some glove materials may be adversely affected by abrasion.

(e) *General use gloves:* Rubber, plastic or knit fabric gloves are flexible, resist cuts and abrasions, repel liquids and offer a good grip. Rubber gloves allow a sensitive touch and give a firm grip in water or wet conditions. Leather, cotton knit or other general purpose gloves are suitable for most other jobs. General use gloves should only be used to protect against minimal risks to health and safety (eg for gardening and washing up and similar low risk tasks).

Maintenance

103 Care should be taken in the donning, use, removal and storage of protective gloves. They should be maintained in good condition, checked regularly and discarded if worn or deteriorated. Gloves should be free of holes or cuts and foreign materials and their shape should not be distorted.

They should fit the wearer properly leaving no gap between the glove and the wearer's sleeve.

104 Gloves should always be cleaned according to the manufacturer's instructions as they may have particular finishes which may make the following general guidance inappropriate. For example, repeated washing may remove fungal and bacterial inhibitors from the lining of the glove which may ultimately lead to skin irritation. And there is also the risk of cross contamination as chemical residues can remain on the gloves even after washing.

105 Contact between the gloves and chemicals should be kept to a minimum as some chemicals can alter the physical characteristics of a glove and impair its protective properties. Gloves contaminated by chemicals should be washed as soon as possible and before their removal from the hands. Grossly contaminated gloves should be discarded. Gloves contaminated on the inside can be dangerous as the chemical contamination will be absorbed by the skin. Wear armlets if there is a danger of chemicals entering the glove at the cuff.

106 When wearing protective gloves do not touch other exposed parts of the body, equipment or furniture as contamination can be transferred to them. Cotton liners can be worn if hands sweat profusely.

Care for the hands when handling chemicals

107 Do not let chemicals come into contact with the skin. Wash hands frequently, dry them carefully and use a hand cream to keep the skin from becoming dry through loss of natural oils. Keep cuts and abrasions covered with waterproof plasters and change the dressing for a porous one after work. Handle and remove gloves carefully to avoid contamination of hands and the insides of the gloves.

Protective clothing for the body

Types of protection

108 Types of clothing used for body protection include:

(a) coveralls, overalls and aprons to protect against chemicals and other hazardous substances;
(b) outfits to protect against cold, heat and bad weather;
(c) clothing to protect against machinery such as chain-saws.

109 Types of clothing worn on the body to protect the person include:

(a) high visibility clothing;
(b) life-jackets and buoyancy aids.

Processes and activities

110 The following are examples of the sorts of processes and activities that require protective clothing for the body. It is not an exhaustive list.

(a) Laboratory work or work with chemicals, dust or other hazardous substances;
(b) construction and outdoor work;
(c) work in cold-stores;
(d) forestry work using chainsaws;
(e) highway and road works;
(f) work on inland and inshore waters;
(g) spraying pesticides;
(h) food processing;
(i) welding;
(j) foundry work and molten metal processes;
(k) fire-fighting.

111 Some relevant British and European Standards:

-   BS 1771:Part I:1989 Specification for fabrics of wool and wool blends
-   BS 1771:Part 2:1984 Specification for fabrics of cellulosic fibres, synthetic fibres and blends
-   BS 1547:1959 Specification for flameproofing industrial clothing (materials and design)
-   BS 6249:1982 Materials and material assemblies used in clothing for protection against heat and flame
-   BS 6249:Part 1:1982 Specification for flammability testing and performance
-   BS 3791:1970 Specification for clothing for protection against intense heat for short periods
-   BS 2653:1955 Specification for protective clothing for welders
-   BS 5426:1987 Specification for workwear and career wear
-   BS 3595:1981 Specification for life-jackets

Note: Many British Standards will be replaced by harmonised European Standards, for example BS 3864:1989 will be replaced by the European Standard EN 443. When the European Standard is introduced it will be prefixed by 'BS' so EN 443 will become BS EN 443 in the United Kingdom. Those with the prefix 'pr' are provisional at the time of going to print. See Appendix 3 for a more comprehensive list of appropriate standards.

Selection

112 Protection from chemicals and hazardous substances:

(a) *Low risk chemicals* can be protected against by wearing chemical-resistant clothing, coveralls and laboratory coats made from uncoated cotton or synthetic material such as nylon or Terylene with a water repellant finish.
(b) *Strong solvents, oils and greases* require heavier protection afforded by coats, overalls and aprons made from neoprene or polyurethane coated nylon, or Terylene or rubber aprons.
(c) *Chemical suits* protect against more potent chemicals. They are totally encapsulating suits which are either vapour-proof or liquid-splash proof and are fed with breathable air. They must be washed in warm

water and a mild soap whenever they have come into contact with chemicals. The suit should be hung up to dry before being stored in cases or hung on hangers. Chemical suits have a life expectancy of three to four years and should be inspected every three months even if not in use. This entails an air test and looking at all of the seams.

(d) *Vapour suits* protect against hazardous vapours and are made of butyl, polyvinyl chloride (PVC), viton, a combination of viton and butyl or teflon. They should be air-tested with the manufacturer's test kit, before being stored in a protective case. Manufacturers of vapour proof suits generally provide a testing and repair service consisting of a visual inspection and air test.

(e) *Splash-resistant suits* are also made from the same polymers but may also be made of limited-use fabrics such as saran coated tyvek and barricade fabric.

(f) *Fibres and dust:* Protection can be obtained by wearing suits made from bonded olefin that forms a dense shield which keeps out fibres and particles.

113 Thermal and weather protection:

(a) *Keeping dry:* Jackets, trousers and leggings made with PVC coated nylon or cotton will offer protection against rain. These materials are also resistant to abrasions, cracking and tearing and will protect against most oils, chemicals and acids. 'Breathable' water-proof fabrics will keep out water while allowing body perspiration to escape. Waxed cotton will also protect against rain.

(b) *Keeping warm:* Minus 25 and Minus 50 suits are available which are guaranteed to protect at these respective sub zero temperatures. More limited protection can be obtained from quilted and insulated coats and vests.

(c) *Keeping cool:*
  (i) Aluminium-asbestos clothing made of dust-suppressed materials is heat-resistant. The outside is made of aluminium and the inside lining is cotton. This type of clothing is suitable for hot work, for example in foundries.
  (ii) Welding and foundry clothing is flame retardant and is mainly of flame retardant cotton or wool materials. Chrome leather is used for aprons etc.
  (iii) Molten metal splash clothing is heat resistant and should resist molten metal splash up to 1600 degrees centigrade.
  (iv) Cotton or cotton and polyester coveralls with flame-retardant finishes are available to protect against sparks and flame.

114 *Food processing:* Food quality overalls and coveralls will protect against splashes from oils and fats. Butchers and slaughterhouse workers should wear lamex or chain-mail aprons if there is a risk of injury to the abdomen or chest, for example when using knives or choppers.

115 *Chainsaw protective clothing:* The front of the leg is most vulnerable to chainsaw accidents although the back of the leg is also at risk. Protective legwear incorporates layers of loosely woven long synthetic fibres. On contact with the saw chain, the fibres are drawn out and clog the chain saw

sprocket, causing the chain to stop. Legwear is available with all-round protection or with protection only for the front of the legs. The legwear with all round protection offers the greatest protection for users. Jackets and gloves are also available with inserts of chainsaw resistant materials at vulnerable points. See paragraph 91(f) in the section on chainsaw boots.

Personal protection worn on the body

High visibility clothing

116 This is made from PVC impregnated with fluorescent pigments. This should be worn by workers on roadsides and other areas where it is important to be seen to be safe. BS 6629 sets out three grades of high visibility clothing:

(a) Class A refers to coats and jackets offering the highest degree of conspicuousness.
(b) Class B refers to waistcoats and tabards and offers a lower level of conspicuousness.
(c) Appendix G is concerned with exposure to a particular risk such as that faced by road workers.

117 Chapter 8 of the Department of Transport Traffic Signs Manual requires all personnel on or near carriageways to wear high visibility garments complying with BS 6629 'Class A or B to Appendix G or better'. The Department of Transport also recommends that Class A with sleeves to Appendix G is used on motorways and other high speed roads.

Personal buoyancy equipment

118 Life-jackets or buoyancy aids should be worn where there is a foreseeable risk of drowning when working on or near water.

(a) *A life-jacket* is a personal safety device which, when fully inflated (if inflatable), will provide sufficient buoyancy to turn and support even an unconscious person face upwards within five seconds (ten seconds if automatically inflated). The person's head will be supported with the mouth and nose well clear of the water.

Some people are reluctant to wear life-jackets as they find them bulky and restrictive. However, either an automatically inflatable life-jacket or a type which is inflated by a manual pull-cord should overcome these problems. These are usually compact and allow for a full range of movement.
(b) *Buoyancy aids* are worn to provide extra buoyancy to assist a conscious person in keeping afloat. However, they will not turn over an unconscious person from a face down position.

Maintenance

119 Protective clothing should only be used for the purpose intended. It should be maintained in good condition and checked regularly. It should be repaired or discarded if damaged.

Appendix 1

Specimen risk survey table for the use of personal protective equipment

Risks

The PPE at Work Regulations 1992 apply except where the Construction (Head) Protection Regulations 1989 apply

The CLW, IRR, CAW, COSHH and NAW Regulations[1] will each apply to the appropriate hazard

			Mechanical				Thermal																		
			Falls from a height	Blows, cuts, impact, crushing	Stabs, cuts, grazes	Vibration	Slipping, falling over	Scalds, heat, fire	Cold	Immersion	Non-ionising radiation	Electrical	Noise	Ionising radiation	Dust fibre	Fume	Vapours	Splashes, spurts	Gases, vapours	Harmful bacteria	Harmful viruses	Fungi	Non-micro biological antigens
P A R T S of the B O D Y	Head	Cranium																					
		Ears																					
		Eyes																					
		Respiratory tract																					
		Face																					
		Whole head																					
	Upper limbs	Hands																					
		Arms (parts)																					
	Lower limbs	Foot																					
		Legs (parts)																					
	Various	Skin																					
		Trunk/abdomen																					
		Whole body																					

(1) The Control of Lead at Work Regulations 1980, The Ionising Radiations Regulations 1985, The Control of Asbestos at Work Regulations 1987, The Control of Substances Hazardous to Health Regulations 1988, The Noise at Work Regulations 1989.

Appendix 2

Legislation on PPE applying in addition to the Regulations

The Coal and Other Mines (Fire and Rescue) Regulations 1956 SI 1956/176
HMSO (regulations 23–25)

The Construction (Working Places) Regulations 1966 SI 1966/94 HMSO
ISBN 011 100264 8 (regulation 38)

The Coal Mines (Respirable Dust) Regulations 1975 SI 1975/1433 HMSO
ISBN 0 11 051433 5 (regulation 10)

The Dangerous Substances in Harbour Areas Regulations 1987 SI 1987/3
HMSO ISBN 0 11 076037 6 (regulation 17(1)(b) & (2)(b))

The Diving Operations At Work Regulations 1981 SI 1981/399 HMSO ISBN
011 016399 0 (regulations 5(1), 7(1), 9(1), 12(1, 4 & 5), 13)

The Docks Regulations 1988 SI 1988/1655 HMSO ISBN 0 11 087655
(regulations 2(1), 19)

The Electricity at Work Regulations 1989 SI 1989/635 HMSO ISBN 0 1
096635 X (regulations 4(4), 14)

*The Offshore Installations (Operational Safety Health and Welfare)
Regulations 1976* SI 1976/1019 HMSO ISBN 0 11 061019
(regulation 16 and Schedule 4)

The Offshore Istallations (Life Saving Appliances) Regulations 1976 S
1977/486 HMSO ISBN 0 11 070486 X (regulation 7)

Provision dealing with entry into confined spaces

The Factories Act 1961 Chapter 34 HMSO 1961 ISBN 0 10 850027
(Section 30)

The Docks Regulations 1988 SI 1988/1655 HMSO ISBN 0 11 087655
(regulation 18)

The Ship Building and Ship Repairing Regulations 1960 SI 1960/193
(regulations 50, 51 and 60)

The Breathing Apparatus etc (Report on Examination) Order 1961 SI 1961
1345 HMSO ISBN 0 11 100320 2 (The whole order)

Appendix 3

British and European Standards

Head protection

BS 3864:1989 *Specification for protective helmets for firefighters* (To be
replaced by BS EN 443)

BS 4033:1966 *Specification for industrial scalp protectors (light duty)* (To be
replaced by BS EN 812)

BS 5240 Part 1:1987 *Industrial safety helmets – specification for construction
and performance* (To be replaced by BS EN 397)

Eye protection

BS 1542:1982 *Specification for equipment for eye, face and neck protection against non-ionising radiation arising during welding and similar operations*

BS 2092:1987 *Specification for eye protection for industrial and non-industrial uses* (To be replaced by BS EN 166, 167 and 168)

BS 6967:1988 *Glossary of terms for personal eye protection* (To be replaced by BS EN 165)

BS 7028:1988 *Guide for selection, use and maintenance of eye protection for industrial and other uses*

BS EN 169 *Personal eye protection: Filters for welding and related techniques: Transmittance requirements and recommended use*

BS EN 170 *Personal eye protection: Ultraviolet filters: Transmittances and requirements for recommended use*

BS EN 171 *Personal eye protection: Infrared filters: Transmittances and requirements for recommended use*

rEN 165 *Personal eye protection: Vocabulary*

rEN 167 *Personal eye protection: Optical test methods*

rEN 168 *Personal eye protection: Non-optical test methods*

Footwear

BS 953:1979 *Methods of test for safety and protective footwear*

BS 1870:Part 1:1988 *Specification for safety footwear other than all rubber and all plastic moulded compounds*

BS 1870:Part 2:1976 (1986) *Specification for lined rubber safety boots*

BS 1870:Part 3:1981 *Specification for polyvinyl chloride moulded safety footwear*

BS 2723:1956 (1988) *Specification for firemen's leather boots*

BS 4676:1983 *Specification for gaiters and footwear for protection against burns and impact risks in foundries*

BS 4972:1973 *Specification for women's protective footwear*

BS 5145:1989 *Specification for lined industrial vulcanised rubber boots*

BS 5462: *Footwear with midsole protection:*

BS 5462:Part 1:1984 *Specification for lined vulcanised rubber footwear with penetration resistant midsoles*

BS 5462:Part 2:1984 *Specification for lined or unlined polyvinyl chloride (PVC) footwear with penetration resistant midsoles*

BS 6159: *Polyvinyl chloride boots:*

BS 6159:Part 1:1987 *Specification for general and industrial lined or unlined boots*

BS 7193:1989 *Specification for lined lightweight rubber overshoes and overboots*

The following will probably replace BS 1870 and BS 953:

rEN 344 *Requirements and test methods for safety protective and occupational footwear for professional use*

prEN 345 *Specification for safety footwear for professional use*
prEN 346 *Specification for protective footwear for professional use*
prEN 347 *Specification for occupational footwear for professional use*
prEN 381 *Protective clothing for users of hand held chain saws: Part 3 Test method for boots*

Gloves

BS 697:1986 *Specification for rubber gloves for electrical purposes*
BS 1651:1986 *Specification for industrial gloves*
BS EN 421 *Protective gloves against ionising radiation to include irradiation and contamination*
prEN 374 (Parts 1 to 5) *Protective gloves against chemicals and micro organisms*
prEN 381 (Parts 1 to 6) *Protective gloves for users of hand held chain saws*
prEN 388 *Protective gloves: Mechanical test methods and specifications*
prEN 407 *Protective gloves against thermal hazards*
prEN 420 *General requirements for gloves*
prEN 511 *Protective gloves against cold*
prEN 659 *Fire-fighters' gloves: Protection against heat and flame*

Protective clothing

BS 1547:1959 *Specification for flameproof industrial clothing (materials and design)*
BS 1771:Part 1:1989 *Specification for fabrics of wool and wool blends*
BS 1771:Part 2:1984 *Specification for fabrics of cellulosic fibres, synthetic fibres and blends*
BS 2653:1955 *Specification for protective clothing for welders*
BS 3595:1981 *Specification for life-jackets*
BS 3791:1970 *Specification for clothing for protection against intensive heat for short periods*
BS 5426:1987 *Specification for workwear and career wear*
BS 6249:1982 *Materials and material assemblies used in clothing for protection against heat and flame*
BS 6249:Part 1:1982 *Specification for flammability testing and performance*
  BS 6629:1985 *Specification for optical performance of high visibility garments and accessories for use on the highway*
prEN 340 *General requirements for protective clothing*
prEN 342 *Protective clothing against cold weather*
prEN 343 *Protective clothing against foul weather*
prEN 366 *Protective clothing: protection against heat and fire: method of test: evaluation of materials and material assemblies when exposed to a source of radiant heat*
prEN 367 *Protective clothing: Method of determining heat transmission on exposure to flame*
prEN 373 *Protective clothing: Assessment of resistance of materials to molten metal splash*

rEN 381 (Parts 1 to 6) *Protective clothing for users of hand held chainsaws*

rEN 393 *Life-jackets and personal buoyancy aids: buoyancy aids, 50 N*

rEN 394 *Life-jackets and personal buoyancy aids: additional items*

rEN 395 *Life-jackets and personal buoyancy aids: life-jackets, 100 N*

rEN 396 *Life-jackets and personal buoyancy aids: life-jackets, 150 N*

rEN 399 *Life-jackets and personal buoyancy aids: life-jackets, 275 N*

rEN 463 *Chemical protective clothing: protection against liquid chemicals: method of test: determination of resistance to penetration by liquids (Jet Test)*

rEN 464 *Chemical protective clothing: protection against gases and vapours: method of test: determination of leak tightness (internal pressure test)*

rEN 465 *Protective clothing: protection against liquid chemicals: performance requirements: type 4 equipment: protective suits with spray-tight connections between different parts of the protective seats*

rEN 466 *Chemical protection clothing: protection against liquid chemicals (including liquid aerosols): performance requirements: type 3 equipment: chemical protective clothing with liquid-tight connections between different parts of the clothing*

rEN 467 *Protective clothing: protection against liquid chemicals: performance requirements: type 5 equipment garments providing chemical protection to parts of the body*

rEN 468 *Chemical protective clothing: protection against liquid chemicals: method of test: determination of resistance to penetration by spray*

rEN 469 *Protective clothing for fire-fighters*

rEN 470 *Protective clothing for use in welding and similar activities*

rEN 471 *High visibility warning clothing*

rEN 510 *Protective clothing against the risk of being caught up in moving parts*

rEN 531 *Protective clothing for industrial workers exposed to heat (excluding fire-fighters' and welders' clothing)*

rEN 532 *Clothing for protection against heat and flame: Method of test for limited flame spread*

rEN 533 *Clothing for protection against heat and flame: Performance specification for limited flame spread of materials*

rEN 702 *Protective clothing: Protection against heat and fire – Test method: Determination of the contact heat transmission though protective clothing or its materials*

Appendix 4

Further reading

This Appendix is not reproduced in this book.

Appendix 5

Manual Handling Operations Regulations 1992

THE REGULATIONS

Regulation 1

Citation and commencement

These Regulations may be cited as the Manual Handling Operation
Regulations 1992 and shall come into force on 1st January 1993.

Regulation 2 *(See p 401 for Guidance notes)*

Interpretation

(1) In these Regulations, unless the context otherwise requires –

'injury' does not include injury caused by any toxic or corrosive substanc
which –
  (a) has leaked or spilled from a load;
  (b) is present on the surface of a load but has not leaked or spille
from it; or
  (c) is a constituent part of a load;
  and 'injured' shall be construed accordingly;
'load' includes any person and any animal;
'manual handling operations' means any transporting or supporting of
load (including the lifting, putting down, pushing, pulling, carrying o
moving thereof) by hand or by bodily force.

(2) Any duty imposed by these Regulations on an employer in respect o
his employees shall also be imposed on a self-employed person in respect o
himself.

Regulation 3 *(See p 402 for Guidance notes)*

Disapplication of Regulations

These Regulations shall not apply to or in relation to the master or crev
of a sea-going ship or to the employer of such persons in respect of th

ormal ship-board activities of a ship's crew under the direction of the
aster.

egulation 4 *(See p 403 for Guidance notes)*

uties of employers

) Each employer shall –

) so far as is reasonably practicable, avoid the need for his employees to
undertake any manual handling operations at work which involve a
risk of their being injured.

) where it is not reasonably practicable to avoid the need for his
employees to undertake any manual handling operations at work
which involve a risk of their being injured –

  (i) make a suitable and sufficient assessment of all such manual
handling operations to be undertaken by them, having regard to
the factors which are specified in column 1 of Schedule 1 to these
Regulations and considering the questions which are specified
opposite thereto in column 2 of that Schedule.

  (ii) take appropriate steps to reduce the risk of injury to those
employees arising out of their undertaking any such manual
handling operations to the lowest level reasonably practicable.

  (iii) take appropriate steps to provide any of those employees who are
undertaking any such manual handling operations with general
indications and, where it is reasonably practicable to do so,
precise information on –

    (aa) the weight of each load, and

    (bb) the heaviest side of any load whose centre of gravity is not
positioned centrally.

(2) Any assessment such as is referred to in paragraph (1)(b)(i) of this
gulation shall be reviewed by the employer who made it if –

) there is reason to suspect that it is no longer valid; or

) there has been a significant change in the manual handling operations
to which it relates;

nd where as a result of any such review changes to an assessment are
quired, the relevant employer shall make them.

egulation 5 *(See p 425 for Guidance notes)*

uty of employees

ach employee while at work shall make full and proper use of any system
f work provided for his use by his employer in compliance with regulation
(1)(b)(ii) of these Regulations.

Regulation 6

Exemption certificates

(1) The Secretary of State for Defence may, in the interests of nationa security, by a certificate in writing exempt –

(a) any of the home forces, any visiting force or any headquarters from any requirement imposed by regulation 4 of these Regulations; or

(b) any member of the home forces, any member of a visiting force or an member of a headquarters from the requirement imposed b regulation 5 of these Regulations;

and any exemption such as is specified in sub-paragraph (a) or (b) of th paragraph may be granted subject to conditions and to a limit of time an may be revoked by the said Secretary of State by a further certificate i writing at any time.

(2) In this regulation –

(a) 'the home forces' has the same meaning as in section 12(1) of th Visiting Forces Act 1952;

(b) 'headquarters' has the same meaning as in article 3(2) of the Visitin Forces and International Headquarters (Application of Law) Orde 1965;

(c) 'member of a headquarters' has the same meaning as in paragraph 1(of the Schedule to the International Headquarters and Defenc Organisations Act 1964; and

(d) 'visiting force' has the same meaning as it does for the purposes of an provision of Part I of the Visiting Forces Act 1952.

Regulation 7 *(See p 426 for Guidance notes)*

Extension outside Great Britain

These Regulations shall, subject to regulation 3 hereof, apply to and i relation to the premises and activities outside Great Britain to whic sections 1 to 59 and 80 to 82 of the Health and Safety at Work etc Act 197 apply by virtue of the Health and Safety at Work etc Act 1974 (Applicatio Outside Great Britain) Order 1989 as they apply within Great Britain.

Regulation 8 *(See p 426 for Guidance notes)*

Repeals and revocations

(1) The enactments mentioned in column 1 of Part I of Schedule 2 to thes Regulations are repealed to the extent specified in the corresponding entr in column 3.

(2) The Regulations mentioned in column 1 of Part II of Schedule 2 t these Regulations are revoked to the extent specified in the correspondin entry in column 3.

Schedule 1

Factors to which the employer must have regard and questions he must consider when making an assessment of manual handling operations

Regulation 4(1)(b)(i)

Column 1 Factors	Column 2 Questions

1 The tasks	Do they involve:
	 – holding or manipulating loads at distance from trunk?
	 – unsatisfactory bodily movement or posture, especially:
	   – twisting the trunk?
	   – stooping?
	   – reaching upwards?
	 – excessive movement of loads, especially:
	   – excessive lifting or lowering distances?
	   – excessive carrying distances?
	 – excessive pushing or pulling of loads?
	 – risk of sudden movement of loads?
	 – frequent or prolonged physical effort?
	 – insufficient rest or recovery periods?
	 – a rate of work imposed by a process?

2 The loads	Are they: – heavy? – bulky or unwieldy? – difficult to grasp? – unstable, or with contents likely to shift? – sharp, hot or otherwise potentially damaging?
3 The working environment	Are there: – space constraints preventing good posture? – uneven, slippery or unstable floors? – variations in level of floors or work surfaces? – extremes of temperature or humidity? – conditions causing ventilation problems or gusts of wind? – poor lighting conditions?

4 Individual capability	Does the job:
	– require unusual strength, height, etc?
	– create a hazard to those who might reasonably be considered to be pregnant or to have a health problem
	– require special information or training for its safe performance?
5 Other factors	Is movement or posture hindered by personal protective equipment or by clothing?

Schedule 2

Repeals and revocations

Regulation 8

Part I Repeals

Column 1 *Short title of enactment*	Column 2 *Reference*	Column 3 *Extent of repeal*
The Children and Young Persons Act 1933.	1933 c.12	Section 18(1)(f) except insofar as that paragraph applies to such employment as is permitted under section 1(2) of the Employment of Women, Young Persons, and Children Act 1920 (1920 c. 65).
The Children and Young Persons (Scotland) Act 1937.	1937 c.37	Section 28(1)(f) except insofar as that paragraph applies to such employment as is permitted under section 1(2) of the Employment of Women, Young Persons, and Children Act 1920.
The Mines and Quarries Act 1954.	1954 c.70	Section 93; in section 115 the word 'ninety-three'.
The Agriculture (Safety, Health and Welfare Provisions) Act 1956.	1956 c.49	Section 2.
The Factories Act 1961.	1961 c.34	Section 72.
The Offices, Shops and Railway Premises Act 1963.	1963 c.41	Section 23 except insofar as the prohibition contained in that section applies to any person specified in section 90(4) of the same Act; in section 63(2) the number '23'; in section 83(1) the number '23'.

Part II Revocations

Column 1 *Title of instrument*	Column 2 *Reference*	Column 3 *Extent of revocation*
The Agriculture (Lifting of Heavy Weights) Regulations 1959.	SI 1959/2120	The whole Regulations.
The Construction (General Provisions) Regulations 1961.	SI 1961/1580	In regulation 3(1)(a) the phrase 'and 55'; regulation 55.

GUIDANCE NOTES

Introduction

1 . . .

2 More than a quarter of the accidents reported each year to the enforcing authorities are associated with manual handling - the transporting or supporting of loads by hand or by bodily force. While fatal manual handling accidents are rare, accidents resulting in a major injury such as a fractured arm are more common, accounting for 6% of all major injuries reported in 1990/91. The vast majority of reported manual handling accidents result in over-three-day injury, most commonly a sprain or strain, often of the back. Figures 1 to 3 illustrate these patterns for over-three-day injuries reported in 1990/91 [not reproduced here].

3 Sprains and strains arise from the incorrect application and/or prolongation of bodily force. Poor posture and excessive repetition of movement can be important factors in their onset. Many manual handling injuries are cumulative rather than being truly attributable to any single handling incident. A full recovery is not always made; the result can be physical impairment or even permanent disability.

4 Figure 4 [not reproduced here], also based on over-three-day injuries reported in 1990/91, shows that the problem of manual handling is not confined to a narrow range of industries but is widespread. Nor should it be supposed that the problem is confined to 'industrial' work: for example the comparable figure for both banking and finance and for retail distribution is 31% and for medical, veterinary and other health services 55%.

5 There is now substantial international acceptance of both the scale of the manual handling problem and methods of prevention. Modern medical and scientific knowledge stresses the importance of an ergonomic approach in removing or reducing the risk of manual handling injury. Ergonomics is sometimes described as 'fitting the job to the person, rather than the person to the job'. The ergonomic approach therefore looks at manual handling as a whole, taking into account a range of relevant factors including the nature of the task, the load, the working environment and individual capability. This approach is central to the European Directive on manual handling, and to the Regulations.

6 The Regulations should not be considered in isolation. Regulation 3(1) of the Management of Health and Safety at Work Regulations 1992 requires employers to make a suitable and sufficient assessment of the risks to the health and safety of their employees while at work. Where this general assessment indicates the possibility of risks to employees from the manual handling of loads the requirements of the present Regulations should be followed.

7 The Regulations establish a clear hierarchy of measures:

(a)   avoid hazardous manual handling operations so far as is reasonably practicable – this may be done by redesigning the task to avoid moving the load or by automating or mechanising the process;

(b) make a suitable and sufficient assessment of any hazardous manual handling operations that cannot be avoided; and

(c) reduce the risk of injury from those operations so far as is reasonably practicable – particular consideration should be given to the provision of mechanical assistance but where this is not reasonably practicable then other improvements to the task, the load and the working environment should be explored.

8 Like the European Directive on manual handling, the Regulations set no specific requirements such as weight limits. The ergonomic approach shows clearly that such requirements are based on too simple a view of the problem and are likely to lead to erroneous conclusions. Instead, an ergonomic assessment based on a range of relevant factors is used to determine the risk of injury and point the way to remedial action.

9 However, a full assessment of every manual handling operation could be a major undertaking and might involve wasted effort. Therefore Appendix 1 [see pp 427ff] offers numerical guidelines which can be used as an initial filter, helping to identify those manual handling operations which warrant a more detailed examination. The guidelines set out an approximate boundary within which manual handling operations are unlikely to create a risk of injury sufficient to warrant more detailed assessment. This should enable assessment work to be concentrated where it is most needed. However even operations lying within the boundary should be avoided or made less demanding wherever it is reasonably practicable to do so. *The guidelines should not be regarded as precise recommendations. They should be applied with caution. Where doubt remains a more detailed assessment should be made.*

10 It is intended that the contents of this booklet should form a general framework within which individual industries and sectors will be able to produce more specific guidance appropriate to their own circumstances.

11 Manual handling injuries are part of a wider family of musculoskeletal problems; the reader may also find it helpful to refer to the Health and Safety Executive's (HSE) booklet Work related upper limb disorders – a guide to prevention.

Regulation 2

Interpretation

Definition of certain terms

Injury
12 The Regulations seek to prevent injury not only to the back but to any part of the body. Account should be taken of any external physical properties of loads which might either affect grip or cause direct injury, for example slipperiness, roughness, sharp edges, extremes of temperature.

13 Hazards from toxic or corrosive properties of loads through spillage or leakage or from external contamination are not covered by these Regulations, though such hazards should be considered in the light of

other provisions such as COSHH – the Control of Substances Hazardous to Health Regulations 1988. For example, the presence of oil on the surface of a load is relevant to the Regulations if it makes the load slippery to handle; but a risk of dermatitis from contact with the oil is dealt with elsewhere.

Load

14 A load in this context must be a discrete moveable object. This includes, for example, a human patient receiving medical attention or an animal during husbandry or undergoing veterinary treatment, and material supported on a shovel or fork. An implement, tool or machine – such as a chainsaw – is not considered to constitute a load while in use for its intended purpose.

Manual handling operations

15 The Regulations apply to the manual handling of loads, ie by human effort, as opposed to mechanical handling by crane, lift truck, etc. The human effort may be applied directly to the load, or indirectly by hauling on a rope or pulling on a lever. Introducing mechanical assistance, for example a sack truck or a powered hoist, may reduce but not eliminate manual handling since human effort is still required to move, steady or position the load.

16 Manual handling includes both transporting a load and supporting a load in a static posture. The load may be moved or supported by the hands or any other part of the body, for example the shoulder. Manual handling also includes the intentional dropping of a load and the throwing of a load, whether into a receptacle or from one person to another.

17 The application of human effort for a purpose other than transporting or supporting a load does not constitute a manual handling operation. For example turning the starting handle of an engine or lifting a control lever on a machine is not manual handling; nor is the action of pulling on a rope while lashing down cargo on the back of a vehicle.

Regulation 2(2)

Duties of the self-employed

18 Regulation 2(2) makes the self-employed responsible for their own safety during manual handling. They should take the same steps to safeguard themselves as would be expected of employers in protecting their employees in similar circumstances.

Regulation 3

Disapplication of Regulations

Sea-going ships

19 Sea-going ships are subject to separate Merchant Shipping legislation administered by the Department of Transport. The Regulations therefore do not apply to the normal ship-board activities of a ship's crew under the

direction of the master. However the Regulations may apply to other manual handling operations aboard a ship, for example where a shore-based contractor carries out the work, provided the ship is within territorial waters. The Regulations also apply to certain activities carried out offshore – see regulation 7.

Regulation 4

Duties of employers

Introduction

20 The present Regulations should not be considered in isolation. Regulation 3(1) of the Management of Health and Safety at Work Regulations 1992 requires employers to make a suitable and sufficient assessment of the risks to the health and safety of their employees while at work. Where this general assessment indicates the possibility of risks to employees from the manual handling of loads the requirements of the present Regulations should be observed, as follows.

Hierarchy of measures

21 Regulation 4(1) establishes a clear hierarchy of measures:

(a) avoid hazardous manual handling operations so far as is reasonably practicable;

(b) assess any hazardous manual handling operations that cannot be avoided; and

(c) reduce the risk of injury so far as is reasonably practicable.

Extent of the employer's duties

22 The extent of the employer's duty to avoid manual handling or to reduce the risk of injury is determined by reference to what is 'reasonably practicable'. Such duties are satisfied if the employer can show that the cost of any further preventive steps would be grossly disproportionate to the further benefit that would accrue from their introduction.

23 This approach is fully applicable to the work of the emergency services. Ultimately, the cost of prohibiting all potentially hazardous manual handling operations would be an inability to provide the general public with an adequate rescue service. A fire authority, for example, may therefore consider that it has discharged this duty when it can show that any further preventive steps would make unduly difficult the efficient discharge of its emergency functions.

A continuing duty

24 It is not sufficient simply to make changes and then hope that the problem has been dealt with. Steps taken to avoid manual handling or

reduce the risk of injury should be monitored to check that they are having the desired effect in practice. If they are not, alternative steps should be sought.

25 It should also be remembered that regulation 4(2) (discussed later) requires the assessment made under regulation 4(1) to be kept up to date.

Work away from the employer's premises

26 The Regulations impose duties upon the employer whose employees carry out the manual handling. However, manual handling operations may occur away from the employer's premises in situations over which little direct control can be exercised. Where possible the employer should seek close liaison with those in control of such premises. There will sometimes be a limit to employers' ability to influence the working environment; but the task and perhaps the load will often remain within their control, as will the provision of effective training, so it is still possible to establish a safe system of work.

27 Employers and others in control of premises at which visiting employees have to work also have duties towards those employees, particularly under sections 3 or 4 of the HSW Act, the Management of Health and Safety at Work Regulations 1992 and the Workplace (Health, Safety and Welfare) Regulations 1992, for example to ensure that the premises and plant provided there are in a safe condition.

Regulation 4(1)(a)

Avoidance of manual handling

Risk of injury
28 If the general assessment carried out under regulation 3(1) of the Management of Health and Safety at Work Regulations 1992 indicates a possibility of injury from manual handling operations, consideration should first be given to avoiding the need for the operations in question. At this preliminary stage a judgement should be made as to the nature and likelihood of injury. It may not be necessary to assess in great detail, particularly if the operations can readily be avoided or if the risk is clearly of a low order. Appendix 1 [see pp 427ff] provides some simple numerical guidelines to assist with this initial judgement, at least in relatively straightforward cases.

Elimination of handling
29 In seeking to avoid manual handling the first question to ask is whether movement of the loads can be eliminated altogether: are the handling operations unnecessary; or could the desired result be achieved in some entirely different way? For example, can a process such as machining or wrapping be carried out in situ, without handling the loads? Can a treatment be brought to a patient rather than taking the patient to the treatment?

Automation or mechanisation

30 Secondly, if load handling operations, in some form, cannot be avoided entirely then further questions should be asked:

(a) can the operations be automated?
(b) can the operations be mechanised?

31 It should be remembered that the introduction of automation or mechanisation may create other, different risks. Even an automated plant will require maintenance and repair. Mechanisation, for example by the introduction of lift trucks or powered conveyors, can introduce fresh risks requiring precautions of their own.

32 It is especially important to address these questions when plant or systems of work are being designed. However, examination of existing activities may also reveal opportunities for avoidance of manual handling operations that involve a risk of injury. Such improvements often bring additional benefits in terms of greater efficiency and productivity, and reduced damage to loads.

Regulation 4(1)(b)(i)

Assessment of risk

33 Where the general assessment carried out under regulation 3(1) of the Management of Health and Safety at Work Regulations 1992 indicates a possibility of injury from manual handling operations but the conclusion reached under regulation 4(1)(a) is that avoidance of the operations is not reasonably practicable; a more specific assessment should be carried out as required by regulation 4(1)(b)(i). The extent to which this further assessment need be pursued will depend on the circumstances. Appendix 1 offers some simple numerical guidelines to assist with this decision. The guidelines are intended to be used as an initial filter, to help to identify those operations deserving more detailed assessment.

34 Schedule 1 to the Regulations specifies factors which this assessment should take into account including the task, the load, the working environment and individual capability. First, however, consideration should be given to how the assessment is to be carried out – and by whom – and what other relevant information may be available to help.

Who should carry out the assessment?

35 In most cases employers should be able to carry out the assessment themselves or delegate it to others in their organisation, having regard to regulation 6 of the Management of Health and Safety at Work Regulations 1992. A meaningful assessment can only be based on a thorough practical understanding of the type of manual handling tasks to be performed, the loads to be handled and the working environment in which the tasks will be carried out. Employers and managers should be better placed to know about the manual handling taking place in their own organisation than someone from outside.

36 While one individual may be able to carry out a perfectly satisfactory assessment, at least in relatively straightforward cases, it can be helpful to draw on the knowledge and expertise of others. In some organisations this has been done informally; others have preferred to set up a small assessment team.

37 Areas of knowledge and expertise likely to be relevant to the successful assessment of risks from manual handling operations, and individuals who may be able to make a useful contribution, include:

(a) the requirements of the Regulations (manager, safety professional);
(b) the nature of the handling operations (supervisor, industrial engineer);
(c) a basic understanding of human capabilities (occupational health nurse, safety professional);
(d) identification of high risk activities (manager, supervisor, occupational health nurse, safety professional); and
(e) practical steps to reduce risk (manager, supervisor, industrial engineer, safety professional).

38 It may be appropriate to seek outside assistance, for example to give basic training to in-house assessors or where manual handling risks are novel or particularly difficult to assess. Possible sources of such assistance are given in the reference section at the back of this document. Outside specialist advice may also help solve unusual handling problems or contribute to ergonomic design. But employers will still wish to oversee the assessment as they have the final responsibility for it.

Employees' contribution
39 The views of staff can be of particular value in identifying manual handling problems and practical solutions to them. Employees, their safety representatives and safety committees should be encouraged to play a positive part in the assessment process. They can assist the employer by highlighting difficulties arising from such things as the size or shape of loads, the frequency with which they are handled or the circumstances in which the handling operations are carried out.

Records of accidents and ill health
40 Well-kept records of accidents and ill health can play a useful part in the assessment process. They should identify accidents associated with manual handling, and careful analysis may also yield evidence of links between manual handling and ill health, including injuries apparently unrelated to any specific event or accident. Other possible indicators of manual handling problems include high levels of absenteeism or staff turnover, poor productivity and morale, excessive product damage, and general dissatisfaction among the employees concerned. Any regular occurrence of back disorders or other ailments possibly associated with unsatisfactory manual handling practices should be investigated. However such indicators are not a complete guide and should be used only to augment other risk assessment methods.

How detailed should an assessment be?

41 Employers' assessments will be 'suitable and sufficient' if they look in a considered way at the totality of the manual handling operations their employees are required to perform. Properly based 'generic' assessments which draw together common threads from a range of broadly similar operations are quite acceptable. Indeed a more narrowly focused assessment may fail to reflect adequately the range of operations encountered.

42 An assessment made at the last minute is unlikely to be 'suitable and sufficient'. In conducting assessments employers should therefore use their experience of the type of work their employees perform, consulting the employees as appropriate. This approach will help with the assessment of work that is of a varied nature (such as construction or maintenance), peripatetic (such as making deliveries) or involves dealing with emergencies (such as fire-fighting and rescue).

43 In the case of delivery operations, for example, a useful technique is to list the various types of task, load and working environment concerned and then to review a selection of them. The aim should be to establish the range of manual handling risks to which employees are exposed and then to decide on appropriate preventive steps where these are shown to be necessary.

44 A distinction should be made between the employer's assessment required by regulation 4(1)(b)(i) and the everyday judgements which supervisors and others will have to make in dealing with manual handling operations. The assessment should identify in broad terms the problems likely to arise during the kind of operations that can be foreseen and the measures that will be necessary to deal with them. These measures should include the provision of training to enable supervisors, and where appropriate individual employees, to cope effectively with the operations they are likely to undertake.

45 This distinction is perhaps most clearly seen in the case of emergency work. Here it will be essential to provide training to enable fire officers, for example, to take the rapid judgements that will inevitably be necessary in dealing satisfactorily with an emergency incident or in supervising realistic training.

Industry-specific data and assessments

46 Individual industries and sectors have a valuable role to play in identifying common manual handling problems and developing practical solutions. Industry associations and similar bodies can also act as a focus for the collection and analysis of accident and ill health data drawn from a far wider base than that available to the individual employer.

Recording the assessment

47 In general, the significant findings of the assessment should be recorded and the record kept, readily accessible, as long as it remains relevant. However, the assessment need not be recorded if:

(a) it could very easily be repeated and explained at any time because it is simple and obvious; or

(b) the manual handling operations are quite straightforward, of low risk, are going to last only a very short time, and the time taken to record them would be disproportionate.

Making a more detailed assessment

48 When a more detailed assessment is necessary it should follow the broad structure set out in Schedule 1 to the Regulations. The Schedule lists a number of questions in five categories including the task; the load; the working environment; and individual capability. Not all of these questions will be relevant in every case.

49 These categories are clearly interrelated: each may influence the others and therefore none can be considered in isolation. However, in order to carry out an assessment in a structured way it is often helpful to begin by breaking the operations down into separate, more manageable items.

Assessment checklist

50 It may be helpful to use a checklist during assessment as an aide-memoire. An example of such a checklist is provided in Appendix 2. This checklist addresses not only the analysis of risk required by regulation 4(1)(b)(i) but also the identification of steps to reduce the risk as required by regulation 4(1)(b)(ii) discussed later. The particular example given will not be suitable in all circumstances; it can be adapted or modified as appropriate.

51 REMEMBER – assessment is not an end in itself, merely a structured way of analysing risks and pointing the way to practical solutions.

The task – making an assessment

Is the load held or manipulated at a distance from the trunk?

52 As the load is moved away from the trunk the general level of stress on the lower back rises. Regardless of the handling technique used, failure to keep the load close to the body will increase the stress. As a rough guide holding a load at arm's length imposes about five times the stress experienced when holding the same load very close to the trunk.

53 In addition, the further away the load, the less easy it is to control. The benefit of friction between the load and the worker's garments in helping to support or steady the load is reduced or lost, and it is more difficult to counterbalance the load with the weight of the trunk.

The importance of posture

54 Poor posture during manual handling introduces the additional risk of loss of control of the load and a sudden, unpredictable increase in physical stresses. The risk of injury is increased if the feet and hands are not well placed to transmit forces efficiently between the floor and the load. A typical example of this is when the body weight is forward on the toes, the heels are off the ground and the feet are too close together.

Does the task involve twisting the trunk?

55 Stress on the lower back is increased significantly if twisted trunk postures are adopted. Still worse is to twist while supporting a load.

Does the task involve stooping?

56 Stooping can also increase the stress on the lower back. This happens whether the handler stoops by bending the back or by leaning forward with the back straight – in each case the trunk is thrown forward and its weight is added to the load being handled.

Does the task involve reaching upwards?

57 Reaching upwards places additional stresses on the arms and back. Control of the load becomes more difficult and, because the arms are extended, they are more prone to injury.

The effect of combining risk factors

58 Individual capability can be reduced substantially if twisting is combined with stooping or stretching. Such combinations should be avoided wherever possible, especially since their effect on individual capability can be worse than the simple addition of their individual effects might suggest. A requirement to position the load with precision can also add to the risk of injury.

Does the task involve excessive lifting or lowering distances?

59 The distance through which a load is lifted or lowered can also be important: large distances are considerably more demanding physically than small ones. Moreover lifting or lowering through a large distance is likely to necessitate a change of grip part way, further increasing the risk of injury. Lifts commencing at floor level should be avoided where possible; where unavoidable they should preferably terminate no higher than waist height.

Does the task involve excessive carrying distances?

60 In general, if a load can safely be lifted and lowered, it can also be carried without endangering the back. However, if a load is carried for an excessive distance, physical stresses are prolonged leading to fatigue and increased risk of injury. As a rough guide if a load is carried further than about 10 m then the physical demands of carrying the load will tend to predominate over those of lifting and lowering and individual capability will be reduced.

Does the task involve excessive pushing or pulling of the load?

61 Like lifting, lowering and carrying, the pushing or pulling of a load can be injurious to the handler. The risk of injury is increased if pushing or pulling is carried out with the hands much below knuckle height or above shoulder height.

62 Additionally, because of the way in which pushing and pulling forces have to be transmitted from the handler's feet to the floor, the risk of slipping and consequent injury is much greater. For this reason pushing or pulling a load in circumstances where the grip between foot and floor is poor – whether through the condition of the floor, footwear or both – is likely to increase significantly the risk of injury.

Does the task involve a risk of sudden movement of the load?
63 If a load suddenly becomes free and the handler is unprepared or is not able to retain complete control of the load, unpredictable stresses can be imposed on the body, creating a risk of injury. For example, the freeing of a box jammed on a shelf or the release of a machine component during maintenance work can easily cause injury if handling conditions are not ideal. The risk is compounded if the handler's posture is unstable.

Does the task involve frequent or prolonged physical effort?
64 The frequency with which a load is handled can affect the risk of injury. A quite modest load, handled very frequently, can create as large a risk of injury as one-off handling of a more substantial load. The effect will be worsened by jerky, hurried movements which can multiply a load's effect on the body.

65 Where physical stresses are prolonged fatigue will occur, increasing the risk of injury. This effect will often be exacerbated by a relatively fixed posture, leading to a rapid increase in fatigue and a corresponding fall in muscular efficiency.

Does the task involve insufficient rest or recovery periods?
66 Research and experience in industry have shown that failure to counter fatigue during physically demanding work increases ill health and reduces output. Consideration should therefore be given to whether there are adequate opportunities for rest (ie breaks from work) or recovery (ie changing to another task which uses a different set of muscles). The amount of work undertaken in fixed postures is also an important consideration since blood flow to the muscles is likely to be reduced, adding to fatigue. This problem is complicated by a large variation in individual susceptibility to fatigue.

Does the task involve a rate of work imposed by a process?
67 Particular care is necessary where the rate of work cannot be varied by the handler. Mild fatigue, which might quickly be relieved by a momentary pause or a brief spell doing another operation using different muscles, can soon become more pronounced, leading to an increased risk of injury.

Handling while seated
68 Handling loads while seated imposes considerable constraints. Use of the relatively powerful leg muscles is precluded and the weight of the handler's body cannot be used as a counterbalance. Therefore most of the work has to be done by the weaker muscles of the arms and trunk.

69 Unless the load is presented close to the body the handler will have to reach and/or lean forward. Not only will handling in this position put the body under additional stress but the seat, unless firmly placed, will then tend to move backwards as the handler attempts to maintain a stable posture.

70 Lifting from below the level of a work surface will almost inevitably result in twisting and stooping, the dangers of which were discussed in paragraphs 55 and 56.

Team handling

71 Handling by two or more people may make possible an operation that is beyond the capability of one person, or reduce the risk of injury to a solo handler. However, team handling may introduce additional problems which the assessment should consider. During the handling operation the proportion of the load that is borne by each member of the team will inevitably vary to some extent. Such variation is likely to be more pronounced on rough ground. Therefore the load that a team can handle in safety is less than the sum of the loads that the individual team members could cope with when working alone.

72 As an approximate guide the capability of a two person team is two thirds the sum of their individual capabilities; and for a three person team the capability is half the sum of their individual capabilities. If steps or slopes must be negotiated most of the weight may be borne by the handler or handlers at the lower end, further reducing the capability of the team as a whole.

73 Additional difficulties may arise if team members impede each others' vision or movement, or if the load offers insufficient good handholds. This can occur particularly with compact loads which force the handlers to work close together or where the space available for movement is limited.

The load – making an assessment

Is the load heavy?

74 For many years legislation and guidance on manual handling have concentrated on the weight of the load. It is now well established that the weight of the load is only one – and sometimes not the main – consideration affecting the risk of injury. Other features of the load such as its resistance to movement, its size, shape or rigidity must also be considered. Proper account must also be taken of the circumstances in which the load is handled; for example postural requirements, frequency and duration of handling, workplace design, and aspects of work organisation such as incentive schemes and piecework.

75 Moreover traditional guidance based on so-called 'acceptable' weights has often considered only symmetrical, two-handed lifts, in front of and close to the body. In reality such lifting tasks are comparatively rare since most will involve sideways movement, twisting of the trunk or some other asymmetry. For these reasons an approach to manual handling which concentrates solely upon the weight of the load is likely to be misleading, either failing adequately to deal with the risk of injury or imposing excessively cautious constraints.

76 The numerical guidelines in Appendix 1 [see pp 427ff] consider the weight of the load in relation to other important factors.

Is the load bulky or unwieldy?

77 The shape of the load will affect the way in which it can be held. For example, the risk of injury will be increased if a load to be lifted from the ground is not small enough to pass between the knees, since its bulk will hinder a close approach. Similarly if the bottom front corners of a load are

not within reach when carried at waist height a good grip will be harder to obtain. And if a load to be carried at the side of the body does not clear the ground without requiring the handler to lean away from the load in order to raise it high enough, the handler will be forced into an unfavourable posture.

78 In general if any dimension of the load exceeds about 75 cm its handling is likely to pose an increased risk of injury. This will be especially so if this size is exceeded in more than one dimension. The risk will be further increased if the load does not provide convenient handholds.

79 The bulk of the load can also interfere with vision. Where restriction of view by a bulky load cannot be avoided account should be taken of the increased risk of slipping, tripping, falling or colliding with obstructions.

80 The risk of injury will also be increased if the load is unwieldy and difficult to control. Well-balanced lifting may be difficult to achieve, the load may hit obstructions, or it may be affected by gusts of wind or other sudden air movements.

81 If the centre of gravity of the load is not positioned centrally within the load, inappropriate handling may increase the risk of injury. For example, much of the weight of a typewriter is often at the rear of the machine; therefore an attempt to lift the typewriter from the front will place its centre of gravity further from the handler's body than if the typewriter is first turned around and then lifted from the rear.

82 Sometimes, as with a sealed and unmarked carton, an offset centre of gravity is not visibly apparent. In these circumstances the risk of injury is increased since the handler may unwittingly hold the load with its centre of gravity further from the body than is necessary.

Is the load difficult to grasp?
83 If the load is difficult to grasp, for example because it is large, rounded, smooth, wet or greasy, its handling will call for extra grip strength – which is fatiguing – and will probably entail inadvertent changes of posture. There will also be a greater risk of dropping the load. Handling will be less sure and the risk of injury will be increased.

Is the load unstable, or are its contents likely to shift?
84 If the load is unstable, for example because it lacks rigidity or has contents that are liable to shift, the likelihood of injury is increased. The stresses arising during the manual handling of such a load are less predictable, and the instability may impose sudden additional stresses for which the handler is not prepared. The risks are further increased if the handler is unfamiliar with a particular load and there is no cautionary marking on it.

85 Handling people or animals, for example hospital patients or livestock, can present additional problems. The load lacks rigidity, there is particular concern on the part of the handler to avoid damaging the load, and to complicate matters the load will often have a mind of its own, introducing an extra element of unpredictability. These factors are likely to increase the risk of injury to the handler as compared with the handling of an inanimate load of similar weight and shape.

Is the load sharp, hot or otherwise potentially damaging?
86 Risk of injury may also arise from the external state of the load. It may have sharp edges or rough surfaces, or be too hot or too cold to touch safely without protective clothing. In addition to the more obvious risk of direct injury, such characteristics may also impair grip, discourage good posture or otherwise interfere with safe handling.

The working environment – making an assessment

Are there space constraints preventing good posture?
87 If the working environment hinders the adoption of good posture the risk of injury from manual handling will be increased. Restricted head room will enforce a stooping posture; furniture, fixtures or other obstructions may increase the need for twisting or leaning; constricted working areas and narrow gangways will hinder the manoeuvring of bulky loads.

Are there uneven, slippery or unstable floors?
88 In addition to increasing the likelihood of slips, trips and falls, uneven or slippery floors hinder smooth movement and create additional unpredictability. Floors which are unstable or susceptible to movement – for example on a boat, a moving train or a mobile work platform – similarly increase the risk of injury through the imposition of sudden, unpredictable stresses.

Are there variations in level of floors or work surfaces?
89 The presence of steps, steep slopes, etc can increase the risk of injury by adding to the complexity of movement when handling loads. Carrying a load up or down a ladder, if it cannot be avoided, is likely to aggravate handling problems because of the additional need to maintain a proper hold on the ladder.

90 Excessive variation between the heights of working surfaces, storage shelving, etc will increase the range of movement and in consequence the scope for injury. This will be especially so if the variation is large and requires, for example, movement of the load from near floor level to shoulder height or beyond.

Are there extremes of temperature or humidity?
91 The risk of injury during manual handling will be increased by extreme thermal conditions. For example, high temperatures or humidity can cause rapid fatigue; and perspiration on the hands may reduce grip. Work at low temperatures may impair dexterity. Gloves and other protective clothing which may be necessary in such circumstances may also hinder movement, impair dexterity and reduce grip. The influence of air movement on working temperatures – the wind chill factor – should not be overlooked.

Are there ventilation problems or gusts of wind?
92 Inadequate ventilation can hasten fatigue, increasing the risk of injury. Sudden air movements, whether caused by a ventilation system or the wind, can make large loads more difficult to manage safely.

Are there poor lighting conditions?
93 Poor lighting conditions can increase the risk of injury. Dimness or glare may cause poor posture, for example by encouraging stooping. Contrast between areas of bright light and deep shadow can aggravate tripping hazards and hinder the accurate judgement of height and distance.

Individual capability – making an assessment

Does the task require unusual strength, height, etc?
94 Manual handling injuries are more often associated with the nature of the operations than with variations in individual capability. Therefore any assessment which concentrates on individual capability at the expense of task or workplace design is likely to be misleading. However, it is an inescapable fact that the ability to carry out manual handling in safety does vary between individuals.

95 In general the lifting strength of women as a group is less than that of men. But for both men and women the range of individual strength and ability is large, and there is considerable overlap; some women can deal safely with greater loads than some men.

96 An individual's physical capability varies with age, typically climbing until the early 20s, declining gradually during the 40s and more markedly thereafter. It should therefore be recognised that the risk of manual handling injury may be somewhat higher for employees in their teens or in their 50s and 60s, though again the range of individual capability is large and the benefits of experience and maturity should not be overlooked.

97 In deciding whether the physical demands imposed by manual handling operations should be regarded as unusual it is not unreasonable to have some regard to the nature of the work. For example, demands that would be considered unusual for a group of employees engaged in office work might not be regarded as out of the ordinary for a group of employees engaged predominantly in heavy physical labour. It would also be unrealistic to ignore the element of self-selection that often occurs for jobs that are relatively demanding physically.

98 As a general rule, however, the risk of injury should be regarded as unacceptable if the manual handling operations cannot be performed satisfactorily by most reasonably fit, healthy employees.

Does the job put at risk those who might reasonably be considered
to be pregnant or to have a health problem?
99 Allowance should be made for pregnancy where the employer could reasonably be expected to be aware of it, ie where the pregnancy is visibly apparent or the employee has informed her employer that she is pregnant. Pregnancy has significant implications for the risk of manual handling injury. Hormonal changes can affect the ligaments, increasing the susceptibility to injury; and postural problems may increase as the pregnancy progresses. Particular care should also be taken for women who may handle loads during the three months following a return to work after childbirth.

100 Allowance should also be made for any health problem of which the employer could reasonably be expected to be aware and which might have a bearing on the ability to carry out manual handling operations in safety. If there is good reason to suspect that an individual's state of health might significantly increase the risk of injury from manual handling operations, medical advice should be sought.

Does the task require special information or training for its safe performance?
101 The risk of injury from a manual handling task will be increased where a worker does not have the information or training necessary for its safe performance. While section 2 of the HSW Act and the Management of Health and Safety at Work Regulations 1992 require employers to provide safety training, this may need to be supplemented to enable employees to carry out manual handling operations safely.

102 For example, ignorance of any unusual characteristics of loads, or of a system of work designed to ensure safety during manual handling, may lead to injury. Remedial steps such as the provision of mechanical handling aids may themselves create a need for training, for example in the proper use of those aids.

Other factors – making an assessment

Personal protective equipment and other clothing
103 Personal protective equipment should be used only as a last resort, when engineering or other controls do not provide adequate protection. Where the wearing of personal protective equipment cannot be avoided its implications for the risk of manual handling injury should be taken into consideration. For example gloves may impair dexterity; the weight of gas cylinders used with breathing apparatus will increase the stresses on the body. Other clothing such as a uniform required to be worn may inhibit free movement during manual handling.

Regulation (4)(b)(ii)

Reducing the risk of injury

Striking a balance
104 It will usually be convenient to continue with the same structured approach used during the assessment of risk, considering in turn the task, the load, the working environment and individual capability.

105 The emphasis given to each of these factors may depend in part upon the nature and circumstances of the manual handling operations. Routine manual handling operations carried out in essentially unchanging circumstances, for example in manufacturing processes, may lend themselves particularly to improvement of the task and working environment.

106 However, manual handling operations carried out in circumstances which change continually, for example certain activities carried out in mines or on construction sites, may offer less scope for improvement of the

working environment and perhaps the task. More interest may therefore focus on the load – for example can it be made easier to handle?

107 For varied work of this kind, including of course much of the work of the emergency services, the provision of effective training will be especially important. It should enable employees to recognise potentially hazardous handling operations. It should also give them a clear understanding of why they should avoid or modify such operations where possible, make full use of appropriate equipment and apply good handling technique.

An ergonomic approach

108 However, health, safety and productivity are most likely to be optimised if an ergonomic approach is used to design the manual handling operations as a whole. Wherever possible full consideration should be given to the task, the load, the working environment, individual capability and the relationship between them, with a view to fitting the operations to the individual rather than the other way around.

109 While better job or workplace design may not eliminate handling injuries, the evidence is that it can greatly reduce them. Particular consideration should be given to the provision of mechanical assistance where this is reasonably practicable.

Mechanical assistance

110 Mechanical assistance involves the use of handling aids – an element of manual handling is retained but bodily forces are applied more efficiently, reducing the risk of injury. There are many examples. A simple lever can reduce the risk of injury merely by lessening the bodily force required to move a load, or by removing fingers from a potentially damaging trap. A hoist, either powered or hand operated, can support the weight of a load and leave the handler free to control its positioning. A trolley, sack truck or roller conveyor can greatly reduce the effort required to move a load horizontally. Chutes are a convenient way of using gravity to move loads from one place to another. Handling devices such as hand-held hooks or suction pads can simplify the problem of handling a load that is difficult to grasp.

Involving the workforce

111 Employees, their safety representatives and safety committees should be involved in any redesign of the system of work and encouraged to report its effects. They should be given the opportunity to contribute to the development of good handling practice.

Industry-specific guidance

112 The development of industry-specific guidance within the framework established by the Regulations and this general guidance will provide a valuable source of information on preventive action that has been found effective for particular activities or types of work.

'Appropriate' steps

113 Above all, the steps taken to reduce the risk of injury should be 'appropriate'. They should address the problem in a practical and effective manner. Their effectiveness should be monitored; if they do not have the desired effect the situation should be reappraised (see also regulation 4(2) 'reviewing the assessment').

Checklist

114 It may be helpful to use a checklist as an aide-memoire while seeking practical steps to reduce the risk of injury. Appendix 2 [pp 430–431] offers an example of such a checklist which combines the assessment of risk required by regulation 4(1)(b)(i) with the identification of remedial steps as required by regulation 4(1)(b)(ii). The particular example given will not be suitable in all circumstances; it can be adapted or modified as appropriate.

The task – reducing the risk of injury

Improving task layout

115 Changes to the layout of the task can reduce the risk of injury by, for example, improving the flow of materials or products. Such changes will often bring the additional benefits of increased efficiency and productivity.

116 The optimum position for storage of loads, for example, is around waist height; storage much above or below this height should be reserved for loads that are lighter or more easily handled, or loads that are handled infrequently.

Using the body more efficiently

117 A closely related set of considerations concerns the way in which the handler's body is used. Changes to the task layout, the equipment used, or the sequence of operations can reduce or remove the need for twisting, stooping and stretching.

118 In general, any change that allows the load to be held closer to the body is likely to reduce the risk of injury. The level of stress at the lower back will be reduced; the weight of the load will be more easily counterbalanced by the weight of the body; and the load will be more stable and the handler less likely to lose control of it. Moreover, if the load is hugged to the body friction with the handler's garments will steady it and may help to support its weight. The need for protective clothing should be considered (see paragraphs 131 and 132).

119 When the lifting of loads at or near floor level is unavoidable, handling techniques which allow the use of the relatively strong leg muscles rather than those of the back are preferable provided the load is small enough to be held close to the trunk.

120 The closeness of the load to the body can also be influenced by foot placement. The elimination of obstacles which need to be reached over or into – for example poorly placed pallets, excessively deep bins – will permit the handler's feet to be placed beneath or adjacent to the load.

121 Where possible the handler should be able to move in close to the load before beginning the manual handling operation. The handler should

also be able to address the load squarely, preferably facing in the direction of intended movement.

122 The risk of injury may also be reduced if lifting can be replaced by controlling pushing or pulling. For example it may be possible to slide the load or roll it along. However, uncontrolled sliding or rolling, particularly of large or heavy loads, may introduce fresh risks of injury.

123 For both pulling and pushing, a secure footing should be ensured, and the hands applied to the load at a height between waist and shoulder wherever possible. A further option, where other safety considerations allow, is to push with the handler's back against the load, using the strong leg muscles to exert the force.

124 The risk of manual handling injury can also be reduced by careful attention to the work routine. Minimising the need for fixed postures dictated by sustained holding or supporting of a load will reduce fatigue and the associated fall-off in muscular efficiency. Attention to the frequency of handling loads, especially those that are heavy or awkward, can also reduce fatigue and the risk of injury. Where possible, tasks should be self-paced and employees trained to adjust their rate of working to optimise safety and productivity.

125 An inflexible provision of rest pauses may not be an efficient method of reducing the risk of injury. The large variation in individual susceptibility to muscular fatigue means that mandatory, fixed breaks are generally less effective than those taken voluntarily within the constraints of what is possible in terms of work organisation.

126 A better solution can often be found in job rotation where this allows one group of muscles to rest while others are being used. Periods of heavy work may be interspersed with lighter activities such as paper work or the monitoring of instruments. Job rotation can also bring advantages in reduced monotony and increased attentiveness. However, where rotation merely repeats the use of the same group of muscles, albeit on a different task, it is generally ineffective in reducing the risk of manual handling injury.

Handling while seated

127 For the reasons given in paragraphs 68 to 70 the loads that can be handled in safety by a person who is seated are substantially less than can be dealt with while standing. This activity therefore demands particular care. Lifting loads from the floor while seated should be avoided where possible.

128 The possibility of accidental movement of the seat should be considered. Castors may be inadvisable, especially on hard floors. A swivel-action seat will help the handler to face the load without having to twist the trunk. The relative heights of seats and work surfaces should be well matched. Further advice on this is given in the HSE booklet *Seating at work*.

Team handling

129 Where a handling operation would be difficult or unsafe for one person, handling by a team of two or more may provide an answer.

However, team handling can introduce additional hazards and caution should be exercised for the reasons given in paragraphs 71 to 73.

130 For safe team handling there should be enough space for the handlers to manoeuvre as a group. They should have adequate access to the load, and the load should provide sufficient handholds; if the load is particularly small or difficult to grasp then a handling aid such as a stretcher or slings should be used. One person should plan and then take charge of the operation, ensuring that movements are coordinated. Team members should preferably be of broadly similar height and physical capability.

Personal protective equipment and other clothing

131 The nature of the load, or the environment in which it is handled, may necessitate the use of personal protective equipment (PPE) such as gloves, aprons, overalls, gaiters or safety footwear. In these cases the protection offered by PPE should not be compromised to facilitate the manual handling operations. Alternative methods of handling may need to be considered where manual handling is likely to lead to risks from the contents of the load or from external contamination.

132 PPE and indeed all work clothing should be well fitting and restrict movement as little as possible. Fasteners, pockets and other features on which loads might snag should be concealed. Gloves should be close fitting and supple, to interfere with manual dexterity as little as possible. Footwear should provide adequate support, a stable, non-slip base and proper protection. Restrictions on the handler's movement caused by wearing protective clothing need to be recognised in the design of the task. Reference should be made to The Personal Protective Equipment at Work Regulations 1992.

Maintenance and accessibility of equipment

133 All equipment provided for use during manual handling, including handling aids and PPE, should be well maintained and there should be a defect reporting and correction system. The siting of equipment can be important: handling aids and PPE that are not readily accessible are less likely to be used fully and effectively. Reference should be made to The Provision and Use of Work Equipment Regulations 1992.

Safety of machinery – European standards

134 Under the Machinery Directive 89/392/EEC (as amended) machinery placed on the market must satisfy certain essential health and safety requirements. This is a product safety Directive made under Article 100A of the EC Treaty and will be implemented by the Department of Trade and Industry. One of the Directive's requirements is that machinery be designed to facilitate its safe handling.

135 In support of this requirement CEN, one of the European standards making bodies, is preparing a harmonised standard entitled Safety of machinery – human physical performance. The purpose of the proposed standards is to assist machinery designers and manufacturers. It has no status in relation to Directive 90/269/EEC on the manual handling of loads

which was made under Article 118A of the Treaty. The standard will therefore have no direct relevance to the Manual Handling Operations Regulations 1992.

The load – reducing the risk of injury

Making it lighter

136 Where a risk of injury from the manual handling of a load is identified, consideration should be given to reducing its weight. For example liquids and powders may be packaged in smaller containers. Where loads are bought in it may be possible to specify lower package weights. However the breaking down of loads will not always be the safest course: the consequent increase in the frequency of handling should not be overlooked.

137 If a great variety of weights is to be handled it may be possible to sort the loads into weight categories so that additional precautions can be applied selectively, where most needed.

Making it smaller or easier to manage

138 Similarly, consideration should be given to making loads less bulky so that they can be grasped more easily and the centre of gravity brought closer to the handler's body. Again, it may be possible to specify smaller or more manageable loads, or to redesign those produced in-house.

Making it easier to grasp

139 Where the size, surface texture or nature of a load makes it difficult to grasp, consideration should be given to the provision of handles, hand grips, indents or any other feature designed to improve the handler's grasp. Alternatively it may be possible to place the load securely in a container which is itself easier to grasp. Where a load is bulky rather than heavy it may be easier to carry it at the side of the body if it has suitable handholds or if slings or other carrying devices can be provided.

140 The positioning of handholds can play a part in reducing the risk of injury. For example, handholds at the top of a load may reduce the temptation to stoop when lifting it from a low level. However, depending upon the size of the load, this might also necessitate carriage with bent arms which could increase fatigue.

141 Handholds should be wide enough to clear the breadth of the palm, and deep enough to accommodate the knuckles and any gloves which may need to be worn.

Making it more stable

142 Where possible, packaging should be such that objects will not shift unexpectedly while being handled. Where the load as a whole lacks rigidity it may be preferable to use slings or other aids to maintain effective control during handling. Ideally, containers holding liquids or free-moving powders should be well filled, leaving only a small amount of free space; where this is not possible alternative means of handling should be considered.

Making it less damaging to hold

43 As far as possible loads should be clean and free from dust, oil, corrosive deposits, etc. To prevent injury during the manual handling of hot or cold materials an adequately insulated container should be used; failing this suitable handling aids or PPE will be necessary. Sharp corners, jagged edges, rough surfaces etc should be avoided where possible; again, where this cannot be achieved then the use of handling aids or PPE will be necessary. In selecting personal protective equipment the advice given in paragraphs 131 and 132 should be noted.

The working environment – reducing the risk of injury

Removing space constraints

44 Gangways and other working areas should where possible allow adequate room to manoeuvre during manual handling operations. The provision of sufficient clear floor space and head room is important; constrictions caused by narrow doorways and the positioning of fixtures, machines, etc should be avoided as far as possible. In many cases much can be achieved simply by improving the standard of housekeeping. Reference should be made to The Workplace (Health, Safety and Welfare) Regulations 1992.

The nature and condition of floors

45 On permanent sites, both indoors and out, a flat, well maintained and properly drained surface should be provided. In construction, agriculture and other activities where manual handling may take place on temporary surfaces, the ground should be prepared if possible and kept even and firm; if possible suitable coverings should be provided. Temporary work platforms should be firm and stable.

146 Spillages of water, oil, soap, food scraps and other substances likely to make the floor slippery should be cleared away promptly. Where necessary, and especially where floors can become wet, attention should be given to the choice of slip-resistant surfacing.

147 Particular care is necessary where manual handling is carried out on a surface that is unstable or susceptible to movement, as for example on a boat, a moving train or a mobile work platform. In these conditions the capability to handle loads in safety may be reduced significantly.

Working at different levels

48 Where possible all manual handling activities should be carried out on a single level. Where more than one level is involved the transition should preferably be made by a gentle slope or, failing that, by well positioned and properly maintained steps. Manual handling on steep slopes should be avoided as far as possible. Working surfaces such as benches should, where possible, be at a uniform height to reduce the need for raising or lowering loads.

The thermal environment and ventilation

49 There is less risk of injury if manual handling is performed in a comfortable working environment. Extremes of temperature, excessive

humidity and poor ventilation should be avoided where possible, either by improving environmental control or relocating the work.

150 Where these conditions cannot be changed, for example when manual handling is necessarily performed out of doors in extreme weather or close to a very hot process, or in a refrigerated storage area, and the use of PPE is necessary, the advice given in paragraphs 131 and 132 should be noted.

Strong air movements

151 Particular care should be taken when handling bulky or unwieldy loads in circumstances in which high winds or powerful ventilation systems could catch a load and destabilise the handler. Possible improvements include relocating the handling operations or taking a different route, provision of handling aids to give greater control of the load, or team handling.

Lighting

152 There should be sufficient well-directed light to enable handlers to see clearly what they are doing and the layout of the workplace, and to make accurate judgements of distance and position.

Individual capability – reducing the risk of injury

Personal considerations

153 Particular consideration should be given to employees who are or have recently been pregnant, or who are known to have a history of back trouble, hernia or other health problems which could affect their manual handling capability. However, beyond such specific pointers to increased risk of injury the scope for preventive action on an individual basis is limited.

154 Clearly an individual's state of health, fitness and strength can significantly affect the ability to perform a task safely. But even though these characteristics vary enormously, studies have shown no close correlation between any of them and injury incidence. There is therefore insufficient evidence for reliable selection of individuals for safe manual handling on the basis of such criteria. It is recognised, however, that there is often a degree of self-selection for work that is physically demanding.

155 It is also recognised that motivation and self-confidence in the ability to handle loads are important factors in reducing the risk of injury. These are linked with fitness and familiarity. Unaccustomed exertion – whether in a new task or on return from holiday or sickness absence – can carry a significant risk of injury and requires particular care.

Information and training

156 Section 2 of the HSW Act and regulations 8 and 11 of the Management of Health and Safety at Work Regulations 1992 require employers to provide their employees with health and safety information and training. This should be supplemented as necessary with more specific information and training on manual handling injury risks and prevention, as part of the steps to reduce risk required by regulation 4(1)(b)(ii) of the present Regulations.

157 It should not be assumed that the provision of information and training alone will ensure safe manual handling. The primary objective in reducing the risk of injury should always be to optimise the design of the manual handling operations, improving the task, the load and the working environment as appropriate. Where possible the manual handling operations should be designed to suit individuals, not the other way round. However as a complement to a safe system of work, rather than a substitute for it, effective training has an important part to play in reducing the risk of manual handling injury.

158 Employers should ensure that their employees understand clearly how manual handling operations have been designed to ensure their safety. Employees, their safety representatives and safety committees should be involved in the development and implementation of manual handling training, and the monitoring of its effectiveness.

159 In devising a training programme for safe manual handling, particular attention should therefore be given to imparting a clear understanding of:

(a) how potentially hazardous handling operations may be recognised;

(b) how to deal with unfamiliar handling operations;

(c) the proper use of handling aids;

(d) the proper use of personal protective equipment;

(e) features of the working environment that contribute to safety;

(f) the importance of good housekeeping;

(g) factors affecting individual capability;

(h) good handling technique (see paragraphs 162 to 164).

160 Employees should be trained to recognise loads whose weight, in conjunction with their shape and other features, and the circumstances in which they are handled, might cause injury. Simple methods for estimating weight on the basis of volume may be taught. Where volume is less important than the density of the contents, as for example in the case of a dustbin containing refuse, an alternative technique for assessing the safety of handling should be taught, such as rocking the load from side to side before attempting to lift it.

161 In general, unfamiliar loads should be treated with caution. For example, it should not be assumed that apparently empty drums or other closed containers are in fact empty. The load may first be tested, for example by attempting to raise one end. Employees should be taught to apply force gradually until either undue strain is felt, in which case the task should be reconsidered, or it is apparent that the task is within the handler's capability.

Good handling technique

162 The development of good handling technique is no substitute for other risk reduction steps such as improvements to the task, load or working environment, but it will form a very valuable adjunct to them. It requires both training and practice. The training should be carried out in conditions that are as realistic as possible, thereby emphasising its relevance to everyday handling operations.

163 The content of training in good handling technique should be tailored to the particular handling operations likely to be undertaken. It should begin with relatively simple examples and progress to more specialised handling operations as appropriate. The following list illustrates some important points, using a basic lifting operation by way of example:

- *Stop and think*. Plan the lift. Where is the load going to be placed? Use appropriate handling aids if possible. Do you need help with the load? Remove obstructions such as discarded wrapping materials. For a long lift – such as floor to shoulder height – consider resting the load midway on a table or bench in order to change grip.
- *Place the feet*. Feet apart, giving a balanced and stable base for lifting (tight skirts and unsuitable footwear make this difficult). Leading leg as far forward as is comfortable.
- *Adopt a good posture*. Bend the knees so that the hands when grasping the load are as nearly level with the waist as possible. But do not kneel or overflex the knees. Keep the back straight (tucking in the chin helps). Lean forward a little over the load if necessary to get a good grip. Keep shoulders level and facing in the same direction as the hips.
- *Get a firm grip*. Try to keep the arms within the boundary formed by the legs. The optimum position and nature of the grip depends on the circumstances and individual preference, but it must be secure. A hook grip is less fatiguing than keeping the fingers straight. If it is necessary to vary the grip as the lift proceeds, do this as smoothly as possible.
- *Don't jerk*. Carry out the lifting movement smoothly, keeping control of the load.
- *Move the feet*. Don't twist the trunk when turning to the side.
- *Keep close to the load*. Keep the load close to the trunk for as long as possible. Keep the heaviest side of the load next to the trunk. If a close approach to the load is not possible try sliding it towards you before attempting to lift it.
- *Put down, then adjust*. If precise positioning of the load is necessary, put it down first, then slide it into the desired position.

Vocational qualifications

164 The development of specific statements of what needs to be done, how well and by whom (ie statements of competence) will help to determine the extent of any shortfall in training. Such statements may be embodied in qualifications accredited by the National Council for Vocational Qualifications (NCVQ) and SCOTVEC (the Scottish Vocational Education Council).

Regulation 4(1)(b)(iii)

The load – providing additional information

165 Regulation 4(1)(b)(iii) can be satisfied in a variety of ways, depending upon the circumstances.

166 The requirement to provide 'general indications' of the weight and nature of the loads to be handled should be addressed during basic training so that employees are suitably prepared for the operations they are likely to undertake.

167 In addition, where it is reasonably practicable to do so, employers should give more precise information. Employers whose businesses originate loads may find that this information is best given by marking it on the loads.

168 The Regulations impose duties on employers whose employees carry out manual handling. However, those who originate loads – manufacturers, packers, etc – that are likely to undergo manual handling may also have relevant duties, for example under sections 3 or 6 of the HSW Act, for the health and safety of other people at work. They should give particular consideration to making loads easy to grasp and handle and to marking loads clearly with their weight and, where appropriate, an indication of their heaviest side.

Regulation 4(2)

Reviewing the assessment

169 The assessment should be kept up-to-date. It should be reviewed if new information comes to light or if there has been a change in the manual handling operations which, in either case, could materially have affected the conclusion reached previously. The assessment should also be reviewed if a reportable injury occurs. It should be corrected or modified where this is found to be necessary.

Regulation 5

Duty of employees

170 Duties are already placed on employees by section 7 of the HSW Act, under which they must:

(a) take reasonable care for their own health and safety and that of others who may be affected by their activities; and

(b) cooperate with their employers to enable them to comply with their health and safety duties.

171 In addition, regulation 12 of the Management of Health and Safety at Work Regulations 1992 requires employees generally to make use of appropriate equipment provided for them, in accordance with their training and the instructions their employer has given them. Such equipment will include machinery and other aids provided for the safe handling of loads.

172 Regulation 5 of the present Regulations supplements these general duties in the case of manual handling by requiring employees to follow appropriate systems of work laid down by their employer to promote safety during the handling of loads.

Emergency action

173 These provisions do not preclude well-intentioned improvisation in an emergency, for example during efforts to rescue a casualty, fight a fire or contain a dangerous spillage.

Regulation 7

Extension outside Great Britain

174 The Regulations apply to offshore activities covered by the 1989 Order on or associated with oil and gas installations, including mobile installations, diving support vessels, heavy lift barges and pipe-lay barges.

Regulation 8

Repeals and revocations

175 The Regulations, like the European Directive on manual handling, apply a modern ergonomic approach to the prevention of injury: they take account of a wide range of relevant factors including the nature of the task, the load, the working environment and individual capability. The Regulations have therefore replaced a number of outdated provisions which concentrated on the weight of the load being handled. The provisions are listed in Schedule 2 to the Regulations.

Appendix 1

Numerical guidelines for assessment

Introduction – the need for assessment

1 Regulation 3(1) of the Management of Health and Safety at Work Regulations 1992 requires employers to make a suitable and sufficient assessment of the risks to the health and safety of their employees while at work. Where this general assessment indicates the possibility of risks to employees from the manual handling of loads the requirements of the Manual Handling Operations Regulation 1992 (the Regulations) should be considered.

2 Regulation 4(1) of the Regulations sets out a hierarchy of measures for safety during manual handling:

(a) avoid hazardous manual handling operations so far as is reasonably practicable;

(b) make a suitable and sufficient assessment of any hazardous manual handling operations that cannot be avoided; and

(c) reduce the risk of injury from those operations so far as is reasonably practicable.

Purpose of the guidelines

3 The Manual Handling Operations Regulations, like the European Directive on manual handling, set no specific requirements such as weight limits. Instead, assessment based on a range of relevant factors listed in Schedule 1 to the Regulations is used to determine the risk of injury and point the way to remedial action. However a full assessment of every manual handling operation could be a major undertaking and might involve wasted effort.

4 The following numerical guidelines therefore provide an initial filter which can help to identify those manual handling operations deserving more detailed examination. The guidelines set out an approximate boundary within which operations are unlikely to create a risk of injury sufficient to warrant more detailed assessment. This should enable assessment work to be concentrated where it is most needed.

5 There is no threshold below which manual handling operations may be regarded as 'safe'. Even operations lying within the boundary mapped out by the guidelines should be avoided or made less demanding wherever it is reasonably practicable to do so.

Source of the guidelines

6 These guidelines have been drawn up by HSE's medical and ergonomics experts on the basis of a careful study of the published literature and their own extensive practical experience of assessing risks from manual handling operations.

Individual capability

7 There is a wide range of individual physical capability, even among those fit and healthy enough to be at work. For the working population the guideline figures will give reasonable protection to nearly all men and between one half and two thirds of women. To provide the same degree of protection to nearly all working women the guideline figures should be reduced by about one third. 'Nearly all' in this context means about 95%.

8 It is important to understand that the *guideline figures are not limits.* They may be exceeded where a more detailed assessment shows that it is appropriate to do so, having regard always to the employer's duty to avoid or reduce risk of injury where this is reasonably practicable. However, even for a minority of fit, well-trained individuals working under favourable conditions any operations which would exceed the guideline figures by more than a factor of about two should come under very close scrutiny.

Guidelines for lifting and lowering

9 Basic guideline figures for manual handling operations involving lifting and lowering are set out in Figure 1 [not included here]. They assume that the load is readily grasped with both hands and that the operation takes place in reasonable working conditions with the handler in a stable body position.

10 The guideline figures take into consideration the vertical and horizontal position of the hands as they move the load during the handling operation, as well as the height and reach of the individual handler. It will be apparent that the capability to lift or lower is reduced significantly, if, for example, the load is held at arm's length or the hands pass above the shoulder height.

11 If the hands enter more than one of the box zones during the operation the smallest weight figure should be used. The transition from one box zone to another is not abrupt; an intermediate figure may be chosen where the hands are close to a boundary. Where lifting or lowering with the hands beyond the box zones is unavoidable a more detailed assessment should be made.

Twisting

12 The basic guideline figures for lifting and lowering should be reduced if the handler twist to the side during the operation. As a rough guide the figures should be reduced by about 10% where the handler twists through 45° and by about 20% where the handler twists through 90°.

Frequent lifting and lowering

13 The basic guideline figures for lifting and lowering are for relatively infrequent operations – up to approximately 30 operations per hour – where the pace of work is not forced, adequate pauses for rest or recovery are possible and the load is not supported for any length of time. They should be reduced if the operation is repeated more frequently. As a rough guide the figures should be reduced by 30% where the operation is repeated

once or twice per minute, by 50% where the operation is repeated around five to eight times per minute and by 80% where the operation is repeated more than about 12 times per minute.

Guidelines for carrying

14 Basic guideline figures for manual handling operations involving carrying are similar to those given for lifting and lowering, though carrying will not normally be carried out with the hands below knuckle height.

15 It is also assumed that the load is held against the body and is carried no further than about 10 m without resting. If the load is carried over a longer distance without resting the guideline figures may need to be reduced.

16 Where the load can be carried securely on the shoulder without first having to be lifted (as for example when unloading sacks from a lorry) a more detailed assessment may show that it is acceptable to exceed the guideline figure.

Guidelines for pushing and pulling

17 The following guideline figures are for manual handling operations involving pushing and pulling, whether the load is slid, rolled or supported on wheels. The guideline figure for starting or stopping the load is a force of about 25 kg (ie about 250 Newtons). The guideline figure for keeping the load in motion is a force of about 10 kg (ie about 100 Newtons).

18 It is assumed that the force is applied with the hands between knuckle and shoulder height; if this is not possible the guideline figures may need to be reduced. No specific limit is intended as to the distance over which the load is pushed or pulled provided there are adequate opportunities for rest or recovery.

Guidelines for handling while seated

19 The basic guideline figure for handling operations carried out while seated is given in Figure 4 [not included here] and applies only when the hands are within the box zone indicated. If handling beyond the box zone is unavoidable or, for example, there is significant twisting to the side a more detailed assessment should be made.

Appendix 2

Example of an assessment checklist

Manual handling of loads
EXAMPLE OF AN ASSESSMENT CHECKLIST

Note: This checklist may be copied freely. It will remind you of the main points to think about while you:
– consider the risk of injury from manual handling operations
– identify steps that can remove or reduce the risk
– decide your priorities for action.

SUMMARY OF ASSESSMENT	Overall priority for remedial action: Nil/Low/Med/High*
Operations covered by the assessment:	Remedial action taken: ....
....	....
....	
Locations:...	Date by which action is to be taken: ....
Personnel involved:	Date for reassessment: ....
Date of assessment:	Assessor's name: .... Signature:...................

*circle as appropriate

Section A – Preliminary:

Q1 Do the operations involve a significant risk of injury?   Yes/No*

If 'Yes' go to Q2. If 'No' the assessment need go no further.

If in doubt answer 'Yes'. You may find the guidelines in Appendix 1 helpful.

Q2 Can the operations be avoided / mechanised / automated at reasonable cost?   Yes/No*

If 'No' go to Q3. If 'Yes' proceed and then check that the result is satisfactory.

Q3 Are the operations clearly within the guidelines in Appendix 1?   Yes/No*

If 'No' go to Section B. If 'Yes' you may go straight to Section C if you wish.

Section C – Overall assessment of risk:

Q What is your overall assessment of the risk of injury?   Insignificant/Low/Med/High*

If not 'Insignificant' go to Section D. If 'Insignificant' the assessment need go no further.

Section D – Remedial action:

Q What remedial steps should be taken, in order of priority?

i ....

ii ....

iii ....

iv ....

v ....

And finally:

– complete the SUMMARY above

– compare it with your other manual handling assessments

– decide your priorities for action

– TAKE ACTION.............AND CHECK THAT IT HAS THE DESIRED EFFECT

Section B – More detailed assessment, where necessary:

Questions to consider:	Level of risk:			Possible remedial action:
(If the answer to a question is 'Yes' place a tick against it and then consider the level of risk)	(Tick as appropriate)			(Make rough notes in this column in preparation for completing Section D)
	Yes	**Low**	**Med**	**High**	

The tasks – do they involve:
- holding loads away from trunk?
- twisting?
- stooping?
- reaching upwards?
- large vertical movement?
- long carrying distances?
- strenuous pushing or pulling?
- unpredictable movement of loads?
- repetitive handling?
- insufficient rest or recovery?
- a workrate imposed by a process?

The loads – are they:
- heavy?
- bulky/unwieldy?
- difficult to grasp?
- unstable/unpredictable?
- intrinsically harmful (eg sharp/hot?)

The working environment – are there:
- constraints on posture?
- poor floors?
- variations in levels?
- hot/cold/humid conditions?
- strong air movements?
- poor lighting conditions?

Individual capability – does the job:
- require unusual capability?
- hazard those with a health problem?
- hazard those who are pregnant?
- call for special information/training?

Other factors –
Is movement or posture hindered by clothing or personal protective equipment?

Deciding the level of risk will inevitably call for judgement. The guidelines in Appendix 1 may provide a useful yardstick. When you have completed Section B go to Section C.

Appendix 3 – References and further information

This Appendix is not reproduced in this book

Appendix 6

Health and Safety (Display Screen Equipment) Regulations 1992

THE REGULATIONS

Regulation 1 *(See p 440 for Guidance notes)*

Citation, commencement, interpretation and application

(1) These Regulations may be cited as the Health and Safety (Display Screen Equipment) Regulations 1992 and shall come into force on January 1993.

(2) In these Regulations –

(a) 'display screen equipment' means any alphanumeric or graphic display screen, regardless of the display process involved;

(b) 'operator' means a self-employed person who habitually uses display screen equipment as a significant part of his normal work;

(c) 'use' means use for or in connection with work;

(d) 'user' means an employee who habitually uses display screen equipment as a significant part of his normal work; and

(e) 'workstation' means an assembly comprising –

    (i) display screen equipment (whether provided with software determining the interface between the equipment and its operator or user, a keyboard or any other input device),

    (ii) any optional accessories to the display screen equipment,

    (iii) any disk drive, telephone, modem, printer, document holder, work chair, work desk, work surface or other item peripheral to the display screen equipment, and

    (iv) the immediate work environment around the display screen equipment.

(3) Any reference in these Regulations to –

(a) a numbered regulation is a reference to the regulation in these Regulations so numbered; or

(b) a numbered paragraph is a reference to the paragraph so numbered in the regulations in which the reference appears.

(4) Nothing in these Regulations shall apply to or in relation to –

(a) drivers' cabs or control cabs for vehicles or machinery;
(b) display screen equipment on board a means of transport;
(c) display screen equipment mainly intended for public operation;
(d) portable systems not in prolonged use;
(e) calculators, cash registers or any equipment having a small data or measurement display required for direct use of the equipment; or
(f) window typewriters.

Regulation 2 *(See p 446 for Guidance notes)*

Analysis of workstations to assess and reduce risks

(1) Every employer shall perform a suitable and sufficient analysis of those workstations which –

(a) (regardless of who has provided them) are used for the purposes of his undertaking by users; or
(b) have been provided by him and are used for the purposes of his undertaking by operators,

for the purpose of assessing the health and safety risks to which those persons are exposed in consequence of that use.

(2) Any assessment made by an employer in pursuance of paragraph (1) shall be reviewed by him if –

(a) there is reason to suspect that it is no longer valid; or
(b) there has been a significant change in the matters to which it relates;

and where as a result of any such review changes to an assessment are required, the employer concerned shall make them.

(3) The employer shall reduce the risks identified in consequence of an assessment to the lowest extent reasonably practicable.

(4) The reference in paragraph (3) to 'an assessment' is a reference to an assessment made by the employer concerned in pursuance of paragraph (1) and changed by him where necessary in pursuance of paragraph (2).

Regulation 3 *(See p 450 for Guidance notes)*

Requirements for workstations

(1) Every employer shall ensure that any workstation first put into service on or after 1st January 1993 which –

(a) (regardless of who has provided it) may be used for the purposes of his undertaking by users; or
(b) has been provided by him and may be used for the purposes of his undertaking by operators,

meets the requirements laid down in the Schedule to these Regulations to the extent specified in paragraph 1 thereof.

(2) Every employer shall ensure that any workstation first put into service on or before 31st December 1992 which –

(a) (regardless of who provided it) may be used for the purposes of his undertaking by users; or

(b) was provided by him and may be used for the purposes of his undertaking by operators,

meets the requirements laid down in the Schedule to these Regulations to the extent specified in paragraph 1 thereof not later than 31st December 1996.

Regulation 4 *(See p 453 for Guidance notes)*

Daily work routine of users

Every employer shall so plan the activities of users at work in his undertaking that their daily work on display screen equipment is periodically interrupted by such breaks or changes of activity as reduce their workload at that equipment.

Regulation 5 *(See p 455 for Guidance notes)*

Eyes and eyesight

(1) Where a person –

(a) is already a user on the date of coming into force of these Regulations; or

(b) is an employee who does not habitually use display screen equipment as a significant part of his normal work but is to become a user in the undertaking in which he is already employed,

his employer shall ensure that he is provided at his request with an appropriate eye and eyesight test, any such test to be carried out by a competent person.

(2) An eye and eyesight test provided in accordance with paragraph (1) shall –

(a) in any case to which sub-paragraph (a) of that paragraph applies, be carried out as soon as practicable after being requested by the user concerned; and

(b) in any case to which sub-paragraph (b) of that paragraph applies, be carried out before the employee concerned becomes a user.

(3) At regular intervals after an employee has been provided with an eye and eyesight test in accordance with paragraphs (1) and (2), his employer shall, subject to paragraph (6), ensure that he is provided with a further eye and eyesight test of an appropriate nature, any such test to be carried out by a competent person.

(4) Where a user experiences visual difficulties which may reasonably be considered to be caused by work on display screen equipment, his employer shall ensure that he is provided at his request with an appropriate eye and eyesight test, any such test to be carried out by a competent person as soon as practicable after being requested as aforesaid.

(5) Every employer shall ensure that each user employed by him is provided with special corrective appliances appropriate for the work being done by the user concerned where –

(a) normal corrective appliances cannot be used; and
(b) the result of an eye and eyesight test which the user has been given in accordance with this regulation shows such provision to be necessary.

(6) Nothing in paragraph (3) shall require an employer to provide any employee with an eye and eyesight test against that employee's will.

Regulation 6 *(See p 458 for Guidance notes)*

Provision of training

(1) Where a person –

(a) is already a user on the date of coming into force of these Regulations; or
(b) is an employee who does not habitually use display screen equipment as a significant part of his normal work but is to become a user in the undertaking in which he is already employed,

his employer shall ensure that he is provided with adequate health and safety training in the use of any workstation upon which he may be required to work.

(2) Every employer shall ensure that each user at work in his undertaking is provided with adequate health and safety training whenever the organisation of any workstation in that undertaking upon which he may be required to work is substantially modified.

Regulation 7 *(See p 460 for Guidance notes)*

Provision of information

(1) Every employer shall ensure that operators and users at work in his undertaking are provided with adequate information about –

(a) all aspects of health and safety relating to their workstations; and
(b) such measures taken by him in compliance with his duties under regulations 2 and 3 as related to them and their work.

(2) Every employer shall ensure that users at work in his undertaking are provided with adequate information about such measures taken by him in

compliance with his duties under regulations 4 and 6(2) as relate to them and their work.

(3) Every employer shall ensure that users employed by him are provided with adequate information about such measures taken by him in compliance with his duties under regulations 5 and 6(1) as relate to them and their work.

Regulation 8

Exemption certificates

(1) The Secretary of State for Defence may, in the interests of national security, exempt any of the home forces, any visiting force or any headquarters from any of the requirements imposed by these Regulations.

(2) Any exemption such as is specified in paragraph (1) may be granted subject to conditions and to a limit of time and may be revoked by the Secretary of State for Defence by a further certificate in writing at any time.

(3) In this regulation –

(a) 'the home forces' has the same meaning as in section 12(1) of the Visiting Forces Act 1952;
(b) 'headquarters' has the same meaning as in article 3(2) of the Visiting Forces and International Headquarters (Application of Law) Order 1965; and
(c) 'visiting force' has the same meaning as it does for the purposes of any provision of Part I of the Visiting Forces Act 1952.

Regulation 9

Extension outside Great Britain

These Regulations shall, subject to regulation 1(4), apply to and in relation to the premises and activities outside Great Britain to which sections 1 to 59 and 80 to 82 of the Health and Safety at Work etc. Act 1974 apply by virtue of the Health and Safety at Work etc. Act 1974 (Application Outside Great Britain) Order 1989 as they apply within Great Britain.

The Schedule

(Which sets out the minimum requirements for workstations which are contained in the Annex to Council Directive 90/270/EEC on the minimum safety and health requirements for work with display screen equipment)

Extent to which employers must ensure that workstations meet the requirements laid down in this Schedule

1   An employer shall ensure that a workstation meets the requirements laid down in this Schedule to the extent that –

(a) those requirements relate to a component which is present in the workstation concerned;

(b) those requirements have effect with a view to securing the health, safety and welfare of persons at work; and

(c) the inherent characteristics of a given task make compliance with those requirements appropriate as respects the workstation concerned.

Equipment

2 (a) *General comment*

The use as such of the equipment must not be a source of risk for operators or users.

(b) *Display screen*

The characters on the screen shall be well-defined and clearly formed, of adequate size and with adequate spacing between the characters and lines.

The image on the screen should be stable, with no flickering or other forms of instability.

The brightness and the contrast between the characters and the background shall be easily adjustable by the operator or user, and also be easily adjustable to ambient conditions.

The screen must swivel and tilt easily and freely to suit the needs of the operator or user.

It shall be possible to use a separate base for the screen or an adjustable table.

The screen shall be free of reflective glare and reflections liable to cause discomfort to the operator or user.

(c) *Keyboard*

The keyboard shall be tiltable and separate from the screen so as to allow the operator or user to find a comfortable working position avoiding fatigue in the arms or hands.

The space in front of the keyboard shall be sufficient to provide support for the hands and arms of the operator or user.

The keyboard shall have a matt surface to avoid reflective glare.

The arrangement of the keyboard and the characteristics of the keys shall be such as to facilitate the use of the keyboard.

The symbols on the keys shall be adequately contrasted and legible from the design working position.

(d) *Work desk or work surface*

The work desk or work surface shall have a sufficiently large, low-reflectant surface and allow a flexible arrangement of the screen, keyboard, documents and related equipment.

The document holder shall be stable and adjustable and shall be positioned so as to minimise the need for uncomfortable head and eye movements.

There shall be adequate space for operators or users to find a comfortable position.

(e) *Work chair*

The work chair shall be stable and allow the operator or user easy freedom of movement and a comfortable position.

The seat shall be adjustable in height.

The seat back shall be adjustable in both height and tilt.

A footrest shall be made available to any operator or user who wishes one.

Environment

3 (a) *Space requirements*

The workstation shall be dimensioned and designed so as to provide sufficient space for the operator or user to change position and vary movements.

(b) *Lighting*

Any room lighting or task lighting provided shall ensure satisfactory lighting conditions and an appropriate contrast between the screen and the background environment, taking into account the type of work and the vision requirements of the operator or user.

Possible disturbing glare and reflections on the screen or other equipment shall be prevented by co-ordinating workplace and workstation layout with the positioning and technical characteristics of the artificial light sources.

(c) *Reflections and glare*

Workstations shall be so designed that sources of light, such as windows and other openings, transparent or translucid walls, and brightly coloured fixtures or walls cause no direct glare and no distracting reflections on the screen.

Windows shall be fitted with a suitable system of adjustable covering to attenuate the daylight that falls on the workstation.

(d) *Noise*

Noise emitted by equipment belonging to any workstation shall be taken into account when a workstation is being equipped, with a view in particular to ensuring that attention is not distracted and speech is not disturbed.

(e) *Heat*

Equipment belonging to any workstation shall not produce excess heat which could cause discomfort to operators or users.

(f) *Radiation*

All radiation with the exception of the visible part of the electromagnetic spectrum shall be reduced to negligible levels from the point of view of the protection of operators' or users' health and safety.

(g) *Humidity*

An adequate level of humidity shall be established and maintained.

Interface between computer and operator/user

4   In designing, selecting, commissioning and modifying software, and
    in designing tasks using display screen equipment, the employer shall
    take into account the following principles:
    (a) software must be suitable for the task;
    (b) software must be easy to use and, where appropriate, adaptable to
        the level of knowledge or experience of the operator or user; no
        quantitative or qualitative checking facility may be used without
        the knowledge of the operators or users;
    (c) systems must provide feedback to operators or users on the
        performance of those systems;
    (d) systems must display information in a format and at a pace which
        are adapted to operators or users;
    (e) the principles of software ergonomics must be applied, in
        particular to human data processing.

GUIDANCE NOTES

Introduction

1–2 . . .

New general Regulations

3 . . .

Structure of this booklet

4 . . .

Regulation 1

Citation, commencement, interpretation and application

5 The definitions of 'display screen equipment', 'workstation', 'user' and 'operator' determine whether or not the Regulations apply in a particular situation.

Which display screen equipment is covered?

6 With a few exceptions (see paragraphs 14-18), the definition of display screen equipment at Regulation 1(2)(a) covers both conventional (cathode ray tube) display screens and other display processes such as liquid crystal displays, and other emerging technologies. Display screens mainly used to display line drawings, graphs, charts or computer generated graphics are included, but screens whose main use is to show television or film pictures are not. Judgements about mixed media workstations will be needed to establish the main use of the screen; if this is to display text, numbers and/or graphics, it is within the scope of the Regulations. The definition is not limited to typical office visual display terminals but covers, for example, non-electronic display systems such as microfiche. Process control screens are also covered in principle (where there are 'users' – see below) although certain requirements may not apply (see paragraphs 38–40).

7 The use of display screen equipment not covered by these Regulations is still subject to other, general health and safety legislation; see paragraphs 2 and 3 above. For example, there are requirements for suitable and sufficient lighting in the Provision and Use of Work Equipment Regulations 1992; and there are general requirements for risk assessment and provision of training and information in the Management of Health and Safety at Work Regulations 1992. Where a display screen is in use but the Display Screen Equipment Regulations do not apply, the assessment of risks and measures taken to control them should take account of ergonomic factors applicable to display screen work. This is also true where these

Regulations do not apply because the display screen is not used by a 'user' – see below.

Who is a display screen user or operator?

8 The Regulations are for the protection of people – employees and self-employed – who habitually use display screen equipment for the purposes of an employer's undertaking as a significant part of their normal work.

9 Regulation 1(2)(d) defines the employees who are covered as 'users' and all the Regulations apply to protect them, as specified, whether they are required to work:

– at their own employer's workstation;
– at a workstation at home;
– at another employer's workstation. In this case that other employer must comply with Regulations 2, 3, 4, 6 (2) and 7, and their own employer with Regulations 5 and 6 (1), as is specified in the Regulations concerned.

Regulations 2, 3 and 7 apply, as specified, to protect self-employed people who work at the client employer's workstation and whose use of display screen equipment is such that they would be users if employed. They are defined in Regulation 1(2)(b) as 'operators' for the purposes of the Regulations.

10 Employers must therefore decide which of their employees are display screen users and whether they also make use of other users (employed by other employers) or of operators. Workers who do not input or extract information by means of display screen equipment need not be regarded as users or operators in this context – for example many of those engaged in manufacture, sales, maintenance or the cleaning of display screen equipment. Whether or not those involved in display screen work are users or operators depends on the nature and extent of their use of the equipment.

11 The need for such a definition stems from the fact that possible hazards associated with display screen use are mainly those leading to musculoskeletal problems, visual fatigue and stress (see paragraph 19 below and Annex B). The likelihood of experiencing these is related mainly to the frequency, duration, intensity and pace of spells of continuous use of the display screen equipment, allied to other factors, such as the amount of discretion the person has over the extent and methods of display screen use. The combination of factors which give rise to risks makes it impossible to lay down hard and fast rules (eg based on set hours' usage per day or week) about who should be classified as a user or operator.

12 In some cases it will be clear that use of display screen equipment is more or less continuous on most days and the individuals concerned should be regarded as users or operators. This will include the majority of those whose job mainly involves, for example, display screen based data input or sales and order processing. Where use is less continuous or frequent, other

factors connected with the job must be assessed. It will generally be appropriate to classify the person concerned as a user or operator if most or all of the following criteria apply:

(a) the individual depends on the use of display screen equipment to do the job, as alternative means are not readily available for achieving the same results;

(b) the individual has no discretion as to use or non-use of the display screen equipment;

(c) the individual needs significant training and/or particular skills in the use of display screen equipment to do the job;

(d) the individual normally uses display screen equipment for continuous spells of an hour or more at a time;

(e) the individual uses display screen equipment in this way more or less daily;

(f) fast transfer of information between the user and screen is an important requirement of the job;

(g) the performance requirements of the system demand high levels of attention and concentration by the user, for example, where the consequences of error may be critical.

Some examples to illustrate these factors are included in the box. This is not an exhaustive list of display screen jobs, but a list of examples chosen to illuminate the above criteria.

Who is a display screen user?

Some examples

Definite display screen users

Word processing pool worker employed on full time text input using dedicated display screen equipment. A mix of checking from screen, keyboard input and formatting. Some change of posture involved in collecting work, operating printer etc. Often five hours in total on the work itself with a lunch break and at least two breaks morning and afternoon. Part-time workers, required to work fewer hours but spending all or most of their working time on this kind of work would also be included.

Secretary or typist who uses a dedicated word processing system and laser printer. Word processing of reports, memos, letters from manuscript and dictation, combined with electronic mail. Some variation in workload with a concomitant degree of control over scheduling throughout the day. Typically around two or three hours daily.

Data Input Operator employed full time on continuous processing of invoices. Predominantly numeric input using numeric key pad. Other keystroke monitoring with associated bonus system. Part-timers, or other staff temporarily assigned to this work to deal with peak workloads, would be definite 'users' while spending all or most of their working time on these duties.

News sub-editor making use of display screen equipment more or less continuously with peak workloads. Some text input to abridge/precis stories, but mainly scanning copy for fact, punctuation, grammar and size.

Journalist whose pattern of work may be variable but includes substantial use of display screen equipment. Information collected by field or telephone interviews (which may involve use of a portable computer) followed by, typically, several hours text input while working on a story. Work likely to be characterised by deadlines and interruptions. Some days may contain periods of less intense work but with more prolonged keyboard text entry and composition.

Tele-Sales/customer complaints/accounts enquiry/directory enquiry operator employed on mainly full-time display screen use while taking telephone enquiries from customers/public.

Air traffic controller whose main task is monitoring of purpose designed screens for air traffic movements combined with communication with air crew on navigation etc. High visual and mental workload. Shift work.

Financial dealer using a dedicated workstation typically with multiple display screens. Variable/unpredictable workload. Often highly stressful situations with information overload. Often long hours.

Graphic designer working on multimedia applications. Intensive scrutiny of images at high resolution. Large screens. Page make-up. Multiple input devices. Colour systems critical.

Librarian carrying out intensive text input on dedicated equipment to add to information held on databases; accessing and checking on records held on databases, eg bibliographic and lending references; creating summaries and reports, combining data held on the equipment and new copy inputted into the system. Display screen work either intensive throughout the day on most days, or more intermittent but still forming at least half of the librarian's total working time.

Possible display screen users – depending on the circumstances

The following are examples of jobs whose occupants may or may not be designated as display screen users, depending on circumstances. In reaching a decision, employers will need to judge the relative importance of different aspects of the work, weighing these against the factors discussed in paragraph 12 and bearing in mind the risks to which the job-holder may be exposed. If there is doubt over whether an individual is a display screen worker, carrying out a risk assessment (see Regulation 2) should help in reaching a decision.

Scientist/technical adviser having use of dedicated display screen equipment. Word processing of a few letters/memos per day. Monitoring of electronic mail for a short period, average 10 minutes, on most days. At irregular intervals, uses display screen equipment intensively for data analysis of research results.

Discussion: This scientist's daily use of display screen equipment is relatively brief, non-intense and he or she would have a good deal of discretion over when and how the equipment was used. Judged against this daily use, he or she would not be a 'user'. However, this decision might be reversed if the periods of use for analysis of research results were at all frequent, of long duration and intensive.

Client manager in a large management accounting consultancy. Dedicated display screen equipment on desk. Daily scanning and transmitting of electronic mail. Typically 1½-2 hours daily.

Discussion: Whether or not this manager is a user will depend on the extent and nature of his or her use of electronic mail. For example, how continuous is use of the screen and/or keyboard during each period of use; is there discretion as to the extent of use of electronic mail; how long is the total daily use?

Building society customer support officer with shared use of office, desk and display screen workstation. Display screen equipment used during interviews with clients to interrogate HQ database to obtain customer details, transactions etc.

Discussion: Decision will be influenced by what proportion of the individual worker's time is spent using the display screen equipment; are there any prolonged and/or intensive periods of use; and what are the consequences of errors (this factor may be relevant if the job involves inputting financial data as well as searching a database).

Airline check-in clerk whose workload in job as a whole varies during day, with occasional peaks of intensive work as flight times get near. Use of display screen equipment follows a predictable pattern; typically, used as part of most transactions but may not be a significant proportion of total working time.

Discussion: There needs to be consideration of how equipment is used and for what purpose. Is the display screen used during most parts of the check-in process or only a few of them? Is the workload of transactions high? What proportion of each transaction involves viewing the screen or keying in data? Is interaction with the screen rushed and intensive? What are the consequences of errors?

Community care worker using a portable computer to make notes during and/or following interviews or visits in the field.

Discussion: Decisions on whether or not those using laptops are 'users' need to be made on the same basis as if they were using non-portable equipment. While some of the specific minimum requirements in the Schedule may not be applicable to portables in prolonged use, as the inherent characteristics of the task may rule them out, it is important that such work is properly assessed, that users are trained, and that measures are taken to control risks.

Receptionist whose job involves frequent use of display screen equipment, for example to check or enter details of each visitor and/or provide them with information.

Discussion: The nature, frequency and duration of periods of display screen work need to be assessed. Some, perhaps most, receptionists would not be users, if most of their work consists of face to face contact and/or phone calls, with a display screen only being used occasionally – see below.

Definitely not display screen users

Senior managers in a large organisation using display screen for occasional monitoring of state of markets or other data, or more frequent but brief enquiries. Low dependency, high control.

Senior manager using display screen equipment at month end for generation/manipulation of financial statistics for board presentation.

Receptionist if work is mainly concerned with customer/public interaction, with the possibilities of interrogating display screen occasionally for limited purposes such as obtaining details of the organisation (telephone numbers, location etc).

13 The following table shows how the criteria in paragraph 12 relate to the job examples in the box.

14 Where any of the exclusions in Regulation 1(4) are operative, none of the specific duties in the Regulations apply to or in connection with the use of the equipment concerned. However, the proviso at paragraph 7 above applies here too. Employers should still ensure that, so far as is reasonably practicable, the health and safety of those using the equipment are not put at risk. The general duties on employers and others under the Health and Safety at Work etc Act 1974, and other general health and safety legislation (see paragraphs 2 and 3), are still applicable and particular attention should be paid to ergonomics in this context.

15 The exclusion in Regulation 1(4)(c) for display screen equipment mainly provided for short-term operation by the general public, such as cashpoint machines at banks and microfiche readers and computer terminals in public libraries. It does not extend to display screen equipment available for operation by the public but mainly provided for use by users.

16 Portable display screen equipment (such as laptop computers) comes under the exclusion in Regulation 1(4)(d) above only if it is not in prolonged use. While there are no hard and fast rules on what constitutes 'prolonged' use, portable equipment that is habitually in use by a display screen user for a significant part of his or her normal work, as explained in paragraphs 11-13 above, should be regarded as covered by the Regulations. While some of the specific minimum requirements in the Schedule may not be applicable to portables in prolonged use, employers should still ensure that such work is assessed and measures taken to control risks.

17 The exclusion in Regulation 1(4)(e) for small data or measurement displays is there because such displays are usually not intensively monitored by workers for long continuous spells. This exclusion covers, for example, much scientific and medical equipment, such as cardiac monitors, oscilloscopes, and instruments with small displays showing a series of digits.

18 The exclusion in Regulation 1(4)(f) is for window typewriters having a small display showing no more than a few lines of text.

Regulation 2

Analysis of workstations to assess and reduce risks

19 Possible risks which have been associated with display screen equipment work are summarised at Annex B. The principal risks relate to physical (musculoskeletal) problems, visual fatigue and mental stress. These are not unique to display screen work nor an inevitable consequence of it, and indeed research shows that the risk to the individual user from typical display screen work is low. However, in display screen work as in other types of work, ill health can result from poor work organisation, working environment, job design and posture, and from inappropriate working methods. As discussed in Annex B, some types of display screen work have been associated with chronic musculoskeletal disorders. While surveys indicate that only a very small proportion of display screen workers are likely to be involved, the number of cases may still be significant as display screen workers are so numerous. All the known health problems that may be associated with display screen work can be prevented altogether by good design of the workplace and the job, and by worker training and consultation.

20 Employers will need to assess the extent to which any of the above risks arise for display screen workers using their workstations who are:

- users employed by them;
- users employed by others (eg agency employed 'temps');
- operators, ie self-employed contractors who would be classified as users if they were employees (eg self-employed agency 'temps', self-employed journalists).

Individual workstations used by any of these people will need to be analysed and risks assessed. If employers require their employees to use workstations at home, these too will need to be assessed (see paragraph 26 below).

If there is doubt whether any individual is a user or operator, carrying out a risk assessment should help in reaching a decision.

Suitable and sufficient analysis and risk assessment

21 Risk assessment should first identify any hazards and then evaluate risks and their extent. A hazard is something with the potential to cause harm; risk expresses the likelihood that the harm from a particular hazard is realised. The extent of the risk takes into account the number of people who might be exposed to a risk and the consequences for them. Analysis of display screen workstations should include a check for the presence of desirable features as well as making sure that bad points have been eliminated. In general, the risks outlined above will arise when the work, workplace and work environment do not take account of worker requirements. Since any risks to health may arise from a combination of risk factors, a suitable and sufficient analysis should:

(a) be systematic – including investigation of non-obvious causes of problems. For example, poor posture may be a response to screen reflections or glare, rather than poor furniture;

(b) be appropriate to the likely degree of risk. This will largely depend on the duration, intensity or difficulty of the work undertaken, for example the need for prolonged high concentration because of particular performance requirements;

(c) be comprehensive, covering organisational, job, workplace and individual factors;

(d) incorporate information provided by both employer and worker.

The form of the assessment

22 In the simplest and most obvious cases which can be easily repeated and explained at any time an assessment need not be recorded. This might be the case, for example, if no significant risks are indicated and no individual user or operator is identified as being especially at risk. Assessments of short-term or temporary workstations may also not need to be recorded, unless risks are significant. However, in most other cases assessments need to be recorded and kept readily accessible to ensure continuity and accuracy of knowledge among those who may need to know the results (eg where risk reduction measures have yet to be completed). Recorded assessments need not necessarily be a 'paper and pencil' record but could be stored electronically.

23 Information provided by users is an essential part of an assessment. A useful way of obtaining this can be through an ergonomic checklist, which should preferably be completed by users. Other approaches are also possible. For example, more objective elements of the analysis (eg nature of work, chair adjustability, keyboard characteristics etc) could be assessed generically in respect of particular types of equipment or groups of worker. Other aspects of workstations would still need to be assessed individually through information collected from users, but this could then be restricted to subjective factors (eg relating to comfort). *Whatever type of checklist is used, employers should ensure workers have received the necessary training before being asked to complete one.*

24 The form of the assessment needs to be appropriate to the nature of the tasks undertaken and the complexity of the workstation. For many office tasks the assessment can be a judgement based on responses to the checklist. Where particular risks are apparent, however, and for complex situations, eg where safety of others is a critical factor, a more detailed assessment may be appropriate. This could include, for example, a task analysis where particular job stresses had been identified, recording of posture, physical measurement of workstations; or quantitative surveys of lighting and glare.

Shared workstations

25 Where one workstation is used by more than one worker, whether simultaneously or in shifts, it should be analysed and assessed in

relation to all those covered by the Regulations (see paragraph 9 above).

Assessment of risks to homeworkers

26 If a display screen user (ie an employee) is required by his or her employer to work at home, whether or not the workstation is provided in whole or part by the employer, the risks must be assessed. An ergonomic checklist which the homeworker completes and submits to the employer for assessment is the most practicable means. The assessment will need to cover any need for extra or special training and information provision for homeworkers to compensate for the absence of direct day to day employer oversight and control of their working methods.

Who should do assessments?

27 Those responsible for the assessment should be familiar with the main requirements of the Regulations and have the ability to:

(a) assess risks from the workstation and the kind of display screen work being done, for example, from a checklist completed by them or others;

(b) draw upon additional sources of information on risk as appropriate;

(c) based upon the assessment of risk, draw valid and reliable conclusions;

(d) make a clear record of the assessment and communicate the findings to those who need to take appropriate action;

(e) recognise their own limitations as to assessment so that further expertise can be called on if necessary.

28 Assessments can be made by health and safety personnel, or line managers with, or trained for, these abilities. It may be necessary to call in outside expertise where, for example, display screen equipment or associated components are faulty in design or use, where workstation design is complex, or where critical tasks are being performed.

29 The views of individual users about their workstations are an essential part of the assessment, as noted in paragraph 23. Employees' safety representatives should be encouraged to play a full part in the assessment process. In particular, they should be encouraged to report any problems in display screen work that come to their attention.

Review of assessment

30 The assessment or relevant parts of it should be reviewed in the light of changes to the display screen worker population, or changes in individual capability and where there has been some significant change to the workstation such as:

(a) a major change to software used;

(b) a major change to the hardware (screen, keyboard, input devices etc);

(c)   a major change in workstation furniture;

(d)   a substantial increase in the amount of time required to be spent using display screen equipment;

(e)   a substantial change in other task requirements (eg more speed or accuracy);

(f)   if the workstation is relocated;

(g)   if the lighting is significantly modified.

Assessments would also need to be reviewed if research findings indicated a significant new risk, or showed that a recognised hazard should be re-evaluated.

31 Because of the varying nature and novelty of some display screen tasks, and because there is incomplete understanding of the development of chronic ill-health problems (particularly musculoskeletal ones), prediction of the nature and likelihood of problems based upon a purely objective evaluation of equipment may be difficult. It is therefore most important that employers should encourage early reporting by users of any symptoms which may be related to display screen work. The need to report and the organisational arrangements for making a report should be covered in training.

Reducing risks

32 The assessment will highlight any particular areas which may give rise for concern, and these will require further evaluation and corrective action as appropriate. The four year lead-in period for the 'minimum require-ments' for workstations which are not new (see paragraph 41) does not apply to the requirement to reduce the risk. Risks identified in the assessment must be remedied as quickly as possible. For typical applications of display screens, such as VDUs in offices, remedial action is often straightforward, for example:

(a)   *postural problems* may be overcome by simple adjustments to the workstation such as repositioning equipment or adjusting the chair. Postural problems can also indicate a need to provide reinforced training of the user (for example on correct hand position, posture, how to adjust equipment). New equipment such as a footrest or document holder may be required in some cases;

(b)   *visual problems* may also be tackled by straightforward means such as repositioning the screen or using blinds to avoid glare, placing the screen at a more comfortable viewing distance from the user, or by ensuring the screen is kept clean. In some cases, new equipment such as window blinds or more appropriate lighting may be needed;

(c)   *fatigue and stress* may be alleviated by correcting obvious defects in the workstation as indicated above. In addition, as in other kinds of work, good design of the task will be important. Wherever possible the task should provide users with a degree of personal control over the pace and nature of their tasks. Proper provision must be made for training, advice and information, not only on health and safety risks but also on the use of software. Further advice is given at paragraphs 31-34 of Annex A.

33 It is important to take a systematic approach to risk reduction and recognise the limitations of the basic assessment. Observed problems may reflect the interaction of several factors or may have causes that are not obvious. For example, backache may turn out to have been caused by the worker sitting in an abnormal position in order to minimise the effects of reflections on the screen. If the factors underlying a problem appear to be complex, or if simple remedial measures do not have the desired effect, it will generally be necessary to obtain expert advice on corrective action.

Sources of information and advice

34 Annex C contains a list of relevant HSE guidance documents, for example on lighting and seating, and other publications. Further advice on health problems that may be connected with display screen work could be obtained from in-house safety or occupational health departments where applicable or, if necessary, from Employment Medical Advisory Service staff in HSE (listed in your local telephone directory under 'Health and Safety Executive'). Expert advice may be obtained from independent specialists in relevant professional disciplines such as ergonomics, or lighting design. Annex C includes some recent publications from relevant professional bodies.

Standards

35 Ergonomic specifications for use of display screen equipment are contained in various international, European and British standards. Further information is given at Annex A. Compliance with relevant parts of these standards will generally not only satisfy, but go beyond the requirements of the Regulations, because such standards aim to enhance performance as well as health and safety.

Regulation 3

Requirements for workstations

Extent to which employers must ensure that workstations meet the requirements laid down in this Schedule

An employer shall ensure that a workstation meets the requirements laid down in this Schedule to the extent that –

(a) those requirements relate to a component which is present in the workstation concerned;

(b) those requirements have effect with a view to securing the health, safety and welfare of persons at work; and

(c) the inherent characteristics of a given task make compliance with those
requirements appropriate as respects the workstation concerned.

36 Regulation 3 refers to the Schedule to the Regulations which sets out
minimum requirements for display screen workstations, covering the
equipment, the working environment, and the interface between computer
and user/operator. Annex A contains more information on those
requirements of the Schedule which call for some interpretation.

37 Regulation 3 and the Schedule must be complied with in respect of all
workstations that may be used by a display screen user or operator. Where
an employer decides that a particular workstation is not used by a display
screen user or operator and is unlikely to be used by one in future, there is
no legal need for that workstation to comply with Regulation 3 or the
Schedule, though, where it is applicable, compliance will in most cases
enhance performance and efficiency. Where employers have workstations
that do not comply they should take steps to ensure that display screen
users or operators do not use them.

They should also bear in mind their general responsibilities under the
Health and Safety at Work Act to ensure health and safety of all those at
work – see paragraph 42.

Application of the Schedule

38 By virtue of paragraph 1 of the Schedule, the requirements apply only in
so far as:

(a) the components concerned (eg document holder, chair or desk) are
present at the workstation. Where a particular item is mentioned in the
Schedule, this should not be interpreted as a requirement that all
workstations should have one, unless risk assessment under Regulation 2 suggests the item is necessary;
(b) they relate to worker health, safety and welfare. For the purposes of
these Regulations, it is only necessary to comply with the detailed
requirements in paragraphs 2, 3 and 4 of the Schedule if this would
actively secure the health, safety or welfare of persons at work. The
requirements in the Schedule do not extend to the efficiency of use of
display screen equipment, workstations or software. However, these
matters are covered, in addition to worker health and safety, in BS
7179 and other standards, and in international standards in
preparation (see Annex A). Compliance with such standards, where
they are appropriate, should enhance efficiency as well as ensuring that
relevant health and safety requirements of the Schedule are also
satisfied;
(c) the inherent requirements or characteristics of the task make
compliance appropriate; for example, where the task could not be
carried out successfully if all the requirements in the Schedule were
complied with. [Note that it is the demands of the task, rather than the
capabilities of any particular equipment, that are the deciding factor
here.]

39 In practice, the detailed requirements in paragraphs 2 to 4 of the Schedule are most likely to be fully applicable in typical office situations, for example where a VDU is used for tasks such as data entry or word processing. In more specialised applications of display screens compliance with particular requirements in the Schedule may be inappropriate where there would be no benefit to, or even adverse effects on, health and safety. Where display screen equipment is used to control machinery, processes or vehicle traffic, it is clearly essential to consider the implications of any design changes for the rest of the workforce and the public, as well as the health and safety of the screen user.

40 The following examples illustrate how these factors can operate in practice. They each include a reference to the relevant part of paragraph 1 of the Schedule:

(a) where, as in some control-room applications, a screen is used from a standing position and without reference to documents, a work surface and chair may be unnecessary [Schedule 1(a)];

(b) some individuals who suffer from certain back complaints may benefit from a chair with a fixed back rest or a special chair without a back rest [Schedule 1(b)];

(c) wheelchair users work from a 'chair' that may not comply with the requirements in paragraph 2(e) of the Schedule. They may have special requirements for work surface (eg height); in practice some wheelchair users may need a purpose-built workstation but others may prefer to use existing work surfaces. Clearly the needs of the individual here should have priority over rigid compliance with paragraph 2 of the Schedule [Schedule 1(b)];

(d) where a user may need to rapidly locate and operate emergency controls, placing them on a detachable keyboard may be inappropriate [Schedule 1(b) and (c)];

(e) where there are banks of screens as in process control or air traffic control for example, individual tilting and swivelling screens may be undesirable as the screens may need to be aligned with one another and/or be aligned for easy viewing from the operator's seat. Detachable keyboards may also be undesirable if a particular keyboard needs to be associated with a particular screen and/or instrumentation in a multi-screen array [Schedule 1(c) and (b)];

(f) a brightness control would be inappropriate for process control screens used to display alarm signals – turning down the brightness could cause an alarm to be missed [Schedule 1(b) and (c)];

(g) screens that are necessarily close to other work equipment (for example, in a fixed assembly such as a control room panel) that needs to be well-illuminated will need carefully positioned local lighting – it may then be inappropriate for the screen to tilt and swivel as this could give rise to strong reflections on the screen [Schedule 1(b)];

(h) where microfiche is used to keep records of original documents, screen characters may not be well-defined or clearly formed if the original was in poor condition or was badly photographed [Schedule 1(c)];

) radar screens used in air traffic control have characters which have blurred 'tails' and hence might be considered to be not well-defined and clearly formed; however long-persistence phosphors are deliberately used in these screens in order to indicate the direction of movement of the aircraft [Schedule 1(c)];

) screens forming part of a simulator for ship or aircraft crew training may have special features that do not comply with the Schedule but are necessary if the simulator is to accurately mimic the features of the exempt display screen equipment on the ship or aircraft [Schedule 1(c)].

Transitional period for existing equipment

1 Employers are required to ensure that workstations, whether or not they are new, which are put into service in their undertakings on or after the coming into force of these Regulations comply with the Schedule where it is relevant. Workstations already in service should comply by 31 December 1996. If new display screen equipment is put into service at an existing workstation, the whole workstation concerned should be regarded as new and brought into compliance with the Schedule straight away. However, if any other part of an existing workstation is changed, only the new component need comply with the Schedule at once; the remainder of the workstation need not comply until 31 December 1996.

42 Where the Schedule does not apply, either because its requirements are not applicable (under paragraph 1) or the workstation is not new, employers must still comply with other provisions of these Regulations as well as with the Health and Safety at Work Act to ensure that risks to users and operators are reduced to the lowest extent reasonably practicable. Thus:

a) if assessment of an existing workstation shows there is a risk to users or operators, the employer should take immediate steps to reduce the risk; or

b) where paragraph 1(a) or (c) of the Schedule is applicable and the minimum requirements in paragraphs 2, 3 and 4 of the Schedule are therefore not being followed, the employer must ensure that the health and safety of users and operators are adequately safeguarded by whatever other means are appropriate, reasonably practicable and necessary.

Regulation 4

Daily work routine of users

3 In most tasks, natural breaks or pauses occur as a consequence of the inherent organisation of the work. Whenever possible, jobs at display screens should be designed to consist of a mix of screen-based and non screen-based work to prevent fatigue and to vary visual and mental

demands. Where the job unavoidably contains spells of intensive display screen work (whether using the keyboard or input device, reading the screen or a mixture of the two), these should be broken up by periods of non-intensive, non-display screen work. Where work cannot be so organised, eg in jobs requiring only data or text entry requiring sustained attention and concentration, deliberate breaks or pauses must be introduced.

Nature and timing of breaks or changes of activity

44 Where the display screen work involves intensive use of the keyboard, any activity that would demand broadly similar use of the arms or hands should be avoided during breaks. Similarly, if the display screen work is visually demanding any activities during breaks should be of a different visual character. Breaks must also allow users to vary their posture. Exercise routines which include blinking, stretching and focussing eyes on distant objects can be helpful and could be covered in training programmes.

45 It is not appropriate to lay down requirements for breaks which apply to all types of work; it is the nature and mix of demands made by the job which determine the length of break necessary to prevent fatigue. But some general guidance can be given:

(a) breaks should be taken before the onset of fatigue, not in order to recuperate and when performance is at a maximum, before productivity reduces. The timing of the break is more important than its length;

(b) breaks or changes of activity should be included in working time. They should reduce the workload at the screen, ie should not result in a higher pace or intensity of work on account of their introduction;

(c) short, frequent breaks are more satisfactory than occasional, longer breaks: eg, a 5-10 minute break after 50-60 minutes continuous screen and/or keyboard work is likely to be better than a 15 minute break every 2 hours;

(d) if possible, breaks should be taken away from the screen;

(e) informal breaks, that is time spent not viewing the screen (eg on other tasks), appear from study evidence to be more effective in relieving visual fatigue than formal rest breaks;

(f) wherever practicable, users should be allowed some discretion as to how they carry out tasks; individual control over the nature and pace of work allows optimal distribution of effort over the working day.

The employer's duty to plan activities

46 The employer's duty under Regulation 4 to plan the activities of users can be satisfied by arranging things so that users are able to benefit from breaks or changes of activity, and encouraging them to do so. The duty to plan does not imply a need for the employer to draw up a precise and detailed timetable for periods of DSE work and breaks.

47 It is generally best for users to be given some discretion over when to take breaks. In such cases the employer's duty to plan activities may be satisfied by allowing an adequate degree of flexibility for the user to organise their own work. However, users given total discretion may forego breaks in favour of a shorter working day, and thus may suffer fatigue. Employers should ensure that users are given adequate information and training on the need for breaks (see paragraphs 64 and 66 below). Where users forego breaks despite this, it may be necessary for employers to lay down minimum requirements for the frequency of breaks while still allowing users some flexibility.

48 The employer's duty is to plan activities so that breaks or changes of activity are taken by users during their normal work. There are a few situations, for example where users working in a control room are handling an unforeseen emergency, where other health and safety considerations may occasionally dictate that normal breaks are not taken.

Regulation 5

Eyes and eyesight

49 There is no reliable evidence that work with display screen equipment causes any permanent damage to eyes or eyesight, but it may make users with pre-existing vision defects more aware of them. This (and/or poor working conditions) may give some users temporary visual fatigue or headaches. Uncorrected vision defects can make work at display screens more tiring or stressful than it should be, and correcting defects can improve comfort, job satisfaction and performance. (Note that some display screen work may also require specific visual capabilities such as colour discrimination).

Eye and eyesight test

50 Regulations 5(1) and 5(2) require employers to provide users who so request it with an appropriate eye and eyesight test. In Great Britain an 'appropriate eye and eyesight test' means a 'sight test' as defined in the Opticians Act legislation.[1] The test includes a test of vision and an examination of the eye. For the purpose of the Display Screen Equipment Regulations, the test should take account of the nature of the users' work, including the distance at which the screen is viewed. Display screen users are not obliged to have such tests performed but where they choose to

---

1 S 36(2) of the Opticians Act 1989 defines testing sight as 'determining whether there is any and, if so, what defect of sight and of correcting, remedying or relieving any such defect of an anatomical or physiological nature by means of an optical appliance prescribed on the basis of the determination'. The test is defined in further detail in the Sight Testing Examination and Prescription (No 2) Regulations 1989.

exercise their entitlement, employers should offer an examination by a registered ophthalmic optician, or a registered medical practitioner with suitable qualifications ('optometrist' and 'doctor' respectively in the paragraphs below). (All registered medical practitioners, including those in company occupational health departments, are entitled to carry out sight tests but normally only those with an ophthalmic qualification do so).

51 Regulation 5(1) gives employers a duty to ensure the provision of appropriate eye and eyesight tests on request:

(a) to their employees who are already users when the Regulations come into force;

(b) and (thereafter) to any of their non-user employees who are to become users.

The Regulations do not give employers any duty to offer eye and eyesight tests to persons not in their employment, such as applicants for jobs. However, where somebody has been recruited and is to work with display screen equipment to the extent that they will become a user, Regulation 5(1)(b) becomes applicable. Hence where a newly recruited employee of this kind – whether or not they have been a user in any previous employment in a different undertaking – requests one, an appropriate eye and eyesight test should be arranged by their new employer. The test should be carried out before the newly recruited employee becomes a user, as required by Regulation 5(2)(b). This does not mean that new recruits must be given a test before doing any display screen work, but they would have to be given a test (if they requested one) before doing sufficient display screen work for this to be regarded as a significant part of their normal work. For guidance on what this means in practice, see paragraphs 10-13 above on the definition of a user.

52 The British College of Optometrists has produced a statement of good practice for optometrists, obtainable from them (see Annex C). Among other things, it makes clear that the purpose of the eye test by an optometrist or doctor under Regulation 5 is to decide whether the user has any defect of sight which requires correction when working with a display screen. It follows that users need to be able to describe their display screen and working environment when they have the eye test. As the College points out, the optometrist will need to make a report to the employer, copied to the employee, stating clearly whether or not a corrective appliance is needed specifically for display screen work and when re-examination should take place. Any prescription, or other confidential clinical information from the eye test, can only be provided to the employer with the employee's consent.

Vision screening tests

53 Vision screening tests are a means of identifying individuals with defective vision who need a full sight test (see paragraph 50). These tests are not designed to screen for eye defects, such as injury or disease, that may not at first affect vision. Where companies offer vision screening facilities,

some users may opt for a vision screening test to check their need for a full sight test. Other users, however, may choose at the outset to exercise their entitlement to a full sight test, and in such cases the employer must arrange for the test specified in paragraph 50 to be provided.

54 Where the user opts for vision screening, the screening instrument or other test method used should be capable of testing vision at the distances appropriate to the user's display screen work, including the intermediate distance at which screens are viewed (normally 50-60 cm). Where test results indicate that vision is defecting at the relevant distances, the user should be informed and referred to an optometrist or doctor for a full sight test.

55 Those conducting eyesight screening tests should have basic knowledge of the eye and its function and be competent in operation of the instrument and/or tests. Both the test results and the need for further referral should be assessed by those with medical, ophthalmic, nursing or paramedical skills.

Regularity of provision of eye and eyesight tests

56 Regulation 5 requires that eye and eyesight tests are provided:

(a) as soon as practicable after display screen users have made a request;

(b) for employees who are to become users, and have made a request. In such cases the test must be carried out before the employee becomes a user;

(c) for users at regular intervals thereafter to check the need for special corrective appliances for display screen work, provided that they want the tests. Employers should be guided by the clinical judgement of the optometrist or doctor on the frequency of repeat testing. The frequency of repeat testing needed will vary between individuals, according to factors such as age. However, employers are not responsible for any corrections for vision defects or examinations for eye complaints which are not related to display screen work which may become necessary within the period. These are the responsibility of the individual concerned;

(d) for users experiencing visual difficulties which may reasonably be considered to be related to the display screen work, for example visual symptoms such as eyestrain or focussing difficulties.

57 Where an eye test by an optometrist suggests that a user is suffering eye injury or disease, the user will be referred to his or her registered medical practitioner for further examination. This examination is free of charge under the National Health Service.

Corrective appliances

58 'Special' corrective appliances (normally spectacles) provided to meet the requirements of the Regulations will be those appliances prescribed to correct vision defects at the viewing distance or distances used specifically for the display screen work concerned. 'Normal' corrective appliances are

spectacles prescribed for any other purpose. It should be noted that experience has shown that in most working populations only a minority (usually less than 10%) will need special corrective appliances for display screen work. Those who need special corrective appliances may include users who already wear spectacles or contact lenses, or others who have uncorrected vision defects.

59 Anti-glare screens, and so-called 'VDU spectacles' and other devices that purport to protect against radiation, are not special corrective appliances (see paragraphs 27-30 of Annex A for advice on radiation).

Employers' liability for costs

60 The provision of eye and eyesight tests and of special corrective appliances under the Regulations is at the expense of the user's employer. This is the case even if the user works on other employers' workstations. Employers are free to specify that users' tests and correction are provided by a particular company or professional. 'Normal' corrective appliances are at the user's own expense.

61 Users needing special corrective appliances may be prescribed a special pair of spectacles for display screen work. Employers' liability for costs is restricted to payment of the cost of a basic appliance, ie of a type and quality adequate for its function. If users wish to choose more costly appliances (eg with designer frames; or lenses with optional treatments not necessary for the work), the employer is not obliged to pay for these. In these circumstances employers may either provide a basic appliance as above, or may opt to contribute a portion of the total cost of a luxury appliance equal to the cost of a basic appliance.

62 If users are permitted by their employers to choose spectacles to correct eye or vision defects for purposes which include display screen work but go wider than that, employers need contribute only the costs attributable to the requirements of the display screen work involved.

Regulation 6

Provision of training

63 In accordance with this Regulation, employers should ensure that all users who make use of their workstations or are required to use other workstations have been provided with health and safety training, in addition to the training received in order to do the work itself. In practice, there may be considerable overlap between general training requirements and specific health and safety ones (for example the development of keyboard skills) and they are best done together. They will then reinforce each other and facilitate efficient and effective use of the equipment as well as avoidance of risk. The purpose of training is to increase the user's competence to use workstation equipment safely and reduce the risk to their or anyone else's health. In considering the extent of any training which will be necessary in a particular

case, the employer needs to make up any shortfalls between the user's existing competence and that necessary to use the equipment in a safe and healthy way. The development of specific statements of what the user needs to do and how well (ie statements of competence) will assist the employer to determine the extent of any shortfall.

64 Training will need to be adapted to the requirements of the particular display screen tasks, be adapted to users' skills and capabilities and be refreshed or updated as the hardware, software, workstation, environment or job are modified. (A workstation should be regarded as having been 'substantially modified' for the purposes of Regulation 6(2) if there has been a significant change to it, as set out in paragraph 30 above). Special training or retraining needs may need to be considered for rehabilitation of people absent for long periods, particularly if ill-health problems are related to the visual, musculoskeletal or stress-related risks referred to earlier. Organisations should develop systems for identifying the occasions when any of these needs for training arise.

65 The health and safety training should be aimed at reducing or minimising the three risk areas outlined at paragraph 19 above and in Annex B, with reference to the part played by the individual user. To do this, six inter-related aspects of training should be covered:

(a) The user's role in correct and timely detection and recognition of hazards and risks. This should cover both the absence of desirable features (chair comfort) and the presence of undesirable ones (screen reflections and glare) together with information on health risks and how problems may be manifested.

(b) A simple explanation of the causes of risk and the mechanisms by which harm may be brought about, for example poor posture leading to static loading on the musculoskeletal system and eventual fatigue and pain.

(c) User initiated actions and procedures which will bring risks under control and to acceptable levels. Training should cover the following:
   - the desirability of comfortable posture and the importance of postural change;
   - the use of adjustment mechanisms on equipment, particularly furniture, so that stress and fatigue can be minimised;
   - the use and arrangement of workstation components to facilitate good posture, prevent over-reaching and avoid glare and reflections on the screen;
   - the need for regular cleaning (or inspection) of screens and other equipment for maintenance;
   - the need to take advantage of breaks and changes of activity.

(d) Organisational arrangements by which symptoms or problems with the workstation can be communicated to management.

(e) Information on these Regulations, particularly as regards eyesight, rest pauses and the contents of Annex A.

(f) The user's contribution to assessments.

66 New users could be given such training at the same time as they are trained on how to use the equipment. The information required to be

provided under Regulation 7 will reinforce the training and could usefully be in the form of posters or cards with pictorial reminders of some of the essential points.

Regulation 7

Provision of information

67 There is a general requirement under the Management of Health and Safety at Work Regulations 1992 for employers to provide information on risks to health and safety to all their own employees as well as to employers of other employees on site, to visiting employees, and to the self-employed. Under Regulation 7 of the Display Screen Regulations specific information should be provided as follows:

68 The information should among other things include reminders of the measures taken to reduce the risks such as the system for reporting problems, the availability of adjustable window covering and furniture, and of how to make use of them. It will thus reinforce any training provided by the employer and be a useful reminder to those trained already.

Annex A

Guidance on workstation minimum requirements

1 The Schedule to the Regulations sets out minimum requirements for workstations, applicable mainly to typical office workstations. As explained in the guidance (paragraph 38) these requirements are applicable only in so far as the components referred to are present in the workstation concerned, the requirements are not precluded by the inherent requirements of the task, and the requirements relate to worker health, safety and welfare. Paragraphs 39-40 give examples of situations in which some aspects of these minimum requirements would not apply.

2 The requirements of the Schedule are in most cases self-explanatory but particular points to note are covered below.

General approach: use of standards

3 Ergonomic requirements for the use of visual display units in office tasks are contained in BS 7179. There is no requirement in the Display Screen Regulations to comply with this or any other standard. Other approaches to meeting the minimum requirements in the Regulations are possible, and may have to be adopted if special requirements of the task or needs of the user preclude the use of equipment made to relevant standards. However, employers may find standards helpful as workstations satisfying BS 7179, or forthcoming international standards (see below), would meet and in most cases go beyond the minimum requirements in the Schedule to the Regulations.

4 BS 7179 is a six-part interim standard covering the ergonomics of esign and use of visual display terminals in offices; it is concerned with the fficient use of VDUs as well as with user health, safety and comfort. BS 179 has been issued by the British Standards Institution in recognition of dustry's immediate need for guidance and is intended for the managers nd supervisors of VDU users as well as for equipment manufacturers. Vhile originally confined to office VDU tasks, many of the general rgonomic recommendations in BS 7179 will be relevant to some non-office tuations.

5 International standards are in preparation that will cover the same abject in an expanded form. BS 7179 will be withdrawn when the uropean standard organisation CEN (Comité Européen de Normalation) issues its multipart standard (EN 29241) concerned with the rgonomics of design and use of visual display terminals for office tasks. his CEN Standard will in turn be based on an ISO Standard (ISO 9241) aat is currently being developed. The eventual ISO and CEN standards ill cover screen and keyboard design and evaluation, workstation design nd environmental requirements, non-keyboard input devices and rgonomic requirements for software design and usability. While the EN standard is not formally linked to the Display Screen Equipment irective, one of its aims is to establish appropriate levels of user health and afety and comfort. Technical data in the various parts of the CEN andard (and currently BS 7179) may therefore help employers to meet the equirements laid down in the Schedule to the Regulations.

6 There are other standards that deal with requirements for furniture, me of which are cross-referenced by BS 7179. These include BS 3044, hich is a guide to ergonomic principles in the design and selection of ffice furniture generally. There is also now a separate standardisation iitiative within CEN concerned with the performance requirements for ffice furniture, including dimensioning appropriate for European user opulations. Details of relevant British, European and international andards can be obtained from the Department of Trade and Industry – e Annex C.

7 Other more detailed and stringent standards are relevant to certain ecialised applications of display screens, especially those where the health r safety of persons other than the screen user may be affected. Some xamples in particular subject areas are:

) *Process control*
   A large number of British and international standards are or will be
   relevant to the design of display screen interfaces for use in process
   control – such as the draft Standard ISO 11064 on the general
   ergonomic design of control rooms.
) *Applications with machinery safety implications*
   Draft Standard pr EN 614 pt 1 – Ergonomic design principles in safety
   of machinery.
) *Safety of programmable electronic systems*
   Draft document IEC 65A (Secretariat) 122 Draft: Functional safety of
   electrical/electronic programmable systems.

Applications such as these are outside the scope of these guidance note
Anyone involved in the design of such display screen interfaces and othe
where there may be safety considerations for non-users should se
appropriate specialist advice. Many relevant standards are listed in the D
publication Directory of HCI Standards – see Annex C.

Equipment

Display screen

8 Choice of display screen should be considered in relation to oth
elements of the work system, such as the type and amount of informatic
required for the task, and environmental factors. A satisfactory display ca
be achieved by custom design for a specific task or environment, or t
appropriate adjustments to adapt the display to suit changing requiremen
or environmental conditions.

Display stability

9 Individual perceptions of screen flicker vary and a screen which
flicker-free to 90% of users should be regarded as satisfying the minimu
requirement. (It is not technically feasible to eliminate flicker for a
users). A change to a different display can resolve individual problen
with flicker. Persistent display instabilities – flicker, jump, jitter or swim
may indicate basic design problems and assistance should be sought fro
suppliers.

Brightness and contrast

10 Negative or positive image polarity (light characters on a dar
background, dark characters on a light background respectively)
acceptable, and each has different advantages. With negative polari
flicker is less perceptible, legibility is better for those with low acuity visio
and characters may be perceived as larger than they are; with positiv
polarity, reflections are less perceptible, edges appear sharper an
luminance balance is easier to achieve.

11 It is important for the brightness and contrast of the display to t
appropriate for ambient lighting conditions; trade-offs between characte
brightness and sharpness may be needed to achieve an acceptable balanc
In many kinds of equipment this is achieved by providing a control c
controls which allow the user to make adjustments.

Screen adjustability

12 Adjustment mechanisms allow the screen to be tilted or swivelled t
avoid glare and reflections and enable the worker to maintain a natural an
relaxed posture. They may be built into the screen, form part of th
workstation furniture or be provided by separate screen support device
they should be simple and easy to operate. Screen height adjustmen
devices, although not essential, may be a useful means of adjusting th
screen to the correct height for the worker. (The reference in the Schedul
to adjustable tables does not mean these have to be provided).

Glare and reflections

13 Screens are generally manufactured without highly reflective surface finishes but in adverse lighting conditions, reflection and glare may be a problem. Advice on lighting is below (paragraphs 20–24).

Keyboard

14 Keyboard design should allow workers to locate and activate keys quickly, accurately and without discomfort. The choice of keyboard will be dictated by the nature of the task and determined in relation to other elements of the work system. Hand support may be incorporated into the keyboard for support while keying or at rest depending on what the worker finds comfortable, may be provided in the form of a space between the keyboard and front edge of the desk, or may be given by a separate hand/wrist support attached to the work surface.

Work desk or work surface

15 Work surface dimensions may need to be larger than for conventional non-screen office work, to take adequate account of:

(a) the range of tasks performed (eg screen viewing, keyboard input, use of other input devices, writing on paper etc);

(b) position and use of hands for each task;

(c) use and storage of working materials and equipment (documents, telephones etc).

16 Document holders are useful for work with hard copy, particularly for workers who have difficulty in refocussing. They should position working documents at a height, visual plane and, where appropriate, viewing distance similar to those of the screen; be of low reflectance; be stable; and not reduce the readability of source documents.

Work chair

17 The primary requirement here is that the work chair should allow the user to achieve a comfortable position. Seat height adjustments should accommodate the needs of users for the tasks performed. The Schedule requires the seat to be adjustable in height (ie relative to the ground) and the seat back to be adjustable in height (also relative to the ground) and tilt. Provided the chair design meets these requirements and allows the user to achieve a comfortable posture, it is not necessary for the height or tilt of the seat back to be adjustable independently of the seat. Automatic backrest adjustments are acceptable if they provide adequate back support. General health and safety advice and specifications for seating are given in the HSE

publication Seating at Work (HS(G)57). A range of publications with detailed advice covering comfort and performance as well as health and safety is included in Annex C.

18 Footrests may be necessary where individual workers are unable to rest their feet flat on the floor (eg where work surfaces cannot be adjusted to the right height in relation to other components of the workstation). Footrests should not be used when they are not necessary as this can result in poor posture.

Environment

Space requirements

19 Prolonged sitting in a static position can be harmful. It is most important that support surfaces for display screen and other equipment and materials used at the workstation should allow adequate clearance for postural changes. This means adequate clearances for thighs, knees, lower legs and feet under the work surface and between furniture components. The height of the work surface should allow a comfortable position for the arms and wrists, if a keyboard is used.

Lighting, reflections and glare

20 Lighting should be appropriate for all the tasks performed at the workstation, eg reading from the screen, keyboard work, reading printed text, writing on paper etc. General lighting – by artificial or natural light, or a combination – should illuminate the entire room to an adequate standard. Any supplementary individual lighting provided to cater for personal needs or a particular task should not adversely affect visual conditions at nearby workstations.

Illuminance

21 High illuminances render screen characters less easy to see but improve the ease of reading documents. Where a high illuminance environment is preferred for this or other reasons, the use of positive polarity screens (dark characters on a light background) has advantages as these can be used comfortably at higher illuminances than can negative polarity screens.

Reflections and glare

22 Problems which can lead to visual fatigue and stress can arise for example from unshielded bright lights or bright areas in the worker's field of view; from an imbalance between brightly and dimly lit parts of the environment; and from reflections on the screen or other parts of the workstation.

23 Measures to minimise these problems include: shielding, replacing or repositioning sources of light; rearranging or moving work surfaces, documents or all or parts of workstations; modifying the colour or reflectance of walls, ceilings, furnishings etc near the workstation; altering the intensity of vertical to horizontal illuminance; or a combination of these. Anti-glare screen filters should be considered as a last resort if other measures fail to solve the problem.

24 General guidance on minimum lighting standards necessary to ensure health and safety of workplaces is available in the HSE guidance note Lighting at Work (HS(G)38). This does not cover ways of using lighting to maximise task performance or enhance the appearance of the workplace, although it does contain a bibliography listing relevant publications in this area. Specific and detailed guidance is given in the CIBSE Lighting Guide 3 Lighting for visual display terminals. Full details of these publications are given in Annex C.

Noise

25 Noise from equipment such as printers at display screen workstations should be kept to levels which do not impair concentration or prevent normal conversation (unless the noise is designed to attract attention, eg to warn of a malfunction). Noise can be reduced by replacement, sound-proofing or repositioning of the equipment; sound insulating partitions between noisy equipment and the rest of the workstation are an alternative.

Heat and humidity

26 Electronic equipment can be a source of dry heat which can modify the thermal environment at the workstation. Ventilation and humidity should be maintained at levels which prevent discomfort and problems of sore eyes.

Radiation

27 The Schedule requires radiation with the exception of the visible part of the electromagnetic spectrum (ie visible light) to be reduced to negligible levels from the point of view of the protection of users' health and safety. In fact so little radiation is emitted from current designs of display screen equipment that no special action is necessary to meet this requirement (see also Annex B, paragraphs 8-10).

28 Taking cathode ray tube displays as an example, ionising radiation is emitted only in exceedingly small quantities, so small as to be generally much less than the natural background level to which everyone is exposed. Emissions of ultraviolet, visible and infrared radiation are also very small, and workers will receive much less than the maximum exposures generally recommended by national and international advisory bodies.

29 For radio frequencies, the exposures will also be well below the maximum values generally recommended by national and international advisory bodies for health protection purposes. The levels of electric and magnetic fields are similar to those from common domestic electrical devices. Although much research has been carried out on possible health effects from exposure to electromagnetic radiation, no adverse health effects have been shown to result from the emissions from display screen equipment.

30 Thus it is not necessary, from the standpoint of limiting risk to human health, for employers or workers to take any action to reduce radiation levels or to attempt to measure emissions; in fact the latter is not recommended as meaningful interpretation of the data is very difficult. There is no need for users to be given protective devices such as anti-radiation screens.

Task design and software

Principles of task design

31 Inappropriate task design can be among the causes of stress at work. Stress jeopardises employee motivation, effectiveness and efficiency and in some cases it can lead to significant health problems. The Regulations are only applicable where health and safety rather than productivity is being put at risk; but employers may find it useful to consider both aspects together as task design changes put into effect for productivity reasons may also benefit health, and vice versa.

32 In display screen work, good design of the task can be as important as the correct choice of equipment, furniture and working environment. It is advantageous to:

(a) design jobs in a way that offers users variety, opportunities to exercise discretion, opportunities for learning, and appropriate feedback, in preference to simple repetitive tasks whenever possible. (For example, the work of a typist can be made less repetitive and stressful if an element of clerical work is added);

(b) match staffing levels to volumes of work, so that individual users are not subject to stress through being either overworked or underworked;

(c) allow users to participate in the planning, design and implementation of work tasks whenever possible.

Principles of software ergonomics

33 In most display screen work the software controls both the presentation of information on the screen and the ways in which the worker can manipulate the information. Thus software design can be an important element of task design. Software that is badly designed or inappropriate for the task will impede the efficient completion of the work and in some cases may cause sufficient stress to affect the health of a user. Involving a sample of users in the purchase or design of software can help to avoid problems.

34 Detailed ergonomic standards for software are likely to be developed in future as part of the ISO 9241 standard; for the moment, the Schedule lists a few general principles which employers should take into account. Requirements of the organisation and of display screen workers should be established as the basis for redesigning, selecting, and modifying software. In many (though not all) applications the main points are:

Suitability for the task
–   Software should enable workers to complete the task efficiently, without presenting unnecessary problems or obstacles.

Ease of use and adaptability
–   Workers should be able to feel that they can master the system and use it effectively following appropriate training;
–   The dialogue between the system and the worker should be appropriate for the worker's ability;
–   Where appropriate, software should enable workers to adapt the user interface to suit their ability level and preferences;

- The software should protect workers from the consequences of errors, for example by providing appropriate warnings and information and by enabling 'lost' data to be recovered wherever practicable.

Feedback on system performance
- The system should provide appropriate feedback, which may include error messages; suitable assistance ('help') to workers on request; and messages about changes in the system such as malfunctions or overloading;
- Feedback messages should be presented at the right time and in an appropriate style and format. They should not contain unnecessary information.

Format and pace
- Speed of response to commands and instructions should be appropriate to the task and to workers' abilities;
- Characters, cursor movements and position changes should where possible be shown on the screen as soon as they are input.

Performance monitoring facilities
- Quantitative or qualitative checking facilities built into the software can lead to stress if they have adverse results such as an over-emphasis on output speed;
- It is possible to design monitoring systems that avoid these drawbacks and provide information that is helpful to workers as well as managers. However, in all cases workers should be kept informed about the introduction and operation of such systems.

Annex B

Display screen equipment: possible effects on health

The main hazards

1 The introduction of VDUs and other display screen equipment has been associated with a range of symptoms related to the visual system and working posture. These often reflect bodily fatigue. They can readily be prevented by applying ergonomic principles to the design, selection and installation of display screen equipment, the design of the workplace, and the organisation of the task.

Upper limb pains and discomfort
2 A range of conditions of the arm, hand and shoulder areas linked to work activities are now described as work related upper limb disorders. These range from temporary fatigue or soreness in the limb to chronic soft tissue disorders like peritendinitis or carpal tunnel syndrome. Some keyboard operators have suffered occupational cramp.

3 The contribution to the onset of any disorder of individual risk factors (eg keying rates) is not clear. It is likely that a combination of

factors are concerned. Prolonged static posture of the back, neck and head are known to cause musculoskeletal problems. Awkward positioning of the hands and wrist (eg as a result of poor working technique or inappropriate work height) are further likely factors. Outbreaks of soft tissue disorders among keyboard workers have often been associated with high workloads combined with tight deadlines. This variety of factors contributing to display screen work risk requires a risk reduction strategy which embraces proper equipment, furniture, training, job design and work planning.

Eye and eyesight effects

4 Medical evidence shows that using display screen equipment is not associated with damage to eyes or eyesight; nor does it make existing defects worse. But some workers may experience temporary visual fatigue, leading to a range of symptoms such as impaired visual performance, red or sore eyes and headaches, or the adoption of awkward posture which can cause further discomfort in the limb. These may be caused by:

(a) staying in the same position and concentrating for a long time;
(b) poor positioning of the display screen equipment;
(c) poor legibility of the screen or source documents;
(d) poor lighting, including glare and reflections;
(e) a drifting, flickering or jittering image on the screen.

Like other visually demanding tasks, VDU work does not cause eye damage but it may make workers with pre-existing vision defects more aware of them. Such uncorrected defects can make work with a display screen more tiring or stressful than would otherwise be the case.

Fatigue and stress

5 Many symptoms described by display screen workers reflect stresses arising from their task. They may be secondary to upper limb or visual problems but they are more likely to be caused by poor job design or work organisation, particularly lack of sufficient control of the work by the user, under-utilisation of skills, high-speed repetitive working or social isolation. All these have been linked with stress in display screen work, although clearly they are not unique to it; but attributing individual symptoms to particular aspects of a job or workplace can be difficult. The risks of display screen workers experiencing physical fatigue and stress can be minimised, however, by following the principles underlying the Display Screen Equipment Regulations 1992 and guidance, ie by careful design, selection and disposition of display screen equipment; good design of the user's workplace, environment and task; and training, consultation and involvement of the user.

Other concerns

Epilepsy

6 Display screen equipment has not been known to induce epileptic seizures. People suffering from the very rare (1 in 10 000 population)

photosensitive epilepsy who react adversely to flickering lights and patterns also find they can safely work with display screens. People with epilepsy who are concerned about display screen work can seek further advice from local offices of the Employment Medical Advisory Service.

Facial dermatitis

7 Some VDU users have reported facial skin complaints such as occasional itching or reddened skin on the face and/or neck. These complaints are relatively rare and the limited evidence available suggests they may be associated with environmental factors, such as low relative humidity or static electricity near the VDU.

Electromagnetic radiation

8 Anxiety about radiation emissions from display screen equipment and possible effects on pregnant women has been widespread. However, there is substantial evidence that these concerns are unfounded. The Health and Safety Executive has consulted the National Radiological Protection Board, which has the statutory function of providing information and advice on all radiation matters to Government Departments, and the advice below summarises scientific understanding.

9 The levels of ionising and non-ionising electromagnetic radiation which are likely to be generated by display screen equipment are well below those set out in international recommendations for limiting risk to human health created by such emissions and the National Radiological Protection Board does not consider such levels to pose a significant risk to health. No special protective measures are therefore needed to protect the health of people from this radiation.

Effects on pregnant women

10 There has been considerable public concern about reports of higher levels of miscarriage and birth defects among some groups of visual display unit (VDU) workers in particular due to electromagnetic radiation. Many scientific studies have been carried out, but taken as a whole their results do not show any link between miscarriages or birth defects and working with VDUs. Research and reviews of the scientific evidence will continue to be undertaken.

11 In the light of the scientific evidence pregnant women do not need to stop work with VDUs. However, to avoid problems caused by stress and anxiety, women who are pregnant or planning children and worried about working with VDUs should be given the opportunity to discuss their concerns with someone adequately informed of current authoritative scientific information and advice.

Annex C

Further sources of information

This Annex is not reproduced in this book.

Index